Modern Chile
1970–1989

Modern Chile 1970–1989

A Critical History

Mark Falcoff

Transaction Publishers
New Brunswick (U.S.A.) and London (U.K.)

Second printing 1991, First paperback reprint 1991

Copyright © 1989 by Transaction Publishers
New Brunswick, New Jersey 08903

Library of Congress Catalog Number: 88-20165
ISBN: 0-88738-257-6 (cloth); 0-88738-867-1 (paper)
Printed in the United States of America

Library of Congress Cataloging-in-Publication Data
Falcoff, Mark.
    Modern Chile, 1970–1989: a critical history/ Mark Falcoff.
      p.   cm.
    Includes bibliographical references and index.
    ISBN 0-88738-257-6
    1. Chile—Politics and government—1970–1973.   2. Chile—Politics
and government—1973–   3. Allende Gossens, Salvador, 1908–1973.
I. Title
F3100.F32   1989   88-20165
983′.06—dc19

For Dennis L. Bark and Roger Kaplan
who believed in this book—and in me.

Contents

Tables

Preface

The twentieth century has been an age of small nations. Indeed, much of Western diplomatic and political history of the past seventy-five years concerns places which, as British Prime Minister Neville Chamberlain once said, "we know nothing"—Agadir, Sarajevo, the Sudetenland, Danzig, Panmunjom, Dien Bien Phu. Such locales may possess little of intrinsic interest to outsiders, but they acquire a disproportionate significance to the extent that they become precipitants of international conflict, or metaphors for the ideological debates which divide more central societies.

This is a book about Chile—one such country which, somewhat improbably, has become one of the great political causes of our time. The immediate precipitant was an unusually violent military coup in September 1973, which overthrew the government of Dr. Salvador Allende, the first freely elected Marxist chief of state anywhere in the world. Such an event inevitably mobilized the radical Left worldwide; but the widespread repression which followed the event itself, the fact that it extinguished the oldest, most important democracy in Latin America, and was followed by revelations of deep U.S. involvement in the internal affairs of that country, widened the circle of concern to socialists and liberals in the United States and Western Europe, who have come to regard the fate of that country under Allende's successor, General Augusto Pinochet Ugarte, as an indictment of the liberal capitalist order and the role of the United States in world affairs. What "happened" to Chilean democracy has thus become part of an ongoing debate within the United States about the nature of our own institutions, and their impact on other countries.

Chile has existed as an independent nation since the early nineteenth century; nonetheless, for international opinion it was created sometime around 1970. Since that year, more books have been published about that country in the major European languages than in the previous one hundred fifty years. Chilean themes now enjoy a market in world literature and in the international cinema—as demonstrated by Costa-Gavras' film *Missing* (1982), or Isabel Allende's *House of Spirits* (1985). Whether as history or political science, film or fiction, much—perhaps most—of what has been produced about Chile since 1970 is organized around the same central idea: that every event in Chilean history ultimately and inevitably led to the election of a Marxist president in 1970 and its socialist transformation by democratic means—a destiny disfigured only by dark, subterranean forces at home and abroad.

This picture is greatly at variance with almost everything known about that country. A sophisticated, largely urban society with a high degree of educational attainment, Chile has long possessed a solid tradition of social science; thus for those who bother to explore the shelves of any good university library, there can be few secrets about its political and social dynamics. While at the time of Allende's election the country possessed two large and well-organized Marxist political parties well-represented in the labor movement, it also had an important, politically articulated middle class, which found expression in parties and forces grouped around the center and center-right. Most Chileans were (and remain) in fact quite conservative, though in a corporatist, rather than liberal sense. Most of the issues which arose during the Allende years had long been debated in Chile, and were the object of comprehensive and far-reaching reforms. What was new after 1970 was the notion that the mere act of electing a Marxist president suddenly and magically released the country from the political and economic constraints which had shaped policy outcomes in the past.

For many years Chile was also something of a theater-in-miniature, where certain Western economic controversies could be played out at a safe distance— particularly those concerning the role of the state in economic development, and the degree to which governments should intervene to assure given outcomes. Chile seemed particularly well-suited for this role, since it closely resembled many Western European countries in political culture and social organization. What many failed to notice was that it possessed a smaller internal market, a greater degree of dependency on one or two exports, and a political community whose expectations ran far ahead of the country's concrete possibilities. Though the Allende regime pushed matters to their ultimate extreme, in many ways it merely carried to their logical conclusion policies long-established and broadly accepted by most people (in theory, though not, as it turned out, in actual practice). The Chilean experience thus points somewhat disturbingly to the high cost exacted from democratic political institutions when the imperatives of equality and growth are too sharply pitted against one another.

Chile has also been a crucial country for the United States, though not in ways generally understood by Americans, and certainly not as depicted in films like *Missing*. Though it had constituted an important source of raw materials during the Second World War and the period immediately thereafter, and though American mining concerns had perceived large profits from their operations there in the 1940s and 1950s, U.S. policy in the more recent period was driven not principally by economic considerations, but by the need to find an alternative political and economic model to the one posed by Castro's Cuba.

This explains the exceptionally intimate relationship which developed between the Kennedy and Johnson administration in the 1960s and the Christian Democratic party. While many of the details of this relationship were revealed by a special congressional investigation headed by the late Senator Frank Church in 1973 and 1975, few Americans have bothered to read the three thick green paper-covered volumes ultimately printed by the Select Subcommittee of the Senate. Instead, careless and tendentious media coverage has perpetuated a series of myths. One of the purposes of this book is to reopen those volumes and examine precisely what they contain.

The truth is that for all its supposed wealth and power, the United States did not get what it wanted in Chile. The Christian Democratic government of the 1960s was succeeded by Popular Unity, not another center-left or center-right coalition. Though the Nixon administration covertly schemed to prevent Allende from taking office in 1970, what it had in mind was not a military coup but a rematch, in which the political forces of the country would more nearly reflect its actual currents of opinion. Doubtless this stretched the definition of respect for self-determination beyond all tolerable limits, but—and this is the point—it still lies very far from the charge of seeking to install a military dictatorship. Chile may indeed be one more example—a quite dramatic one at that—of the law of unintended outcomes as it operates in the international arena, or of the limits of hegemony.

This book began as a history of the Allende regime. Very quickly it became apparent to the author that no aspect could be adequately explained within the span of three years. Most of the issues needed to be explored topically, and on their own terms. This required sinking "shafts," as it were, into the Chilean past at different angles. To follow the mining metaphor, sometimes the tunnels crisscross one another; taken as a whole, they provide a revealing look at a remarkably complex and interesting society.

I was able to begin work on the book as a national fellow of the Hoover Institution at Stanford University, 1979–80. I appreciate particularly the sympathetic interest of Dr. Glenn Campbell, its director, and Dr. Dennis L. Bark, then associate director and chief of its national fellows program, as well as the support of Dr. John Wirth, then director of Stanford University's Center for Latin American Studies. A subsequent fellowship from the Council on Foreign Relations in New York in 1986–87 allowed me to complete it with a minimum of obligations, thanks to the Council's president, Peter Tarnoff, and the director of its Latin American program, Susan Kaufman Purcell. As work-in-progress, I have been able to discuss it over the years with many people, including some who participated in the events described. Except for the late President Eduardo Frei, whose comments are reproduced in the Appendix, and those whom I quote directly in the text, I have generally abstained from identifying them, so as to make it clear that however much I have benefited from their perspectives, the interpretations are mine alone.

Finally, my thanks to Professor Irving Louis Horowitz, president of Transaction Publishers, and Anita Stock, my editor, who have seen the importance of the subject, and been willing to commit energy and resources to make the work accessible to the public.

Acronyms

BIH	Basic Irrigated Hectares
CEPRO	Centers of [Agricultural] Production
CERA	Centers of Land Reform
CODE	Confederation of Democratic Organizations
CODELCO	Chilean Copper Corporation
CORA	Agrarian Reform Corporation
CORFO	Chilean State Development Corporation
CUT	Unified Confederation of Labor
ENDESA	National Electrical Company
ENU	Unified National School Curriculum
FRAP	Front of Popular Action
IC	Christian Left
INDAP	Institute for Aid to [Agricultural] Production
JAPs	Price and Supply Boards
MAPU	Movement of Unified Popular Action
MCR	Revolutionary Peasant Movement
MIR	Movement of the Revolutionary Left
ODEPLAN	National Planning Office
SOQUIMICH	Chilean Chemical Company
SOFOFA	Society for the Promotion of Industrial Growth
VOP	Organized Vanguard of the People

1

Chile, 1970: Ripe for Revolution?

On September 4, 1970, Chileans went to the polls and elected a Marxist physician, Salvador Allende—a Socialist in coalition with his country's Communist party and other, smaller groups—to a six-year presidential term. In so doing, they suddenly and unwittingly propelled a remote South American republic from the margins to the very center of Western consciousness. A month before, few Europeans or North Americans could even have located Chile on a map; within a matter of weeks, Santiago regularly figured as a dateline on front pages around the world—a position it still occupies, and for related reasons, nearly two decades later. The Chilean capital—then nearly eleven hours flying time from New York and between eighteen and twenty-two hours from Western Europe—abruptly became a new center of revolutionary pilgrimage, for a time displacing China, North Vietnam, and Cuba. Though the moment was brief, it was extremely intense: everything that happened during the next three years in Chile acquired vast international relevance.

Of what did that relevance consist? In the first instance, Chile was the oldest and firmest democracy in Latin America, complete with a multiparty system and the fullest range of civic and political rights. Up until that point, no such country had ever freely opted for socialism, at least in the Marxist sense of the word; that it could apparently do so was profoundly unsettling to those who believed in the central lesson of the immediate postwar period, namely, that democracy provided its own antibodies to the challenge of communism. But Allende's election was also a beacon of hope to the left wing of all Western European Socialist parties, as well as to advocates of an emerging "theology of liberation" within the Roman Catholic church. Since the 1950s, these people had been searching for a "historic compromise" between two models of development, one which placed its highest priorities on "political and civil rights" as understood and practiced in Western countries; the other on what the Soviets and their allies called "economic and social rights." If

1

this possibility could be demonstrated in an environment reasonably similar to Western Europe, the consequences would be far-reaching indeed. As a group of Italian sympathizers told Allende shortly after his election, "If you can show in Chile that a second road to socialism is possible, that it is possible to create a symbiosis of Christian *values* and socialist *institutions*, then the next country to advance along that road will be Italy, and very soon others in Latin America, and later, in one or two generations, half the world."[1] Such was the burden—and the glory—visited upon Allende and his people by well-wishers around the world; and such, also, the stuff of subsequent legend.

Up until 1970 few people expected Chile to be cast into such a heroic role. It was a small and somewhat impoverished country which had clearly seen better days; its political civility, like much else in its public life, had a slightly shabby-genteel quality. Chileans themselves were modest in their expectations for their country and for themselves. As retiring President Eduardo Frei Montalva was fond of remarking, in Chile to produce wealth required enormous effort; his countrymen could not risk the luxury of outlandish experiments such as those to which the Argentines (far richer in natural resources, and also in bizzare ideological tendencies) were periodically prone. Since the Great Depression there had been several cautious attempts at social reform in Chile, rendered all the more tentative by scarce resources and the constraints of the political system. In spite of the presence of a vigorous and even interesting Left, the dominant tone of political life was unmistakably gray. In the decade before Allende's election it was common to hear people say, "Nothing ever *happens* in Chile."

When something finally did, the country was overrun by legions of foreigners who arrogated to themselves the job of explaining to the world how Allende's election, and consequently the advent of the Chilean road to socialism, was inevitably prefigured in all that had come before it.[2] Whole decades of Chilean history were ransacked to find the supporting evidence. Italian Marxists, German Social Democrats, American liberals, and left-wing Catholics from everywhere suddenly found themselves subscribing to what used to be called the Whig interpretation of history. The problem with such explanations—they quickly became writ and to some degree remain so today—was that they confused a specific outcome with the conditions which had made it possible. They also ignored, or glossed over, the central questions posed by the particular context: Who voted for Allende and who did not? What did the result say about the values and preferences of the majority? In short, did Chileans really opt in 1970 for a social revolution? If so, why? If not, why not? And how could one know? These questions, in any event, are our point of departure here.

The Context: Economic, Social, Political

Sudden dramatic events have a way of altering the landscape of our perceptions, and in this regard Chile was no exception. Thus, before September 1970 the country's most salient feature—certainly, the only thing highly educated foreigners knew about it—was its success at replicating Western democratic practices. Once Allende had triumphed at the polls, however, the country's image was totally altered. Quite literally overnight, its most salient aspect became the deficiencies of its economic and pervasive social inequalities. Actually, however, economic backwardness and extreme poverty were not new to Chileans. Indeed, in few Latin American countries had these subjects been so extensively and learnedly discussed, in large measure because the country had experienced so many cycles of boom-and-bust throughout its one hundred fifty years of independent existence. During the nineteenth century, the country enjoyed a modest prosperity based upon the export of wheat, wines, silver, and copper. After 1880, however, it underwent a phenomenal economic boom following the forcible annexation from Bolivia and Peru (in the War of the Pacific, 1879–1883) of territories rich in nitrates. These nitrates produced a highly-prized fertilizer and were a vital element in the manufacture of explosives. The nitrate bonanza not only enriched the country's coffers manyfold, but encouraged neglect of agriculture and other forms of social investment. Instead of diverting revenues from mining into capital goods, income from the nitrate camps of the northern desert was channeled into public works, military and naval expenditures, and salaries for South America's best–paid bureaucracy, or expended on luxury imports and on purchases of the very foodstuffs which Chile itself had once produced in abundance.

The development of synthetic nitrates by the Germans during the First World War, and the collapse of world commodity markets in 1930, brought an end to the nitrate era, but left Chile saddled with an infrastructure narrowly based on mining exports. The country survived the Great Depression and subsequent travails through the substitution of copper for nitrates, but with some very significant differences. Like nitrates, copper had once been mined by Chilean entrepreneurs; but by the turn of the century, the more easily accessible deposits had long since been exhausted. The rich reserves which were known to lie underground could be extracted only through the massive infusion of an extremely expensive technology. Hence the substitution of copper for nitrates facilitated the entry into Chile of North American mining concerns; and what is more important from the point of view of Chile's subsequent political history, the surrender of its basic resources to foreign corporations.[3]

Although in subsequent years Chile would attempt to break free from dependence on copper exports, diversification—no less than survival itself—depended upon the flow of royalties from the mining sector. It was out of these revenues that the country had to pay for industrial machinery, patent royalties, credit, technology, and for the very food to sustain its people until the transition was completed. By 1970, Chile could be said to have proceeded about halfway toward industrialization, with extremely problematical results. Apart from the centrality of mining and an unfinished industrial plant, the Chilean economic landscape after 1930 was dominated by an inefficient agriculture, a growing foreign debt, recurrent bouts of inflation, and income inequalities which pointed to a genuine social crisis.

Just how acute that social crisis had become by 1970 was, of course, the subject of considerable controversy. Development surveys habitually placed Chile in the very bottom of the top third of all nations, and somewhere in the top quarter of all Latin American republics. Such rankings were (and are) of limited value, since they average out qualitative and quantitative factors—in the Chilean case, excellent scores for literacy (90 percent), urbanization (31.5 percent in 1960, third in Latin America after Argentina and Uruguay), and political participation (78 percent of eligible voters cast ballots in the 1965 congressional elections), with surprisingly mediocre comparative figures for infant mortality (thirteenth among twenty-four Latin American nations), and life expectancy (sixty-two years, tied for twelfth in the same group).[4] As one distinguished American scholar put it, Chile in 1970 was a society "in which the range of income differences was too wide, the contrasts were too great, not only between the misery belts of the marginals [in Santiago and other cities] and the golden living standards of the rich, but also between the middle classes and the very poor."[5] Chile's small size and high urbanization and population density made its citizens more aware of these differences than might otherwise have been the case. Many who were far from Marxist in sympathy shared the frequently-quoted view of Christian Democrat Jorge Ahumada that there was "nothing intrinsic in the mentality of the Chilean people, in the nature of its territory and resources, or in any other of its permanent characteristics, that make it impossible to build in this area a society that can function without hatred, without shameful misery, and with opportunity for all."[6] Without discounting the sheer human cost provoked by discontinuities in Chile's economic development, it is necessary to stress the unusually high degree of political awareness and critical intelligence which were brought to bear in the discussion of economic and social issues. It was this awareness, rather than the statistics themselves, which explained much of the course of Chilean public life.

Perhaps the most remarkable feature of those decades up until the 1970 election, was the persistence of democratic institutions in the face of uneven growth, stagnation, and sometimes near-catastrophic and social conditions. Except for a period of turmoil in the mid-1920s, followed by the dictatorship of Colonel Carlos Ibáñez del Campo (1927–1931), Chile had experienced no serious disruption of its public life since 1891. Civilian rule continued to be the order of the day; constitutional forms were rigorously respected; freedom of speech, assembly, and press was generally observed; and there was ample opportunity for citizens of all political persuasions to express themselves through a multiplicity of parties and groupings.

Historically, the interests of the Right were represented by the Liberal and Conservative parties,[7] which spoke for the large landowners, industrialists, importers, and upper professional classes. The Center was embodied by the Radical party, whose constituency was drawn from public employees, school-teachers, and urban middle sectors, and which overlapped to some degree with the Chilean Masonic order. The Left was divided between the Communist and the Socialist parties, whose mainstay of support were the miners of the north, Chile's industrial proletariat, and sectors of the lower-middle class and the intelligentsia. Although the Communist party had been outlawed in Chile from 1948 to 1957, the Socialists continued to function legally, and no Chilean election since 1918 failed to offer voters some sort of left-wing slate.

The diversity of electoral choices was considerably enriched after 1941 with the emergence of the Christian Democratic party. Product of a schism between the youth movement of the Conservative party and its parent body, the Christian Democrats slowly climbed to a position of prominence in electoral politics, so that by 1958 it was clear that the next presidential contest would be a confrontation between their standard-bearer and his opposite number on the left. The Christian Democrats brought to Chile the traditions of European Catholic social thought, and they staked out an ideological position somewhere between the Radicals and the Left. They spoke of the need to transform Chile's economic and social structure, and to establish a system which would constitute something of a "middle way" between capitalism and communism, all within the framework of parliamentary democracy. At times this system sounded as if it would resemble that of Sweden; at times, that of Yugoslavia; at still others, that of West Germany. This studied ideological vagueness was of itself a source of appeal, permitting the Christian Democrats to knit together a broad coalition of forces which proved resoundingly successful in the 1964 presidential contest, though it carried within it the seeds of future interparty conflict.

Perhaps of greater long-term significance for Chilean electoral politics, the Christian Democrats crowded out the Radicals at the Center-Left of the spectrum, causing that party to decline in size and split between left and right wings. However, it should be noted that Christian Democracy drew its growing strength in the 1960s not merely from electors lured from other parties, but from the increasing incorporation of new voters, particularly peasants and urban squatters in the slums of Santiago and other cities.

Even more remarkable than the wide range of choices and the open environment in which to make them, was the diversity of responses by the Chilean electorate to the country's economic and social problems. Thus, between 1938 and 1964, four distinct ideological tendencies were given a turn at the presidency: *Center-Left* (the Popular Front government of Radical Presidents Pedro Aguirre Cerda [1938–1941], Juan Antonio Ríos [1942–1946], and Gabriel González Videla [1946–1952]); *Populist* ("Independent" General Carlos Ibáñez del Campo [1952–1958]); *Conservative* (Liberal Jorge Alessandri [1958–1964]); *Social-Catholic* (Christian Democratic Eduardo Frei [1964–1970]).[8] Although the Socialist and Communist parties supported (and, at the beginning, participated in) the Popular Front government of Aguirre Cerda and Rios, it was generally conceded that the regime was dominated by Radicals. President González Videla proved as much in 1948 when he turned on the Communists, broke up the coalition, and drove the party into jail, exile, or hiding.[9] Thus, in spite of ample opportunities at the ballot box between 1938 and 1948, and again between 1957 and 1970, combined with an economic and social environment throughout the entire period supposedly propitious for the rise of communism (or some other left-wing movement), Chileans preferred more moderate alternatives.

Particularly significant in this connection was the reform-minded government of President Eduardo Frei (1964–1970), which captured the imagination of much of Latin America and was widely regarded in Washington (with mixed results in Chile) as a "showcase" for the Alliance for Progress. Frei's program in 1964 had called for a thoroughgoing agrarian reform, and an increasing participation of the Chilean state in the foreign-owned copper industry ("Chileanization"). It envisioned tax reforms, economic diversification, modernization of education, and the increasing incorporation of the country's "marginals" into its political and social structures. On the farthest fringes of Christian Democratic ideology, there was even some talk about worker participation in the management of industry.

During his six years in office, Frei accomplished a fair number of these campaign promises, an achievement due partly to his enormous energy and personal popularity, partly to a congressional majority after 1964, partly to heavy U.S. economic assistance, and partly to the fact that much of his presidency coincided with the Vietnam War, which (though officially deplored by the president's party and many other sectors of Chilean life) raised the world price of copper and significantly increased revenues from the mining sector. By 1970, majority ownership of most of the country's copper mines had been transferred to the Chilean state, and the government had moved into the areas of steel and electricity. Tax collections were increased in real terms by fifty percent. Perhaps most important of all, the Christian Democrats had transformed the Chilean countryside. Thirty thousand families had been settled on the land. Peasants were unionized, and for the first time, the minimum wage was extended to rural laborers. One hundred thousand small farmers had joined cooperatives. In the cities, a reform of nearly equal; magnitude was evident in the organization of 600,000 shanty-town dwellers into social-purpose organizations, closely affiliated with the government (in effect, with the Christian Democratic party). Primary education was expanded, and some attempts were made at reforming the curricula of the country's antiquated universities and higher technical institutions.[10]

Impressive as these gains were, they fell somewhat short of the 1964 Christian Democratic program. For example, its provision for land reform originally envisioned settling fully 100,000 families on the land. To some degree, Frei's incomplete success was due to inflation, which he, like so many of his predecessors, had failed to control. He was not always deft in his dealings with Congress, particularly with the Right. And at times his course of action was seriously constricted by the legal inhibitions built into the Chilean system, which generally precluded drastic measures in areas affecting private property. On the other hand, all public opinion polls in 1969 and 1970 attested to the president's continuing personal popularity, and it is generally thought that if Chilean law had not precluded consecutive presidential terms, Eduardo Frei would have been re-elected in 1970 by a comfortable majority.

Hence it is not surprising that prior to 1970 Chile was not precisely a major focus of attention for the international Left. In fact, those of its number who visited the country in the 1960s tended to express consternation at the obvious relish with which Communist and Socialist parliamentarians settled comfortably into their upholstered benches, elbow-to-elbow with representatives of Chile's landed aristocracy and "*comprador*-bourgeoisie," while outside the chambers a potentially revolutionary situation was held to be in the making. A case in point was that of two American Marxists visiting Chile in 1963, who could not help wondering aloud if somehow the Left ever won an election there, it would be psychologically as well as politically capable of consolidating its gains and creating a viable regime.[11]

In Cuba, where a Marxist government had come to power after 1959 as the indirect consequence of a successful guerrilla movement, the subject of Chile and its Left habitually evoked responses of controlled skepticism. The Castro regime, trapped in an ideological fog of its own making, rigidly insisted upon the universal applicability of its own, peculiar road to power,[12] and only infrequently could it be persuaded to concede the possibility of an electoral road to socialism (and this, only for Chilean domestic consumption). Far more typical, however, was Premier Fidel Castro's annual vituperative denial of the possibility of peaceful revolution in Latin America, delivered on the revolutionary holiday of July 26, while the principal advocate of the course he was attacking, Senator Salvador Allende, sat smiling several feet away on the platform.[13]

Writing after Allende's victory, but expresssing views common to the Cuban leadership before 1970, French Marxist Régis Debray held that in Chile "liberal bourgeois democracy . . . has demonstrated an exceptional capacity for absorption, recuperation, and conciliation." Its myths "of Liberty and Law with capital L's," he added tartly, were "lived at the humblest level . . . [penetrating] the attitudes of the exploited." Such a regime would not disappear "in the blink of an eye, not even if the present state were overthrown tomorrow; the whole of 'civil society' is steeped in it."[14] These comments and many others like them, scattered throughout Marxist journals in Latin America, Western Europe, and even in Chile itself, deplored the gap of "false consciousness" which prevented Chileans from seeing that a revolution was necessary, and from taking the measures—by ballot box or otherwise—which would achieve its consummation.

The Left Explains Allende's Victory

Now that the impossible had nonetheless occurred, the international Left abruptly shifted ideological gears and pushed forward to provide a framework for undertstanding the new turn of events in Chile. In general, its analyses fell into two broad categories, emphasizing either short- or long-range considerations. Short-range hypotheses recurred to that hoary Marxist standby, the "increasing immiseration" thesis, combined, however, with what should have been its methodological polar opposite, the "rising expectations" thesis of bourgeois social science. Longer-range explanations emphasized a rising Marxist wave at the ballot box which finally peaked victorious in 1970. Of course, neither short- nor long-range explanations were necessarily mutually exclusive; both, however, were fraught with serious factual difficulties.

The notion of revolution as the consequence of acutely worsening social and economic conditions has appealed to revolutionary historians from time immemorial; it was merely left to Karl Marx and Friedrich Engels to give it its most eloquent literary expression in *The Communist Manifesto*. In truth, however, no Marxist regime has ever come to power under the circumstances outlined in that document, including the one in Chile. Yet there seems to be something about the picture of a growing popular desperation naturally exploding into revolt—something, perhaps, left over from Victorian notions of natural science?—which left-wing commentators cannot quite abandon, regardless of the facts. Here are some examples in the case of Chile:

> Instead of improving, the lot of Chilean workers deteriorated during this period of purported progress.[15]

Thanks to the growth of the population at a more rapid rate than opportunities for work, the army of unemployed and sub-employed was also growing. The total result was a relentless pressure for more extreme measures to change the quality of life by changing the rules of the game, a pressure which expressed itself in the plurality for the coalition headed by Salvador Allende in the 1970 presidential election.[16]

From the election of Ibáñez in 1952 on to 1970, economists of every school and political persuasion would attempt to solve the huge problems of underdevelopment in Chile . . . Each would have limited success, with perhaps the most positive contribution being the negative one of eliminating for the new incumbent one more alternative. . . . As each new palliative was tried, the people of Chile awakened further to the need for their organization and participation in power.[17]

[In the 1960s] the rich were actually getting richer, while the poor were getting relatively—and sometimes absolutely—poorer. . . . Is it any wonder, then, that most Chileans were not fond of the capitalist system, nor of the class structure which was its natural corollary?[18]

If by these statements what the authors really *mean* to say is that as late as 1970, a significant percentage of the Chilean population was still lacking in the essentials of a decent life as known in most Western countries—access to housing, employment, education, and self-respect—then there are many and eloquent proofs to bear them out. This situation was far from new, however, and begs the question of why 1970 should have been the year of a Marxist victory in Chile, rather than 1964, 1958, or even (theoretically) 1976. Or, if one is supposed to infer that in spite of the efforts of Christian Democracy, by 1970 social conditions in Chile still had not risen to levels satisfactory to development economists, social workers, and humanitarians—again, there is little reason to quibble.

But if these commentators insist, as they seem to, that Chile was literally moving in the direction of a vast social transformation during the Frei administration, then they are wrong. Insofar as it is possible to discern broad trends during the 1960s, the indicators tend to cancel each other out. On one hand, the *rate* of economic growth dropped (from 5.4 percent [1960–1965] to 4.6 percent [1965–1970]), and unemployment *rose* (from 5.4 percent [1964] to 6.2 percent [1970]). However, Chile's gross national product *increased* (from E^0s 5,755 million [1965] to E^0s 7,201 million [1970]), as did the per capita share, thereof (from E^0s 658 [1965] to E^0s 741 [1970]), and as did the annual *rate of increase* in per capita income (from 1.4 percent [1940–1960] to 2.6 percent [1960–1970]).[19] Insofar as income distribution is concerned, there was no significant improvement in the Christian Democratic years—in fact, the Gini coefficients[20] show no substantive change (Table 1.1). Thus it

TABLE 1.1
Gini Coefficients for Chile, 1958–1970

Period	Distribution of Family Income	of Personal Income
1959–1964 (Alessandri)	.4656	.4977
1965–1967 (Frei)	.4713	.4986
1968–1970 (Frei)	.4943	.5175

Source: Juan Carlos Méndez G., *Chilean Socioeconomic Overview* (Santiago, 1980), p. 27, based on Isabel Heskia, *Distribución del ingreso en el Gran Santiago, 1957–1978* (Santiago, 1979).

is possible to argue that things in Chile had not significantly improved in the decade prior to Allende's election, but their figures offer no overwhelming quantitative evidence of large-scale regression, or increasing immiseration.

These figures fail to capture, however, two distinctive qualitative factors of the Chilean economic and social scene. One is the degree to which large segments of the urban population had managed to insulate themselves from the vagaries of economic slump, and more important, the measure to which that privileged circle was being widened during the Christian Democratic years of power. Since the Great Depression, Chile's middle class and organized urban proletariat had succeeded in creating for itself what one student has called "an elaborate structure of legal privilege," whose principal feature was forty or fifty different social security systems, special pay clauses and benefits, tax exemptions and annual adjustments for inflation. The result was a rather peculiar kind of income redistribution, in which the burden was borne not by the rich, but by "the lower income groups"—prototypically, non-organized workers and rural laborers—"through indirect taxation and forced transfer of income through the inflationary process."[21] The Christian Democrats recognized this anomaly, and during the Frei years sought to alter it by enlarging the perimeter of groups served by the system. (There was an obvious political payoff here: not merely the recruitment of new constituencies, but the swamping of rival ones traditionally loyal to the Radicals and to the parties of the Left.)

The first steps in this direction were the unionization of the rural working class, which for the first time brought an important sector of the Chilean peasantry into the bargaining system, and the organization of slum-dwellers into a quasi-official economic and social organization known as *Promoción Popular*. It is difficult to measure precisely the degree to which these efforts actually succeeded in ameliorating the lot of these long-neglected groups, but they cannot be brushed aside simply because there are no reliable units of measure. For one thing, the Christian Democrats did very well among both groups in the 1970 elections, and one cannot dismiss the unprecedented efforts of that party—often, admittedly, with massive financial assistance from the United States—in the areas of housing, health, education, and land reform, however incomplete, as being of no import to ordinary Chileans.

The point which needs to be stressed above all, however, is that no discussion of "the lot of the Chilean workers" or "the Chilean people" or "the poor" makes much sense without taking fully into account the critical distinction between the country's privileged and non-privileged proletariats. Further, no accurate statement about the direction in which the country was moving can fail to reflect the efforts of Christian Democracy—however slightly or inadequately—to enlarge the boundaries of the former.

Short-Term Trends

Since the Second World War, the "rising expectations" thesis has been a short-hand expression for roughly the following statement: The world revolution in communications and popular political consciousness since 1945 in many underdeveloped countries has raised levels of political, social, and economic expectations to the point of placing local governments (and their foreign allies) under strong, even revolutionary pressures. The thesis is subject to a number of possible refinements, all of relevance here: (a) that governments which fail utterly to meet those expectations will be subject to revolutionary pressures; (b) that governments which succeed in meeting them partially, but incompletely, will be subject to revolutionary pressures; (c) that governments which succeed in meeting them completely will be subject to equal or *even greater* revolutionary pressures by raising popular awareness of what is actually possible, and therefore introducing a new upward spiral of expectations.

The problem with this theory is that it "explains" revolutionary upheavals under virtually *all* circumstances, and condemns to instability governments which do nothing at all to better the lot of their people no less than those which undertake a full-blown program of reform. In other words, its predictive value is not very great. On the other hand, there is a certain common-sense appeal to the thesis, since it evokes instinctive assumptions many people hold about human nature (though one would not expect those same assumptions to be shared by Marxists, for whom "consciousness" presumably follows, rather than precedes, material conditions).

Nonetheless, in the case of Chile it is interesting to note that many of the same proponents of the increasing immiseration theory cannot be altogether convinced of their own arguments, since so many of them also wish to subscribe to a variant of the rising expectations thesis. Among other things, this forces them to admit, at least indirectly, that the Frei regime might well have been more a victim of its successes than its failures.[22] It also contradicts the gloomy picture of Chile in the 1960s which they already sketched out for us. Thus, some of the arguments are rather torturous in their logic:

> If the Socialists had won in 1964, their victory would probably never have been consummated. Faced with a society almost feudal in many respects, the difficulties of jumping into socialism would probably have been overwhelming. But by permitting Frei to legitimate the concepts of socialism and to begin marching toward a reformation of Chilean society, the Socialists by 1970 found much less resistance to their victory.

> Yet, ironically, as the masses began making the very types of demands that Frei had encouraged, and, indeed, spawned, internal and international factors limited the government's will and power to respond.[23]

> The techniques used by the Christian Democrats to enlist a mass following had drawn great numbers of both rural and urban workers to the center of the political process in which they had previously been marginal, a change which quickly rebounded to the benefit of the extreme Left and permanently enlarged its power base.[24]

> Frei's administration was to some extent successful in achieving its political goals . . . Yet the Frei administration also unwittingly caused stirrings among the people of Chile. By talking about the need for structural change, it helped make the idea that it was necessary a commonplace. The rhetoric of "Chileanization" and the perception that it was a fraud helped spread the desire to see copper truly nationalized . . . The land reform awakened expectations among the *campesinos*. In one place after another—impatient at the slowness of reform—they began to seize land themselves.[25]

> With slow growth and very limited redistribution, the rising expectations of the poor created in the 1964 campaign had to go largely unmet.[26]

The one thing most of these arguments have in common is a studied reluctance to admit that anything of real importance happened in Chile during the Christian Democratic years except for the introduction of new points of reference into political discourse. Actually, however, overblown rhetoric and sweeping promises were not new in Chilean presidential campaigns, and the Christian Democratic program of 1964 was far less sweeping than that of the Popular Front of 1938 (which promised "Food, Clothing and Shelter" to every Chilean), or that of General Carlos Ibáñez del Campo (who also had a great following among Chile's poor) in 1952. As a matter of fact, the accomplishments of Frei's government *did* ultimately prove its undoing, but not—as the authors cited would have it—so much by increasing the powers, appeal, or constituency of the Left, as by seriously alienating (and significantly expanding the political base of) the Right. They also introduced a serious division within the Christian Democratic leadership itself as to how fast and how far to go, particularly after inflation began to rise again in 1967 and President

Frei found it necessary to trim the sails of his program. That division led to the exodus of a number of left-wing Christian Democratic leaders, who formed a new party. Both of these developments were of crucial relevance to the outcome of the 1970 presidential elections.

Longer-Term Trends

So much for short-term explanations. What if one took a longer prospect, and examined the trends in Chilean politics in the ten or twenty years prior to Allende's election? Here is the way our commentators explain things:

> In the past decade [1960–1970] the ranks [of the Left] had been slowly but steadily swelling. In 1952, with the Socialists split and the Communists openly persecuted, leftist factions could give Allende only 52,000 votes (5.5 percent of the total). Just six years later, however, a united Left delivered 357,000 Allende ballots (28.9 percent). In 1964, with the field narrowed down to two, Allende and Frei, the Left had continued its rapid rise, winning 978,000 votes (38.9 percent).[27]

> As the imagination behind Christian Democracy wavered, the people of Chile pressed forward . . . social protest touched almost all facets of society . . . Chilean society was speeding towards an upheaval. No longer was there enough largesse in the society to buy off a few large groups.[28]

> As the electorate broadened and increasingly larger groups of people have been organized into local and regional groups linked and tied into national political parties, the entire country has responded by moving slowly leftward.[29]

> The electoral result [of 1970] was just one further episode in a much wider phenomenon: the general crisis of the dependent capitalist system and of its expression, the system of political rule. [Chile's social crisis] stretched the *status quo* to its limit, and despite the psychological campaign mounted by the Right . . . two thirds of the electorate were agreed as to the necessity to replace it.[30]

Thanks to the work of political scientists James Prothro and Patricio Chaparro, it is very easy to demonstrate that these characterizations of the Chilean electorate are quite untrue.

Table 1.2 illustrates several interesting points. First, while the Right obviously declined between 1952 and 1964, it was not the Left but the Center which was the principal beneficiary. Since the 1950s, the left-wing vote in Chilean presidential elections hovered at about 36 percent, a figure which "was not greatly increased or decreased by the number of parties or candidates contesting the election."[31] Second, the Marxist wave which our authors repeatedly suggest was moving the electorate could just as well have peaked in 1958, when Allende came within a shadow of winning the presidency. His triumph in that year was blunted only by the rival candidacy of a defrocked left-wing priest, Antonio Zamorano, who deprived him of a handful of critically-

TABLE 1.2
Distribution of Popular Votes in Chilean Presidential Elections, 1952–1970

Year	Candidate/Party(ies)	Percentage of Vote
1952	Carlos Ibáñez (Independent)	46.8
	Arturo Matte (Right: Conservative, Liberal)	27.8
	Pedro E. Alfonso (Center: Radical)	19.9
	Salvador Allende (Left: Socialist)	*5.5*
1958	Jorge Alessandri (Right: Conservative, Liberal)	31.6
	Salvador Allende (Left: Socialist, Communist)	*28.9*
	Eduardo Frei (Center: Christian Democrat)	20.7
	Luis Bossay (Center: Radical)	15.6
	Antonio Zamorano (Independent Left)	3.3
1964	Eduardo Frei (Center-Right: Christian Democrat, Conservative, Liberal)	56.09
	Salvador Allende (Left: Socialist, Communist)	*38.93*
	Julio Durán (Center-Right, Radical)	4.99
1970	*Salvador Allende (Left: Socialist, Communist MAPU, Radical Left)*	*36.6*
	Jorge Alessandri (Right: Independent, National)	35.2
	Radomiro Tomic (Center: Christian Democrat)	28.1

Source: Dirección del Registro Electoral, Chile, reproduced from James W. Prothro and Patricio E. Chaparro, "Public Opinion and the Movement of the Chilean Government to the Left, 1952–72," in A. and S. Valenzuela., eds., *Chile: Politics and Society* (New Brunswick, N.J., 1976), p. 91.

needed radical ballots. Third, Allende's victory in 1970 was due largely to a division between the Center and Right, each of which chose to run a candidate of their own. Even so, running in 1970 with the additional support of several new groups (the most important of which were the Movement of Unity Popular Action (MAPU) and the Left-Radicals, both schismatic remnants of Christian Democracy and the Radical party, respectively), *Allende actually won a smaller percentage of the vote in the year of his victory than in 1964, when he was defeated by Eduardo Frei.*

These facts speak all the more eloquently when one considers that the Chilean electorate had grown considerably since 1952, partly through the introduction of feminine suffrage (1952), the introduction of the secret ballot in rural areas (1958), obligatory voter registration (1962), and the enfranchisement of illiterates (1970).[32] Further, the decline of the Conservative political machine in the Chilean countryside was reflected not only in an overall decline of right-wing strength nationally, but the entry into the political arena of a constituency which, if not new to voting itself, was able for the first time to speak its own mind. Thus, the argument that Allende's victory was due to the increased participation of new, formerly-neglected marginal elements simply is not true. As Arturo and Samuel Valenzuela have shown, while the percentage of the Chilean population registered to vote virtually doubled

TABLE 1.3
Presidential Election Returns, Chile 1970

Candidates (Parties)	Popular Vote	Percentage
Jorge Alessandri		
(Independent, National)	1,036,279	35.2
Salvador Allende		
(Popular Unity [Socialist, Communist,		
MAPU, Left-Radical)	1,075,616	36.6
Radomiro Tomic		
(Christian Democrat)	824,849	28.1

Source: See Table 1.2

between 1957 and 1970, "increases in participation did not benefit any particular party to the detriment of others." In fact, they continue, "Allende received at most *13 percent* of the new voters that were added to the rolls from 1964 to 1970, with the bulk going to the candidate of the Right."[33] This fact alone goes a long way towards explaining why Allende received a smaller percentage of the total vote in 1970 than he had in 1964.[34]

It is true that over the previous three presidential elections, there were scattered pieces of evidence which allowed some commentators to assume that in due course Allende (or his successor) might improve the Left's share of the vote. For example, there was a noticeable gain among female voters, only 4.6 percent of whom favored the Socialist candidate in 1952. In 1958, this percentage increased dramatically to 22.3 and in 1964 continued to rise to 32.08.[35] On the other hand, it dropped back to 30.5 in 1970, which suggests that the newly-enfranchised female voter was settling into the long-term pattern established by her male counterpart.[36]

Likewise, in 1964 there appeared to be some qualitative breakthrough for the Left when Allende transcended his traditional fiefdoms in the copper mining areas of the north and the coal mining areas of the south, and for the first time obtained male majorities in the Central Valley provinces of Talca, Linares, and O'Higgins. However, in the 1970 elections, Allende won a lower percentage of the vote "in every province of Chile except [the mining provinces of] Tarapacá and Atacama in the extreme North, and Chiloé and Llanquihue in the extreme South." Particularly disappointing was the drop he suffered in the agricultural provinces of the Central Valley, where he had made considerable progress in 1964; of lesser impact, but of considerable symbolic significance, was his loss of the Anaconda mine in Chuquiquimata, which went to the candidate of the Right, former President Jorge Alessandri![37] Thus on balance it appears that Robert Ayres is fully justified in stating that Chile "has not experienced a critical election at the national level in many years—in the sense of one which produced a durable realignment of party loyalties on behalf of change or innovations."[38]

TABLE 1.4
Ideological Identification of Chileans, 1958–1970

Tendency	1958	1961	1964	1970
Right	31.4	23.8	17.4	26.6
Center	17.8	28.2	29.0	24.2
Left	24.5	26.5	32.0	26.0
No Opinion	26.3	21.5	21.6	23.2
Total	100	100	100	100

Source: Adapted from Carlos Huneeus, *Los chilenos y la política* (Santiago, 1987), p. 163

The illusion that 1970 constituted a meaningful departure from established Chilean voting patterns would seem to be seriously challenged by the presidential election returns themselves (Table 1.3). The most striking aspect is the slim difference between the vote received by Alessandri, running as both an Independent and as the candidate of the right-wing National party, and that of the victorious candidate of Popular Unity—a mere 39,000 votes out of a total of two million ballots cast.

There is, admittedly, a way to interpret these figures in a way favorable to Popular Unity. In a paroxysm of misplaced opportunism, the Christian Democratic candidate, Radomiro Tomic, had run on a shrill left-wing platform of his own (actually it was even more radical than that of his Socialist rival!). Therefore, one could argue that by combining his own 36.3 percent of the vote with Tomic's 28.1, nearly 65 percent of the electorate had given Allende an "ideological majority" for socialism. This is precisely what our authors do:

> It was ultimately this recognition of economic dependence resulting from a capitalist system which denied them a fair share of the benefits of their own economy that persuaded an overwhelming majority of Chileans to vote for a president who promised to start the country on the road to socialism.[39]

> However programatic and demagogic these statements [of Tomic's] may have been, they nonetheless reflected a level of consciousness shared by the majority of the country.[40]

> Tomic chose the Right as his main enemy [in the campaign], thus becoming an objective and personal ally of the Popular Unity candidate, behind the back and even the will of his own governmental apparatus.[41]

Obviously, it is impossible to fully explain the motives behind every Christian Democratic ballot, but some general trends can be identified, and certain possibilities eliminated from the outset. Insofar as broad tendencies are concerned, the most notable development in the period 1964–1970 was a momentary resurgence of the Right in Chile at the expense of both the Center and the Left. This can plausibly be read as a middle-class backlash against the property and tax policies of the Christian Democrats, the resurgence of inflation after 1967, as well as the inability of the party to produce a moderate successor to Frei himself (Table 1.4).

Insofar as the Christian Democratic party itself was concerned, those within its ranks who favored a program similar to Allende's had already departed by 1970. Concretely, in May 1969, a number of left-wing Christian Democratic leaders, including Agriculture Minister Jacques Chonchol and two senators, resigned from the party over what they regarded as its excessive rightward course. They were followed by most of the leaders of the party's youth movement and of its peasant and trade union affiliates. Chonchol referred to these as constituting "about 30 percent of the force of the party,"[42] but more probably the figure represented 30 percent of the *leadership*. The vast majority of their followers remained, as evidenced by the fact that MAPU, the new schismatic movement which Chonchol founded and which became part of Popular Unity, attracted only two percent of the Christian Democratic vote in 1970. It would appear, then, that Christian Democrats who voted for Tomic did so in spite of—rather than because of—his overheated leftist rhetoric.

Perhaps most important of all, survey research demonstrated that Allende could win *only* in a three-way race. A few weeks before the 1970 elections a poll conducted in Santiago found that in any two-way contest—against either Alessandri or any well-known Christian Democrat—the Socialist politician was bound to lose. "Although Allende won more than any other candidate," Prothro and Chaparro report, "the relative clarity of his ideological position made him, at the same time, the last choice of the majority."[43] Indeed, most polls throughout 1969 and early 1970 showed Alessandri as an easy victor. Presumably, it was this large lead which persuaded his sponsors to present a right-wing candidate of their own, rather than to try to forestall a Marxist victory at the polls by repeating what they had done six years before, that is, by lining up behind the Christian Democrats. It was only when Alessandri, who was 73 years old at the time, was revealed in the course of the campaign (the first in Chile in which television played a part) to be somewhat decrepit and lacking in vigor, that his lead began to drop in the polls and an Allende victory became a clear possibility. Too late: the Right had no choice but to hope for the best and push on.

Thus, what we know about the conduct of the Chilean electorate over time does not support the view that Allende's election represents a culminating moment in the rise of the Left. Nor does it does support the notion of an "ideological majority" for socialism. Instead, it establishes the existence since 1952 of a remarkably resilient multiparty system in which the Right, Center and Left held onto significant (and roughly equal) segments of the electorate. No single economic or social development, or series of developments, seems to have been as crucial a determinant of electoral outcomes as the particular configuration of party alignments or rivalries—in effect, whether the Center and Right were united or split. Had Alessandri (or any other candidate of his stature) run in a three-way race in 1964, Allende might well have won six years ahead of time; had Tomic withdrawn in 1970, in all probability Allende would have lost.

A Closer Look at the Electorate

In the face of rising expectations and slow economic growth, inflation, and widespread misery in some urban and rural areas, one might well wonder why such large segments of the Chilean electorate continued to support parties and forces of the Center and Right. Much of the answer can be found in the country's particular social structure. Although most national income was generated by mining and manufacturing, the work force in those sectors amounted to no more than a quarter of what the 1970 census classified as "working class."[44] By way of contrast, an extraordinary number of Chileans— about 24 percent of the labor force in 1969—were classified as "self-employed." Even more suggestive was the persistence in Chile of an artisanal economy well into the recent period. As late as 1957, "almost half of industrial employment and eight percent of total labor was in . . . 70,000 small establishments" employing four persons or less, a figure which had only dropped to 34.2 percent in 1968.[45] The rest of the Chilean working class was widely dispersed, either in the countryside or throughout an unusually large service sector. The service sector was "the most important in the economy in terms of income and employment contribution"—40.5 percent in 1970.[46]

Thus, although most Chilean workers, whether dependent or "self-employed," earned very modest incomes, only a small minority in 1970 were subject to the (presumptively radicalizing) political and social stimuli generated by the classic industrial environment.[47] "Workers in artisanal or semi-artisanal industries in thousands of small units scattered about the country," Jacqueline Roddick reports, were "an almost impossible sector to penetrate politically on any permanent basis except insofar as they themselves [made] contact with other sectors of the working class." Although artisanal workers in Chile had been among the founders of the Socialist party in the early 1930s, by 1970, she found, "the connection [seemed] to have been lost."[48]

Chile's middle class had a long history of political involvement in reform movements, and most of the leaders of the parties of the Left were drawn from this group. As a whole, however, by the 1960s, most of its members preferred to vote for the Radicals or Christian Democracy. This is not really surprising, since the middle class was the principal beneficiary of all important labor legislation since the 1930s (white collar unions were common in Chile). Its members now had something to protect, as the figures on income distribution clearly show. In 1967, while 9 percent of the population possessed 39 percent of the total income, "the richest 10 percent included . . . 47 percent of all office workers [and] 20 percent of those working on their own account."[49] Another way of putting it was that 46 percent of the economically active population received about 50 percent of all income.[50]

In theory, the unorganized urban and rural poor—for whom the system offered so few of its benefits—should have constituted a new and powerful addition to the constituency of the Left. As shown in our analysis of electoral trends, in actual practice this was far from the case. The reasons, again, were sociological and structural. In the countryside, the peasantry was divided into tenants (many of whom were subemployers), migrant workers (*afuerinos*), and provisional smallholders who were recipients of land under Frei's agrarian reform.[51] The Christian Democrats had made good use of their mandate, and through a combination of expropriation, parcelization, and peasant unionization, they possessed by 1970 "a substantial popular base in the countryside." This combined with the traditional cultural environment such as could then be found in almost any Latin American country, meant that even after his election Allende had to deal with an agricultural working class in which "Christian Democratic and right-wing influence [continued to be] strong."[52]

Even greater gains were anticipated from urban sub-proletariat—the inhabitants of the shantytowns (*poblaciones callampas*) of the capital and other major cities. Most of these were former peasants whose displacement to the relative affluence of urban centers was supposed to afford edifying political lessons which would inevitably rebound to the benefit of the Left. Clearly, the parties of Popular Unity did enjoy some success with this group, but by no means enough to tip the electoral scales decisively in their favor. The theoreticians of relative deprivation had cogent arguments; these, however, were often belied by certain harsh realities of Chile's culture of poverty.

For example, in a survey of four representative lower-class slums in Greater Santiago (1968–69), sociologist Alejandro Portes found *no immediate linkage* between socioeconomic frustration and the acquisition of a radical political orientation. Much depended on the length of time the *poblador* had been in the city, and other influences to which he had been exposed in the intervening period. Newcomers, for whom the change was an immediate improvement, were far less likely to affiliate with parties of the Left than those who had been in this setting for a generation of more—in other words, sufficient time for the first illusions of long-term improvement to fully fade. Even more important than length of residence, Portes found, was the situation in the workplace. Thus, the *poblador* who worked in a factory and was subject to the ideological influences of the Marxist trade union movement was the one who voted for Popular Unity, rather than his neighbor who sold shoelaces on the street or worked as a domestic servant in some middle-class household.[53] Given the high rate of rural-urban migration between 1960 and 1970, and the constantly shifting composition of the *poblaciones* themselves, it is not surprising that the Left failed to establish a firm footing in this sector—firm enough at least by 1970, to form a consensus for socialism.

These structural considerations are amply supported by survey data on political opinions. When Portes asked his *pobladores* to indicate their party preferences (again, in 1968–69), the Socialist and Communists received only 38.5 percent of the "vote"–only slightly more than the amount they received two years later in the presidential elections. The Christian Democrats garnered 31 percent, a figure somewhat higher than the percentage obtained in 1970, when Tomic was pitching his rhetoric far to the Left. Portes also notes that if one moved away from party identification to general ideological orientation, "those expressing radical [opinions] in the sample are, without exception, a minority usually less than one-third of the total."[54] When he attempted to correlate leftist radicalism and levels of stratification within his sample, none of the six coefficients was statistically significant, and in many cases they moved in directions opposite to those one might have predicted.[55] Among other things, this suggests that even some of those who voted for the parties of the Left in 1970 may have envisioned something rather different from what they got.

What Did Chileans Want?

Was Chile, then, "ripe for revolution" in 1970? If by that question one means, Was Chile in need of some rather thoroughgoing restructuring of its pattern of income distribution, social expenditures, tax and tariff policies, and national saving, the answer is an undeniable yes.

If, on the other hand, the question is whether these changes were what the Chilean electorate consciously and unambiguously had in mind when it facilitated the rise of Salvador Allende and Popular Unity, then the answer must be an equally categoric no.

Like most Latin American countries, Chile in 1970 represented a curious hybrid—a society whose economic system contained elements of the corporatist structure inherited from the Spanish colony, and areas in which nineteenth-century liberalism had established a freer play of markets and social forces. Specifically, part of the population, probably just under one-half, enjoyed a certain amount of economic security, either through the possession of large urban and rural property (with corresponding subsidies, tax exemptions, tariffs, free ports, low-interest government loans, and so forth), or through functional representation in the government bureaucracy or the trade union movement (annual salary adjustments, social security, housing subsidies).

Through the years these groups had carved out for themselves a perimeter of safety within which, through a variety of means, they could survive inflation, devaluation, and periods of low or negative economic growth. Outside this privileged circle, however, stood the other half of Chile: the urban and rural poor, abandoned to the vagaries of the free market, where—in the context of a system in which the "commanding heights" were corporatist—they were subject to all of the vices of capitalism, but beneficiaries of few or none of its virtues.

For many years, the potential for acute social conflict enclosed within this system was mediated by the relative freedom offered by the political arena— that is, through a multiparty system which presumably allowed Chileans to advance their economic interests at the polling place. In later years, much of the tensions generated within Chilean society could be vented externally—by blaming the United States, whose copper corporations controlled the country's basic national resource. The corporations were alleged to be taking out of the country huge sums which, if retained in Chile, could have bought social peace, and would have precluded the need to alter the dual structure described above. What Chileans did *not* wish to do, however, was to break decisively with the corporatist structure and move toward a full free market economy. Nor were they capable of drawing the entire population into the existing system of functional rewards. The middle class and even the Marxist trade unions had a vested stake in that system, and those outside of it were torn between wanting to destroy it altogether and wanting to enter it on an individual or sectoral basis (such as that achieved by the unionized peasantry under Christian Democracy).

It is indeed possible that by 1970 the Chilean system had reached a point of crisis, though not in the sense of clearly pointing the way to socialism. Markos Mamalakis has summarized the problem brilliantly in a few lines.

> Under Eduardo Frei it became evident that the system's low capacity to convert internal and external resources into physical, human, and institutional capital remained the foremost bottleneck to growth and economic independence. The transformation policies required increasing national savings, sacrifices, and investment. Neither Eduardo Frei's policies towards this end, nor the response to these policies by the people, was of a magnitude close to the one needed for success.[56]

The fact that Chilean reformism might have reached an intellectual and systematic dead-end under Christian Democracy does not, however, of itself prove that the country as a whole had abandoned the illusion of an easy or painless solution to its problems. Up to 1970, Chileans preferred to postpone as long as possible—and by just about any means possible—the decision to radically alter their inherited economic and social structures. They wanted them to work better, but they did not want to change them. Allende's victory on September 4, 1970—the product of vagaries of the Chilean party system, and thus, in the end, an accident—forced them into a context in which sharp choices would have to be made. This in turn unleashed all of the demons secreted into the interstices of the country's economic and social system.

Notes

1. Quoted in Radomiro Tomic, "Christian Democracy and the Unidad Popular," in Federico G. Gil et al., *Chile at the Turning Point: Lessons of the Socialist Years, 1970–1973* tr. John S. Gilitz (Philadelphia, 1979), p. 211.
2. A typical example of such hyperbole was the affirmation of Gary MacEoin that Allende's victory was "but a logical step in the upward thrust of a people." Gary MacEoin, *No Peaceful Way: Chile's Struggle for Dignity* (New York, 1974), p. 28
3. For a more extended discussion, see Chapter Six.
4. Ruth Leger Sivard, *World Military and Social Expenditures, 1978* (n.p., n.d.), pp. 24–25; C. L. Taylor and M. C. Hudson, eds., *World Handbook of Political and Social Indicators*, 2d ed. (New Haven, Conn., 1972), pp. 54, 219.
5. Markos J. Mamalakis, *The Growth and Structure of the Chilean Economy from Independence to Allende* (New Haven, Conn., 1976), p. 243. I have followed Mamalakis closely in my discussion of Chilean economic history.
6. Jorge Ahumada, *En vez de la misera* (Santiago, 1958), cited in ibid., p. 89.
7. The two were fused into the National party in 1966.
8. These designations refer not to the policies specifically pursued once in office, but to the ideological orientation offered to the public at the time of election.
9. The proscription of the Communist party had generally been attributed to the Cold War and pressures from Washington. There is, however, evidence that the move responded to certain considerations of domestic politics. See Paul W. Drake, *Socialism and Populism in Chile, 1932–1952* (Urbana, Ill., 1978), pp. 283–290.
10. Paul E. Sigmund, *The Overthrow of Allende and the Politics of Chile, 1964–76* (Pittsburgh, Pa., 1977), p. 124.
11. Leo Huberman and Paul Sweezy, "Notes on Latin America," in Carlos Fuentes, et. al., *Whither Latin America?* (New York, 1963), pp. 132–134.
12. Ernesto Ché Guevera, "Cuba—Exception or Vanguard?", in John Gerassi, ed., *Venceremos: The Speeches and Writings of Ernesto Ché Guevara* (London, 1968), pp. 131–138.
13. See for example, *El Siglo* (Santiago), July 27, 1966; *El Mercurio* (Santiago), July 27, 28, 1966.
14. Régis Debray, *The Chilean Revolution: Conversations with Allende* (New York, 1971), p. 28.
15. McEoin, *No Peaceful Way*, p. 47.
16. Ibid., p. 57.
17. David J. Morris, *We Must Make Haste—Slowly: The Process of Revolution in Chile* (New York, 1973), p. 25.
18. Richard Feinberg, *The Triumph of Allende: Chile's Legal Revolution* (New York, 1972), pp. 81–82.

19. Kenneth Ruddle and Mukhtar Hamour, eds., *Statistical Abstract of Latin America, 1970* (Los Angeles, 1972), p. 94 (unemployment); Mamalakis, *Growth and Structure*, pp. 90–92 (growth and income). E^0s = escudos, the then-current unit of Chilean currency.

20. Gini coefficients are used to measure distribution or concentration of income. They range between 0, when there is perfect equality, and 1, when there is perfect concentration of income (i.e., 100 percent of income is concentrated in the hands of a single person or sector).

21. Osvaldo Sunkel, "Change and Frustration in Chile," in Claudio Véliz, ed., *Obstacles to Change in Latin America* (London, 1965), pp. 132–133.

22. This also compels left-wing commentators to subscribe, willy-nilly, to the notion of Chile's extreme Right, namely, that Frei was the "Chilean Kerensky." A book by this title, penned by a right-wing Brazilian journalist, was banned in Chile in 1966.

23. Morris, *We Must Make Haste*, pp. 35, 36.

24. MacEoin, *No Peaceful Way*, p. 13.

25. Edward Boorstein, *Allende's Chile* (New York, 1977), pp. 39–40.

26. Feinberg, *The Triumph of Allende*, p. 85.

27. Ibid., p. 88.

28. Morris, *We Must Make Haste*, pp. 38–39, 41.

29. Ibid., p. 7.

30. Debray, *The Chilean Revolution*, p. 41.

31. James Prothro and Patricio E. Chaparro, "Public Opinion and the Movement of the Chilean Government to the Left, 1952–72," in A. and J. S. Valenzuela, eds., *Chile: Politics and Society* (New Brunswick, N.J., 1976), p. 93. The same author also points out that this trend is even more clearly in evidence in congressional elections since 1941 (pp. 94—95).

32. In 1971 suffrage was extended to 18 year olds.

33. Arturo Valenzuela and J. Samuel Valenzuela, "Party Oppositions under the Chilean Authoritarian Regime," in A. and J. S. Valenzuela, *Military Rule in Chile* (Baltimore, 1986), pp. 196–197. Emphasis added.

34. "Among [the] squatters in Santiago, many of whom voted for the first time in the 1960s, the Christian Democrats [in 1970] received about the same number of votes as the Communists and Socialists combined." Arturo Valenzuela, "Political Constraints to the Establishment of Socialism in Chile," in A. and J. S. Valenzuela, eds., *Chile: Politics and Society*, p. 12. Likewise, among the peasantry, correlational analysis "does not confirm the expectation that the propertyless were voting for the parties of the Left." While the Socialists showed some improvement over time (−.54 to −.34), the chief beneficiary of changes in the countryside were the Christian Democrats (−33. to +.33). Robert L. Ayres, "Unidad Popular and the Chilean Electoral Process," in ibid., pp. 54, 56–57. Ayres' figures do not go beyond 1967, and thus do not reflect some modest additional gains in rural Chile by parties of the Left in 1970. In time, all things being equal, they might well have risen to about a third of the vote, that is, their historical national share of the electorate.

35. Institute for the Comparative Study of Political Systems, *The Chilean Presidential Election of September 4, 1964, Part II* (Washington, D.C., 1965), pp. 11, 28, 30. Male and female voters were tabulated separately in Chile.

36. Sigmund, *The Overthrow of Allende*, p. 107.

37. Ibid. This may have been the result of Allende's visit to the region in the 1970 campaign, when he told the assembled members of the mining community that once in office he planned to prohibit the practice of paying Chilean workers in American dollars, a proposal which, according to Allende's private secretary, was understandably ill-received. Osvaldo Puccio, *Un cuarto de siglo con Allende* (Santiago, 1985), p. 216.

38. Ayres, "Unidad Popular," in A. and J. S. Valenzuela, eds., *Chile: Politics and Society*, p. 33.

39. MacEoin, *No Peaceful Way*, p. 54.

40. Debray, *The Chilean Revolution*, p. 41.

41. Ibid., pp. 20–21. At times Debray slips—or could it be the atrocious translation?—and credits Allende with the "first majority" ever won by a left-wing candidate (p. 40). Richard Feinberg parts company here with his ideological confrères, and admits that Tomic's "radical" rhetoric was not taken seriously by many moderate voters of his own party. Feinberg, *The Triumph of Allende*, pp. 134–135. Eduard Boorstein, the author closest ideologically to the Chilean Communist party, does not seem to think that it matters: for him Tomic was one more Christian Democratic fraud, and he rejoices that "the Chileans," not to be fooled again, chose Allende. Boorstein, *Allende's Chile*, p. 40.

42. Quoted in Lester Sobel, ed., *Chile and Allende* (New York, 1974), p. 18.

43. Prothro and Chaparro, "Public Opinion . . .," pp. 88–89.

44. Jacqueline Roddick, "Class Structure and Class Politics in Chile," in Philip O'Brien, ed., *Allende's Chile* (New York, 1976), pp. 7–8.

45. Mamalakis, *Growth and Structure*, pp. 145–146, 233.

46. Ibid., p. 158.

47. By one estimate, "only 30 percent of salaried workers over the age of eighteen belonged to the trade union movement, but this included not merely factory workers but members of peasant unions and white collar workers—particularly civil servants and employees of state-owned industries, since 90 percent of the public sector was unionized." Monica Threfall, "Shantytown Dwellers and Peoples Power," in O'Brien, ed., *Allende's Chile*, pp. 168–169.

48. Roddick, "Class Structure and Class Politics . . .," p. 10.

49. Mamalakis, *Growth and Structure*, p. 234.

50. Alejandro Foxley and Oscar Muñoz, "Income Redistribution, Economic Growth, and Social Structure: The Case of Chile," *Oxford Bulletin of Economics & Statistics* XXXVI, 1 (1974):21–44.

51. For a fuller discussion, see Chapter Four.

52. Roddick, "Class Structure and Class Politics . . .," pp. 10–12.

53. Alejandro Portes, "On the Logic of Post-Factum Explanations: The Hypothesis of Lower-Class Frustration as the Cause of Leftist Radicalism," *Social Forces*, L, 1 (1971):42–3.

54. Alejandro Portes, "Occupation and Lower-Class Political Orientations in Chile," in A. and J. S. Valenzuela eds., *Chile: Politics and Society*, pp. 214–215.

55. Alejandro Portes, "Status Inconsistency and Lower-Class Leftist Radicalism," *Sociological Quarterly*, XIII (Summer, 1972):361–381.

56. Mamalakis, *Growth and Structure*, p. 98.

2

Allende in Power:
The Nature of the Coalition

The program which Salvador Allende was committed to carry out once in the presidency was one of the most thorough and comprehensive ever offered to the Chilean electorate—indeed, one might say, ever offered to the voters of any democratic nation. It was also one of the most radical, both in its critique of the existing social and economic system, and in the nature of the solutions it offered. Its principal economic objective, succinctly stated, was the abolition "of the power of foreign and national monopoly capital and of large units of agricultural property, in order to initiate the construction of socialism."[1] Although the precise juridical mechanisms by which this was to be accomplished were stated only in barest outline, there was certainly no equivocation about the precise measure to be taken. Popular Unity promised to nationalize outright Chile's mines, banks, foreign trade, large distribution firms and strategic industrial enterprises; its electric power, rail, air, and sea transport agencies; its communications, petroleum, iron and steel industries; petrochemicals and heavy chemicals; cellulose and paper. It also called for a drastic extension in the existing system of land reform.

Leaving aside for the present the program's other proposals—which basically envisioned a populist-welfarist approach to income transfers, educational reforms, and the diffusion of opportunities for housing, leisure time, and culture—one cannot but be struck at the enormous gap between the drastic nature of these measures, and the actual number of Chileans (a little more than one out of three) willing to vote for them. Or to put it another way, Chile had had frequent experience with minority governments, but since no previous administration had contemplated such a total transformation of Chilean society, the lack of a clear majority did not pose insuperable problems.[2]

To be sure, many countries in the twentieth century have experienced serious alterations in their social and political fabric, though not typically through democratic procedures. Such changes as have been accomplished by

25

open political communities have normally rested on clear-cut mandates at the ballot box, such as the victory of the Labour party in the British elections of 1945. Chile's political system was certainly far ahead of its social structure, and probably even more farther ahead of the broader values of its society. But to have expected it to deliver through a minority government what even more resilient sytems in Britain, Sweden, and elsewhere had only imperfectly produced through majoritarian regimes seems in retrospect to have been remarkably naive. Unless, of course, the democratic aspect of the Chilean experiment was to be regarded as a mere prelude to more expeditious (that is, more authoritarian) methods.

However, the paradox of Allende's victory went a bit further than that; the Popular Unity was not merely a minority regime, but a coalition government as well. For in order to reach the few thousand votes to pass Alessandri on the right, it had proven necessary to knit together a consortium of six parties, only two of which were Marxist. This coalition was the product of enervating negotiations between August and December 1969, in which conflict centered on both the common program and the identity of the presidential candidate. Even after both were announced, it was clear that some fundamental differences remained—differences arising not only out of varying ideological and international commitments, but also from the distinctive social bases of the parties themselves. It thus appears useful to review the nature of the governing coalition and its membership prior to turning to the specific issues which united it in opposition, and then confused and divided it in power.

The Parties of Popular Unity

The Communists

In 1970 the Communist party of Chile was the largest, best-organized, most disciplined organization of its kind in Latin America. Unlike its counterpart in Cuba, it was no quasi-creation of a victorious regime, not did it resemble other parties in the region, which were more often than not cenacles of declassed intellectuals with tenuous links to a fragmented labor movement. Rather, the Chilean party came close to being what such organizations habitually claim to be: the political expression of the industrial working class, and such of its allies among the middle class, the intelligentsia, and the peasantry committed to the transformation of society along Marxist lines.

The history of the Chilean party is rich in paradox. On one hand, it has been unswervingly faithful to the Soviet line in domestic and foreign affairs, siding with Moscow over the Nazi-Soviet Pact, the Cold War, Yugoslavia, the Sino-Soviet dispute, even the 1968 invasion of Czechoslovakia, which it was the first party outside the bloc to endorse. On the other, it was a truly Chilean party, with deep roots in that country's social struggles. It could claim rightful descent from the Workers' Socialist Party, founded in 1912 by typographer Luis Emilio Recabarren, who led his followers into the Comintern in 1922, the only Latin American socialist party to respond affirmatively to Lenin's invitation. Although by 1970 its organizational structure reached into virtually all sections of Chile, its greatest strength geographically lay in the centers where it first exercised influence, the desolate mining regions of Tarapacá and Antofagasta in Chile's Great North, and the Lota coal mining district in the southern province of Concepción. Although over the years it had attracted a fair number of middle-class lawyers and intellectuals (the most famous of whom was poet Pablo Neruda, 1968 Nobel laureate), it remained overwhelmingly working class in membership; its leaders dominated the national labor federation, the Central Unica de Trabajadores de Chile (CUT).

Historically, the stern requirements of loyalty placed upon the Communist parties of Latin America by the Soviet Union have seriously impaired both their freedom of action and their credibility. That such has not been the case in Chile is due largely to a series of fortuitous coincidences. Since the 1930s, Soviet policy in the region has favored legalistic approaches to power; and Chile, for most of this period, possessed a political structure uniquely open to Communist participation. Thus it was possible for the Chilean party to satisfy its Soviet mentors abroad without seriously challenging the existing parliamentary system at home, although in the decade prior to Allende's assumption of power this role exposed it to increasing criticism from other, more nationalistic or radical movements to its left.

If electoral and parliamentary participation has been one dominant strand in the recent history of the Chilean party, another has been a predilection for broad fronts, and, where possible, coalition governments, particularly with reformist parties of the Center-Left. Here again, the imperatives of Soviet foreign policy and the practical realities of Chilean politics have meshed. Such had not always been the case. In the early days of the party, it pursued Moscow's ultraradical "Third Period" line, isolating itself from other left-wing forces, and facilitating its near-extinction during the dictatorship of Colonel Carlos Ibáñez del Campo (1927–1931). During the early 1930s, it forfeited much of its influence in the labor movement to the newly-founded Socialist party, and Communist fortunes did not recover until after Moscow's Popular Front policy (1935) made it possible to explore the concrete possibilities on the ground. The party was instrumental in the formation of Latin America's only Popular Front government, led by Radical Pedro Aguirre Cerda, who assumed the presidency in 1938. Although the chief beneficiaries of the Aguirre Cerda administration were the Radicals and their middle-class constituency, the Communists' crucial role in its creation afforded them a new respectability in Chilean politics, and what was perhaps even more important, opportunities to expand their hold within the labor movement.

After the Front disbanded in 1941, the Communists set about bringing the Socialists into another Radical-led coalition, the Democratic Alliance. Their high point of success came in 1946, when Radical President Gabriel González Videla named three Communists to his nine-man cabinet. The following year, however, a combination of foreign and domestic pressures led González Videla to turn suddenly against the party and eject its representatives from his administration.[3] The Communists responded by fanning a wave of strikes in the Lota coalfields; the Chilean President then sponsored a series of severely repressive measures, embodied in the so-called Law for the Defense of Democracy (1948). This document proscribed the Communist party and jailed or exiled its leaders. The Communists did not openly re-enter Chilean public life until the law's repeal some ten years later. But even during its underground period in the late 1940s and 1950s, the party continued to participate in conventional politics, even running parliamentary candidates under different party labels, often that of the Socialists. After 1959 it returned to electoral activity under its own name; by the 1969 congressional elections its membership had risen to 15.9 percent of the electorate.

Over the years the Communists had proven remarkably successful in defending their position on the "peaceful road" to power, as well as encouraging the concept of broad coalitions uniting Marxist parties with bourgeois reformist elements. This was no mean accomplishment in the light of considerable internal stresses generated within the movement, first, by the repressive policies of various Chilean governments during the early and mid-1950s, and then in the 1960s, by new external challenges from the Cuban example and the Chinese. However, probably the Communists' most significant achievement in this regard was their successful sponsorship—overcoming strong initial Socialist objections—of the Radical party's admission to the Popular Unity coalition. Although by the 1970s the Radicals were a much-diminished force in Chilean politics, without votes it would have proven impossible to put Socialist Salvador Allende over the top.

Indeed, in more than one respect Allende's victory was a Communist triumph. It vindicated the party's long-standing assumptions about the possibilities afforded by the Chilean political system, and it demonstrated its capacity to create successful coalitions. It allowed the Communists to prove their indispensability to other left-wing forces and parties (80 percent of the 14,800 Popular Unity committees in Chile during the campaign were controlled by the Communists).[4] It also encouraged many middle-class elements not normally friendly to Communism to regard the party as serious and responsible, the center of gravity and the source of stability in an otherwise mercurial governing coalition.[5] This was certainly true during Allende's first year in office. However, after the 1971 municipal elections, when the Socialists suddenly replaced the Communists as the most numerous party in the government, the latter's capacity to play this stabilizing role quickly diminished.

The history of the party before 1970 thus provided several clues to its future role in the Popular Unity government. First, having experienced severe repression under two Chilean governments (1927–1931; 1948–1958), it acquired a healthy respect for the limitiation of the political process. Both this experience and the lessons learned from it were not shared by the Socialists. Second, the need to defend the party's revolutionary credentials against increasingly vocal criticism on the left—not merely from the Socialists, but from smaller pro-Cuban and pro-Chinese groups—led the party in the 1960s to sound more radical than in fact it was. Although it spoke dialectically, it often thought and acted incrementally. In some ways this was to be expected of a party which was firmly based in the labor movement, where, ideology notwithstanding, most of the work of its trade union branch was absorbed in day-to-day struggles against inflation and the confines of an extremely archaic labor code. Moreover, after thirty years of participation within the system, the party had acquired, willy-nilly, something of a stake in its continuance. It possessed, for example, a network of commercial enterprises which provided an important source of domestic financing, a national daily, *El Siglo,* and (for its leaders) the comforts and perquisites of parliamentary and municipal office.

In the Congress, this incrementalist approach was evident in the late 1960s when the party joined the Radicals in offering qualified support for some of President Frei's reform legislation. This was in contrast to the Socialists, who were reluctant to do anything which might add to the Christian Democrats' record of success. Once again, party economic and parliamentary strategy meshed with Soviet policy, which at that point was aimed at strengthening and supporting "bourgeois nationalist" governments in Latin America, with a view to isolating the United States in the region. Moreover, given Chile's strong identification with Western culture and a social structure roughly equivalent to that of Southern Europe, this tactic also served the Soviets with a useable metaphor, presumptively capable of reassuring Center-Left parties in France and Italy then flirting with the nation of a "historic compromise" (e.g., parliamentary coalitions with local Communist parties).

Third, its experience in the Popular Front era of the late 1930s had taught the Chilean Communist party to anticipate the moderating effects of power. Although the program on which Aguirre Cerda was elected was seen as so advanced by his opponents that there was actually some question as to whether he would be allowed to take office, in practice his government was an exercise in prudent retreat from its initial positions. From this precedent the Communists could anticipate that the Popular Unity program would undergo adjustments in practice in order to take more fully into account the political realities of Chilean society. In fact, a close reading of that program suggests that the Communists contributed most of the sections emphasizing the legalistic nature of the transition to socialism, and they well may have played an even larger role than the Radicals in drafting the portions which assured the lower-middle and middle classes, small businessmen and farmers, that their interests would remain untouched or even enhanced under Popular Unity. The Communists could presumably view these provisos as openings to blunt the generally radical thrust of that program. If this was so, they failed to recognize that comparisons with the Popular Front period were seriously misplaced: Allende was not Aguirre Cerda, and even more, this time not the Radicals, but the Socialists, controlled the government.

The Socialists

If the Communist party of Chile was unique among Latin American branches of the Third International, the Socialists were an even more interesting anomaly — a Marxist party which was neither a precursor nor an offshoot of the Communists. In fact, the Chilean Socialist party was a genuinely indigenous, nationalist, radical social movement. Founded in 1932 by, among others, Colonel Marmaduke Grove, the dashing commander of the Chilean Air Force, the party was the product of the economic and social crisis unleashed in the country by the Great Depression. Much of its early growth and development was due to its capacity—in contrast to the "sectarian" Communists of the period—to absorb the broadest range of militants: anarcho-syndicalists, Trotskyists, Evangelical Protestants, even Freemasons. Its extremely heterogeneous origins were reflected in a wide diversity of ideological influences; in recent years the party's eclectic Marxist tradition had been further enriched by such disparate examples as Peronism in Argentina, Titoism in Yugoslavia, and the Chinese and Cuban revolutions.

Several distinctive features set Chilean Socialists apart from their Communist rivals. They possessed far less internal discipline or ideological homogeneity. They could claim to be a truly national party, in the sense that they had no formal affiliations outside of the country (the party had never been part of the Second International). And their social base was slightly different. Although it labelled itself a working-class party (which in a certain measure it was), almost half its membership at the time of Allende's election was middle or lower-middle class.[6]

Socialist party history falls rather conveniently into two distinct periods. In the first, from 1932 to 1952, the party worked in what one historian has termed an "uneasy alliance" with the Communists, and through membership in the Popular Front government (1938–1941), became integrated into the existing political system.[7] If for the Communists these were years of recovery and growth prior to their setback in 1948, for the Socialists they were ones of disillusionment and frustration. Although Aguirre Cerda had not been elected on a socialist platform, implicit in some of his campaign promises were plans to tilt the country's structure of economic opportunity more in the direction of the lower classes. Instead, once in power, his government emphasized economic development rather than the redistribution of income or social power. Through the Chilean Development Corporation (CORFO), founded in 1938, industry experienced very significant growth, opening up scores of new avenues to the middle class and to Chilean professionals, many of whom were, not surprisingly, members of the president's own party. While the Communists could bask in the warm approval of their Soviet friends for having successfully organized an "anti-fascist" front in Chile, and avail themselves of new opportunities in the labor movement, for the Socialists and their followers there was no comparable reward. From the Popular Front experience it was easy for many Socialists to conclude that working-class alliances with bourgeois parties inevitably worked to the benefit of the latter, and to the detriment of the former. When the Radical-led coalition finally dissolved in 1952, the Socialists were ready to strike out in a new direction, although it took four more years of division, debate, and reunion to firmly establish new political line.

During the second phase of its history from 1952 to 1973, the party was far more "revolutionary" in its rhetoric, program, and appraisal of the Chilean scene. This did not prevent it from participating in conventional politics, but it effectively ended the era of subordination to bourgeois parties and alliances, with or without Communist participation. Beneath that apparent consensus, however, two fundamental differences persisted: one, a conflict between those who favored peaceful, parliamentary roads to power, and those who believed that ultimately only force and violence could usher in a new and better social order; and two, a division between partisans of a populist, multi-class coalition (presumably led by the Socialists and Communists) versus advocates of a government composed *exclusively* of working-class parties, or at least, parties that styled themselves as such.

Neither of these tensions were ever resolved, even to the last day of the Allende regime. The president himself had long been identified with the party's "electoral" wing, but his administration was replete with comrades from the other side, notably his first Foreign Minister Clodomiro Almeyda, and his party chief Senator Carlos Altamirano. While Allende's embrace of the peaceful road obviously made him the most attractive Socialist candidate from the point of view of the Communists, it undermined his hold on important sectors of his own party. In fact, Allende was the only candidate of any of the Popular Unity parties not to win a majority vote from his coreligionists in the August 1969 pre-selection balloting.[8] (The Altamirano group had actually favored electoral abstention.) It was his solid support from the Communists that assured Allende his nomination.

Nor could the Socialists escape their own populist heritage. Although doctrinally Marxist from the beginning, the party had been built by Colonel Grove and his followers in the 1930s by formulating broad-based appeals, pitched as much to small farmers and merchants, civil servants and schoolteachers, as to members of the industrial working class. Further, over the years Socialist parliamentarians had learned to appreciate the usefulness of machine politics and patron-client networks. And concretely, those who favored electoral strategies recognized that only by drawing support from outside its own ranks and that of the Communists could the party hope to win a presidential election, and after that, effectively govern. (Those who, like Almeyda and Altamirano, professed not to believe in elections at all, were obviously unconcerned with this problem.) The eventual inclusion, at Communist insistence, of non-Marxist parties (particularly the Radicals) in the governing coalition, masked the fact that this issue, too, had not been definitively settled. After Allende's election, the Socialists found themselves engaged in a continual and sharpening intraparty war, in which advocates of the harsher "classist" line, while usually unsuccessful in imposing their views, nonetheless retained an effective veto power, which they used—sometimes with devastating effect—to sabotage moderate or conciliatory policies.

From this admittedly cursory survey, it is easy to appreciate that the Socialists were an extremely problematical ally for the Communist party. The two had long been locked in contest at the ballot box and in the trade union centrals, where the tightly-organized, well-financed Communists had often emerged triumphant, bequeathing to their Marxist rivals a residue of resentment and suspicion. (As of 1969, the Socialists had captured 12.2 percent of the Chilean electorate.) Even when rivalries could be set aside, serious tactical dilemmas remained. For the Communists, the problem posed by Allende's party was not so much its intransigently revolutionary nature, as the fact that it was so divided and undisciplined as to be unpredictable and unreliable. There were many opportunities to observe its erratic nature prior to Allende's assumption of power. For example, when the Frei regime was faced by a rather ineffectual attempt at a military coup in 1969, the Communists lept to the government's defense, threatening a general strike if the rebellion showed signs of gaining ground. Not only did the Socialists refuse to endorse this effort; they were highly critical of the Communists for their support, however indirect, of a "bourgeois-oligarchical" regime unworthy of the blood of the working class. Likewise, within the trade union movement, the two parties periodically differed over the use of the strike weapon. The Socialists generally favored stoppages of unlimited duration, which they hoped would mount to general strike proportions; Communists preferred to avoid all-out confrontations with employers, and favored strikes of limited duration for more concrete economic gains.[9]

In effect, the Chilean Socialists never fully ingested the anarcho-syndicalist and Trotskyist theories to which they were exposed by elements which entered their ranks in the party's early years. Quite the contrary, these strains were continually revivified in later decades, both by the frustrations of Chilean parliamentary politics, and the successes of more violent models elsewhere. Precisely how the party could reconcile these differences and execute a Marxist program through populist and even democratic, legal means — an act which would seem to defy the laws of political gravity — was a question which fascinated its admirers abroad and mystified its more radical critics at home. For the very fashion in which his party reluctantly handed Allende its nomination strongly implied a lack of fundamental consensus to support his efforts.

The Radicals

The Chilean Radical party was the oldest, strongest, and best-established of the non-Marxist parties in Allende's government. As the quintessential representative of Chile's "old" (preindustrial) middle class, it was expected to play a vital role, both before and after the assumption of power. On one hand, it was hoped that it would deliver the votes to assure Allende's victory in the 1970 elections; on the other, it was expected to facilitate implementation of his program once in office, by neutralizing elements which habitually fell within the sphere of the traditional Right. The first of these it managed, although with some difficulty; the second it utterly failed to produce.

Founded in the nineteenth century as an offshoot of the Liberals, the Radicals had begun as the expression of an emerging elite of mining entrepreneurs in Chile's northern provinces, and a coalition of southern landowners. By the First World War, however, its constituency had come to be centered among Chile's bureaucratic middle class and petty bourgeoisie — schoolteachers, civil servants and other white collar employees, small town merchants and professional men, even (before 1930) a handful of industrial workers and provincial aristrocrats. Uniting these disparate groups was a devotion to government employment as the principal avenue of social mobility (for their sons and nephews, if not for themselves), Freemasonry and anticlericalism, and often, a provincial resentment against the domination of Chile by the Santiago-Valparaíso-Central Valley complex, where most of the country's wealth and power were concentrated.

In the 1920s and 1930s, the Radicals were Chile's largest party, normally accounting for about 20 percent of the electorate. Their solid base and their domination of the Center made them the indispensable key to successful coalitions, an advantage which allowed them to control the Chilean presidency from 1938 to 1952—first (1938–1948) with the backing of the parties of the Left, and then (1948–1958) with support from the Socialists and parties of the Center and Right. During the 1950s and 1960s, the party experienced a slow but perceptible decline; by the 1969 congressional elections, it had dropped to 13 percent of the electorate. Even more dramatic than shrinking percentages were certain qualitative factors. In spite of their anticlerical heritage, some Radical voters were deserting their party for the Christian Democrats, who were gradually displacing it at the center of the Chilean political spectrum. Further, the Radical share of the vote was declining at a time when the overall size of the Chilean electorate was undergoing enormous growth. This meant that the Radicals were not merely losing some of their old supporters, but were failing to attract their share of newly-enfranchised voters—women, peasants, urban slum-dwellers, who were opting in disproportionate numbers for the Christian Democrats, and to a lesser degree, for the parties of the Left. The Radical decline was not merely relative but absolute, and if matters continued after 1970 as they appeared to be tending in 1968 and 1969, the Radical party would ultimately be drowned in a sea of universal suffrage.

Such prospects invariably provoke any political movement to a good deal of soul-searching, and during the latter half of the 1960s, the Radical party was pervaded by what might be called an acute crisis of ideological identity. A small but well-disciplined element within its leadership concluded that Chilean politics were moving ineluctably to the Left, and as the historic party of the Center, the Radicals should reshape their own role accordingly. In the forefront of this struggle was the party's youth wing, which represented between 20 to 30 percent of the votes at any Radical convention, and whose leader, Francisco Valdés, was actively cultivated by the Communists throughout the 1960s. Yet another factor pushing the party leftwards—difficult to measure, but the subject of wide and authoritative comment[10]—was the undisguised preference of the United States for the Christian Democrats—a predilection so obvious as to push the Radicals towards the local allies of the Soviet Union as an expression, however proximate, of anticlerical *revanche*.

Towards the end of the 1960s the party established formal affiliation with the Second International, although it little resembled a social democratic organization, either in its constituency or its basic ethos. A leftist Radical, Senator Hugo Miranda, had already been elected to head the party in 1965, and a voting alliance was concluded with the Communist party to effect joint action in Congress. For their part, the Communists supported a self-styled Marxist Radical, Professor Alberto Baltra, for the Senate in 1967; two years later, Senator Baltra was the Radicals' nominee to head the Popular Unity ticket. In 1969, the same leftist faction gained control of the party's convention and expelled its more conservative elements, led by Senator Julio Durán. (Durán and his followers later formed the Democratic Radical party, which supported Alessandri.) In amputating their party's right wing, the leftist Radicals were now in a position to bargain more advantageously for entry into Popular Unity. What few noticed at the time—it would become apparent only when the presidential election returns were in—was that Durán had taken a majority of the rank-and-file with him.[11]

The ideological conflicts and the infighting of the 1960s had not, then, actually resolved the question of what role the Radicals would play in Chilean politics. Nor, as we shall see, was this uncertainty and confusion resolved by the expulsion of Durán and his more conservative followers. Much of the problem resided in the fact that if the Radical constituency had benefited historically from expansion of the public sector in Chile, this did not make it "socialist," at least in the Marxist sense of the term. The distinction had been somewhat blurred over the years by the tendency of various Radical bodies to employ sometimes quite scarifying left-wing rhetoric in order to pressure various Chilean governments into meeting their essentially incrementalist, short-term economic goals.

To pursue this point a bit further: the party's left-wing base was generally thought to reside in its trade union branch, but the Radicals' hold on the labor movement was limited largely to syndicates of white-collar employees *(empleados)*, especially government bureaucrats. White-collar workers in Chile enjoyed a status vastly superior to their blue-collar counterparts *(obreros)*, and much of their collective energies in recent years had been devoted to defense of their differential status, their pensions, and their annual adjustments for inflation. As one observer put it neatly, for such elements, support of the Radical party was the political expression of their desire to maintain the socioeconomic division between the two branches of the Chilean working class.[12] If this was indeed what the "left" in the Radical party represented, then it was somewhat to the right of the Popular Unity program, which committed itself to ending such distinctions within the labor force.[13]

What, then, did the Radicals expect to gain from participation in the Popular Unity government? At a minimum, they anticipated a share of government patronage, which would presumably afford the party an opportunity to rebuild some of its following lost since last in power nearly two decades before. It envisioned itself acting as a representative of the middle class within the regime, a role which it may have imagined would be larger and more potent than in fact turned out to be the case. It may have expected to function as moderator and arbiter between other members of the coalition, and to put them in a position to water down some of the more radical notions of the

Popular Unity program.[14] It hoped to even scores with the Christian Democrats, who had displaced it at the center of the spectrum, "an arena that [the Radicals] had long regarded as their special preserve."[15] Some of the Radical unions, resentful of President Frei's increasingly conservative wage policies, may even have imagined that they could advance their own corporate interests more successfully in a government in which their own party was a participant, regardless of ideological labels or programs. At the beginning, there may even have been a lingering illusion that the Radicals could provide the presidential candidate for the coalition, since in the 1969 elections they had outperformed the Socialists by almost a percentage point, and since before the split they had the largest representation of any Popular Unity party in the Senate and Chamber of Deputies.[16]

Without doubt, the Radicals' thinking—again, like that of the Communists— was dominated by the experience of the Popular Front, which had worked so well to both parties' advantage. However, those who evoked such memories failed to deal realistically with the changed context of Chilean public life. In the late 1930s the Radicals were eminently equipped to play the role of "swing party" in Chilean politics; in 1970, however, they found themselves positioned at the weak center of a left-wing coalition, *but not the center of Chilean politics generally.*

If the Radicals did impart to Popular Unity a patina of bourgeois respectability which neither Marxist party could give, nonetheless their contribution to Allende's movement was not as crucial as they (and the Communists) imagined that it would be. To be sure, the Radicals delivered the votes which assured Allende's election, but not in sufficient quantities to constitute a clear majority.[17] In the April 1971 municipal elections, their own share of the electorate continued to drop, and a year later the Radicals left the government altogether and joined the opposition. The apparent cause was President Allende's veto of a constitutional amendment that would have prevented the government from expropriating any enterprise without legislative approval. At the time, the Chilean chief executive expressed satisfaction at the party's departure, since, he asserted, it had been guilty of "opportunism and demagoguery."[18] This was certainly true, although it did not touch upon the heart of the matter. The alliance of the Radicals and Popular Unity resembled an improbable marriage. Based on illusions and misunderstandings on both sides, it was only a matter of time before the true nature of the relationship became clear.

MAPU, API, PSD

MAPU (Movement of Unity Popular Action) was an offshoot of the Christian Democratic party notable more for the quality and character of its leadership than the size of its constituency. Its principal personality, as noted in Chapter One, was agronomist Jacques Chonchol, who had served as head of the national land reform agency (INDAP) during the Frei administration. Although he styled himself a technician rather than a political figure, during his tenure at INDAP Chonchol had been extremely active in developing peasant unions and in carrying out the early phases of Frei's land reform program. These activities placed him at the very storm center of controversy between the government and the parties of the Right. When he left Christian Democracy, Chonchol took with him a substantial number of leaders of the party's nascent peasant movement. Other former Christian Democrats in MAPU were Senators Rafael Gumicio and Alberto Jérez, Deputy Julio Silvia Solar, most of the party's youth leaders, and some trade unionists.

The defining feature of the MAPU leadership was its heavily ideological bent. Most of its personalities had drunk deeply at the wells of Christian Democratic theory, which had sketched out the model of a "communitarian" society—a rather murky compromise between capitalism and communism, in which large-scale enterprises would be jointly owned and managed by workers and their employers. This utopia quickly dissolved during the first year or two of Christian Democratic rule, when it became clear that in practice President Frei would have settled for a democratic, capitalist welfare state. When even this more modest goal faded into the distance under the joint impact of inflation and a growing opposition on the Right, the dissident Left of Christian Democracy began to draw more freely upon Marxist categories of analysis. (To some degree this was also a reflection of the general Marxist-Christian "dialogue" then underway in Western Europe.)

In many ways, the MAPU people hoped to play the same role vis-a-vis the Catholic middle classes that the Radicals played for their anticlerical brethren, although Chonchol and his associates often displayed considerably greater ideological sophistication—or, if one will, more outright cynicism and frankness. For example, in a newspaper interview granted shortly after Allende's inauguration, MAPU Secretary-General Rodrigo Ambrosio admitted that it would be difficult to draw small farmers and members of the petty bourgeoisie into active support of the government, but he condemned the "Trotskyist" fallacy of making "gratuitous awards of followers to the enemy." The point, he added, would ultimately become academic in any case. Once large-scale enterprises had passed under the control of the state, there would be nothing small and medium property owners could do about it. Ambrosio also hinted that MAPU support in the future for electoral processes was conditional upon their producing the correct result. Although he admitted that the Chilean political system afforded opportunities rare in Western societies, he insisted that "the destruction of the bourgeois state" could not be accomplished "without confrontations." The definitive struggle of social classes would have to be repeated in Chile, "as in all the great revolutionary processes elsewhere." And, he added, emphatically, "Chile, then, is not an exception case. The destruction of the bourgeois state continues to be a requisite."[19]

Thus, although supposedly a non-Marxist party with the self-imposed task of winning over (or neutralizing) sectors of the middle class to Popular Unity, in reality MAPU came closer ideologically to the left wing of the Socialist party in its overall conception of the Chilean process. Moreover, during Allende's first year in power, MAPU dropped its self-styled "Christian" identity to become uninhibitedly Marxist-Leninist. Whatever ideological satisfaction its militants might have derived from this action, it precluded Chonchol's movement from playing the role most useful to the government, namely, "enticing away the Left militants still adhering to the Christian Democratic party . . . [who could] not throw in their lot with the Popular Unity without ceasing to be Christians."[20] Thus, without attracting more than a handful of voters to Allende's side in 1970, MAPU remained for the next three years an additional perturbing factor within a coalition where public credibility depended to a great degree on commitment to constitutional and democratic norms.

API (Independent Popular Action) was a small party, founded in 1969 by Rafael Tarud, a landowner and businessman of Sirio-Lebanese origin. Only two points about it need be made. Ideologically populist, with some base in the country's Arab community, among police and army officers, and among the provincial petty bourgeoisie, API was basically a personalist machine designed to promote Tarud's political ambitions. Further, during the deliberation over the identity of Popular Unity's presidential candidate, Tarud enlisted the support of the Radicals and the PSD (the tiny Social Democrat party, whose petty-bourgeois origins resembled that of the API). At one point Tarud clung so obstinately to his presidential dreams that the grand coalition almost failed to be born. What was remarkable, as one sympathetic source later commented, was that "even at this early stage, the middle class parties clearly aspired to a controlling position" within the proposed new government.[21] When it became clear that the Marxist parties would prefer to strike out on their own rather than to permit this, the API and PSD fell into line, and finally, along with the Radicals, threw their support to Allende. The episode illustrated once more how sharply opposed were the ambitions and expectations which together formed the cement of Allende's future regime.

The "Loyal Opposition"

Coalition governments have an internal dynamic of their own, but much of their movement can often be explained by their relationship to outside forces. This was particularly true in Chile, where the fortunes of the Allende government were strongly affected by groups to its immediate left and right—by what constituted, at least in the beginning, a quasi-loyal opposition. Under this heading, from very different perspectives, there figured the Movement of the Revolutionary Left (MIR), and the Christian Democrats.

The MIR was perhaps the closest expression of the Cuban revolutionary line. Founded in 1964 by dissident members of the Socialist party and a handful of Trotskyists and independent radicals, by the time Allende took office it had long since passed under the control of students at the traditionally leftist University of Concepción. Although the MIR saw itself as the only significant Marxist party to openly preach the necessity of violent revolution in Chile, it was not at first clear precisely how the Cuban model could be applied in a highly urbanized country, whose overall geographical characteristics did not easily lend themselves to rural guerrilla warfare. During the first two years of its existence, then, the MIR differentiated itself from more traditional left-wing forces largely through the tone of its ideological pronouncements ("Revolución o misera") rather than by any overt revolutionary activity.

In 1967, however, the MIR struck out in a new and more resolutely violent direction. This was partly due to the influence of the founding congress of the Cuban-sponsored Organization of Latin American Solidarity (OLAS), to which MIR had sent a deputation. But perhaps ultimately of greater significance was the example of the Tupamaro urban guerrillas in Uruguay, a country which Chileans often regarded within Latin America as most nearly resembling their own. Like the Tupamaros, the MIR soon began to stage bank robberies in order to capture public attention for their message, to obtain funds for party work, and for largesse to lavish, Robin Hood style, upon selected squatter settlements in Santiago and other cities. Mounting miristas activity led to a police counter-offensive by the Frei government, and most MIR members spent the last two years before Allende's election in hiding or in jail.

During the presidential campaign, MIR made no secret of its contempt for the electoral process ("nothing more than a mechanism of self-preservation for the ruling class, a more refined or subtle method than brute coercion . . . not a road toward the conquest of power")[22] and for Popular Unity, which it labelled "essentially leftist reformist" rather than authentically revolutionary.[23] The fundamental task of the day, it argued emphatically, was a combination of "armed revolutionary actions and militant mobilization of the masses."[24] To prove that this was not idle rhetoric, during the mid-summer of 1970 MIR escalated its activities from its underground command posts. More dramatic than its bank robberies was the discovery in June by national police agents of what they called a "guerrilla school" in Santiago, "with quantities of explosives and material for the preparation of bombs."[25] The Communist party recognized the potentially alienating effect of this sort of thing on the electorate, and at its XIVth Congress in 1969, various delegates stepped forward to denounce the MIR for its "lack of confidence in the masses . . . lack of calmness in struggle . . . lack of organization spirit, discipline, and strength." For his party, Secretary-General Luis Corvalán referred to the group as a collection of "terrorists, adventurers, renegades, and declassed elements," a charge he was pleased to repeat often during the course of Allende's presidential campaign.[26] The Socialists were somewhat more muted in their response to MIR's activities, for many leaders of the party's left wing were known to be closer ideologically to the MIR than to the Communists. Characteristically, one of the students arrested in connection with the "guerrilla school" affair turned out to be the son of a Socialist senator.

The MIR had long maintained that victory at the ballot box was an impossibility for Popular Unity, or that in the very unlikely event of its occurrence, such a government would not be allowed to take power. In October 1970, MIR found itself forced to admit that it had misjudged the situation, although it insisted that the election had merely postponed the inevitable—armed struggle. It warned Allende that once the "euphoria of triumph" had passed, he would have to "satisfy the desires of the masses concretely, and in a short time."[27] In the meanwhile, it pledged the regime its conditional support. Shortly after his inauguration a month later, Allende had all political charges dropped against members of the group, and the organization once again surfaced to public view.

Reconciliation between Allende and the MIR seemed complete, but an undercurrent of hostility persisted between the latter and the Communist party. On December 2, Communist students and *miristas* clashed on the campus of the University of Concepción, resulting in the death of one student participant. The two groups were brought together by the president himself and forced to compose their differences temporarily; the compromise was purchased through dividing shares of power in the student federations at Concepción and the larger University of Chile in Santiago. The potential for conflict between the MIR and Allende's government had not been totally defused, although during the regime's first twelve months it did not appear to be a serious problem. In the meanwhile, in a climate of greater official tolerance, MIR militants fanned out to the countryside and to the squatter settlements of Santiago and other cities for further organizational work. Members of MIR (along with militants from other ultra-left groups) also made up Allende's personal bodyguard.[28]

At the beginning, Allende found it relatively easy to placate his critics on the Left.[29] He had proven that he knew more about Chilean politics than they did, and he was magnanimous in his treatment of the discredited theoreticians and practitioners of the violent road. For their part, they were forced now to take the Socialist leader somewhat more seriously than had previously been their wont. Then, too, the blanket release of imprisoned revolutionaries bought a long period of cooperation, or at least, of nonresistance. With the Christian Democrats, the process was somewhat different.

Tomic's party was not, of course, a member of Popular Unity, even on an informal basis. But without its support Allende could never have assumed office. This was so because Popular Unity had not received a majority in the 1970 elections. According to Article 64 of the Chilean constitution, under such circumstances the Congress was charged to choose by majority vote between the two candidates receiving the largest pluralities—in this case, between Allende and Alessandri. It was customary for that body to award the presidency to the candidate with the largest popular vote, but the situation was far from normal, and nobody failed to grasp the point that this decision would probably be the most important in Chilean history. If the Christian Democrats could be persuaded to throw their support in Congress to Allende, his victory was assured; if they voted for Alessandri, then Popular Unity would be denied what it had won at the polls, and the country would face the prospect of a civil war.

After a long internal debate on September 30, 1970, the Assembly of the Christian Democratic party agreed in the principle to vote for Allende, in exchange for support by the Popular Unity parties for a series of congressionally-mandated constitutional amendments known collectively as the Statute of Democratic Guarantees. These affirmed the right to free association in political parties, which in turn were granted equal access to state-controlled communications media, and to ink, paper, and other materials vital to the diffusion of information. Newspapers and other forms of mass media could be expropriated only by law approved by an absolute majority of the full membership of both houses of Congress. Private education was guaranteed the right of survival, even of government financial support if necessary, and freedom from ideological supervision of any kind. In addition, only Congress could authorize alteration in the size of the armed forces or national police (Carabineros). Paul Sigmund has explained the import of these measures very lucidly:

> The Statute of Democratic Guarantees was an attempt to bind Allende publicly and explicitly to what he had always supported verbally, the maintenance of the norms of pluralistic constitutional democracy. It seemed to guarantee to the opposition that Chile could not become another Cuba by means of a similar process of takeover of the trade unions, universities, political parties, and the media. Of particular importance in the maintenance of these guarantees was the independence and commitment to the constitution of the armed forces, since both sides understood that if constitutional norms were respected, the military would remain out of politics, however much they might disagree with Allende's

policies. If, on the other hand, the more extreme elements among Allende's supporters . . . were to bring about a situation in which Allende might be tempted to violate the guarantees, the military could appeal to the constitution in preventing or dissuading him from such a move.[30]

Several additional points about this agreement seem worth making. First, it was a compromise over what the Christian Democrats had originally wanted. For example, their draft had called for an absolute guarantee against the expropriation of newspapers (and other mass media) rather than allowing the matter to be decided by circumstantial congressional majorities. Also, the provision assuring a nonpolitical military had originally contained a section which would have limited Allende's power to choose subordinate commanders of the military and the national police. Second, Allende entered into the dialogue with the Christian Democrats with the support of the Communists, but over the strong objections of his own party, who then and later insisted that the Statute of Democratic Guarantees surrendered the revolution to its enemies in advance. (MAPU justified Allende's adhesion to the Statute on tactical grounds; Secretary-General Ambrosio compared it to Soviet acceptance in 1919 of the Treaty of Brest-Litovsk—which, considering Lenin's attitude towards treaties, was not a very comforting analogy.[31] Third, built into the Chilean political system was a complicated network of constitutional restraints which circumscribed the discretionary power of any executive. What did not fall within the specific ken of the Statute of Constitutional Guarantees might nonetheless clash with the constitution and laws of Chile, which the Christian Democrats could be expected to cite, chapter and verse, when the opportunity presented itself.

The goodwill of the Christian Democrats was something more, however, than a passing necessity in order to install Allende in the presidential palace. For, as two Chilean political scientists have pointed out, from the very beginning Popular Unity "lacked the power needed to enforce [its] policies within the framework of the existing constitutional system." The Congress with which the new President would have to work until March 1973, was dominated by the opposition; only by winning the collaboration of its Christian Democratic members could his government effect its proposed reforms with a minimum of controversy. Although the Communists repeatedly urged this course upon him, Allende's own party continually vetoed initiatives which would have effected a relationship of this sort, whatever its ultimate prospects of success.

It is true that the new government had originally contemplated avoiding this problem altogether. The Popular Unity program had called for the eventual elimination of the Chilean Congress altogether—through a plebiscite which would create in its place a unicameral "Assembly of the People." But such a drastic departure presupposed that the government had *already* won the support of the majority of Chileans. That majority never materialized, and Allende, recognizing as much, prudently avoided putting the matter to a popular vote.[32] This left him no alternative, however, but to abandon his program altogether, or to rely upon extralegislative devices to push it through. By opting for the latter, he provoked an unexpected and even improbable rapprochement between the Christian Democrats and the parties and forces of the Right.[33]

In retrospect it is clear, then, that Allende's road to power was exceedingly narrow—hemmed in on the right by the lack of a decisive popular mandate, by limitations inherent in the Chilean system, in the lack of a working majority in Congress, and by commitments he was forced to make in order to take office; and continually threatened on the left by a revolutionary exuberance that could be seen, at best, as but temporarily contained. The nub of the problem was that what would placate one wing of the "loyal" opposition would inevitably inflame the other. Yet short of total immobilism, it is difficult to see how Allende could have avoided making costly choices once in power. This, combined with a potentially quarrelsome coalition government, pointed out the extremely fragile and problematic nature of his mandate to effect a Chilean transition to socialsim.

Allende's problems were not merely "structural," however, but psychological and cultural as well. Both supporters and opponents understood that the Popular Unity governemnt was not merely one administration elected for six years, to be followed by whatever happened to come along afterwards. Rather, it represented a sharp break with the Chilean past—far sharper than the Christian Democratic government it replaced. Allende and his supporters continually referred to their mandate as a "process" which was to be "irreversible." in spite of their relatively narrow base, they appeared intoxicated with a sense of historical inevitability, sweeping aside, as it were, all restraints and everything which they had inherited. Such *triunfalismo*—to use a useful Spanish word—was bound to heighten the anxieties of the opposition, particularly when it found expression in concrete acts. It was as if after September 4, 1970, there had been a sudden, unexpected expropriation—not so much of property in the immediate sense as of self-esteem and a sense of possessing a stake in the nation's future—by one half of Chile to the disadvantage of the other. There had been an election, true, but not a decisive mandate at the ballot box—certainly not sufficient to underpin the kinds of radical changes envisaged by the Popular Unity program. Too many of Allende's supporters and collaborators seemed not to notice this at all, which explains why so many were convinced that they were being victimized by a cosmic confidence game which would alter once and for all the terms of Chilean politics and society. This darkening public mood—an ephemeral but pervasive phenomenon—must be constantly kept in mind in order to understand why Allende's repeated assurances and ritual affirmations of support for the democratic process and the rule of law were incapable of satisfying certain concrete political necessities.

Who Was Salvador Allende?

Salvador Allende was crucial to the creation of Popular Unity, since he alone was capable of cojoining the traditional and revolutionary strands of Chilean politics. Born in Valparaíso in 1908 into a professional family active in the Radical party, he had been active in politics since his student days, when as a medical student he entered into conspiracies against dictator Carlos Ibáñez del Campo. He was briefly jailed for subversive activities in the chaotic days following the fall of Ibáñez in 1931. And by the time he received his degree in 1933, he had accumulated a police dossier so impressive as to prevent him from obtaining a government medical post. He settled for a job doing autopsies, but spent most of his time helping to organize the Socialist party, which he had helped to found the year he left medical school.

By 1937 he was the leader of the Socialist party in Valparaiso and also its deputy in the National Congress. When Radical President Pedro Aguirre Cerda formed Chile's first Popular Front government in 1938, in conjunction with the Communist and Socialist parties, Allende, then 30 years of age, became Minister of Health, and subsequently directed the Chilean Workers' Social Security Fund. In 1945 he was elected to the Senate, where he served continuously for twenty-five years until elected President in 1970.

In 1952 the Socialists divided over the question of supporting the presidential bid of Carlos Ibáñez, who had returned to political life in a populist guise; instead, Allende ran for the presidency himself with the support of dissident Socialists and the (then) outlawed Communist party. In 1956 he served as the first president of the Popular Revolutionary Action Front (FRAP), the joint Communist-Socialist coalition, and was its presidential candidate in 1958 and 1964. Allende ran a strong second in a five-man race in 1958, and was the unsuccessful candidate of the unified Left against Eduardo Frei in 1964.

At the time of his inauguration, there was little about Salvador Allende's political career, personality, inclinations, or associations which was unknown in Chile. Certainly he had functioned as a normal, democratic politician in the give-and-take of parliamentary life for many years; at the time of his election he was, in fact, President of the Chilean Senate. In the view of one who knew him well, it was quite possible that he took "bombastic revolutionary slogans" somewhat less seriously than did his followers.[34] Insofar as his habits and lifestyle were concerned, there was nothing to differentiate him from dozens of other successful Chilean politicians. He had a well-known fondness for fine art, wines, and beautiful women; he was self-indulgent and even a bit cynical; he was on good terms with a wide range of personalities, including leaders of Chilean industry, agriculture, the armed forces, and the press. He was active in Chilean Masonry, not precisely a revolutionary organization, but one which opened up important avenues of friendship and influence with Radical party politicians and voters.

In some ways Allende's candidacy in 1970 was a bit of a surprise. By the late 1960s he was considered somewhat "over the hill" as a politician—having run unsuccessfully for the presidency three times before, no longer a young man, and somewhat the worse for wear. In fact, he probably would not have run at all had not the Communists insisted upon putting him forward. Precisely because of his acceptability to non-Marxist political forces, Allende was the only politician within the Socialist party who could reasonably expect to preside successfully over a relatively broad coalition of the Left. The Socialist leadership itself was unenthusiastic about the idea of a broad coalition in the first place, particularly one including so patently bourgeois a party as the Radicals, preferring instead an alliance of exclusively Marxist parties openly avowing their revolutionary intentions. The Communists would have none of this. They insisted upon including the Radicals, winning the day by threatening to nominate a presidential candidate from their own ranks (such as poet Pablo Neruda, who obviously could not have won), rather than supporting a candidate from another party (e.g., a Socialist). Whereas Senator Carlos Altamirano or some other representative of the ultra-Left would have been a likely candidate on a Socialist (or Socialist-dominated) ticket, a broad coalition required a more conventional political figure. Hence, the Communists ended up not merely writing the program and determining the width and breadth of the coalition, but also imposing Allende upon his own reluctant party.[35]

All of this—but particularly what was widely known of Allende himself—should have been somewhat reassuring to the parties and forces of the Center and Right. Why was it not? In the first place, it was evident that Allende had no real idea of how he was going to accomplish his task. As President Eduardo Frei put it some years later, Allende "expected to be able to out-manipulate and out-maneuver everyone, pull all the strings, and somehow ride out the internal contradictions of his own government." But whenever he met with obstacles, particularly in the last phase, he would sink into the deepest depression, with "much talk about death and suicide, about the example of Balmaceda, etc."[36]

Second, Chilean politics had changed since Allende had begun his career some four decades before, and to a certain extent, he had changed as well. Paradoxically, the President's own bourgeois lifestyle, far from moderating his view, "only reinforced his compulsion to be true to his leftist attachments,"[37] all the more so in the particular period in which he was called upon to rule. The late 1960s were a turbulent time in many Western countries, with a rise in revolutionary romanticism expressed, among other ways, through the cult of youthful violence. The creation of the MIR was one manifestation in Chile; the persistence and even growth of Leninist strains within the Socialist party, yet another. Moreover, Allende was at an age when his own children and younger relatives were most susceptible to these trends. His youngest daughter, Beatriz ("Tati") with whom Allende was especially close and who was also a medical doctor, had accompanied her father on his trips to Cuba in the 1960s and been deeply impressed by Ché Guevara, a physician-turned-revolutionary. She herself was identified with the farthest left of the Socialist party, and often described herself as her father's "political conscience." As President, Allende was at considerable pains not to disillusion her.[38]

Third, during this same period Allende began to travel frequently, particularly to Cuba, but also to North Korea, North Vietnam, and East Germany. According to his private secretary, his visit to North Vietnam in 1969, where he was an honored guest of Ho Chi Minh, was "one of the most important experiences of his life."[39] While he was emphatic in his belief that the Cuban revolution could not be replicated in Chile,[40] this did not prevent him from becoming the first president of the Latin American Organization of Solidarity (OLAS). [41] All of this raised questions, not about Allende's commitment to the electoral road to power—which was never in doubt—but about his ultimate purposes once in office. Many Chileans who were far from reactionaries found it deeply disturbing that Allende saw no contradiction between his own stated democratic convictions, and the practices of "socialist" states and causes he espoused, or at any rate, with which he felt entirely comfortable.

Fourth, even in the presidency Allende continued to maintain ties to the violent or would be-violent Left. Even apart from his daughter Beatriz, the links within his own family were considerable: his sister Laura Allende, a Socialist deputy, was a close ally of Senator Carlos Altamirano; his nephew Andrés Pascal Allende was a leader of the MIR, and most of his bodyguards were drawn from that same formation. President Frei, who had gone to see Allende shortly after his inauguration, warned him that he and many others doubted the new president's ability to control the MIR and other groups of a similar nature; but Allende waved his objections aside.[42]

Finally, Allende was determined not to go down in Chilean history in the same way as Gabriel González Videla, who had been elected in 1946 as a Popular Front candidate with the support of the Communists, only to turn against them the following year and govern with the support of the Center and Right.[43] This was self-evidently the case when, shortly after his inauguration, he frankly declared, "I am *not* the President of all Chileans." In and of itself this did not prove that Allende was intending to break with legality, but it was profoundly unsettling. It suggested that he was not interested in the kinds of compromises which had given Chilean politics its peculiar civility and had made it possible for institutions to breach wide gaps in economic and social power.

A Euphoric First Year, 1970-1971

Many of the difficulties prefigured above were not apparent during Allende's first year in office. From November 1970, and for approximately eleven months thereafter, the government embarked upon a major redistribution of income by allowing wages to rise 30 percent. Price controls made it possible to temporarily curb inflation, and wage increases led the workers' share of national income to rise from 50 to 59 percent. These increases, together with a 100 percent growth in the money supply, lead to a rise in demand, and then, in production.

Chile's gross national product increased significantly during Allende's first year in office, "producing one of the Chile's best growth rates in several decades."[44] Equally important, though little noted at the time, was the existence of a large fund of foreign exchange. This was an unusual situation for Chile, the consequences of rising copper prices promoted by the Vietnam war. These reserves constituted an additional buffer which allowed the regime to pursue economic policies—particularly in the areas of public spending, the subsidizing of state enterprises, or the purchase of foodstuffs—on a scale which normally would have been impossible.

Those policies are explored in some detail in the following chapter. In the present context, however, we should note their two most immediate political consequences. During Allende's euphoric first year, differences within the government coalition remained largely buried under a sea of freshly-printed currency; there was plenty of patronage for all deserving elements, and few unpleasant decisions to make. Further, the regime received—not surprisingly—a warm endorsement from the Chilean electorate in the municipal elections of April 1971, rising to 49.73 percent of the vote. This marked the high point of performance at the ballot box for Popular Unity. And what was probably of greater import for the future, the results transformed the Socialist party into the most powerful member of the coalition.

However, at the end of 1971 certain economic realities began to reassert themselves—inflation resumed; the government was forced to decree price increases; a decline in new investment began to make itself felt; copper prices began to drop; there was a crisis of agricultural productivity; foreign exchange reserves were exhausted. By November 1971, the government found it necessary to declare a moratorium on its foreign debt. At this point the debate began to sharpen, both inside and outside the government. All of the potential for fragmentation and conflict, which had temporarily receded from public view, now surfaced to become the most critical factor determining the survival of the Allende government.

Notes

1. "The Popular Unity's Programme," in J. Anne Zammit, *The Chilean Road to Socialism* (Brighton, Sussex, 1973), pp. 255–284.
2. Significantly, the Frei administration was the first Chilean government since 1938 to govern with a clear mandate from the voters, which is precisely why it felt capable of attempting more far-reaching reforms than its predecessors. Much of its subsequent frustration arose from the reluctance to recognize that many of its votes—certainly those that pushed it well above 50 percent—came from members of the Conservative and Liberal parties, who regarded Christian Democracy as the lesser evil when faced with the prospect of Marxism, but possessed no enthusiasm whatever for Frei's political and economic program.
3. See note 7, Chapter One.
4. William E. Ratliff, ed., *Yearbook on Latin American Communist Affairs, 1971* (Stanford, Conn. 1971), p. 43.
5. In 1969, just before Allende's election, the Communist party had an estimated 45,000 members, 68 percent of whom it claimed were workers. By 1973 that figure had risen to 120,000, 76 percent of whom it claimed were workers. It would appear that the three-fold increase in membership was matched by a less than ten percent increase in worker membership. Obviously, many middle-class Chileans must have been joining the party during Allende's years of power, and precisely for conservative (as well as opportunistic) reasons. The parallels with the Spanish party in the civil war of 1936–1939 are striking, although perhaps they should not be; both parties played roughly similar roles, and pursued roughly congruent Soviet-conceived policies. The data is from William Ratliff, *Castroism and Communism in Latin America, 1959–76* (Stanford, Conn. 1976), pp. 58–59, and Paul W. Drake, *Socialism and Populism in Chile, 1932–52* (Urbana, Ill, 1978), pp. 328–329.
6. Drake, *Socialism and Populism*, p. 328.
7. Ibid., pp. 3-5.
8. Ian Roxborough, et. al., *Chile: The State and Revolution* (New York, 1977), pp. 66–67. In the nominating council Allende received 12 votes as against 13 abstentions.
9. Ben G. Burnett, *Political Groups in Chile* (Austin, Tex., 1970), p. 157. It would be tempting to conclude that the key to Socialist and Comminist divisions lay within the labor movement. That is, it would seem logical to assume that ideological differences expressed slightly different working-class constituencies—say, Communists in the better-organized and more powerful unions (particularly the copper miners), Socialists in the newer and weaker federations. Or, Communists among the better-paid industrial workers, Socialists among the most exploited. However, a British political scientist has established rather convincingly that (a) while the Socialists were generally critical of the "economism" of Communist trade union secretaries, in fact their own labor leaders had to look to bread-and-butter issues just as vigorously, in order to maintain (and enlarge) their own followings; (b) the real "ideologists" of the parties were not found in the union movement, but in their parliamentary leadership; and that vertical linkages be-

tween the two were extremely weak. Angell found that "even if union leaders obeyed party orders [which even the highly disciplined Communist party affiliates did but imperfectly], it does not follow that they could translate them automatically into union action; the rank-and-file of Chilean unions can hardly be mobilized for action outside of a threat to their economic interests. Union leaders may be able to amalgamate a union issue with a party one, but there are fairly strict limits to the number of occasions on which this can be done." While differences between the unions were real enough, Angell points out that they often reflected intense competition for the same constituency (ordinary party rivalries), or disagreements over quasi-tactical issues, such as admission of non-Marxist unions to the CUT. Alan Angel, *Politics and the Labour Movement in Chile* (London, 1972), esp. pp. 116, 121, 125, 232.
10. See the remarks of former U.S. Ambassador Edward Korry, in U.S. Senate, Committee on Foreign Relations (95th Congress, 1st Sess.), *Hearing . . . . on the Nomination of Hon. Cyrus R. Vance to be Secretary of State* (Washington, 1977), p. 52. The present author, a student in Chile in 1966 at a private university with strong Radical and Masonic connections, can recall the acute resentment felt by the administration at the high-handed and crude attempts of then-Ambassador Ralph Dungan to bludgeon it into closer cooperation with the Christian Democratic Ministry of Education. There were many jokes in Chile about Ambassador Dungan, whose personality and qualifications lent themselves easily to ridicule, emphasizing in near–pornographic terms his closeness to the government.
11. Edward W. Glab, Jr., "Christian Democracy, Marxism, and Revolution in Chile: The Election and Overthrow of Salvador Allende." Ph.D. diss., Northern Illinois University, 1975, pp. 243–44.
12. Angell, *Politics and the Labour Movement . . . .*, p. 168
13. "The Popular Unity's Programme," in Zammit, ed. *The Chilean Road*, p. 271.
14. Although these hopes proved illusory, they were based on very real experience in the 1940s and 1950s . . . . As one student observes, "the premium the Radicals placed on elected office had, in the past, frequently provided them with a strong incentive to engage in wide swings in electoral alignments, and had encouraged a great flexibility in adopting those slogans, rhetoric, and appeal that appeared necessary to remain in power." Robert R. Kaufmann, *The Politics of Land Reform in Chile, 1950–1970* (Cambridge, Mass., 1972), p. 50.
15. Angell, *Politics and the Labour Movement . . .*, p. 168
16. Ratliff, *YLACA, 1971*, p. 41. However, even had the two wings of the party held together, it is exceedingly doubtful that the Socialists would have consented to Radical entry into Popular Unity if one of the conditions were to be that Baltra (or some other Radical) head the ticket.
17. In the 1969 congressional elections, the Communist, Socialist and Radical parties combined won 41 percent of the vote. Had the Radicals remained united, and assuming that Allende would have received the same number of votes in 1970 from the smaller parties of Popular Unity and from independents, it is possible he would have approached 50 percent.
18. Sobel, ed., *Chile and Allende*, p. 82
19. *Documents of the Chilean Road to Socialism* (Philadelphia,1977), vols.1–2, pp. 19, 23–24.
20. Alain Joxe, "Is the 'Chilean Road to Socialism' Blocked?," in Zammit, *The Chilean Road*, p. 231.
21. Roxborough, *Chile: The State and Revolution*, p. 67.

22. Quoted in Ratliff, *Castroism and Communism . . ., pp. 172–173.*
23. Quoted in Ratliff, *YLACA, 1971,* pp. 49–50.
24. Source note 22, above.
25. Paul Sigmund, *The Overthrow of Allende and the Politics of Chile, 1964–76* (Pittsburgh, Penn., 1977), p. 84.
26. Quoted in Ratliff, *YLACA, 1971,* p. 46.
27. Ibid., pp. 49–50
28. Known rather colorfully as the GAP ("Group of Personal Friends").
29. These initially included not only the ultras in his won party and the MIR, but the Revolutionary Communist party (PCR) and nearly a dozen other small organizations, ranging from Trotskyist nuclei to armed and underground groups whose objectives were limited to direct action. Though small, the PCR had enjoyed a certain influence among students in Santiago and the south in the late 1960s, partly because it disposed of greater financial and propaganda resources than its other sectarian rivals, probably from the Peoples Republic of China or North Korea, or both. Its monthly magazine, *Cause M-L* had called for abstention in the 1970 elections. Once Allende recognized the Peoples Republic of China, however, the PCR sharply declined in influence, and many of its partisans probably drifted into the MIR or the left-wing of the Socialist party. For a sympathetic evaluation, see A Correspondent, "Chile: September 4 to November 3, 1970," in Paul M. Sweezy and Harry Magdoff, eds., *Revolution and Counter-Revolution in Chile* (New York, 1974).
30. Sigmund, *The Overthrow of Allende,* p. 120.
31. *Documents on the Chilean Road,* cited note 19 (above).
32. It remains something of a mystery just why Allende thought that this would solve all of his problems. Assuming that democratic choice remained open in Chile, the same Assembly might be returned at a later date dominated by the opposition, which would presumably, dismantle the socialist structures in place. These are the sorts of contradictions that neither Allende nor his associates ever thought through clearly. Either that, or they were so convinced of the superiority of the socialist system as to discard altogether even the theoretical possibility that opinion might react against it.
33. These two paragraphs owe much to J. Biehl del Rio and Gonzalo Férnandez R., "The Political Prerequisites for a Chilean Way," in Kenneth Medhurst, ed., *Allende's Chile* (London, 1972), pp. 51–72 .
34. Claudio Véliz, "Continuidades y rupturas en la historica chilena: otra hipótesis sobre la crisis chilena de 1973," *Estudios Públicos,* No. 12 (1983), p. 61.
35. Julio Silva Solar, "The Program of the Unidad Popular," in Federico Gil et. al., *Chile at the Turning Point: Lessons of the Socialist Years, 1970–73,* tr. John S. Gilitz (Philadelphia,1979), p. 194.
36. Interview with President Eduardo Frei, March 28, 1980. See Appendix I for the full text.
37. This is the view of Ambassador Nathaniel Davis, *The Last Two Years of Salvador Allende* (Ithaca, N.Y., 1985), p. 52.
38. Véliz, "Continuidades y rupturas . . . ," pp. 62–63. Señorita 'Allende subsequently married a Cuban intelligence officer assigned to the Embassy in Santiago, returned with him to Cuba after the coup, subsequently separated from him and committed suicide.
39. Osvaldo Puccio, *Un cuarto de siglo con Allende* (Santiago, 1985), p. 196.
40. Ibid., p. 96.

41. According to Puccio, the very concept of OLAS was Allende's, not Castro's. Ibid., p. 167.
42. Interview with President Frei, cited.
43. Davis, *The Last Two Years* . . . , p. 51.
44. Arturo Valenzuela, "Political Constraints to the Establishment of Socialism in Chile," p. 5.

3

Economic Policy: Expansion and Redistribution, Boom and Bust, 1970–1973

⌐One of the very few points upon which both partisans and critics of the Allende regime are agreed is that its economic policy led it to lose control over a volatile political situation. This still leaves open, of course, the question of why and whose fault it was that Popular Unity's economic program did not yield its expected results. At the end of this chapter we shall return to that debate, and explore its broader ideological implications. To provide an adequate framework for discussion, we begin, however, with a review of the political and economic assumptions that inspired the government's program, followed by a commentary on the performance of the Chilean economy during each of the three years Allende was in power.

Economic Planning and Socialist Politics

One of the pitfalls any historian of Allende's Chile must avoid is attributing to the regime's economic policies an internal logic they never possessed. The government's program, as one of its economists has subsequently admitted, "was neither openly reformist, nor a blueprint for a transition to socialism."[1] Instead, it occupied a murky ideological ground somewhere between socialism and populism, touching upon and criss-crossing both territories.

Two basic assumptions, however, can be singled out at once. First, the Chilean Left firmly believed that since the country's economy was largely monopolistic, and (except for agriculture) foreign-controlled, a policy of punitive taxation or even expropriation would affect a relatively small number of individuals, many of them not Chileans at all. This argument seemed all the more compelling given the sharply asymmetrical distribution of income; while Chile possessed a relatively large middle sector, the gap between the top and bottom quintile—as in most Third World countries—was simply enormous.

Second, socialism was at once a method and an objective: the nationalization of banks, heavy industry, mineral resources, strategic economic activi-

53

ties, as well as foreign trade would give the government new resources with which to "buy" the neutrality or even the support of hundreds of thousands of Chileans who were self-employed or owned small and middle-sized enterprises. Unfortunately, the line between public and private areas of the economy was never firmly established, either before the 1970 elections or thereafter. Chapter Five illustrates some of the political problems which this ultimately engendered.

Evidently, the economic aspects of Allende's program were subordinated to its major political objective, which was to produce that majority for socialism which had not been obtained at the ballot box in 1970. Between the presidential elections and the constitutionally-demarcated end of Allende's term in 1976, there were two possible moments when such a majority, if it materialized, could express itself. One was in the congressional elections due to take place in March 1973. The other, for which Allende himself repeatedly expressed a preference, was a plebiscite which would alter the rules of the game and give the President wider powers over political and economic life.[2]

How precisely would a plebiscite accomplish this? According to Allende's campaign program, it would replace Chile's existing two-house legislature, most of whose members were elected in staggered terms and therefore reflected political opinion as it existed before 1970, with a unicameral "Assembly of the People." This body would have regional and local counterparts that is, provincial and municipal chambers, elections for which would be held simultaneously "to establish the necessary harmony between the different expressions of the Popular Will, and to ensure that these are expressed coherently."

Each component of this network of legislative bodies would have economic and social as well as political functions. But perhaps most important of all, they would be empowered to make significant changes in Chile's judicial system. As the program set forth, the national Peoples' Assembly would replace the existing Supreme Court with appointees of its own choosing,[3] which in turn would be free to determine "the initial personal or corporate powers of the judicial system." More than that, "under the Popular Government," it rather provocatively asserted, "a whole new concept of judicial process will replace the existing individualistic and bourgeois one."[4]

It is not easy to see why President Allende thought that a plebiscite would provide the master key for a transition to socialism. Assume that all future elections in Chile were to be free, fair, and open, what was to prevent the same electorate from reversing itself at some future date if the results proved disappointing—precisely as occurred in Mitterand's France a decade later? Either Allende simply assumed that socialism, once established, simply could not fail to generate an economy of abundance. Or, as he hinted to French Marxist Régis Debray a few weeks after he took office, even if he failed to win power through the traditional avenues afforded by the existing legal order, once a "major portion" of the economy had passed under state control, the transition to socialism would be an accomplished fact.[5]

It should be strongly emphasized, however, that Allende's economic policies were not merely conceived for short-run political advantage. They were actually expected to work. There is certainly no other *economic* explanation for the tenacity with which they were applied, once they were shown to produce results very different from those anticipated. Like most of their Latin American contemporaries, Allende's economists led by Minister Pedro Vuskovic (November 1970–June 1972) were exponents of Marxist and "structuralist" theory, particularly in that version developed after World War II by the United Nations Economic Commission for Latin America (ECLA), whose headquarters were in Santiago.

As applied to Chile, this school of analysis held that the principal domestic roadblock to economic growth was lack of consumer demand; hence, the country's most pressing economic necessity was redistribution of income. This would not merely have socially desirable results, but would unleash a self-sustaining cycle of economic growth without inflation. Redistribution would be accomplished through a combination of full employment and wage-and-price policies, whose effectiveness would presumably be assured by the state's acquistion—through purchase or expropriation—of all major economic enterprises.

On the international front, the chief obstacle to development was alleged to be Chile's "dependent" insertion into the international capitalist order. This, it was said, prevented it from effectively formulating policies either of growth *or* of distribution. Hence, a reordering of those relations was necessary to give the Popular Unity government sufficient freedom of action to effect domestic reforms. A new international policy would also entail a diversification of foreign trade and borrowing, nationalization of foreign-owned enterprises, and a transfer to the state of all important economic decisions formerly left to foreign capital (as well as to major domestic enterprises allied to it through technology or investment).

Taken together, both lines of attack—redistribution and expansion at home, a reordering of relations abroad—were expected to yield an immediate increase in living standards. At the same time, they would generate sufficient savings for new investment and continued economic expansion. Since consumption and savings are pretty universally regarded as conflicting choices in early industrial economies such as Chile's, it is worth noting why Allende's people thought that the rules of classical economics could be ignored.

First, the expropriation of foreign enterprises—particularly the American-run copper mines—was expected to save Chile millions of dollars annually in profit repatriations. Second, expansion of state ownership to cover the "com-

manding heights'' of the economy would presumably capture economic surpluses which previously passed into private hands, domestic and foreign.
Third, expansion and intensification of the agrarian reform begun under the
Christian Democrats was expected to yield an increase in domestic food
production; this would relieve Chile of its existing bill for imported foodstuffs, running several hundreds of millions of dollars each year. Finally, a
new system of taxation, credit, and foreign exchange controls would indirectly force money formerly expended on luxury goods, conspicuous consumption, and foreign tourism, into ''socially necessary'' areas of investment. This would also have the effect of saving valuable foreign exchange.[6]

These assumptions formed the framework for what was advertised as the
regime's Six Year Plan (1971–1976) for economic development. In its published form, the plan occupied sixteen folio volumes, including annexes for
each of the country's twelve regions. Gonzalo Martner, chief of Allende's
National Planning Office (ODEPLAN) described these volumes somewhat
delphically as containing ''a diagnosis, some projections within the national
strategy, and groups of projects at various stages of progress.'' In reality, they
were largely made up of projections, many of which were wildly optimistic.
The most sanguine of all was the prediction that Chile's gross domestic
product would increase approximately 50 percent during Allende's presidency, that is, at an annual rate of seven percent, which would have out-
stripped all previous growth records for any corresponding period in the
nation's history.

This somewhat cavalier approach to planning evoked rather pointed criticism from the regime's socialist friends abroad. At an international meeting
convoked in Santiago in early 1972 to discuss such problems, several Eastern
European representatives emphasized the importance of having ''a clear and
unambiguous central plan which determined the main priorities and allocations of the nation's resources.'' On this occasion Allende's people confessed
that this criticism was ''difficult to answer.''

> Not all participants [the conference report read] were convinced that the 1971-
> 76 Six Year Plan constituted an operational and integrated plan. It was agreed
> that the aims had been clearly set out, but there was some doubt about whether
> the plan was integrated so that all the sectoral targets were mutually consistent,
> and how well the aims were adapted to the available resources.
>
> Nevertheless [it went on to say] it seemed to some participants that, in changing
> the priorities, or strategy, the planners had tried to wish away certain important
> and long-standing problems, or alternatively, had not fully worked out the
> overall resource limitations.[7]

When Soviet planning methods were suggested, Popular Unity representatives to the gathering protested that these could not be applied to Chile
because the regime was only ''trying to plan the transitional stage to social-

ism'' (e.g., did not yet possess sufficient political power to unambiguously impose socialist planning criteria), and that, in any event, the "restricted size of the public sector" posed serious obstacles to information gathering necessary for planning purposes.

This discussion highlights the relationship between politics and economics as understood by Allende's people. First, it was believed that there was no contradiction between the regime's short- and long-term goals; one led ineluctably to the other. Second, any serious (that is, potentially conflicting) economic decisions could be postponed until *after* the total conquest of power. All problems which arose in the intervening period ("the transition to socialism") could be explained away in terms of the lack of that total power, and underscore once again the need for the government to broaden its political base in order to achieve it. Third, that the widest possible expansion of public ownership was a *sine qua non*, not merely for political success (to render the "transition to socialism" irreversible), but also to assure a favorable economic performance. Some members of Allende's economic team recognized the degree to which these assumptions worked at cross-purposes, but once put into operation, there was little they could do to change them.

One way of understanding the Allende experiment is to see it as an attempt to achieve a long-term political strategy by means a short-term economic plan. When the latter did not work, the regime proved incapable of replacing it, partly because it was still religiously believed to have some potential for success, but also because all of the other options which presented themselves were bound to shrink, rather than expand, the governement's base of political support. We now turn to the data on specific economic performance to see how these contradictions revealed themselves in actual practice.

1971: The Boom Year

Allende's first year was one of the best in Chilean history. The country's gross domestic product increased approximately 7.7 percent—nearly a point higher than the annual average anticipated by the Six Year Plan.[8] All sectors— agriculture, mining, construction, but especially manufacturing—showed significant gains in output. Unemployment dropped from 1970 levels in at least all three urban complexes for which figures were collected: from 7.1 to 5.5 percent in Greater Santiago; from 10.1 to 9.0 percent in Concepción-Talcahuano; and from 16.6 to 14.2 percent in Lota-Coronel. Nor were these advances cancelled out, as they had so often been in the past, by a general increase in the cost of living. Quite the contrary, the annual rate of inflation actually dropped between December 1970 and December 1971 from 34.9 to 22.3 percent.

Of equal significance was the government's deliberate policy of income redistribution. The objective here was to compensate all but the highest-paid Chileans for loss of income suffered as the result of inflation since January 1, 1970. This turned out to be an average across-the-board wage increase of 35 percent, but the amount was larger still for the lowest-paid workers. By the end of Allende's first year, the share of total income going to the working population (wage and salary earners) had risen from 53.7 to 58.6 percent; some estimates put the figure even higher.[9] This meant that by the end of 1971, the regime was approaching a goal which it had anticipated meeting only by 1976.

A considerable measure of income was also redistributed indirectly, particularly to the neediest sectors of the population. This was accomplished by closing the gap in fringe benefits, pensions, family allowances, and so forth, which had long prevailed between the best- and worst-paid members of the work force, and by extending cheap housing loans to the poor, which subsequently became "open giveaways as escalator clauses were eliminated amid the tidal inflation [which followed] in 1972 and 1973."[10] In addition, the regime sponsored a dramatic acceleration of existing social programs, and created many new ones. These included day-care centers, school lunch programs, and health and welfare services generally. One campaign promise which Allende rigorously fulfilled—ironically, with the help of the United States government—was the delivery to every Chilean infant of a liter of milk a day.[11] As a result, during 1971 there was a drop in the country's scandalously high infant mortality rate.

How had President Allende achieved, by the end of his first year in office, what legitimately appeared to be an economic and social miracle? Part of the answer lies in the nature and extent of assets inherited from the previous presidential period. At the time of Allende's inauguration in November 1970, the dollar reserves held by the nation's Central Bank had reached a record high of $333 million. Of itself this was a very unusual situation, since Chile's external accounts had shown a deficit most years since 1956[12]; in this case, the surplus was the consequence of higher copper prices generated by the Vietnam war, an event Allende himself profoundly deplored. Further, the 1970-71 harvest (planted in 1970, before the outcome of the presidential elections could be known) was one of the best in Chilean history.[13] Finally, a large stock of consumer goods was already on hand, stored away in factory inventories, unsold because of an economic recession which had marred the last two years of the Frei regime.

The rest of the explanation lies in the deliberately expansionary policies pursued by the Allende economic team. These were based on ODEPLAN estimates that idle capacity in industry ranged somewhere in the neighborhood of 25 percent. The exact figures are in dispute, but no doubt considerable slack did exist—due not only to the recession, but to a climate of acute uncertainty following Allende's election. Reactivation was effected in part by the government's incomes policy; it was also promoted by putting the government printing presses to work (the money supply was more than doubled the first year), and by a strict policy of price controls, enforced by the government and also by neighborhood vigilance committees.[14] The result was that hundreds of thousands, possibly millions of Chileans, had more spending power than ever before in their lives.

In Popular Unity theory, the cause of Chile's endemic inflation had been the excessive surplus value appropriated by capital; hence, in the future, industrialists were to earn what government planners deemed a "fair" profit— if, that is, they increased production, which they very nearly had to in order to survive. Although some discomfort and uncertainty remained throughout 1971, a goodly number of industrialists may indeed have managed to enjoy what many must have regarded as the roseate twilight of Chilean capitalism. One American economist, who visited the country in the middle of that year, was "surprised to find that there was little complaint from businessmen that they were being squeezed by wage increases and forced stabilization of prices of their goods." He was further assured on good authority that most industrialists and merchants handling consumer goods were benefiting substantially from the situation."[15]

The regime's full employment goals were met not only through an expansion of demand, of liquidity, and of industrial production, but through the gradual acquistion by the state of some of the principal economic enterprises in Chile. Through a combination of purchase, expropriation, "intervention," and "requisition,"[16] at least 150 industries had passed under government control by the end of 1971, including twelve of the country's twenty largest firms.[17] As the government expanded its hold on the nation's industrial apparatus, it was increasingly able to enlarge payrolls to comprehend an ever-greater number of wage-earners. It is probable that many if not most of the unemployed who found work in industry in 1971 did so in the expanded public sector, the so-called Area of Social Property.[18]

The wave of consumption made possible by these produced a widespread public euphoria utterly without equal in the history of Chile; to do it full justice would require the descriptive talents of a first-rate novelist. Whatever the ultimate unwisdom of Allende's actions, public response to them at this stage was fully understandable. Chile was, and remains, a poor country at once blessed and cursed with a high degree of sophistication; its excellent system of education and communications had done much since World War II to publicize living standards of Western Europe and the United States, and it was these models which formed the reference points for a very broad spectrum of the population.[19] What Allende seems to have proven during his first year in office was that with a bit of tampering with the printing press, and with the discretionary powers of the executive branch, he could pull aside the veil which had long separated most Chileans from the lifestyles they coveted. Some must have thought that the milennium had arrived.

Equally dramatic was the reaction of the country's upper and upper-middle classes. A foreign visitor with extensive experience in the country subsequently recalled that the Chilean *haute bourgeoisie* "lived in a *fin de siècle* mood; tomorrow we die. Instead of saving, everybody spent. One had to phone to find a seat in a luxury restaurant." Santiago, which many remembered from the 1960s as one of the stuffiest of South American capitals, "almost became a swinging town whose ambience was reminiscent of the unreal atmosphere that pervaded Vienna in the midst of the despair and doom of the 1920s."[20] Both the euphoria and the despair of this brief moment left its mark on subsequent events.

The political consequences of this sudden shift in national mood were not long in coming. In the municipal elections held throughout Chile in April 1971, the new government received a striking endorsement. Its standing with the electorate had risen in little more than five months from just under 37 percent to slightly above 50 percent.[21] The Christian Democrats were in confusion and disarray; a few weeks after the municipal elections, six of their congressional deputies left to form a grouping of their own, the Christian Left (IC), which applied for admission to the Popular Unity coalition. For its part, the Chilean Right, represented by the National party, was at its lowest point, isolated and demoralized; some of its members spoke openly of emigration.

Buttressed by the electoral vote of confidence, Allende moved ahead with his plans to nationalize the American-owned copper compaines. On July 11, the Chilean Congress voted unanimously to authorize the President to seize the assets of Kennecott, Anaconda and Cerro corporations, and on September 28 Allende announced that he would deduct what he determined to be the companies' "excess profits" from the book value of compensation due them. Less than a month later, the Comptroller-General, the official responsible for determining indemnification in such cases, ruled that the "excess profits" found by the Chief Executive effectively cancelled out the companies' outstanding claims for compensation.

Once again there was talk of holding a plebiscite to give Allende the expanded powers he desired; in early September, the President announced his intention of holding such a referendum, but there was further delay until it was clear in late November that the Congress could not be persuaded to enact such a reform through normal legislative procedures. Attention was then focussed on by-elections in O'Higgins, Colchagua, and Linares provinces, scheduled for January 16, 1972, whose outcome would determine whether the government's popular support had risen sufficiently to risk an all-or-nothing vote on political institutions.

The most important consequence of the 1971 boom was to reinforce the views originally held by Allende's economic team. The results of Popular Unity's first year, the National Planning Office declared, "confirm the validity of a planned program to confront rapidly and directly the vices of the capitalist system." They "firmly refute all the forecasts of economic catastrophe and chaos made by the reformist [e.g., Christian Democratic and Democratic Radical] political movements." The performance of the Chilean economy in 1971, ODEPLAN added, "also proves that, with a minimum of social cost, it is possible to give a substantial proportion of production a social connotation, [and to achieve] a significant expansion of economic activities at the same time."[22] From this position Allende's planners proved difficult to budge, even when the signals began to point elsewhere. Their refusal to come to terms with the costs of their 1971 policies in 1972 and 1973 was as much the cause of the regime's precipitous decline as any other single factor.

1972: The Year of Decision

During Allende's second year in office almost all of the favorable trends of 1971 reversed themselves except employment and social services. The rate of economic growth fell below one percent, registering a decline in almost all rubrics—industry, agriculture, construction, even the country's fishing industry. Mining did better than most sectors, although there was a drop in iron and iodine production; the newly-nationalized copper mines registered a slight rise (3 percent), which would have been higher still except for labor difficulties. Still and all, this figure fell somewhat short of the government's needs and expectations.

The most important indicator of economic crisis was the sudden reappearance—with unaccustomed virulence—of inflation. In 1972, the rate reached 163 percent, the highest for any twelve-month period in Chilean history. The regime's artifically-imposed price structure encouraged a flourishing black market, and panic buying and hoarding, particularly in foodstuffs and certain essential consumer items. The transformation from milk-and-honey abundance to a virtual siege economy was as rapid as it was devastating, and it once again turned the political tables, throwing the initiative back to Allende's opponents.

Why had Popular Unity's economic miracle proven so short-lived? In part, the answer lay in conditions beyond the government's control. But to a larger degree, its reverses (as its earlier successes) were the consequences of its deliberate actions. The world price of copper, which had reached a record high of sixty four cents a pound in 1970, dropped to forty nine cents in 1971, inflicting a loss of export revenues of approximately $240 million.[23] At the same time, a world rise in food prices (+ 8 percent in 1971; +41 percent in

1972), forced the government to devote a significantly greater amount of foreign exchange to these vital imports.[24]

These two factors, particularly the first, had much to do with a drastic reversal in the country's balance of payments situation; Chile possessed a trade surplus the year Allende took office variously estimated at between $134 and $139 million, but showed a deficit of $427 million two years later.[25] The movement of world commodity prices were not of themselves sufficient to create a trade or current account deficit—at least, not one of these proportions— but they must be taken into account in order to understand the unfavorable economic environment in which Allende was operating.

However, most of the downward movements of economic indicators in 1972 were nothing more than 1971 policies come home to roost. During Allende's first year, the government spent all the foreign exchange reserves inherited from the Christian Democrats, either by buying up majority shares in banks and other enterprises, or drastically increasing imports of foodstuffs and light consumer articles.[26] The high level of imports enjoyed by Chileans in 1971 remained roughly the same in 1972, but were "paid" for by borrowing heavily from a new range of foreign creditors. With reserves exhausted, a growing trade deficit, and a declining rate of growth, as early as January 1972, the regime found it necessary to request a three-year moratorium on the servicing of the "old" (pre-Allende) foreign debt, which had stood at approximately $2.5 billion in late 1970.

By 1972 it was also clear that the period of industrial expansion, the most dramatic in more than a decade, was quite over. Whatever idle capacity had existed in 1970 had been taken up—indeed, in some lines, exceeded—in 1971. While there can be little doubt that there was an actual increase of production during the first year, much of the increased consumption of articles was facilitated by nothing more than a liquidation of inventories. By early 1972 both preexisting production and that which was elaborated in 1971 had disappeared from warehouses and retail shelves, and shortages were becoming ubiquitous.

There could be no immediate revival of industrial production because, quite simply, there had been no new investment in 1971 and there were no domestic resources available to devote to it in 1972. The traditional source of new foreign investment had been the United States, but even before the expropriation of the copper mines in July 1971 (and the subsequent refusal of compensation in September and October), it was apparent that nothing more could be expected from that quarter. Far from regarding this as an obstacle, the Allende regime welcomed the opportunity to diversify Chile's range of foreign partners, but it would be another year before a new mix of loans could make themselves felt. Meanwhile, private Chilean capital remained in hiding or abroad.

This apparently came as something of a surprise to members of the economic team, although at an international round table organized by the Institute of Development Studies (IDS) of the University of Sussex and ODEPLAN in March, 1972, Popular Unity economists seemed at least aware of the dilemma facing the Chilean private investor. The conference report paraphrased the remarks of the ODEPLAN representatives thus:

> A large number of private capitalists had been warned that there was little future for them, yet, they still had been left in control, at this stage, of a sizeable proportion of production and income. Naturally, they were reluctant to invest, as were smaller enterprises, who despite government assurances, felt unsure about their future. Any tendency of the Government's prices and income distribution policies to squeeze profits would provide even less encouragement to invest.[27]

Even if the Chilean investor had been tempted to ignore the signs of the times (and his lower profit margins), he would have experienced serious difficulty acting the way he was supposed to according to the Six Year Plan. A system of exchange controls imposed during the first weeks of the regime made it more difficult to buy dollars for export-related activities than for food and popular consumer goods; for mineral exports, crucial to the nation's balance of payments, the situation was "entirely unfavorable," in the words of one European economist sympathetic to the government. And he adds, "the exchange rate policy must have greatly discouraged many of the private small and medium-sized producers,"[28] to whom the government was dispensing its assurances. As it was, imports of capital goods in 1971 fell 16.8 percent below 1970; by 1972, serious shortages of critical raw materials and spare parts were felt throughout Chilean industry, large and small.

To be sure, the private sector was supposed to play a relatively subordinate role in the generating of investment capital in Allende's Chile. "It was foreseen," the National Planning Office reported to the IDS-ODEPLAN conference, "that local private investment would continue to decrease as it had done during the preceeding years, but that this decrease would be partly offset by a substantial increase in public sector investment."[29] This was a tacit acknowledgement that under the Christian Democrats, the public sector had in fact increased, though at the cost of mounting foreign indebtness.[30] Popular Unity expected to avoid this trap by expanding state ownership to all of the vital areas of the economy on the presumption that the surpluses thus captured would generate new capital for further investment.

Instead, the expanded public sector (the Area of Social Property) lost money. And as it expanded (from 150 enterprises at the end of 1971 to at least 250 at the close of 1972), it lost more money. The few new investments the government was able to make in 1971 fell under the heading of "housing and public works," but however laudable from a social point of view, not necessarily "productive" (e.g., self-liquidating). Hence, far from generating new capital, the enlarged public sector became one more charge upon the government, whose only option was to subsidize it at a growing loss.

In the face of a declining rate of economic growth and the return of inflation in 1972, the government was forced to confront renewed pressures from the labor movement for wage increases. Allende had decreed his 1971 across-the-board increment, confident that it would not prove inflationary largely because prices were expected to remain below government-decreed ceilings. This attempt to circumvent (or repeal) the pressures of the marketplace simply forced them underground to a "black economy" of hoarding and illegal exchange which, by the end of 1972, amounted to something close to a complete alternative to the formal economic system.

The matter was particularly acute in foodstuffs. A drastic acceleration in the agrarian reform had led to an apparent drop in production; in reality, artificially low prices discouraged farmers from sending what they produced to official markets.[31] The shortages were there, nonetheless. In August and September 1972, the government finally recognized the need to bring "official" prices more in line with the realities of supply and demand, if for no other reason than to undercut the flourishing black economy. The formula decreed was "stabilization at a higher level," but even with large price increases (averaging between 100 and 200 percent for basic foodstuffs), the shortages, lines, and black market persisted.

The sudden and sharp rise in the cost-of-living index made it extremely difficult for the government to control its allies in the labor movement. Even in 1971, many plant wage settlements exceeded government guidelines, as employers attempted to "buy off" possible demands for expropriation.[32] With the rate of inflation rising to over 160 percent by the end of 1972, union demands leaped ahead of government plans, partly because "union leaders at the plant level did not believe that inflation could be kept down for another year, and so were determined to protect their members by asking for larger increases." Even Communist and Socialist trade union secretaries sympathetic to the government's stabilization program found it difficult to limit their wage requests, caught as they were between the pressures of their own membership, and the sudden competition with their Christian Democratic rivals.[33] Consequently, in October 1972, a few days after what was supposed to be a once-and-for-all price rise, the government was forced to decree a 100 percent increase in wages, which generated a new inflationary spiral.

In order to meet these wage demands and the the mounting deficits of the public sector, and to finance continued expansion of social welfare programs, the government recurred once again to the printing press. In 1972 the money supply increased 165 percent, which made it possible to meet the regime's expenses (and payroll which approached full employment), although with bills of geometrically declining value. The tripling of the country's money supply by the end of Allende's second year—conceived as a short-run response to inflationary pressure—afforded virtually no respite. Instead, it succeeded in imparting to those pressures a redoubled vigor and force. By early 1973, a series of misguided and mutually reinforcing policies had pushed the inflationary process beyond recall.

In retrospect, it is clear that the year 1972 was the critical moment in the history of the Allende regime in the sense that at that point the Popular Unity government was faced with all of the hard decisions necessary to its survival. Those decisions it desperately tried to avoid making, since they required resolution of tactical and ideological differences which—beneath the surface—had divided the members of the government, its economic team, and its supporters among the electorate from the very start. Indecision was also fostered by a continuation of wishful thinking and a reluctance to acknowledge the errors of the expansionary policies of 1971. As one surviving member of the economic team has written, the atmosphere of that period in government circles was clouded by considerable "uncertainty. . . . How long [people asked one another] would the recessive effects last? When and how would the private sector resume normal behavior as an investor?" That confusion, he explains, "circumscribed the degree to which one could successfully plan each subsequent measure. Analytical capacity was also somewhat lacking," he adds, "and the vacuum tended to be filled with appreciations heavily colored by ideological pleading."[34]

By the middle of the year it was impossible to ignore the existence of two distinct lines or camps within the government. What might be called a moderate group (President Allende, the Communists, the Radicals, and a minority of Socialists) was moving toward a tacit recognition of some of the errors of 1971. Consequently, it now favored "consolidation" (a favorite term) of the public sector, and concentration on raising production in order to generate surpluses for reinvestment.

On the other side, a radical element (most of the President's own Socialist party, as well as MAPU and the Christian Left, and from outside the government, the MIR) believed that the process had not gone far enough. That is, they argued that the Area of Social Property had not shown a profit because it was still not large enough. For these people, enlargement of the state's share of industry would somehow mysteriously remove the expropriated enterprises "from the operation of the market and the 'law of value'."[35] There was also a difference of opinion as to which industries should receive the lion's share of government resources. The radicals favored a continuation of the 1971 policies, with their emphasis on basic consumer goods, while the moderates preferred industries capable of generating foreign exchange—mining, iron and steel, wood and paper, fishing and agro-industry.

Likewise, there was considerable disagreement over the causes of inflation. The moderates, particularly the Communists, set themselves firmly against further expansion of the money supply. As party functionary Orlando Millas remarked in a report to the Central Committee in March 1972, the existing policy of unrestricted printing of escudo bills was "equivalent to sitting down on the crater of a volcano . . . It is a matter of life and death not to permit a repetition of the inflationary cycle to which bourgeois governments have accustomed us." To this end, Millas proposed a number of stringent financial measures, including the imposition of a strict ceiling on government expenditures.[36] To the radicals, such proposals bore a chilling resemblance to the monetarist policies pursued by Chile's conservative governments of times past, often at the behest of foreign (largely American) experts; for the left opposition within the government, the causes of inflation had been and remained structural, that is, due to the persistence of large pockets of economic power in private hads. Therefore, they tirelessly insisted, price rises could be effectively combated only by enlarging the state's hold on the economy.

These disagreements over investment and monetary policies spilled over into the question of wages and prices. The radicals strongly opposed the price increases of August–September 1972, and the government's largely non-discriminatory (across-the-board) pay increases. Such increases, they maintained (not without foundation), actually favored the middle class, which already received a disproportionate share of the national income. The radicals also criticized the government's failure to put an end to the black market. Allende and the Communists hoped that increases in production would gradually displace the underground economy; in the meanwhile, they preferred to rely upon the vigilance committees, the Price and Supply Boards (JAPs). Their opponents within the coalition saw no reason to wait: they urged a greater control over marketing mechanisms through the nationalization of wholesale distribution firms and the major transportation companies. Even at this stage there was some talk about the desirability of imposing some sort of outright rationing, an idea which Allende himself strongly opposed.

In reality, these differences turned less on economic policy as such, than on the role which economics itself should play in the quest for power. Allende's "moderate" stance was inspired by a desire to broaden his political base—or, at any rate, to do nothing which would diminish it. Hence, his continuing pursuit of populist policies, long past the point where the preconditions for their success had disappeared. The radicals, on the other hand, regarded overall economic performance, even in the short run, as basically unimportant. What they sought to do was to strengthen the government's control over the economy and its support among the have-nots of the Chilean population. Although they recognized that this was unlikely to produce an electoral majority, it was expected to solidify support among the cadres and troops for a confrontation in which they expected Chileans to definitively resolve their political differences.[37]

In June 1972, all elements of Popular Unity were summoned to a conference on economic policy held at Lo Curro, a suburb of Santiago. Apparently differences were fully ventilated, yet no firm decisions could be made; even the subsequent cabinet changes were difficult to interpret. Although Pedro Vuskovic, a self-described "independent Marxist" with no party affiliation (but strongly identified with the radical line) stepped down as Economy Minister, he remained within the government as head of the "Economic Coordinating Committee." His place was taken by Carlos Matus Romo, a Socialist drawn from the more moderate wing of the party; Communist Orlando Millas became Minister of Finance. The sense of stalemate was underlined by the speed with which the upward price adjustments of August–September were followed by wage increases in October.

It is difficult to see how the Lo Curro deliberations could have solved Allende's problems in any case. However much he and the Communists might have wished to consolidate their populist political gains, they still had to meet the costs of those socialist aspects of their program initiated in 1971, e.g., expanded government services and a vastly enlarged public sector. The process was not merely irreversible, but literally out of control. The radicals who failed to fully impose their views at Lo Curro in 1972 could nonetheless provoke factory occupations by workers, thus continuing to enlarge, willy-nilly, the public sector (and its deficits). And, of course, even the most moderate political elements within Popular Unity feared the political consequences of cutting back employment rolls. Hence, the regime took refuge in pious exhortations to the workers for greater productivity, hoping against hope for a sudden rise in copper prices, while frantically searching about for new sources of foreign credit, printing still more paper money in the meanwhile.

While the government and its allies drifted on a sea of confusion and growing discord, the economic crisis of 1972 fostered a near-miraculous revival in the political fortunes of the opposition. On January 16, the government sustained a sharp defeat in by-elections in O'Higgins, Colchagua, and Linares provinces. The loss strengthened the opposition's majority in the Congress, and also led Allende to shelve plans for a plebiscite.

In early April, Felipe Herrera, former President of the Inter-American Development Bank and a close personal friend of President Allende, was defeated in his bid for rectorship of the University of Chile; the opposition also captured control of that foundation's governing council. While the outcome of university elections in themselves could neither help nor hinder the government, they were an important bellweather of middle-class opinion. The defeat of the Popular Unity slate—headed by one of the strongest candidates ever fielded by the Left—suggested that the generation gap which had historically divided Chilean students from their more conservative parents was closing rapidly.

In early October a quarrel between the government and the owners of small trucking concerns in the remote southern provinces of Aysén exploded into what quickly became a nationwide strike, as sympathetic members of Chile's professional and business classes walked off their jobs or closed their shops. Attempts to force the strikers to resume their tasks led to violence, imposition of states of siege, and subordination of twenty-one Chilean provinces to temporary military rule. President Allende's negotiations with the confederation of truckowners broke down on October 25, leading to new waves of disorder in Santiago and other cities. The crisis was finally resolved on November 5, but only after Allende had agreed to a cabinet reorganization in which three of the portfolios would be held by ranking members of the armed forces. Civil war had been averted by military mediation, but the opposition had been persuaded to return to normal channels of political activity largely in anticipation of the opportunity to defeat the government in congressional elections scheduled for the following March.

1973: Economic Chaos and Political Collapse

Almost all of the indices of economic performance continued their downward movement in 1973. Agriculture and mining output dropped, the first very sharply; construction declined; manufacturing, which began the year with a negative figure and then stagnated at low levels in February and March, began a precipitous descent in April, from which it was not to recover in the life of the regime.

Investment continued to fall as a percentage of GDP; by 1973, it had dropped to 11.4 percent (Table 3.1), not through saving but through new infusions of foreign credit. Employment continued to show improvement, and it is probable that—with the help of the printing press—government services either experienced a modest increase or held steady. Imports of foodstuffs and light consumer articles actually increased in 1973 over 1972, at a cost of the continued rapid growth of the short-term foreign debt. (Table 3.2) Nonetheless, even heavy import bills could not cancel out short-falls in agriculture and industry, thus forcing Chileans to queue for basic goods, or recur to the ubiquitous black market.

The indicator which showed the greatest rate of change was the cost-of-living index, which by the end of the Allende period had scaled astronomic heights—officially in excess of 500 percent a year. (Table 3.3) The precise

TABLE 3.1
Major Aspects of Chilean Economic Performance, 1970–1973

GDP	Annual avg. 1964–1970	1971	1972	1973
Total GDP (%)	4.1	7.1	–.08	–3.62
Gross National Saving (E^{0}s millions, 1965 constant prices)	3,052	3,119	2,072	2,633
CONSUMPTION AND INVESTMENT				
Total consumption (%)	3.1	14.7	0.9	–2.4
Gross fixed investment/GDP (coefficient)	15.5	14.3	13.6	11.4
FISCAL SPENDING & DEFICIT, DEFICIT/SPENDING RATIO	**1970**	**1971**	**1972**	**1973**
Fiscal spending (millions 1976 US$)	2,393	2,959	2,936	3,931
Deficit/Spending Ratio (% deficit to spending)	10.3	34.7	41.9	55.1

Sources: National Planning Office (ODEPLAN); Markos J. Mamalakis, *Historical Statistics of Chile: Volume One, National Accounts* (Westport, Conn., 1978); Ministry of Finance, Budget Office; Ian Roxborough et. al., *Chile: The State and Revolution* (New York, 1977)

figure can only be guessed at, given the inability to measure the full extent of the black market, where prices were considerably higher than those decreed by the government.[38] Apart from shortages induced by declining production and market and price distortions, the consumer price index was strongly affected by a quantum increase in the country's money supply.

These figures quietly chart the dimensions of a social earthquake. In 1973, Chileans were subject to world's highest rate of inflation and shortages of basic goods reminiscent of a country in the last stages of a military defeat. An American Marxist who had come to Chile to work for the Central Bank has recalled that during these months it was "impossible" to buy meat, and that "many goods—coffee, tea, sugar, toilet paper, detergents, bedsheets—were available only sporadically, or not at all."[39] Economics became an issue of everyday survival, as the supply situation each day grew more chaotic and difficult.

The year began with an uncharacteristically forthright attempt by the government to deal with food shortages. On January 10 it proposed a new system of distribution, based on a list of thirty essential items (the so-called *canasta popular,* or people's market basket), to be established for each Chilean family. These items would be sold at controlled prices under the vigilance of the Price and Supply Boards (JAPs). The latter, composed of government supporters, were authorized "to determine the local needs for essential goods, supervise supplies, and denounce merchants and speculators who subverted

TABLE 3.2
Selected Aspects of Chile's International Finances, 1970–1973

	1970	1971	1972	1973
Curent Account Balance (millions 1976 US$)*	−134.3	−303.2	−593.9	−390.5
Foreign Debt (millions 1976 US$) "Traditional" (middle and long-term debits)	2,533	2,640	2,880	3,159
Short-term credits	48	83	219	381
Surplus on external account (E^0s millions, current prices)	−1,209	−2,604	−7,536	−34,416

Note: * = deflated by U.S. wholesale price index
Sources: Central Bank of Chile; Markos J. Mamalakis, *Historical Statistics of Chile: Volume One, National Accounts* (Westport, Conn., 1978).

the plan.''[40] Actually, the proposal fell somewhat short of full rationing, since it contemplated control only of wholesale distribution; retailers were allowed to continue their operations, although they were instructed to restrict their food sales to regular customers.

Overall responsibility for the execution of this plan was assigned to a new agency, the Secretariat of Distribution and Trade (DIRINCO), which Allende prudently placed in the hands of the armed forces. The opposition immediately attacked the plan as an attempt to utilize food supplies as political blackmail, but the President's decision was instantly buttressed by the affirmation of his three military ministers that these measures were urgently necessary. However, symptomatic of a growing dissatisfaction even among government supporters was the protest strike on January 16–17 at the Chuquiquimata mine, in which 8,000 workers walked off their jobs to protest serious food shortages and new restrictions on consumption.

By mid-year, the controversy over food supplies had reached a stalemate. The poor, particularly those residing in urban settlements known to be loyal to the government, were receiving regular dispatches of the most essential foodstuffs through their own liaisons with the DIRINCO. The well-to-do could provision themselves through the black market. "But," as the Economist Intelligence Unit reported, "the government has not yet come up with a single distribution policy acceptable to all, and consequently those in the middle are forced to queue.''[41] Behind the scenes a furious debate raged within government councils between radicals and moderates over whether to extend DIRINCO's authority to the retail trade. This, everyone knew, would require the imposition of frank and outright rationing—coupon books and all.

More violent still was the conflict over wage adjustments to compensate for hyperinflation. In 1973, for the first time the govenment abandoned its across-

TABLE 3.3
Money Supply and the Consumer Price Index (CPI), 1970–1973

Year	M1*	M1 % change	CPI Dec–Dec
1969	6,057	35.2	29.3
1970	10,068	66.2	34.9
1971	21,488	113.4	22.1
1972	54,111	151.8	163.4
1973	250,477	362.9	508.1

Note: * = nominal balances in E^os millions each year
Sources: Central Bank of Chile; National Planning Office (ODEPLAN); National Bureau of Statistics.

the-board approach to wage increases and proposed in its March-April deliberations with the CUT that only the poorest paid workers be fully compensated for inflation between October, 1972 and March, 1973; those in higher brackets would receive increases according to a sliding scale, declining to zero for those at the top.

The proposal led to a new round of recriminations between Allende and the Chilean Congress. The latter refused the President the necessary legislation, enacting in its place a generous across-the-board increase, which Allende promptly vetoed. This attempt to break past populist wage policies was inspired by acute financial constraints, radical preachments, and a sobering recognition that the Chilean middle class had by now drifted so far into the ranks of the opposition that its goodwill was no longer worth attempting to purchase.

An unforseen consequence of the new incomes policy was a major protest within the labor movement. On May 10, the copper miners of Chuquiquimata, who figured among the better-paid members of the blue-collar work force, went on strike to demand increases sufficient to compensate them for inflation. The walkout lasted 74 days, climaxing in a dramatic march on Santiago and a clash with the police strikingly similar to those which had occurred under right-wing governments in times past. It also led to a wave of sympathy strikes by truckers, professionals, and small businessmen, as well as a loss to the treasury of approximately $70 million in foreign exchange. The workers returned to their jobs on July 2, having won most of their demands; however, because of dislocations, the state copper company (CODELCO) announced that no ore would be available for sale for another month.

In the midst of these tumultuous events, Chileans went to the polls on March 4 to elect a new congress. The results did not point to a political resolution of the country's economic problems. The forces of the opposition, grouped together on a single list, retained their solid majority—54.7 percent; on the other hand, Allende's Popular Unity slate received 43.4 percent, which meant a slight improvement in its congressional representation. Both sides claimed victory, though in fact the elections at best registered a stalemate; the opposition failed to obtain enough seats to impeach the government, but Popular Unity's showing in the population as a whole showed a sharp decline since the last election in April 1971. Theoretically Chileans could iron out their differences three years hence, in the 1976 presidential elections; in practice, no one expected things to wait that long. After the March elections, it was obvious that the country faced only two choices—either a military coup or a civil war.

Why Did Allende Fail? Three Hypotheses Examined

Allende's economic difficulties were the product of the simultaneous pursuit of mutually exclusive goals: investment *and* consumption, full employment *and* a balanced budget, price disincentives *and* greater productivity, inflation *and* redistribution, economic independence *and* a quantum increase in the foreign debt. Between 1970 and 1973 orthodox economists of both the socialist and capitalist worlds stood aghast at Chile's reckless insistence upon proving the viability of an unworkable economic model. Indeed, those from the Eastern bloc might well have been the more appalled; whatever else can be said about those societies, in recent history they have demonstrated a tenacious commitment to capital accumulation, as several generations of hapless consumers consumers could readily attest. To the Soviets, to the Chinese, above all to the Cubans, long inured to a stern and cheerless rationing, there was something almost obscene in Chile's hedonistic road to socialism. As Fidel Castro is supposed to have ruefully remarked, "Marxism is a revolution of production; Allende's was a revolution of consumption."[42]

In some ways, of course, Popular Unity's policies were not socialist at all, but rather welfarist. But, as David Lehmann has observed, they *were* socialist at one very critical level—that of institutions (state ownership of the means of production).[43] The result was the worst of two systems: a welfare state run at a loss, based on a public sector, which, as things turned out, also ran at a loss. As such, the Allende experiment in redistribution could not but quickly devour the means of its own subsistence.

No doubt Allende made a serious attempt to close the gap between the country's lowest-paid workers and its organized labor force; thus it is just possible that to the very end those Chileans at the bottom of the scale were still better off in 1973 than they had been in 1969. If so, this was due not so much to wage increases (which were largely cancelled out by inflation) as to indirect transfers (expanded government services) and even, in an involuted sense, privileged access to essential foodstuffs at controlled (artificially low) prices. If by 1973 there were still some citizens better off than they had been in 1969, this would constitute a devastating comment on the state of the nation's poor at the time of Allende's election. But it would not ratify Popular Unity's economic model. For how much longer could even the poorest of the poor hold on to their post-1970 gains depended almost wholly upon the regime's capacity to procure foreign subsidies (from whatever quarter), or to purchase foodstuffs and cheap consumer goods on unlimited short-term credits.

Since Allende's fall, there has been a studied reluctance on the part of many commentators to recognize these facts for what they are. None seems willing to insist outright the Popular Unity's model could have worked, but many hedge their arguments with claims that the *decisive* factor was the opposition, either at home or abroad. Since these arguments constitute so central a portion of the mythological history of Allende's Chile, it seems worthwhile to devote some space to each.

First, there is the issue of taxation:

> Control over finances [writes one author] became a major tool in the bourgeois battle against the UP; by refusing to provide finances for wage increases and social programs, the opposition-controlled Congress forced the government to print money, raising the inflation rate and eating up much of the wage increases that had been granted.[44]

In reality, Allende's recourse to the printing press was inspired by a far more complex set of motives. The initial decision in 1971 to more than double the money supply was not taken under any particular budgetary duress, but as an integral part of the government's program to redistribute income and reactivate the economy. The monetary expansion was not expected to have an inflationary effect, because—owing to the existing slack in Chilean industrial capacity—"it placed much faith in an econometric estimate which showed that 'a growth rate of liquid assets as high as 40 percent would not increase pressure on prices.'"[45] The actual *drop* in the inflation rate in 1971 provided further support for this view, and for the hoary argument of the Chilean Left that the country's inflationary condition was due to purely "structural" conditions; once the structures were altered, presumably the rate of inflation would drop further still.

When this suddenly proved untrue in 1972 and 1973, the economic team divided between those who thought that monetary expansion must be curtailed, and those who refused to see any connection between the money supply and the inflation rate. Edward Boorstein, an American Marxist economist politically close to the Chilean Communist party and who worked at the Central Bank during these years, has left us a vivid account of this controversy, which—even in the extremely opaque tones in which he paints it—evokes something far closer to a theological disputation than a debate over economic strategies.

Moreover, Allende's team was not "forced" to print paper money; this was the method that it *chose,* initially and thereafter, to finance a quantum increase

in government expenditures. The government could just as easily have reduced its budget and corresponding deficits. Admittedly, this would have led
to some very serious political difficulties within the ruling coalition, but
probably no more serious than the ones which Allende ultimately faced. As it
was, the unrestrained increase in paper money, though less costly in the very
short run, was devastating in the middle-term, which lay only twelve to
eighteen months away.

Would a tax increase—if it had been obtained from the Chilean Congress—
have resolved Allende's problems? By turning to Chile's national accounts for
the year prior to Popular Unity's assumption of power, it is fairly easy to
arrive at a very rough calculation of how much income was deliberately and
voluntarily forfeited by Popular Unity's policies of wholesale nationalization
of industrial properties. (All figures are given in U.S. dollars converted at the
1970 rate of exchange [E^o 15.8/1].)

In 1970 the Chilean state perceived approximately $513 million in "direct
taxes," a category which covered (a) personal income tax; (b) corporate
income tax; (c) taxes on copper mining operations; (d) taxes on property. Of
this $513 million, copper's share was approximately $227 million. The figures for personal and corporate income taxes have been aggregated in the
materials available; together they come to $244 million. Under the Christian
Democrats, personal and corporate income tax yields had been brought nearly
in tandem by 1969; it is therefore a reasonable guess that in 1970 approximately half of the $244 million—let us say, $122 million—represented the
corporate contributions.[46]

By the end of 1971, the copper industry, as well as 150 of the principal
enterprises of Chile had passed into the hands of the state; indeed, at the time
President Allende's ideologue-in-residence Joan Garcés was reporting to the
world that the "financial industrial bourgeoisie" had been virtually eliminated in Chile as a socioeconomic category.[47] This meant that as of the
beginning of the regime's second year, it had permanently renounced *no less
than 65 percent of its inherited direct tax base,* which in 1970 had amounted
to approximately $349 out of $513 million. The percentage of what might be
called tax renunciation would have been far higher for 1972, when the number
of nationalized or "intervened" enterprises climbed to at least 250, and for
1973, higher still.[48]

How much of this could have been replaced by a combination of higher
taxes on personal income and property? Since the legislation repeatedly requested by President Allende was never passed, the figure can never be
known. However, it is possible to venture some intelligent guesses. Insofar as
a personal income tax is concerned, a 400 percent increase (far more than the
government ever proposed) would have done nothing more than replace the
corporate tax revenues necessary to finance Chile under the Christian Dem-

ocrats, where the level of government expenditures never remotely approached that of Popular Unity.[49] Moreover, to the degree to which upper-class incomes rested upon shares of stock in major industrial enterprises, by 1972 this source had been largely eliminated by expansion of the public sector.

This still left considerable private wealth. In a general sense, the well-to-do in Chile followed the widespread Latin American practice of investing heavily in urban real estate and in keeping much of their liquidity in banks outside the country. Not surprisingly, the government focused much of its attention on the former. For example, in 1973 it announced plans to drastically increase tax appraisals on large houses and mansions. As reported by the Economist Intelligence Unit, the government had decided that such properties would "increase in value by 300 percent this year [1973] and another 200 percent in 1974, giving [a property presented assessed at E^o 100,000] a value of E^o 1,200,000 [strictly for tax purposes]. Taking account of this increase, taxation next year is estimated at E^o 400,000."[50]

Congress never passed this legislation. But even if it had, far from enhancing government revenues, it would simply have led to the dumping of massive amounts of property on a market where nobody would wish to acquire it — along with its tax burden based on fictitious assessments. (Ironically, fear of outright expropriation caused this to happen anyway.) Further, even assuming that wealthy Chileans had been willing to patriotically liquidate their foreign bank accounts to meet their property taxes at home, the most the government could have hoped for would have been a one-year windfall, not unlike its liquidation of inherited foreign exchange reserves in 1971; after that, it would be broke once again. No one will ever be able to say how much Chilean money reposed in foreign banks in 1972 and 1973, but a figure of one billion dollars would not quite stretch to cover the regime's foreign trade deficit for its three years in power. It would not cover one penny's worth of the massive revenue shortfalls necessary to finance its domestic operations.

Of itself, tax reform in Chile was long overdue. During the 1960s the Frei administration had done much to raise personal and corporate rate, although the levels of revenue produced (as well as efforts to close avenues of tax evasion) were far from adequate. However, contrary to superficial appearances, the major difference between the Christian Democrats and Allende was not so much the magnitude of the tax burden they sought to impose, as it was their contrasting economic and social goals. Frei attempted, not without success, to force Chile's capitalist class to make a more meaningful contribution of national saving. Allende nationalized the major corporate holdings in Chile; his tax proposals could therefore contemplate little more than the liquidation of what private wealth remained, in order to finance (temporarily) higher levels of popular consumption. Ironically, had Popular Unity allowed Chilean industrialists to retain their properties, it is conceivable that there would have been something left to tax, and the country's upper class would have remained isolated politically—which, by the way, was the government's original intention.[51]

The second argument in defense of Allende's economic policies emphasizes the punitive role of foreign credit, specifically that proceeding from the U.S. government, U.S. private banks, and the multilateral lending agencies. For example, it is held that

> as [U.S.] bilateral and multilateral aid was withdrawn, Chile's ability to service its debts declined by definition, surely part of the Nixon-Kissinger plan . . .
>
> The credit blockade [also] began to cause supply problems in certain sectors of industry, and the interrelated nature of the industrial sector itself, as well as its key role with respect to the rest of the economy, meant that these problems soon had a ripple effect elsewhere.[52]

Without doubt United States lending agencies withdrew confidence from Chile after Allende came to power. This had the potential for creating some rather serious difficulties because, among other things, the new regime inherited a large foreign debt from the Christian Democrats, servicing of which required a steady flow of new credit and investments. However, to describe the situation which followed as a "credit blockade" distorts the language. For, far from sealing Chile off from credit generally, the "Nixon-Kissinger plan," if it existed, merely led President Allende to embark upon an unprecedented wave of borrowing from nontraditional sources. In rapid order New York and Washington were replaced by Moscow, Peking, Bucharest, East Berlin, and Pyongyang, as well as by Paris, Tokyo, Sydney, Ottawa, Buenos Aires, Mexico City, Madrid, Brussels, Stockholm, Amsterdam and Helsinki. As noted in Table 3.2 Chile's foreign debt increased in slightly more than three years from $2.6 billion to 3.5 billion. When coupled with the expended reserves of foreign exchange accumulated under the Christian Democrats, this substantially exceeded the total indebtedness incurred from the previous presidential term. "In fact," Paul Sigmund has pointed out, "on August 30, 1973, Allende had more short-term credits available to him . . . than at the time of his election to office."[53]

The use of foreign credit to cover government deficits in Chile was not an innovation of the Allende regime, but the latter subjected the practice to several new twists. The Frei administration's borrowing practices were at least based upon the expectation of continued creditworthiness, and more important still, were largely directed toward an increase in Chile's industrial productivity, particularly in the mining sector.[54] Popular Unity's borrowing practices were of a completely different order. Allende's preference for confiscating foreign capital (particularly U.S. copper properties) virtually eliminated Chile's links to its traditional credit sources, and rendered it vulnerable to lenders whose concern with the country's long-term economic potential was extremely questionable. Although some credits, particularly those from the Eastern bloc, were intended to increase overall industrial capacity, they were overshadowed by obligations to cover imports of foodstuffs and consumer items, which were running at $700 million a year in the final days of the regime.

Those who allege that the United States, by closing credit lines to Chile, "forced" Allende into irresponsible practices which he otherwise would have been inclined to avoid, overlook the fact that a sound investment policy would have required choices (between savings and consumption, wages and prices) which for political reasons he preferred to avoid. For reasons of its own, the United States refused to underwrite Allende's boom-and-spend populism, but then neither would anyone else. Most of the loans Allende obtained between 1970 and 1973 were tied to the immediate purchase of goods from export-driven economies, socialist and capitalist, often on terms which bordered on the usurious. As Markos Mamalakis crisply remarks, during the Allende years the Chilean government accepted "any trade or credit deal, however uneconomical," and those willing to export to Chile on credit "emerged as a privileged class of foreigners enjoying returns far beyond those deserved realistically under competitive market conditions."[55] If these sorts of loans were not what Chile required for sustained growth, neither were the economic policies they were intended to underpin.

How long Allende could have continued to find even such makeshift credit arrangements to subsidize his day-to-day operations remains a matter of serious doubt. After Allende's first year, both the Russians and the Chinese were sternly lecturing him on the need to end his reckless borrowing practices — the Soviets through the ubiquitous medium of the Chilean Communist party, and also on the occasion of the President's visit to Moscow in December, 1972;[56] the Chinese in a remarkable letter from Premier Chou En-lai to Allende which the government made public a few weeks prior to its overthrow.[57]

One final point about the so-called "credit blockade." While Allende frequently attributed his difficulites to the imposing foreign debt contracted by the previous regime, as a matter of fact after 1971 his government ceased to make regular service payments on its inherited obligations.[58] Further, nationalizing the principal foreign-owned industries in Chile, while depriving the government of massive tax revenues, did in fact save it some millions of dollars through profit repatriations, patent royalties, and other related outflows; this constituted something of a "credit blockade" in reverse. That plugging such leakages did not yield more impressive results attests to the enormous size of the foreign trade deficit such operations were expected to offset.

A third hypothesis puts the blame for Allende's economic failure on his opposition, which, it is said, "deliberately intervened in the economic process, bringing about the 'predicted' decline." Those who offer this argument single out the Chilean middle class for especial opprobrium, particularly as regards its penchant for hoarding, speculation, and recourse to the black market. In this view, the Chilean bourgeoisie resisted Popular Unity's economic policies not because they were failing, but precisely because they threatened to work so effectively.[59]

This argument purposely obscures important considerations of sequence and context. In the first place, Popular Unity's own strategy was expressly predicated on a middle class which would either remain neutral, or find itself benevolently disposed to the new order of things. Writing in 1971, Joan Garcés made clear that the Allende government aimed at putting an end to "the economic power of the higher bourgeoisie and the *latifundistas* (large landowners), but desired "neither conflict nor confrontation" with Chile's middle sectors. Indeed, he added, "every economic and legislative policy of the government has sought to give them security and to prevent them being drawn into violent opposition in the service of the dominant class." These political objectives he linked to Popular Unity's short-term economic program. "The political power of the Popular government," he insisted, "is indissolubly linked with its short-term economic success . . . The [political] road followed by the Chilean government [therefore] requires economic effectiveness as a *sine qua non*."[60]

At the time these words were written, the economic performance of Popular Unity was at its peak, and Garcés projection of a middle class detached politically from what he called "the higher bourgeoisie and the *latifundistas*" seemed a reasonable possibility. The sudden lurch to the right by Chile's petty bourgeoisie was the product of an abrupt decline in its living standards the following year, when even presidential wage decrees failed to compensate white-collar workers for a rise in the cost of living. These same decrees, of course, could not affect those whom the Chilean census habitually classified as "self-employed" or "own account" workers, which by one authoritative estimate, embraced approximately 568,000 persons in urban areas, and something between 300 and 400,000 in the countryside—almost half the rural labor force.[61]

The evident recourse by the middle class to hoarding, speculation and the black market was inspired far less by greed than simple economic logic. Since the purchasing power of Chilean currency declined daily in 1972 and 1973, it became more prudent to keep one's liquid assets in easily negotiable form— canned food, toilet paper, soap, cooking oil (and, where possible, foreign currency). The sheer magnitude of this informal economy speaks not so much to the ultimate political intentions of the Chilean bourgeoisie—whatever those might have been—as to the enormous subterranean pressures generated by the government's unrealistic price and supply policies. Since middle-class Chileans could not depend on the supply of goods made available to working-class settlements through DIRINCO and the JAPs at controlled prices, they had no choice but to pay whatever the underground market would bear—normally a figure far above the official cost-of-living estimates or government guidelines for the *canasta popular*.

Finally, the government's peculiar system of currency controls did much to alienate Chile's numerous small business class. British economist Alec Nove, a specialist in the socialist economies of Eastern Europe who visited Chile in 1972 and again in 1973, provides a graphic illustration. Citing the hypothetical example of a petty manufacturer, shopkeeper, or owner of two or three trucks, he writes:

> If he required spare parts, materials or commodities from abroad, these were subject to strict import licensing, owing to a desperate shortage of foreign exchange. Or it might be available at one of the large number of widely varying exchange rates, according to the category of essentiality judged by the Central Bank to apply to the proposed transaction.
>
> By 1972 the would-be importer might or might not be called upon to make a deposit in Escudos [the Chilean unit of currency] worth 10,000 percent of the value of the imports for three months ...
>
> Insofar as imports were involved, therefore, a high degree of uncertainty and frustration prevailed, both as regards the cost and availability of the necessary permit.[62]

Whatever the government's intentions, such difficulties over an extended period of time could not proffer credible proofs of "security, and to prevent" such persons from "being drawn into violent opposition," although by late 1972, whether "in the service of the dominant class" or upon their own behalf, had become a meaningless distinction. To heap vituperation upon the Chilean middle class for turning against the Allende government implies that it had some responsibility to support a government which—regardless of its programs, statements, even its intentions—was implementing policies demonstrably contrary to the interests of that class. Why Marxists (or all people) should wish to separate analytically economic motivation from political action must be left to one of their number to explain.

Was There a Chilean Road to Socialism?

If the economic policies of Popular Unity—half socialist, half-populist—were incapable of effecting a "transition to socialism" in Chile, what chance remained for a more rigorously Marxist alternative? Since 1973 this is a question which many members of the Chilean Left have put to themselves; it is also one which has been frequently addressed by their foreign sympathizers. One, who holds a major university chair in the United States, has stated the case for the ultra-Left: "with more attention to political education and a chance for planning and distribution (rationing) mechanisms to actually begin to operate, it would not seem farfetched for an alliance to be built around a more solid socialist model."[63]

Just how plausible is this argument? Leaving aside the question of "political education" (whatever that might mean), the practical possibilities of implementing full-dress rationing in Chile were never very great. The country did not possess the sheer economic resources to support such a system, least of all in 1973. Moreover, as one member of the economic team has written, "the political preconditions for this . . . course simply did not exist."[64] Rationing was repeatedly discussed at the cabinet level as an alternative, and just as repeatedly discarded as likely to alienate the peasantry and the nation's extremely numerous small merchant class. As Edward Boorstein wrote to Jaime Barrios, President of Chile's Central Bank, such options lacked broad political support, and if they were nonetheless imposed, "will not work well. We could see ourselves forced to recur more and more to coercive measures, even against sympathizers, to our political disadvantage."[65]

If Allende's people had set about building "an alliance . . . around a more solid socialist model," what would that model have been able to offer? As one of the better left-wing studies puts it, "in September 1973, Chile was in a state of economic confusion. Whoever won the battle for power, a realistic program of austerity and realism would have been required." Chilean socialism, it concedes, "would not have been able to offer abundance. But . . . better the socialism of poverty than the misery and rank horror of Chilean capitalism."[66] The question, however, was not whether "the socialism of poverty" was preferable to its capitalist alternative, but whether an electoral majority could be expected to opt for it. Chile was and remains a poor country where austerity is an unpopular political choice. As Allende himself must have known, a forced savings plan of his own stood no chance of faring better at the hands of the electorate than earlier attempts at capital formation under Presidents Alessandri and Frei.

Nor is the matter disproved by the government's capacity to retain 44 percent of the electorate as late as March 1973. It has been argued that this relatively strong showing, against the background of a fall in real wages in 1972 and 1973, proves that "the workers . . . did not need immediate increases in consumption to commit them to a transition to socialism."[67] It proves nothing of the sort. The good times of Allende's first year were still a vivid memory in 1973, and a vote for Popular Unity symbolized a desire for their resumption at the hands of the government originally responsible for them. In contradistinction, many of those voters who deserted Allende in 1973 (nearly six percent of the electorate, compared to 1971) did so not because they objected to his populist economic policies so much as because they had lost confidence in his capacity to successfully implement them.

Of course, if one maintains that by 1973 matters in Chile had reached such an impasse that socialism could not be achieved there except through armed confrontation (under various euphemisms), which would have done away with elections, parliaments, and opportunities to participate in political life, then it is indeed possible to discuss the feasibility of "a more solid socialist model." Such a "solution," however, would not have constituted the "Chilean road" (legal, constitutional and pacific) to socialism, consonant both with that country's democratic traditions and the liberal values of the West to which Allende's supporters so often appealed. Rather, it would have resembled something far closer to Czechoslovakia in 1948, with its attendant details and subsequent political legacy.

In effect, then, there *was* no Chilean road to socialism, in the sense that there never was a socialist political majority in that country for which the economic term normally applies. There *was* a Chilean road to soak-the-rich populism (as there is in most capitalist countries); unfortunately, it did not and could not work in economic terms. At best it could make life extremely difficult for Chilean capitalism, but a capitalism rendered inoperable does not ineluctably yield to a functioning alternative. As Foxley and Muñoz put it in the technical language of economists, "a lasting redistribution in favor of workers engaged in marginal services of no social benefit will not be possible unless there is an increase in the labor-absorbing capacity of the more socially productive sectors, which would modify the structure of employment and ensure a genuine economic base for increasing the income of these groups."[68] Stated simply, no welfare state can exist over time without an economic surplus, either inherited or on-going. Under Popular Unity, Chile quickly liquidated what it possessed of the first source, but for political reasons found it impossible to generate the second.

Notes

1. Pablo Lira (pseud.), "The Crisis of Hegemony in the Chilean Left," in Philip O'Brien, ed., *Allende's Chile*, p. 30.
2. In theory, a third opportunity might be expected in the presidential elections of 1976, but even at the outset not many Popular Unity partisans expected the critical question of power to be postponed for six years. Even the Communists, who acted as the moderates within the governing coalition, apparently expected the "correlation of forces" to alter so dramatically between 1970 and 1976 that the transition to socialism would be complete by the time Chileans once again had the oppor-

tunity to chose a new chief executive. (He could not be Allende, who was constitutionally barred from succeeding himself.) See Alain Joxe, "Is the 'Chilean Road to Socialism' Blocked," in Zammit, ed., *The Chilean Road to Socialism*, p. 225.

3. Chile's Supreme Court was even more independent than its North American counterpart. Not only were its judges appointed for life; they were empowered to nominate their own successors.

4. "The Popular Unity's Programme," in Zammit, *The Chilean Road to Socialism*, pp. 264-265. It is difficult to overestimate the importance Popular Unity's political strategists attributed to reform of the judiciary. Chile's 1925 Constitution reflected nineteenth-century values of order and property, and both its codes and interpreters—as well as the broader concepts it embodied—were seen as a serious obstacle to the transition to socialism. As Eduardo Novoa, chief theorist of Allende's new "socialist legality" put it, "within the confines of their conservative legal training, the members of the judiciary are unfit for the needs of the day and are unable to understand that laws need to be applied in a way which makes them useful to the existing society in which they live." "The Constitutional and Legal Aspects of the Popular Unity Government's Policy" in ibid., p. 29.

5. Debray, *The Chilean Revolution: Conversations with Allende*, p.83.

6. Robert Ayres, "Economic Stagnation and the Emergence of the Political Ideology of Chilean Underdevelopment," *World Politics*, XXVI, 1 (1972), pp. 34–61; Gonzalo Martner, "The Economic Aspects of Allende's Government: Problems and Prospects," in Kenneth Medhurst, *Allende's Chile* (London, 1972), pp. 143–147; Sergio Bitar, "Interacción entre economía y política," in Federico G. Gil et. al., *Chile, 1970–73: lecciones de una experiencia* (Madrid, 1977), pp. 118–119; "Discussions on the Popular Unity Economic Policy," in Zammit, *The Chilean Road to Socialism*, pp. 76–77.

7. "Discusson on the Popular Unity's Planning Efforts," in Zammit, ed., *The Chilean Road to Socialism*, pp. 95–96.

8. Markos J. Mamalakis, *Historical Statistics of Chile: Volume One, National Accounts* (Westport, Conn., 1978), p. 164.

9. These figures are taken from the official government statistics as presented by Stefan DeVylder in *Allende's Chile: The Political Economy of the Rise and Fall of Unidad Popular* (Cambridge, England, 1976), pp. 60 et seq. See also Alejandro Foxley and Oscar Muñoz, "Income Redistribution, Economic Growth, and Social Structure: The Case of Chile," *Oxford Bulletin of Economics and Statistics*, XXXVI, 1 (1974), pp. 21–44.

10. Mamalakis, *Growth and Structure*, pp. 21–44.

11. More than 10 million pounds of powdered milk were delivered to Chile in 1971 under the United States' Food for Peace Program; as a matter of fact, total food shipments from this source acutally *rose* during the Allende regime. Paul E. Sigmund, "The 'Invisible Blockade' and The Overthrow of Allende," *Foreign Affairs*, LII, 2 (1974), p. 334.

12. Mamalakis, *Growth and Structure*, p. 327.

13. Still and all, the regime doubled food imports during its first year, producing an even greater abundance in the marketplace, and obviously affecting the declining rate of inflation.

14. The so-called *Juntas de Abastecimineto y Precios*, or JAPS.

15. Robert Alexander, *The Tragedy of Chile* (Westport, Conn., 1978), p. 175.

16. The meaning of these terms is explained in Chapter Five.

17. Barbara Stallings, *Class Conflict and Economic Development in Chile, 1958–1973* (Stanford, CA., 1978), p. 131.

18. Alexander, *The Tragedy of Chile*, p. 174.

19. It is not without significance that although the Chilean Communist party was very closely tied to the Soviet Union, the socialist country its Santiago daily *El Siglo* most often pointed out as a showcase was not the USSR—or even Cuba—but East Germany ("Alemania Democrática"), whose living standards more closely approximated those of Western Europe than any other Marxist state.

20. Paul Rosenstein-Rodan, "Why Allende Failed," *Challenge*, XVII, 2 (1974), p. 8.

21. The actual figure was 50.86 percent, although the critical one percent which put the government over the top was cast for Raúl Ampuero's ultra-leftist Popular Socialist Union, which supported Popular Unity but was not a formal member of the coalition.

22. "Analysis of the Chilean Economy in 1971," in Zammit, *The Chilean Road to Socialism*, pp. 320–321.

23. Each penny in the pound price of copper represented a loss/gain to Chile of $16 million.

24. David Lehmann, "The Political Economy of Armageddon: Chile, 1970–73," *Journal of Development Economics*, V, 2 (1972), p. 115.

25. Jonathan E. Sanford, "The Multilateral Development Banks and the Suspension of Lending to Allende's Chile," in F. Orrego Vicuña, ed., *Chile: The Balanced View* (Santiago, 1975), p. 132.

26. Chile had devoted $120 million of its foreign exchange in 1970 to importing foodstuffs; the figure more than doubled to $261 million in 1971, obviously far in advance of the modest price rise in foodstuffs internationally for that year. Alberto Baltra Cortés, *Gestion económica del gobierno de la Unidad Popular* (Santiago, 1974), p. 14.

27. "Discussion on the Popular Unity's Economic Policy," in Zammit, *The Chilean Road to Socialism*, p. 81. This is the meeting referred to earlier (pp. 6–7); hereinafter it will be referred to as the IDS-ODEPLAN Round Table.

28. DeVylder, *Allende's Chile*, p. 101.

29. "Analysis of the Chilean Economy in 1971," in Zammit, *The Chilean Road*, pp. 320–321.

30. This was so because CORFO, the State Development Corporation, financed its operations through foreign borrowing. For further details, see Chapter Five.

31. For further discussion, see Chapter Four.

32. Alec Nove, "The Political Economy of the Allende Regime," in O'Brien, *Allende's Chile*, pp. 59–63.

33. Stallings, *Class Conflict and Economic Development*, p. 129. With their Marxist confreres now saddled with overall responsibility for the country's economic performance, the Christian Democrats could savor for the first time the pleasures of unbridled militancy. Stallings adds the rather peculiar comment, "This was the tragic legacy of many years of CUT concentration on economistic demands; now the UP was to be plagued by what its own supporters had fostered." One cannot help wondering what policy in the pre-Allende years would have served the political purposes of the CUT's Marxist unions better than "concentration on economistic demands."

34. Bitar, "Interacción entre economia y politica," pp. 119–120.

35. Nove, "The Political Economy," p. 66.

36. Quoted in Boorstein, *Allende's Chile*, pp. 120–121.
37. Stallings, *Class Conflict and Economic Development*, p. 143; Bitar, "Interacción entre economia y politica," pp. 124–125; James Petras, "The Transition to Socialism in Chile," pp. 68–69; "The Political Economy," p. 62.
38. Official estimates always attempted to guess at a figure somewhere between official and black market prices.
39. Boorstein, *Allende's Chile*, p. 194.
40. Quoted in Sobel, ed., *Chile and Allende*, p. 194.
41. *Quarterly Economic Review: Chile* (No. 2, 1973), p. 6.
42. Quoted in Rosenstein-Rodan, "Why Allende Failed," p. 10.
43. "The Political Economy of Armageddon," p. 114.
44. Stallings, *Class Conflict and Economic Development*, p. 203.
45. Sanford, "The Multilateral Development Banks . . .," p. 132.
46. I am using the figures published by the Allende government in República de Chile, Oficina de Planificatión Nacional, *Balances económicos de Chile, 1960–1970* (Santiago, 1973), pp. 138–139.
47. Joan Garcés, "Chile, 1971: A Revolutionary Government Within a Welfare State," in Medhurst, *Allende's Chile*, p. 31.
48. For problems of estimation, see Chapter Five.
49. In fact, it would not even done this, since those revenues were not quite adequate to finance the Christian Democrats' programs; hence, Frei's recurrence to foreign borrowing.
50. *Quarterly Economic Review: Chile* (No. 2, 1973), p. 18.
51. The case is not significantly altered by the frequent argument that Allende failed to win congressional approval of a package of tax bills which would have raised *indirect* taxes as well. To be sure, this category certainly had the *potential* of producing considerable revenue, since in 1970 it yielded about 51 percent ($683 million) of the Christian Democrats' total tax returns. However, the context in which the Allende government was operating radically altered its prospects.

   The category "indirect taxes" embraced both sales taxes and taxes on production. In Chile sales taxes were far less regressive than in many countries, since they were traditionally levied on items of luxury consumption (automobiles, for example). How much revenue a sharp rise in sales taxes would have yielded is difficult to say, since—if the increase was sharp enough to cover a meaningful portion of the government's deficits—it would have acted as a serious disincentive to consumption. Further, to the degree to which the items subject to tax were imported (as luxury articles often were in Chile), the government's own foreign exchange policies sternly militated against much movement.

   To make the best possible case for Allende: had *all* of his proposals for indirect tax increases been proposed and passed in 1971, this would have produced a rather handsome sum for that year. How such income would have been spent can never be known, but that it would have been applied either to the foreign debt or to national saving runs sharply counter to everything we know about the ideological and political atmosphere in which economic decisions were being made in 1971. More than likely such increases, if obtained in 1971, would have granted the regime an additional year of good times before it had to face the same hard decisions. As a matter of fact, however, most of Allende's proposals for indirect tax increases were made in 1972 and 1973, when the inflationary effect of his monetary policies could no longer be denied, and when their social base (a class of luxury consumers) was well on its way to extinction.

Production taxes (which were not quantitatively a large item under this heading in 1970) could not be expected to significantly increase in an environment in which (After 1971, at least), most indices were moving downward. And, of course, one could expect nothing in the way of contributions from the sizeable (and growing) state-controlled industrial sector, which required direct subsidies merely to survive.

52. Stallings, *Class Conflict and Economic Development*, p. 134.
53. Sigmund, "The 'Invisible Blockade' . . .," pp. 336–337.
54. Allende was the beneficiary of this policy in 1971 and 1972, when—in spite of mismanagement in the nationalized mines—copper production actually increased, as projects begun under his predecessor came on stream.
55. Mamalakis, *Growth and Structure*, p. 242.
56. James Theberge, "Kremlin's Hand in Allende's Chile," *Soviet Analyst* (London), III, 17 (1974), pp. 2–3.
57. Among other things, Chou told Allende that while developing countries had a moral obligation to help one another whenever possible "what is of fundamental importance is that [they] achieve development by relying upon their own forces, that is to say, regard self-sustained growth as the principal means, and foreign aid as a complimentary measure. It is very dangerous to rely excessively on foreign aid, particularly on credits from the great powers, in place of basing one's economy on one's country's own efforts." Text in *El Mercurio* (international edition), July 23–29, 1973.
58. For further details, see Chapter Seven.
59. James Petras, "Chile after the Elections," in Paul Sweezy and Harry Magdoff, eds., *Revolution and Counter-Revolution in Chile* (New York, 1974), p. 117.
60. Garcés, "Chile, 1971 . . .," pp. 31, 44.
61. Foxley and Muñoz, "Income Redistribution . . .," pp. 63–64.
62. Nove, "The Political Economy . . .," pp. 63–64.
63. Stallings, *Class Conflict and Economic Development*, p. 237.
64. Bitar, "Interacción entre economía y politíca," p. 125.
65. Boorstein, *Allende's Chile*, pp. 196–197.
66. Roxborough et al., *Chile: The State and Revolution*, pp. 159–160.
67. Ibid., p. 146.
68. Foxley and Muñoz, "Income and Redistribution . . .," p. 32.

4

Agrarian Reform

The land question is one of the oldest and most enduring issues in Chilean history, though its significance has varied considerably over nearly four centuries. During the colonial period, it was closely related to native policy, centering around the complex obligations of labor and service imposed upon conquered peoples through the institution of the *encomienda*[1]. During the struggle for Chilean independence in the second and third decades of the nineteenth century, the debate over entailed estates divided an entire generation of patriot leaders. The most outstanding of these, Supreme Director Bernardo O'Higgins, favored the abolition of entails, for which cause he is generally thought to have been overthrown and permanently exiled in 1828. O'Higgins had believed, with the simple faith of land reformers then and since, that a change in the structure of ownership would radically transform Chilean society, replacing an aristocratic republic of landowners with a Jeffersonian commonwealth of yeoman farmers. His victorious enemies agreed with his analysis, but feared its consequences if put into practice. In the end, however, both were proven wrong. Entails were abolished in the "liberal" constitution of 1828, restored in the "conservative" charter of 1833, and finally lifted forever in legislation sponsored by President Manuel Montt in 1852. But their changing juridical fortunes had no perceptible effect on the pattern of land ownership, much less the broader structure of Chilean society. In 1860, indeed in 1910, Chile remained what it had been in O'Higgins' time—a land of great estates, a political communtiy dominated by their owners.[2]

Alongside the permanence of latifundia, however, another trend was at work. After the War of the Pacific and the annexation of huge nitrate reserves formerly the patrimony of Bolivia and Peru, an unprecedented economic boom led to massive rural migration and the rapid growth of Chilean cities. "The urban population, only 27 percent of the total in 1875, had risen to 43 percent in 1907. From 1885 to 1895, the population of Santiago went up over 30 percent, and by 1907 had increased an additional 22." During the same two time periods, Antofagasta rose 58 and 73 percent; Iquique 76 and 16 percent; Concepción 50 and 27 percent; Valparaíso 15 and 25 percent. The entire period from 1885, a distinguished historian concludes, "witnesses the most dramatic population shift in Chile's history."[3]

The implications for Chilean agriculture of a rapidly depopulating countryside were obvious. As early as 1911, conservative intellectual Francisco Encina noted with alarm that "notwithstanding some recent advances in productivity," due largely to the expansion of agro-pastoral activities to former Indian territories in the Chilean south, "national agriculture and stockraising scarcely produce enough for domestic consumption."[4] This phenomenon was all the more striking for being a drastic reversal: until the opening of the Argentine pampas after 1880, Chile had been a South American leader in agricultural exports—particularly wheat, which it shipped not only to England, but even to Australia and to California during the Gold Rush.[5]

What Encina feared most—that Chile would ultimately lose its agricultural self-sufficiency altogether—became a conspicuous fact of life after 1940. The annual average agricultural growth rate, which had hovered around 3 percent between 1910 and 1933, *halved* to 1.5 between 1932 and 1955. In the 1960s, it redounded to a modest 2.6 percent, which did not always clear the nation's rising population curve. Between 1940 and 1970—the year of Allende's election—agriculture's share of the gross domestic product dropped from 14.9 to 8.6 percent. In all Latin America, only Venezuela did worse, but unlike Chile, it could redress matters through massive petroleum exports.[6] Meanwhile, a continuing increase in Chile's urban population, as well as a long-term improvement in its living standards, meant that shortfalls in agricultural production had to be met through imports, largely from the United States.[7] Chile's international balance of payments in agricultural products turned negative for the first time in 1942, and consistently rose to its disfavor; by 1970, the bill for imported foodstuffs came to $146 million.[8]

That a nation like Chile should squander such large amounts of precious foreign exchange on items which clearly could be produced at home, dominated much of the discussion of the land question during the Alessandri and Frei administrations. The matter was all the more compelling because in spite of massive and growing imports, a significant percentage of the population still subsisted on an inadequate diet, reflected, among other things, by a high rate of infant mortality. During this period it was common to hear it remarked that Chile could feed three times its population, and some estimates placed the country's agricultural possibilities considerably beyond that point.

What was the cause of Chile's unsatisfactory agricultural performance? The answer depended entirely upon the source to which one addressed the question. Landowners' associations, both the aristocratic National Agricultural Society (SNA) and the independent producers' federations, as well as some economists, held that low productivity was due to neglect or even discrimination against the agricultural sector. Such policies of neglect were embodied in a low or negative level of investment in social overhead, foreign exchange constraints, and a variety of economic disincentives. They particularly singled out price controls, which had been imposed on a number of basic farm products in the urban marketplace since 1940, combined with import subsidies for foreign foodstuffs. "The ill-conceived attempt," as Markos J. Mamalakis has called it, by Chile's predominantly urban population "to extract a surplus through these instruments became doubly counterproductive. Agricultural living standards fell in relative and sometimes even absolute terms, and the transferable surpluses shrank."[9]

A quite different view was advanced by the "structuralist" economists associated with Chilean universities and international organizations, and in time, by Christian Democratic and Marxist politicians. These insisted that the root cause of agricultural inefficiency in Chile was a land tenure structure "which left landless *inquilinos* [resident workers] without the means or incentives to make improvements." Thus if one analysis suggested the need to remove government controls and allow Chilean agriculture to do its work, the other pointed to the need to "take landed property away from the unproductive aristocrats" and to redistribute it to "a more potentially enterprising class of peasants."[10]

Nothing illustrates more pointedly the highly-charged ideological environment in which these discussions took place, than the fact that neither party to the debate was willing to recognize and separate the elements of truth that reposed on both sides. Price controls alone could not explain the low productivity of Chilean agriculture, for—as studies repeatedly showed—they were often ineffective.[11] In many cases, the problem was less prices as such than the fact that the cost of essential inputs—fertilizer, machinery and so on—rose far more rapidly.[12] On the other hand, studies of commercial poultry, sugar beet, and rice enterprises produced persuasive evidence that some Chilean landowners did in fact respond to economic incentives when made available.[13]

Likewise, the relationship between land tenure structures and productivity was by no means as simple and direct as many claimed. Of the extremely inegalitarian structure of land ownership in Chile—particularly before the Christian Democratic reform of 1967—there can be little doubt. The 1955 agricultural census, which was probably still broadly accurate the year Eduardo Frei assumed office, showed that 78 percent of all agricultural land, 65 percent of all arable land, and 79 percent of all irrigated land was found on 7 percent of all farms. Since many large landowners possessed more than one farm, the concentration of ownership was even higher than these figures would suggest.[14]

For many land reformers and urban social theorists, the fact of an inefficient agriculture dominated by large holdings established that the intensity of
land use was inversely correlated with the size of farms. This was not,
however, a conclusion supported by economic or agricological data. Almost
nowhere were land and water resources fully utilized, but while units of less
than family size (*minifundia*) did indeed cultivate a larger percentage of their
land than large estates (*latifundia*), the latter in turn cultivated a larger percentage of their land than did family-sized tracts. The property least efficient
of all was not the great estate, but the medium-size multifamily farm. Even
so, "the only clear difference between size groups with respect to the intensity
of land use," reported economist Pierre Crosson in 1970, "was between these
three groups [large estates, family and multifamily tracts] on one hand, and
the sub-family-sized farms on the other. As far as it goes, this scarcely
suggests a continuous relationship between efficiency of land use and size."[15]

The 1965 agricultural census contained additional data which weakened
still further the case against latifundia. It showed that in the previous ten
years, productivity per hectare [one hectare = 2.471 acres] for most crops had
risen more sharply on the large farms than on the smaller ones. This reflected
the large-scale introduction of fertilizers into Chilean agriculture, which in
turn was a function of access to credit—always heavily weighted in favor of
the larger rural entrepreneur. Such findings pointed to the need for a more
equitable spread of technical assistance and financing, but did little to support
the notion that larger holdings and low productivity went hand in hand.[16]

The key to Chile's agricultural dilemma lay not so much in the structure of
tenancy (however unsatisfactory that may have been in many respects), as in
the complex sociology of its landowning class. Perhaps indeed this group
once possessed the homogenity of outlook and interest depicted in nineteenth-
century Chilean novels (*Casa Grande*) and twentieth-century political folk-
lore, but by the early 1960s, it comprehended a bewildering multiplicity of
elements. Some large landowners presided over huge agribusiness operations
which were highly capitalized, while others used land strictly for purposes of
social prestige, as a hedge against inflation, or as a source of credit which they
habitually (and illegally) applied to urban enterprises. Somewhere in the
middle fell a group which was not well-connected enough (or fortunately
situated geographically) to pursue agriculture as a big business, and yet,
desirous of turning a profit, was dependent upon quasi-feudal obligations
imposed on a resident tenantry.

Chile also possessed a small but very significant group of middle-sized
agricultural entrepreneurs, particularly in its southern provinces, where col-
onies of Germans and Yugoslavs (or their descendants) were given over to
pastoral activities or highly scientific experimental farms. This category also
comprehended many of Chile's vineyards, one of the few sectors of rural

activity which—among other things, because it represented an important source of foreign exchange—received preferential treatment from all governments. Middle-sized agricultural enterprises, a tiny minority of the whole during the late 1950s, for reasons to be explained shortly, became the fastest-growing and most dynamic sector of Chilean agriculture after 1964.

Alongside all of these groups there languished inefficient family farmers or poverty-striken minifundistas, forced to work on neighboring properties part of the year to supplement their own meager yields. The performance of each of these groups (as well as within them) often varied considerably, but by concentrating on merely one or two, it was entirely possible to produce cogent evidence in favor of (or in opposition to) land reform—understood here as a change in tenure patterns. For example, if one studied the large agribusiness enterprises and some of the productive middle-sized operations, a strong case could be made for the disincentives of price controls. If one confined attention to the unproductive estates held by some of Santiago's society families, it was possible to evince incontrovertible proof of the economic irrationality of latifundia. The intensive nature of minifundia cultivation, combined with the large and growing number of sharecroppers (*voluntarios*) and migrant laborers (*afuerinos*) who possessed no land at all, argued for the desirability of dividing some, perhaps even most, great estates among sectors of the Chilean peasantry. None of these arguments, however, needed to be mutually exclusive. As Crosson concluded on the eve of Allende's election, "to achieve healthy development of its agriculture over the long run," Chile needed to "reform its land tenure system, expand and modernize the marketing and transport systems serving agriculture, rationalize agricultural pricing policies, and adopt an agricultural tax system which rewards efficiency."[17] This could not be accomplished, however, by any agrarian reform law which failed to take full cognisance of the differences and distinctions which characterized the Chilean rural sector. At least, one could not do so if one believed that the purpose of land reform was to make Chile realize to the fullest its food-producing potential.

The Land Reform Issue

Resolution of the land question was long postponed in Chile because rural issues were habitually subordinated to the nation's urban agenda. This reflected not only the growing preponderance of cities as centers of population and decision making, but also the residual power of landowners. Deprived of their dominant voice in national politics after the 1880s, *hacendados* continued to exercise unquestioned authority within their own domains, and indirect attempts to circumscribe their corporate prerogatives were doomed to be either ineffective or counter-productive. Thus, the Chilean Congress could pass a comprehensive labor code in 1931, but find it impossible to apply it to the countryside for the next three decades.[18] Governments of the Center-Right and Center-Left could introduce price controls on selected agricultural staples, but they could not prevent rural proprietors from relocating their profit margins in the reduced living standards of the unskilled rural labor force.[19] Nor could they dissuade smaller agricultural entrepreneurs from selling what became unprofitable operations to urban speculators, thus increasing the amount of land left fallow.[20]

The principal line of defense for landed magnates was their control of the rural electorate, which permitted their own interests to be vastly overrepresented in the Chilean Congress, artificially prolonged the life of the Conservative party, and forced reformers to concentrate on what could be accomplished in Chile's factories and mines, its cities and ports. Thus, the Popular Front government of Pedro Aguirre Cerda and its successors (1938–1952), which at times included ministers from the Radical, the Socialist, and the Communist parties, found that the industrialization of Chile, the growth of the labor movement, and significant improvements in urban social services, could be purchased only through an agreement with the Conservative party and the landowners' associations to halt rural unionization.[21]

Paradoxically, the sudden movement of the land question to the forefront of political discussion in Chile during the late 1950s and early 1960s was inspired by the same urban concerns which had determined its neglect in times past. The international example of the Cuban Revolution, the Alliance for Progress, and the growing embrace of doctrines of social reform by the Roman Catholic church, meshed with the increasing conviction of Chilean economists and public figures that the issue of inflation—which had dominated every election between 1932 and 1958—was intimately related to the country's unsatisfactory agricultural performance.[22] Land reform thus became a panacea for the two principal threats to Chile's urban population: a supposedly incipient rural revolution, and the eroding living standards of its middle and organized working classes.

At the same time, in 1958 a new law sponsored by retiring President Carlos Ibáñez del Campo introduced the use of the secret ballot in rural elections, almost overnight depriving the landed classes of what had once been their most important political resource. For the first time, the rural vote was worth competing for, and Christian Democratic and Marxist parties, already locked in a decisive contest to expand their urban electoral bases, took to the countryside with promises of a new day.

The notion that a new majority coalition in Chilean politics could be permanently constructed upon an alliance of peasants on one hand, and urban workers—both blue-collar and white—was based on a good deal of ideological confusion and even wishful thinking. The fact that latifundia, inflation, landlessness, and low productivity existed side by side was not sufficient of itself to establish their precise relationships to one another. Nor did it mean that expropriation of large properties (even those most inefficiently exploited) and their transfer to new owners would automatically lead to higher food production, lower prices, and social justice for all. As Robert Kaufmann has pointed out, while the *slogans* of land reform were well-received by the urban population (partly as a way of punishing the hated "oligarchy," partly to promote a generalized notion of progress),

> the concrete *demands* that were actively pursued by these groups tended at many points to conflict with the necessities of a land reform program. A government which spent time resolving wage disputes had less time to spend on the agricultural sector; funds spent on urban jobs, social security, and pensions meant fewer funds for the expropriation of rural property and for the disbursement of credit and extension aid to peasants.
>
> A general urban interest in cheaper food conflicted in the short run with the need to provide market incentives to old and new rural proprietors. The paradox of urban society was that while a majority was probably weakly inclined toward land reform, it was strongly opposed to paying the costs that would be incurred in such a program.[23]

Yet it was in the urban arena—with countless unsatisfied demands of its own—that all land reform projects would have to originate, where they would have to justify themselves in concrete economic terms, and where they would necessarily rely for funding and political support. This contradiction, in different degrees, was to trouble the agrarian policies of both the Christian Democratic and Popular Unity governments.

Reform Under Alessandri and Frei, 1962–1970

In 1962 Public Law 15.020 launched what was ultimately to become one of the most sustained and significant periods of land reform in Latin American history.[24] The fact that the law itself was hedged in by countless restrictions and limitations did not detract from its wider significance; that it could be sponsored at all by the government of President Jorge Alessandri—himself a cheerless and austere businessman with no taste for social innovation— indicates the degree to which the idea of land reform had taken hold of the Chilean public imagination.

The key provision of this legislation was redefinition of the rights and obligations of rural proprietorship. Landowners were now required as a matter of public policy to increase the fertility and productivity of their properties; land which was found to be "abandoned" or "badly managed" was subject to expropriation under certain conditions.[25] The law also disallowed owner-ship of land by juridical personalities who did not directly cultivate it; this provision affected some organisms of the Chilean government and the Roman Catholic church.

Under the Constitution of 1925, still in force at the time, the government was obligated to compensate expropriated parties in cash, normally based on the land's current commercial value. An amendment passed in 1963 made it possible to remunerate them on a long-term basis—20 percent in cash, and the balance over a minimum of 10 years at 4 percent interest, with annual read-justments for inflation. The law also created a new government agency, the Agrarian Reform Corporation (CORA) to oversee the evaluation and expro-priation of properties, an extension service (INDAP) to assist new cultivators with technical assistance and credit, and a new system of land tribunals, to adjudicate differences between CORA and landowners threatened with ex-propriation. The decisions of these courts were subject to appeal through the regular system of Chilean courts.

The 1962 law made possible a variety of proprietary arrangements, but in practice land acquired under its authority was parcelled into family-sized plots, or "economic units" (unidades económicas). Since land quality and access to irrigation varied widely in Chile, these units were defined in terms of economic capacity (sufficient to provide an adequate income for one farm family) rather than size; however, lower and upper limits were established. The government prohibited private subdivision of new properties into parcels of land less than fifteen hectares of irrigated and fifty of unirrigated land. Expropriated landowners were allowed to select and keep a reserve equivalent to eighty irrigated hectares, but in no case could it exceed twenty economic units.

The new government originally declared its intention of settling 5,000 new proprietors per year on the land, or about 10,000 in total between November 1962 and November, 1964 (when Alessandri left office). The administrative costs of such a change were estimated at 77 million escudos (US $35,814,000 at 1963 rates of exchange). Instead, only about 1,200 new proprietors were settled during this period, and of the approximately 60,000 hectares affected, 40,000 had belonged to a single publicly-owned hacienda in the province of Talca. Between this and church properties voluntarily surrendered by the Episcopate, nearly 70 percent of the "reformed" properties under Alessandri had belonged to public or quasi-public agencies. Only about 18,000 hectares were acquired from private owners, who voluntarily sold them to the land reform agency. The expropriation provisions of Law 15.020 were thus never actually invoked during the life of the Alessandri administration.[26]

The slow pace of agrarian reform under Alessandri was due partly to the government's ambivalent feelings about the entire project from the very start.

But other factors were involved. The constitutional amendment permitting deferred payments was not passed until July 1963, at which point only fourteen months remained in the six-year life of the administration. President Alessandri possessed neither the capacity (nor, probably, the inclination) to extract from the Congress the funds necessary to fully finance the resettlement of 10,000 families. Additionally, the land reform agency's limited budgetary resources were stretched further by the tendency to offer favorable prices for private land, and also rather generous terms of payment (20 percent cash and the remainder in three rather than the mandated ten years). Although no landowner found it necessary to appeal to the new agrarian tribunals during the Alessandri years, the mere existence of such a lengthy and complicated recourse led CORA officials to concentrate on projects where no resistance would be encountered.

Nonetheless, the Alessandri reform was not without considerable long-term impact. It led many large landowners to begin voluntarily subdividing their properties (usually among their progeny) to avoid future grounds for expropriation, particularly as the likelihood of a new government headed by a Christian Democrat increased in late 1963 and early 1964. In fact, private parcelization proceeded at so rapid a rate that after Frei's election it became necessary to explicitly prohibit it. Moreover, Law 15.020 armed the new Christian Democratic administration with the instrument to carry out wide-ranging expropriations until it could obtain a land reform of its own design from Congress. Between 1964 and 1967, when the Christian Democratic legislation was finally passed, the Frei government was able to acquire 500 private estates, making land available to 8,000 rural families. Although CORA could not yet force landowners to accept compensation in the form of long-term bonds, the threat of a new and presumably more stringent law was sufficient to encourage numerous compromise settlements out of court.

Public Law 16.640 (1967) contained a number of new provisions which facilitated a more expeditious transfer of properties. It enumerated detailed criteria to determine efficiency or inefficiency of exploitation. It redefined· "poorly exploited land" in social terms; a landowner's properties could be taken from him if he failed to meet his obligations to his workers under existing labor legislation. The law also established an entirely new basis for expropriation. In the future *all* agricultural land belonging to the same owner— no matter how efficiently worked—would be limited to tracts no larger than 80 standard hectares of irrigated land (herinafter abbreviated as BIH, or basic irrigated hectares), calculated according to a complicated conversion table.[27] Landowners were allowed to retain a reserve of this size, to which they could move machinery, livestock, and tools. However, the avenue of appeal of decisions by the agrarian tribunals to the higher courts was narrowed very considerably.

As this law was written, the grounds on which a property was expropriated were critical to determining the future fortunes of the landowners—and, in an inverse fashion, that of his successors. If "bad management" was the cause rather than sheer size, the owner was not entitled to a reserve. In theory, this afforded considerable grounds for landowner apprehension, since the laborers on a given farm would have a vested interest in stirring up a labor dispute, just to prevent the present owners from carrying vital capital resources off to some future reserve. In practice, however, before 1970 this was not a problem, since CORA officials decided to limit expropriation proceedings to considerations of size alone, thus avoiding the lengthy court proceedings to which landowners would inevitably have recurred.

The conditions of expropriation also determined the nature and extent of compensation. The law reduced maximum cash payment to 10 percent of the value of the property, the rest to be paid in interest-bearing bonds only partially adjusted for inflation. However, whereas Law 15.520 used the marked value of the property as the basis for compensation, Law 16.640 calculated value according to the tax rolls, where an outdated system of appraisals drastically reduced the financial obligations of the expropriating agencies.

Expropriated properties were reorganized into a new transitional form of tenure, the *asentamiento*.[28] Its stated purpose was to prepare newly enfranchised peasants (*asentados*) for independent proprietorship. The transitional period was defined as three to five years, during which time the farm was run under INDAP officials. At the end of the period, whose precise moment depended upon an evaluation made by land reform functionaries under a lengthy point system, asentados were permitted to determine whether the reformed tract was to be subdivided into family-owned parcels, or run as a cooperative. Under certain circumstances, the period of asentamiento status could be prolonged an additional two years, or even indefinitely, at the discretion, again, of the authorities. Preference for asentado membership was given to heads of families of resident tenants (*inquilinos*) at the time of expropriation.

Law 16.640 was the result of an elaborate compromise within the Christian Democratic party, between pragmatic reformers who favored a capitalism that worked, and "communitarian" theorists who looked to some vaguely-defined postcapitalist society which would nonetheless avoid the tyrannical features of Marxian collectivism. This compromise was apparent in the decision to allow both a "reformed" and "unreformed" (privately-owned but productive) agriculture to exist side by side. It was also evident within the very allocation of expropriated properties—between a "collective" section upon which all asentados were expected to work, and small family house-and-garden plots (*huertos*), where asentados were permitted to run their own peasant economies. The land reform agencies were virtually colonized by communitarians; INDAP chief Jacques Chonchol, and archetypical example, had worked with the United Nations in Cuba during Castro's second land reform. INDAP and CORA functionaries used all of the considerable resources of the government to persuade asentados of the advantages of collective expropriation.[29]

On the other hand, it was no secret that the government's apparent commitment to the ideal of private ownership was the source of much peasant support in the 1964 elections, and—despite the growing ambiguities inherent in the actual administration of the reform itself—even thereafter.[30] Since Law 16.640 was passed only in 1967, the vast majority of asentamientos formed under the Christian Democrats would be eligible to determine the final disposition of their properties only after 1970, that is, within the life of the next administration.[31]

The Frei government also took decisive steps to organize the rural labor force. Between 1965 and 1967, for the first time this long-neglected group was permitted and even encouraged to organize and bargain collectively. Also, the urban minimum wage was finally extended to the countryside, and a complex system was established to protect land workers from arbitrary dismissal. By June 1970, nearly 500 new rural unions existed, with a combined membership of more than 125,000 members. Although there was acute competition among the Christian Democrats and the parties of the Left for the allegiance of these new organisms, INDAP initiative in bringing about their formation, combined with the judicious allocation of government resources to those which proved loyal to it, led a significant majority to opt for Christian Democracy, at least before 1970. The fact that unionization went hand in hand with an agrarian reform law which made improper labor practices one of the principal grounds for expropriation, illustrated the way in which the various parts of the agrarian program of the Frei administration were supposed to (and in fact did) reinforce one another. An annex to this legislation permitted the formation of employers' unions in the countryside as well, although the full political significance of this innovation was not demonstrated until after Allende came to power.

By the end of 1970 the Christian Democrats had expropriated approximately 1,400 farms, reorganized into nearly 1,000 asentamientos. The transfers involved slightly more than 3.5 million hectares, about 17 percent of the country's irrigated and 12 percent of its non-irrigated land. Qualitative distinctions were even more important. Reformed properties no longer consisted— as they had in Alessandri's time—exclusively of marginal lands of little or no interest to their owners. Many of the farms expropriated under the Christian Democrats lay in the country's privileged Central Valley, historic seat of the nation's landed aristocracy. Further, whereas before 1968 the Christian Democrats preferred to rely upon considerations of size alone in determining criteria for expropriation—which led to many voluntary transfers by landowners—

after 1968 the number of properties seized for ''poor exploitation'' increased. Under the existing system of compensation, this made it possible to reduce the cost to the government of each property acquired, and thus to stretch finite budgetary resources over a wider geographical base. Apart from definitive land assignments to 5,600 peasant families, the Frei administration completed its mandate with 24,000 new proprietors residing on asentamientos.[32] This was far below the 100,000 figure which the Christian Democrats had promised to achieve during their presidential campaign in 1964. Since the partial failure of the Frei administration in this area was the source of heated polemics — both with Christian Democracy itself, where it led to the formation of the schismatic MAPU, and between the administration and its Marxist opponents — it is worth examining why reform under Law 16.640 fell so short of initial projections. The fact that it took three years of enervating negotiations with Congress — half the life of the government — to obtain a new law was an obvious consideration. There is some evidence, too, that Chile's total agricultural endowment simply was not sufficient; there was enough land for all only in a rough mathematical sense, not in terms of the man-land equivalencies upon which the asentamiento was based.[33]

But the principal obstacle to meeting even more modest goals was cost. During the years 1965–1967, CORA and INDAP together spent approximately $100 million dollars, which came to $12,500 for each of the families affected by the reform. And this, of course, was at a time when the figure hovered below 10,000 families, since the government was still constrained by the limits of Alessandri's law. To have fully benefited 100,000 families would have run to an astronomical sum, well beyond the reach of any Chilean government.[34] Granted that some resources were misallocated in the Christian Democratic land reform process, even a more austere and tightly managed operation ''would have required an effort to squeeze funds from non-agricultural income sectors and [the establishment of] broad political controls over a disaffected urban population.'' Such a recourse was highly unlikely, Kaufmann points out, given the determination of the Frei government ''to build onto, rather than destroy, urban social institutions, and to operate within the framework of constitutional norms.''[35] If the Christian Democrats did not quite expect their land reform to finance itself from the very start, their urban constituencies almost certainly did, and in reality the government often acted as if it shared their views. For example, the percentage of the budget dedicated to agricultural investment increased only slightly during the Frei years.

The real significance of the Christian Democrats reform was not quantitative, however, but sociological. Into the already complicated class structure of the Chilean countryside it inserted a new class of rural proprietor — a sort of freeholder-in-waiting. The ultimate political potential of a privileged group of peasants suddenly granted land ownership was not lost on the history-

TABLE 4.1
Index of Agricultural Production, 1966–1970

(1961–1965 = 100)	
1966	115
1967	114
1968	119
1969	114
1970	121

Source: Food and Agriculture Organization of the United Nations, *Production Yearbook, 1975* (Rome, 1975), Table 8.

conscious Marxist parties. This process, they feared, would further divide the rural proletariat and provide a permanent economic base for what they like to call "petty bourgeois tendencies"; it would also create a lasting political clientele for Christian Democracy; and in the event that some future government further to the left were to come to power, this group, combined with a new class of "kulaks" drawn from the ranks of the former estate owners now confined to their reserves, would provide the rank-and-file for a Chilean Vendée. This was certainly not the intention of the agrarian ideologues of Christian Democracy, particularly those associated with CORA and INDAP; nonetheless, it is very possible that this was precisely what the main stream of the party's leadership had in mind when it sponsored Law 16.640 in the first place.[36]

If the Christian Democratic reform was to be judged by the criterion of food production, it was by no means the dismal failure its critics often made out. If food production did not rise very sharply during the first three years of the reform, neither did it drop very much, particularly if one took into account a serious drought in the 1968–69 agricultural year, which made the 1969 harvest smaller than would otherwise have been the case. The 1970 performance was the best in many years.

The relationship between reform and performance was somewhat less than direct, however. Two academic studies of the reformed sector (that is, the asentamientos) published on the eve of the Allende government stated their conclusions with extreme caution:

> In 1967 about all that could be said of the economic results of the Chilean land reform was that the asentamientos had not led to the spectacular *drops* in production which many rightists had predicted. Overall production in the agricultural sector neither improved markedly nor declined during the period from 1965 through 1967.[37]

> [As of 1969] there is little evidence . . . that output had increased under asentamientos management . . . [It would appear that] the increased use of idle land [is] perhaps the most fruitful effect of the reform.

> There is no doubt that production on some asentamientos increased, but it has
> declined or remained the same on others . . . We . . . do not state positively
> that there has been no change, but rather claim that there is insufficient evidence
> to support a claim that there has been a change.[38]

It was often remarked in their defense that the asentamientos began their
existence under the handicap of decapitalization; that is, the provision for a
reserve allowed the expropriated owner to carry out his livestock and machinery. The conversion table used to arrive at what constituted the equivalent
of 80 basic irrigated hectares for the reserve itself was also said to be strongly
biased in favor of the expropriated parties. The other side of the coin, however, was the growing productivity of commercial agriculture in Chile during
the very period when the reformed sector was in a virtually incipient state. As
of 1970 there were still some 3–4,000 private farms over 80 BIH which, for
reasons of efficiency, cost, or political expendiency (or some combination
thereof) had not yet been "reformed";[39] these, along with more than 1,000
successor-parcels to expropriated latifundia, carried the principal load of the
country's food producing burden. Threats of expropriation on one hand, and
ample agricultural credit for those willing to exploit their properties more
fully, combined to produce almost as an afterthought what the reform itself
had posited as a principal goal.

What the Christian Democrats had *not* succeeded in doing by 1970 was
devising a land reform which would benefit the entire Chilean peasantry.
Outside the charmed circle of asentados, there stood the sharecroppers and
wage workers *(voluntarios)* of the expropriated properties, for whom no immediate prospect of land ownership was held out. Further still were the
migrant laborers *(afuerinos)* and the Mapuche Indian communities in the
South, most of whom did not benefit even from rural unionization. It is not
clear, however, that Frei's people ever intended—in spite of their campaign
rhetoric—to give land to all who worked it. Rural migration, after all, had
been accepted as a fact of life in Chile for many years; agriculture played a
relatively minor role in the gross national product; there was considerable
optimism (by no means wholly without foundation) about the possibilities of
industrial expansion. Obviously, these assumptions had to go unspoken. Nonetheless, it is very likely that they were operative, and not only under Frei, but
even, in a considerably attenuted form, under Allende. If the design of Law
16.640 was not, to Christian Democrats, necessarily an indictment on its own
terms, for its enemies on the Left it pointed to new opportunities for peasant
mobilization. Whether that and the broader objectives of agrarian reform were
immediately compatible was not discussed among the Marxist parties until the
process was well-advanced.

Agriculture Under Popular Unity

Although the parties of the Left had advocated some sort of land reform in Chile for many years, at the time of Allende's election it was not possible to say with any certainty what form socialist agriculture would assume. Popular Unity's 1970 electoral program did not shed much light on the matter; it merely spoke of accelerating the process begun under the Christian Democrats, applying more rigorously the criteria of size in determining expropriations, abridging the disenfranchised landowner's right to a reserve, and subjecting to transfer the formerly exempted vineyard and orchards. "Expropriated land," it declared, "will be organized preferably on the basis of cooperative forms of ownership." But this went no further than to state in principle what the Christian Democrats had very largely followed in practice. The program hinted at some future for small and medium-sized cultivators, without explicitly committing itself to their defense. "In certain qualified cases, land will be allocated to small farmers, tenants, sharecroppers, and trained agricultural workers . . . Small and medium peasants will be given access to the advantages and services provided by cooperatives operating in their geographical area." It affirmed that "lands [would be] allocated to create state agricultural enterprises using modern technology," but it did not reveal how much (or how little) importance would be given to such holdings within the total mix of properties. Significantly, it made no direct reference to the asentamiento at all, nor did it mention the need to increase food production as a motivation for the reform itself.[40]

Behind these phrases hovered vague aspirations to collective exploitation along Soviet or Cuban lines. Apart from a certain ideological coherence within the government's general economic policies, such a solution appeared to hold out important economic and political dividends. It would permit a significant increase in the number of peasants brought within the sphere of INDAP and CORA operations; it would presumably facilitate the development of large state agribusiness enterprises; it would prepare the way for the creation of a single peasant class purged of the "petty bourgeois" mentality inherent in land ownership. It would also create an additional base of support for the government's urban programs. At a minimum, such a process ("proletarianization of the peasantry") would immerse those who opposed Popular Unity in a sea of new partisans recruited from the lower strata of the rural population.[41]

To forge a thoroughgoing socialist agriculture would require an entirely new land reform law. The government knew this to be unattainable unless a different and vastly more favorable Congress were returned (at the earliest, March 1973), or a plebiscite could be staged to alter drastically the structure of Chile's representative institutions. Its hand was further stayed by the frank recognition by many Popular Unity leaders that a premature public embrace of collective agriculture would alienate much, if indeed not all, of the peasantry. Finally, the parties which made up the ruling coalition could not agree among themselves upon the transitional form which expropriated property should assume, or even the size of the parcels to be exempted from the reform process. From the start, the asentamiento was rejected as an appropriate form of agrarian reorganization, although, paradoxically, while the government parties themselves haggled over the shape of a replacement, land reform officials found it expedient to implement a modified version to the properties which passed into their competence during the first half of 1971.

Expropriations

If Law 16.640 could not provide the Allende regime with the power to refashion Chilean agriculture entirely to its liking, it did bequeath it sufficient authority to accelerate vastly the rate of expropriation. Between November 1970 and May 1972, 2,944 farms covering 344,022 BIH had entered the reform sector, more than double the number of units and about a third again as much land as was transferred under the Christian Democrats.[42] At the time Popular Unity was overthrown, the Chilean state was declared by its new military rulers to be in "legal possession of 60.84 percent of all the irrigated farmlands in the country, and also [to hold] title to 37.78 percent of all nonirrigated but arable rural land" — some 10 million hectares.[43] "There were scarcely twelve properies left in the country large enough [under Law 16.640] to be taken," a prominent foreign export on Chilean agriculture has recalled, "and these had not been for special reasons — typically, because they were too remote, subject to flooding, or otherwise of no interest to the campesinos."[44]

The rapid growth of the reformed sector was achieved by recourse to existing legislation, but also to methods of marginal or questionable legality. The size provisions of the Christian Democratic law were applied unswervingly to all properties above 80 BIH, regardless of efficiency. Further, landowners were generally compelled to accept reserves of 40 rather than 80 BIH, sometimes even less.[45] In addition, Article 171 of Law 16.640 — what one historian has called an "overlooked provision" of the Christian Democratic reform — made it possible to acquire additional properties in the event of labor disputes. The article was originally designed to mitigate the economic effect of rural work stoppages; in the event of either a lockout or an illegal strike, the President of the Republic was empowered both to appoint an interventor (personal representative) to take over management until the conflict was settled, and to order the workers to resume their tasks. "As written," Loveman has pointed out, "Article 171 provided the basis *either* for governmental repression of the labor movement or for worker-pressured governmental takeovers of private property." It could also, of course, be applied impartially in genuine cases of labor-management conflict. As employed by Allende, however, "it provided a quasi-legal alternative to expropriation."[46]

The third method of transferring land was simply to seize it. During the first eighteen months of the Allende regime more than 1,700 rural properties were occupied by peasants, either spontaneously or under the tutelage of the rural wing of the MIR, the Movimiento Campesino Revolucionario (MCR). The seizures *(tomas)* were by no means confined to large estates; indeed, half of them took place on properties smaller than 80 BIH. In most cases the government responded to these actions by appointing an interventor to run the farm in conjunction with its occupiers. Although the parcels themselves were not formally incorporated into the reformed sector, in practice they became "almost a new type of reformed units, as they often remained intervened for long periods and were slowly expropriated."[47]

The official explanation for the seizures was that they were provoked by "outstanding labor conflicts, such as frequent cases where workers had seized the land on which they worked as a means of forcing the employer to pay the family benefits which they were due, or the obligatory social security contributions."[48] This glossed over the fact that the Christian Democrat reform had specifically designated transgressions of the labor code as legal ground for expropriation; this presumably obviated the necessity of dramatic actions by the peasantry, all the more so under a socialist government determined to pursue matters to the letter of the law, indeed beyond it. Moreover, since owners of intervened properties *prima facie* were denied the right to a reserve, the peasants would have had to have been very dense indeed not to perceive the advantage of seizing a property rather than waiting for land reform officials to get around to it. This was particularly the case if it fell below the size limitations prescribed by Law 16.640, in which case there was no legal way of expropriating it at all. Some properties were obviously marked for future expropriation, but seized nonetheless "when workers knew that expropriation was imminent and wanted to prevent the landowner from removing all his capital."[49]

Much controversy surrounded these land seizures. The government condemned them from the housetops, but in the private places of power opinions were presumed to be different. Popular Unity leaders repeatedly insisted that the *tomas* were spontaneous, and that they were without power to prevent them, save by stepping up the pace of the reform itself. This rather disingenuous posture was belied by these facts: (a) the operational relationship in the countryside between the MIR and the President's own Socialist party was far closer than officially acknowledged[50]; (b) the socialists and the MAPU were publicly in favor of the seizures, and also of staged confrontations with landowners to provoke intervention under Article 171; indeed, by 1972 "unofficial organization of *tomas* by Socialists and the MAPU had become a regular part of the expropriation process, even though the official position of [Popular Unity] as a government remained unchanged'';[51] (c) Allende's dogged refusal to use force to dislodge peasants who had seized properties was read— quite properly—as an open invitation to continue the practice. Although the Communists were vociferously opposed to the seizures both publicly and privately on the grounds that they provided explosive material for the opposition press and media, they were unable to impress their views upon the other parties within the ruling coalition. While his supporters quarreled among themselves or simply took the initiative, President Allende quietly abdicated any serious responsibility for order in the country's rural areas, confident that the flow of forces there could not but move in a direction generally favorably to his government.

Civil War in the Countryside

Events proved Allende wrong. With force the only sure arbiter, the Chilean countryside became the backdrop for a civil war in miniature, complete with costly engagements and losses of major political terrain to the opposition. The rash of seizures led owners of confiscated or occupied properties to seek redress in the courts, where they could count upon favorable decisions from a generally conservative judiciary; enforcement, however, was quite another matter, since the police power was centralized in the Ministry of Interior, at the very heart of the Executive Branch. In areas where the provincial administration was headed by a Communist, sporadic attempts were made to convince peasants to peacefully withdraw—with mixed success. Landowners who could not obtain satisfaction through legal channels, or were impatient with their slow workings, or who had not yet been confronted with the loss of property but feared that they were next, combined to form vigilante groups. There were occasional incidents of violence between these and the peasantry, particularly in attempting "retakings" *(retomas)* of occupied properties.

As in all rural settings where order has suddenly dissolved—Cuba during the war of 1895, or Spain in July–August, 1936—in Chile there were incidents where old scores were settled under the lofty cover of ideology, or long-nourished feelings of envy were finally purged in the catharsis of confiscation. CORA Vice-President David Baytelman, himself a Communist, has described in mordant tones how peasants in the province of Ñuble approached him on a routine visit in 1971 "to help resolve a problem which they had with a 'rich man' whose lands bordered on their farm." Once on the site, "we . . . discovered to our consternation," he reported, "that the 'rich man' was in reality an extremely poor minifundista, whose only wealth, in addition to his heavily eroded and impoverished bit of earth, was a team of oxen, a horse, and his guitar."[52] In relative terms, of course, the peasants were not wrong about this man's wealth,[53] and the incident itself may have been unique; it illustrates in exaggerated relief, however, the degree to which, in an environment in which the permissible boundaries of ownership were constantly shifting—or better put, resisting definition—all differences became subject to political conflict.

Landowner resistance often assumed passive or indirect forms whose consequences would be quickly devastating. Insecurity of tenure and the increasing use of seizures to separate proprietors from their moveable assets led to a significant depletion of Chile's livestock population—through illegal slaughter or through smuggling of cattle on the hoof across the remote and poorly-policed southern border with Argentina. It was also responsible for a decline in capital investment in the nonreformed agrarian sector. The Christian Democrat law had specifically promised compensation for recent improvements in expropriated properties, but the general thrust of Allende's policies (as well as countless specific examples), deprived that proviso of all meaning. In the event, there was no new investment in the private agricultural sector during the Allende years: instead truly wealthy landowners took their dollars and abandoned the countryside altogether, leaving their less fortunate colleagues to fight on whatever terms they could.

The unleashing of class war in the countryside also led to a rapid realignment of rural political forces. The parties of the Left improved their footing within the rural labor movement, both by expanding its size, and by employing the same patronage techniques which had served the Christian Democrats so well at an earlier point. Eventually that movement split, and Christian Democracy was left with the smaller half. At the same time, the Christian Democrats and the forces of the Right, now represented by the National party, achieved a reconciliation of sorts. The Christian Democrats did not repudiate their own reform, still the object of much rancor on the part of landowners, but they suddenly discovered the unqualified virtues of private property in land. From this vantage they accused Popular Unity of plotting to deprive the peasant of any possibility of obtaining individual title, and to merge all reformed properties into a system of state farms *(haciendas del estado)*—a message which met with considerable resonance not only among asentados but minifundistas as well.

To these attacks the government responded, in tones of hurt commingled with indignation, that its position was being cynically misrepresented. It appeared, however, that the opposition had happened upon a fatal opening in Popular Unity's defenses. Without doubt the government wished to calm the apprehension of smallholders, asentados, and peasants who aspired to land ownership. But it steadfastly refused to do the one thing that could have accomplished that goal—namely, to commit itself unambiguously to a pluralistic system of land tenure. Nor would it frankly reveal the shape which it hoped land exploitation in Chile would ultimately assume. This was possibly because, given differences within the National Agrarian Commission, it could not, but just as likely, because it dared not.

Finally, when revisions of Law 16.640 were discussed in Congress, the conduct of the government did not provide much reason to think that the accusations of the opposition were particularly ill-founded. Popular Unity proposed (without success) that size as a criterion for expropriation be replaced by "economic importance" (soil quality, access to irrigation, location with respect to markets); likewise, a mere request by workers on agricultural enterprise would be sufficient cause for incorporation into the reformed sector. Conversely, President Allende's veto of a Christian Democratic bill which passed both houses in the final days of the regime was not very reassuring. It would have lowered the permissible size of rural holdings from 80 to 40 BIH, which was, ironically, nothing more than Popular Unity's official position in the March 1973 congressional elections. This bill, however, contained two additional provisions which were apparently unacceptable to the government. One would have assured that peasants were given title to expropriated property within two years; the other would have required that small and medium-sized landowners from whom property was taken be compensated in cash. If a totally nationalized agriculture was not what Allende had in mind, he seemed oddly unwilling to foreclose the possibility.

The Collective Economy in Agriculture

In the second half of 1971, the government finally unveiled its own transitional model for reformed agriculture, the Centro de Reforma Agraria (CERA). Like the asentamiento, the CERA was the fruit of a painfully-fashioned compromise—in this case, between different elements of the regime represented on the National Agrarian Commission, and what the government ultimately wanted, and what it thought it could sell to the peasantry. On paper the CERA's had several advantages over the Christian Democratic asentamiento. They were larger, grouping together several expropriated enterprises, thus encompassing a wider pool of livestock, machinery, and such other capital resources as were retained (or acquired) by INDAP management. And they were more inclusive: membership and voting rights were extended beyond the heads of households of resident tenantry to women and children eighteen years or older, and also to all landless laborers within a designated geographical compass. At times, the CERA was even intended to "blanket in" minifundistas scattered on plots between or around newly-reformed enterprises.

Although elaborate agricological arguments were used to justify the creation of the CERA's, it is fairly clear that they were shaped largely in accordance with an ideological goal—namely, to create a classless society in the Chilean countryside.

It is generally conceded that the CERA's were not well-received by the peasantry; there is less agreement as to why. Some credit resistance to the success of opposition propaganda,[54] others to the "class selfishness" of peasants who otherwise would have qualified for the relatively privileged status of asentado.[55] Both, of course, might be true, without necessarily proving that the CERA was well-conceived. As David Lehmann has pointed out, the CERA rested upon "a number of crucial assumptions about the political and administrative conditions prevailing in the countryside." It was, above all, "a political and administrative model, not an economic one. It [depended] for its success on a very high level of egalitarianism, collectivist consciousness, and mutual trust among the workers who [made it up] . . . It [depicted] an organization of a 'transitory character' . . . yet it [took] as a given a profound transformation of the consciousness of the workers involved."[56] To which Loveman adds:

> contrary to the declarations of some coalition ideologues, the [CERA] did not eliminate proprietorship, and therefore privilege; it merely transferred more prerogatives of proprietorship to [CORA and INDAP] bureaucrats, while removing from the individual enterprise or group of campesino enterprises control over the surplus generated in the rural sector.[57]

Because peasant opposition to the CERA was so pervasive, few were ever formed; by June 1972, the government acknowledged the existence of only 150. Other expropriated properties were run under the *ad hoc* rubric of "peasant committees" (which bore strong operational resemblance to the asentamiento, but lacked the juridical possibilities of eventual parcelization), or without any formal organization at all. In some areas, peasants went ahead and established unauthorized asentamientos, probably at the instigation of Christian Democratic rural organizations. By so doing, they effectively foreclosed the possibility of annexation by some future CERA, or absorption by a state farm.[58]

The collective economy in agriculture did not perform very well under Popular Unity, but neither had it done so under Christian Democracy. The asentamientos were largely run at a loss, with the real difference made up indirectly by CORA loans and advances, whose real value for repayment purposes was seriously discounted by inflation. Often asentamientos simply defaulted on their debts to the government, and under neither Frei nor Allende was it thought politically expedient to press the matter. Even when agricultural credit was shifted in 1972 from CORA to the State Bank, presumably to facilitate more rigorous collection of obligations, the land reform agency habitually rushed in to compensate for the asentamientos' inability to show a profit.

The unimpressive performance of the asentamientos was due both to undercapitalization and a lack of economic incentives. Left-wing critics habitually complained about the higher quality of land which expropriated proprietors were allowed to keep for their reserves, and (under Frei) the right to deplete the reformed units of moveable assets prior to their transfer. Yet except for a highly controversial agreement to purchase 100,000 tractors from the Soviet bloc, President Allende did very little to redress the balance by allocating significantly greater resources for the replenishment of reformed units; instead, *enlargement of the reformed sector*, rather than its overall performance, became the principal focus of agrarian policy, at least until late 1972, when expropriation had been pushed as far as the law allowed (or indeed, even farther), and it began to dawn on some members of the government that considerations of productivity could no longer be ignored.

The problem of incentives was long-standing. Under the Christian Democrats, the asentados received a regular wage which was officially designated an *anticipo*— that is, an "advance" on the profits of the collective enterprise. In practice, however, the reformed peasants came to regard the anticipo as a wage (and a political right as well), and they neglected the collective plot for their own gardens (*huertos*). The practice continued under Popular Unity, both on the asentamientos, and even in the CERA's. Agrarian reformers of both "communitarian" and Marxist persuasion hoped against hope that the peasants' consciousness could be raised sufficiently to recognize their obligations to the collective enterprise; however, in a context in which competition for the peasant vote overrode all over considerations in the countryside, no meaningful sanctions against the pursuit of self-interest could be contemplated.

The general economic policies of the Allende regime did nothing to improve incentives to agricultural productivity, and added several new elements whose effect was to undermine them even more. Imports of foodstuffs more than doubled by value between 1970 and 1973; this was not intended, of course, to discourage domestic production, but it could hardly act as a stimulus, particularly when the government distributed imports at artificially low prices. Even more important was the extension of a stricter system of price controls to virtually all locally-produced foodstuffs. This led peasants to turn to their own plots with redoubled dedication, since the fruits thereof could easily be sold on the black market. When the government attempted to close that avenue by instituting a state purchasing monopoly for specific crops, such as wheat and sugar beets, peasants quietly shifted to other cultivations, and both the amount of land sown for the desired items, and the actual yields, dropped by nearly one-quarter.

Nor is it possible in any evaluation of socialist agriculture in Chile to exclude sociological considerations, however difficult they may be to measure. The atmosphere in which Popular Unity carried out its land reform—part jacquerie, part carnival—led inevitably to a breakdown of labor discipline on many reformed units. Even the most sanguine accounts of the countryside during the Allende years find it impossible to deny serious mismanagement in the reformed sector—misappropriation of seeds, tools, livestock; failure to maintain machinery; absenteeism, frequently due to drunkenness. The matter was so serious, indeed, that the Communist party's Secretary-General Luis Corvalán found it necessary to call it publicly to the government's attention. By way of contrast, the most successful reformed units under Popular Unity appear to have been the Centros de Producción (CEPROs), which were nationalized agribusiness enterprises, vertically integrated, with a large salaried work force which was organized hierarchically according to skills and functions—in other words, units on which, from an administrative and economic point of view, relations of production strongly resembled their former capitalist configuration.[59]

The Balance Sheet, 1970–1973

By 1973, Law 16.640, as interpreted and applied successively by Christian Democratic and Marxist administrations, had finally achieved one of the major purposes for which entails had been abolished in 1852. Chile no longer possessed a class of large landowners with political and economic interests reaching to the very summit of the nation's urban power structure. Instead, no privately-owned farm was larger than 80 BIH, and many, perhaps most, were smaller. The only large estates which remained in Chile were the reformed units of production under the control of CORA and INDAP bureaucrats. Whatever the political and ideological virtues of this transformation, its effect on food production did not appear to justify the predictions of land reformers, ancient or modern. (Table 4.2)

An exceedingly long list of extenuating circumstances has been drawn up to justify the view that these figures unfairly represent Chile's agricultural performance under Popular Unity. It is said that the period is too short to reflect any definitive trends. It is also held that the existence of the ubiquitous black market prevented accurate measurement of food production; therefore, these figures are too low. We are reminded that the October strike in 1971 came in the midst of the planting season, and therefore prevented distribution

TABLE 4.2
Index of Agricultural Production, 1970–1973

Year	(1961–1965 = 100) Index	% Previous
1970	118	+5
1971	113	–4
1972	113	n/c
1973	95	–15

[*Note:* Only 1972 and 1973 can be considered "Popular Unity harvests, since 1971 was planted in 1970, before the outcomes of the election could be known.]

Source: Food and Agriculture Organization of the United Nations, *Production Yearbook, 1974* (Rome, 1975), p. 27.

of seeds and fertilizers at a critical moment. Bad weather conditions prevailed throughout the 1971 agricultural year. The economic constraints attendant upon a foreign exchange shortage made some drop inevitable, since many critical inputs were imported and finally, when one considers the dislocations which historically have accompanied agrarian reform in many parts of the world in the twentieth century, Popular Unity did not do so badly after all.[60]

These arguments require some sorting out. The only failure for which Popular Unity can without reservation be relieved of all responsibility pertains to the weather. The October strike, whatever its eventual purpose, began as a response to the government's nationalization policies. Similarly, the black market was the result of an unrealistic price structure for agricultural products, not a deliberate attempt at sabotage. The shortage of foreign exchange was the consequence of the government's spending spree in 1971, not an act of God. There is a plausible quality to the statement that 1971–1973 is too short a period to gauge definitely the direction in which Chilean agriculture was heading, but the argument cuts both ways: if continued, it could just as easily have declined even further (as we shall discuss below). Likewise, if one assumes that the black market absorbed a very large quantity of foodstuffs missing from the official production tables for 1972 and 1973, the production record of Popular Unity is probably not much worse than that of the Christian Democrats—may indeed, even have been better. But if this is so, it would be *only thanks to the incentives provided by the black market.* Had the government succeeded in its goal of taking full control of the rural sector, what we know of the "offical" market suggests that the figures would have plunged still further.

Moreover, some embarrassing sociological and economic facts lie behind the production figures: by 1973, by far the most productive agricultural units in Chile were the privately-owned farms of between 40 and 80 BIH, operating under the quasi-incentive of the black market. We can be certain, then, that output would have been far lower under Allende had not Law 16.640 established certain size limitations to expropriation and frustrated the government's desire to "complete" the agrarian reform—that is, to dismantle these existing centers of productive agriculture altogether.

Nor is it clear that the future of the Allende experiment in the countryside, if permitted to continue, would have yielded more impressive results over the longer term. In the days before land reform, estate owners could shift the burden of price controls onto their work force, and from low wages and the non-payment of social security contributions, hope to collect the profits denied them in the marketplace. By 1973, however, Chile had no landed aristocracy; the peasantry was organized into unions; and the agricultural work force—whether on the asentamientos. CERAs, or elsewhere—was virtually guaranteed a decent minimum wage. Hence, there was no longer a way of pretending that low productivity was due to latifundia; to increase food production, the problem of incentives would have to be faced.

This would have been an unpleasant task for any Chilean government, but for a Marxist regime, it posed uniquely distasteful ideological dilemmas. As David Baytelman has explained, within the government throughout the Allende years there existed what he terms "a persistent minority view" (which was nonetheless also the view of the majority of the president's own party):

> that economic incentives would destroy the principal of equality and deform the objective of a socialist agriculture, which was to form a 'new man'. Therefore, economic incentives should not be applied under any conditions. There were even some who proposed the total elimination of money in the reformed sector.[61]

This mentality encouraged government functionaries to look anywhere else for a solution to the problem of productivity: to a new reform law; to a still further reduction in the permissible size of holdings; to intensified "political education" for peasants on reformed properties; to more stringent controls on transportation, marketing, and distribution; to selective granting of INDAP benefits to "cooperative" asentamientos; and so on. What lay behind this vision was the conviction that agricultural production was fundamentally a matter of political power rather than management; that it could be increased by expanding the government's authority over additional resources, rather than by making a more intelligent use of the ones it already possessed. Such a solution, James Wilkie has written in a cross-national study of land reform in Latin America, "is more often than not self-defeating." Knowledge about "subtleties of diversity and about contradictions in policy is lost," he continues, "and the problems generated in policy are compounded. Rather than seek more power in such cases, leaders might often profitably undertake to understand the impact of their programs."[62] There are no indications that at the time of Allende's overthrow such pragmatism was in the offing for Chilean agriculture.

Some Concluding Observations

There is no reason why a society cannot embark upon a land reform which does not immediately pay for itself—*provided that this is what it wishes to do*. Such a decision requires the investment of significant resources in long-term agricultural development, and a willingness to wait. During an indeterminate period it must be prepared (and able) to acquire much if not most of its foodstuffs elsewhere, while new tenure structures are rendered operational, and an enfranchised peasantry given the tools and skills necessary to maximize the benefits of ownership. Existing productive units must be encouraged to continue, to minimize the cost of imports and allow the allocation of foreign exchange to newer, "reformed" sectors of agriculture, so that the gap between domestic capacity and foreign supplies can be closed as quickly as possible. Admittedly, this ideal scenario has never been realized anywhere, but there are few cases that stray farther from it than that of Chile.

There, under all recent regimes—Alessandri, the Christian Democrats, the Marxist—land reform was embraced as a cure for urban ills, either food shortages, foreign exchange constraints, political unrest, or any combination. Thus the land question in its final, definitive phase in Chilean history was approached in terms of what could be extracted from the countryside, rather than what needed to be given to it. All of the delusions which informed land reform legislation since at least 1962 simply reached an apex under Allende. Having preached for so many years that the sole cause of inadequate production was latifundia, Popular Unity could imagine no other prescription than to abolish large private property in agriculture. And when this did not yield the expected results, connive at the further reduction or even abolition of private property in land altogether. Of course, there were professional agronomists within the government who knew better, but apparently they were not able to make their influence sufficiently felt. As Baytelman—who was certainly in a position to know—has said, "there were important leaders [within Popular Unity] who placed a kind of mystic faith in Chilean agriculture's ability to produce a miracle in a short period of time."[63] One of them was Gonzalo Martner, chief of the National Planning Office, who told an international conference in early 1972 that the government was "confident that *in the short term*, through agrarian reform and import substitution, $300 million of foreign exchange could be liberated for other uses, even taking into account the social problems in the countryside."[64] Instead, the regime ended up spending at least $243 million for food imports in 1971; 315 million in 1972; $449 million in 1973. The figure projected for 1974 before Allende's fall was nearly $700 million.[65]

Although the need to increase food production was always the *stated* reason for agrarian reform in Chile, in practice that goal was habitually subordinated to other, more narrowly political agendas. Both the Christian Democrats and Popular Unity looked upon expropriations and peasant unionization as a means of expanding their urban base to a newly-enfranchised rural electorate. In this, ironically, they did not differ markedly from the Conservatives of old, for whom the peasantry constituted so many voters whose suffrage could be manipulated to advantage. Of course, the latter-day reformers gave the rural work force more than a meal of meatpies and wine in exchange for its ballot; they had to.

As long as there was a large landowning class in Chile against which to focus peasant grievances, this was a relatively inexpensive strategy. The Christian Democrats were saved from potentially negative consequences in the area of production by the multi-class nature of their own party, their ambivalence about property rights, a lingering carrot-and-stick pragmatism, and a respect for the financial and political constraints within which they were operating.

None of these factors particularly inhibited the leaders of Popular Unity. Their principal concern was not with legal niceties or balancing interests (or budgets), but with consciousness and mobilization. Some thought these two things would somehow solve the problem of production; others professed not to care. Both sides were united in the fear that "petty bourgeois" tendencies would take root among the reformed peasantry; and that a new class of "kulaks" created as the result of the Christian Democratic reform would come to dominate the rural scene, and provide a model (and perhaps a demonstration effect) of functioning capitalist relations in agriculture. These ideological goals were pursued so singlemindedly that in the end, the Allende regime preferred to give (or borrow to give) half a billion dollars to foreign food exporters rather than to transfer a smaller amount within Chile in the form of higher prices to a politically undesirable agribusiness class.

In the very short run, this strategy seems to have yielded some modest political results. By expanding their base in the rural union movement, increasing social services, and stepping up the rate of expropriations, the government improved its standing among the rural electorate, particularly peasant women. Nonetheless, in the congressional elections of March 1973—the last ballot in the life of the regime—the majority of peasants "continued to vote for the Right, or more likely, the Christian Democrats."[66] Whether one chose to regard this showing as disappointing or encouraging, it pointed to an acceleration of the process, rather than to a consolidation of existing gains.

Even if a majority could somehow be coaxed out of the peasant electorate at some future date, tipping the scales nationally in favor of Popular Unity, the government would still have faced serious problems within the rural sector. It is far easier to expropriate land than to advance literacy, agricultural skills, entrepreneurial ability, and habits of discipline and work. The same kinds of urban-rural resource choices which constrained the Christian Democrats, and before them, the Popular Front, would have persisted within a victorious socialist Chile. So would controversies over incentives, tenure, and title. The examples of Hungary, Poland, East Germany, the Soviet Union, and other closed political environments do not suggest that power alone—even uncontested power—is sufficient to increase agriculture productivity while fully satisfying Marxian values.[67] What sorts of compromises would have been necessary after the "transition to socialism" in Chile cannot be known; those necessary to arrive at that point were never found, principally because they were never sought in the first place.

Notes

1. Arnold J. Bauer, *Chilean Rural Society from the Spanish Conquest to 1930* (Cambridge, England, 1975), pp. 8–12. The *encomienda* was a grant of land and of the labor of a given community of Indians to cultivate it.
2. Ibid., pp. 20–21; Simon Collier, *Ideas and Politics of Chilean Independence, 1808–1833* (Cambridge, England, 1967), p. 247.
3. Fredrick B. Pike, *Chile and the United States, 1880–1962* (Notre Dame, 1963), pp. 118–119.
4. *Nuestra inferioridad económica [1911]* (Santiago, 3rd ed., 1972), p. 236.
5. *The Growth and Structure*, pp. 120–128.
6. Ibid., pp. 128–132; Jeannine Swift, *Agrarian Reform in Chile: An Economic Study* (Lexington, Mass., 1971), pp. 12–13.
7. Markos J. Mamalakis and Clark W. Reynolds, *Essays on the Chilean Economy* (Homewood, Ill., 1965), pp. 122–123.
8. Jacques Chonchol, "The Agrarian Policy of the Popular Government," in Zammit, ed., *The Chilean Road to Socialism*, pp. 112–113; James W. Wilkie and Peter Reich, eds., *Statistical Abstract of Latin America, 1977* (Los Angeles, 1977), p. 381.
9. *Growth and Structure . . . , p. 348*. See also James O. Bray, "Demand, and the Supply of Food in Chile," *Journal of Farm Economics*, XLIV, 4 (1962), pp. 1005–1020.
10. Robert R. Kaufmann, *The Politics of Land Reform in Chile, 1950–1970* (Cambridge, Mass., 1972), pp. 32–33.
11. Swift, *Land Reform . . .* , p. 13.
12. Pierre Crosson, *Agricultural Development and Productivity, Lessons from the Chilean Experience* (Baltimore, 1970), pp. 8–11.
13. Mamalakis and Reynolds, *Essays on the Chilean Economy*, pp. 141–143.
14. Swift, *Agrarian Reform . . .* , pp. 17–18.

15. Crosson, *Agricultural Development and Productivity* . . . , p.38 . See also Swift, *Agrarian Reform* . . . , pp. 17, 19–23, and Mamakis and Reynolds, *Essays on the Chilean Economy*, p. 147.
16. Crosson, *Agricultural Development*, p. 43.
17. Ibid., p. 103.
18. Brian Loveman, *Struggle in the Countryside: Politics and Rural Labor in Chile, 1919–1973* (Bloomington, Ind., 1976), pp. 69–112.
19. Mamalakis and Reynolds, *Essays on the Chile Economy*, pp. 144–147.
20. Ibid., pp. 138–139.
21. Loveman, *Struggle in the Countryside*, pp. 118–124.
22. Kaufmann, *The Politics of Land Reform*, pp. 46–58.
23. Ibid., p. 228. Emphasis added.
24. We omit here discussion of the activities of the Agricultural Colonization Bank, created in 1928, whose charter had mandated the purchase of agricultural land which to settle "colonists." By 1960 only one percent of all Chilean rural families had benefited from its operation, and although designed to favor administrators, foremen, and other persons with prior experience in cultivation, apparently many recipients of land from the bank were persons with no established agricultural connections. Swift, *Agrarian Reform*, pp. 33–34.
25. Specifically excluded from the law were fruit orchards and vineyards, which did not lend themselves easily to parcelization, as well as dry lands being developed into artificial pastures. These categories, critics often pointed out, comprehended some of the most valuable agricultural land in Chile. However, they also included some of the most efficiently worked rural properties.
26. Kaufmann, *The Politics of Land Reform*, p. 67; Loveman, *Struggle in the Countryside*, p.235.
27. There were some exceptions to this law. Persons who ran an unusually well-managed farm could hold as much as 320 BIH, and the 80 BIH limit could also be exceeded by owners of vineyards under certain circumstances.
28. Actually an earlier version had been developed on church lands divided up by the dioceses of Talca and Greater Santiago under the Alessandri reform.
29. Similar pressures were brought to bear on the smallholders (minifundistas). By 1970 more than 100,000 of them had been gathered in cooperatives where, from their point of view, the chief benefit was access to INDAP subsidies and credits which would otherwise have been unavailable to them. Loveman, *Struggle in the Countryside*, pp. 275–276.
30. In 1966, while Frei's agrarian legislation was working its way through Congress, a Socialist physician in the province of Concepión, a close personal friend of Salvador Allende, frankly confessed to me that the defeat of the Left in the 1964 presidential elections had been due in large part to the FRAP's studiously vague outline of the land tenure structures it advocated. In tones of an angel describing the Fall of Man, he mused that the Christian Democrats "held out something more attractive than just 'land reform', and that was the prospect of making every peasant a little capitalist in his own right."
31. All but 14 of the 109 asentamientos which had completed the statutory three years before 1970 and which were permitted by land reform officials to vote upon their definitive mode of organization, opted for cooperatives rather than parcelation. This could be (and in fact was) often cited as evidence of a preternatural urge to collectivism on the part of the Chilean peasantry, but the matter was not so simple. The 109 permitted to vote actually constituted less than half the total

number of asentamientos which had reached three years of life by 1970; it is difficult to believe that the principle of selection by CORA and INDAP personnel was not influenced by the likely outcome of the vote. Also, asentamientos which opted for parcelization had to pay off outstanding debts to INDAP. Since few of them operated in the black, it was easier to extend the life of the cooperative at government expense, rather than to find the resources to meet outstanding obligations. The figures are from David Lehmann, "Agrarian Reform in Chile, 1964–72: An Essay in Contradictions," from his *Peasants, Landlords and Governments: Agrarian Reform in the Third World* (New York, 1974), p. 107.

32. John Strasma, "Campesinos, Land, and Employment under Unidad Popular," in Federico G. Gil et. al., *Chile at the Turning Point: Lessons of the Socialist Years, 1970–73,* tr. John S. Gilitz (Philadelphia, 1979), p. 195: Kaufmann, *The Politics of Land Reform,* pp. 102–103; Loveman, *Struggle in the Countryside,* pp. 271–272.

33. Strasma, "Campesinos, Land, and Employment . . . ," pp. 195–196. From this excellent article I draw rather different conclusions than its author. For him the data demonstrates the unsuitability of the asentamiento as the proper form of reformed agriculture in Chile, and therefore, by indirection, points to the need for some form of state or collective farms. He takes as a given the political and economic possibilities of such a reorganization; I do not.

34. Such progress as was made, in fact, depended largely upon massive amounts of aid under the Alliance for Progress, much of it earmarked for this specific purpose.

35. Kaufmann, *The Politics of Land Reform,* p. 99.

36. There can be no doubt whatever that this is what made the Chilean land reform so fascinating to the United States government, which put up much of the resources for it during the Frei period.

37. Kaufmann, *The Politics of Land Reform,* pp. 116–117.

38. Swift, *Agrarian Reform in Chile,* pp. 102, 196.

39. Lehmann, "Agrarian Reform in Chile . . . ," p. 85; Loveman, *Struggle in the Countryside,* pp. 276–278.

40. "The Popular Unity's Programme," in Zammit, *The Chilean Road to Socialism,* pp. 267–268.

41. Lehmann, "Agrarian Reform in Chile . . . ," pp. 97–115; Strasma, "Campesinos, Land and Employment . . . ," pp. 195–205; David Baytelman, "Problems of Collective Land Exploitation in Chilean Agriculture," in Gil, *Chile at the Turning Point,* pp. 121–159; Peter Winn and Cristóbal Kay," Agrarian Reform and Rural Revolution in Allende's Chile," *Journal of Latin American Studies,* VI, 1 (1974), pp. 135–159.

42. Lehman, "Agrarian Reform in Chile . . . ," p. 80.

43. Loveman, *Struggle in the Countryside,* p. 305.

44. Strasma, "Campesinos, Land, and Employment . . . ," p. 196.

45. Typically, the peasants were invited by land reform officials to determine the size and selection of the reserve. "Once the government had demonstrated its ability and will to employ its discretionary power with respect to the granting of reserves," two pro-Allende writers have reported, "it was in a good position to bargain with the owner for the purchase of the working capital of the farm at a reasonable price—particularly when the peasants had recommended no reserve and seized the property." Winn and Kay, "Agrarian Reform and Rural Revolution . . . ," p. 144.

46. *Struggle in the Countryside,* p. 271. Emphasis added.

47. Cristóbal Kay, "Agrarian Reform and the Transition to Socialism," in Philip O'Brien, ed., *Allende's Chile* (New York, 1976), p. 90.
48. "Discussion on the Agrarian Reform and Agrarian Policy," in Zammit, *The Chilean Road to Socialism*, pp. 129–130.
49. Lehmann, "Agrarian Reform in Chile . . . ,"p. 105.
50. Loveman, *Struggle in the Countryside*, pp. 280–281; see also Alistair Horne's account of his 1971 visit with MIR's "Comandante Pepe" in the province of Valdivia, *Small Earthquake in Chile* (New York, 1972), pp. 184–201. The Comandante claimed to be a close friend of Chonchol (by then Allende's Minister of Agriculture), who had apparently recently visited the areas he controlled.
51. Winn and Kay, "Agrarian Reform and Rural Revolution . . . ," p. 143.
52. "Problems of Collective Land Exploitation . . . ," p. 159.
53. "A house may be large or small; as long as the surrounding houses are equally small it satisfies all social demands for a dwelling. But let a palace arise beside the little house, and it shrinks from a little house to a hut . . . . Our desires and pleasures spring from society; we measure them, therefore, by society and not by the objects which serve for their satisfaction. Because they are of a social nature, they are of a relative nature." Karl Marx, *Wage Labour and Capital*, from Marx and Engels, *Selected Works* (Moscow, 1962), Vol. 1, pp. 93–94.
54. Baytelman, "Problems of Collective Land Exploitation . . . ,"p. 130.
55. Strasma, "Campesinos, Land, and Employment . . . ,"p. 200; Jacques Chonchol, "The Agrarian Policy of the Popular Government," p. 112.
56. "Agrarian Reform in Chile . . . ," p. 108.
57. *Struggle in the Countryside*, pp. 294–295.
58. The case of the Mapuche Indians really requires an entirely separate chapter. These were indigenes who had been dispossessed of their land generations before by the Spaniards and their Chilean creole successors, and whose idea of land reform was simply to take back what they had once owned in common. This was what *they* had in mind when they engaged in a *toma*. A wholly disproportionate number of seizures, particularly in the province of Cautín, where undertaken by Mapuche communities, but not with a view to joining up with some larger system of state agriculture. Quite the contrary "many . . . never had much to do with the State in any case, and saw no reason why, once they had seized the land and begun to work on it, this outside authority should interfere and seek to start the process all over again, with expropriation and furthermore to acquire the land for itself," in whatever form it might prefer. As time went on, and the Mapuches became dependent upon CORA for advances, inputs and machinery, their councils "born in such an [apparent] revolutionary spirit, devoted their energies more and more to . . . bureaucratic guerrilla" warfare. Lehmann, "Agrarian Reform . . . ," p. 104.
59. Apart from the sources already cited, this section draws upon materials presented in Kay, "Agrarian Reform and the Transition to Socialism," esp. pp. 89–96; Ian Roxborough et. al., *Chile: The State and Revolution* (New York, 1977), pp. 135–143; Kyle Steenland, *Agrarian Reform under Allende: Peasant Revolt in the South* (Alburquerque, N.M., 1977), esp. pp. 131–139. For Corvalán's statement, see *El Siglo* (Santiago), August 14, 1972.
60. Baytelman, "Problems of Collective Land Exploitation . .," pp. 137–139; Roxborough, *Chile: The State and Revolution*, p. 142; Stefan de Vylder, *Allende's Chile: The Political Economy of the Rise and Fall of the Unidad Popular* (Cambridge, 1976), pp. 198–200; Edward Boorstein, *Allende's Chile* (New York, 1977), pp. 149–159.

61. Baytelman, "Problems of Collective Land Exploitation," p. 147.
62. James Wilkie, *Measuring Land Reform* (Los Angeles, 1974), p. 97.
63. Baytelman, "Problems of Collective Land Exploitation . . . ," p. 156.
64. "Discussion on Payments and Balance of Trade Policy," in Zammit, *The Chilean Road to Socialism*, pp. 162–163. Emphasis added.
65. James Wilkie and Peter Reich, eds., *Statistical Abstract of Latin America, 1977* (Los Angeles, 1977), p. 381.
66. Baytelman, "Problems of Collective Land Exploitation . . . ," p. 137.
67. Alec Nove, "Can Eastern Europe Feed Itself?", in *Political Economy and Soviet Socialism* (London, 1979), pp. 166–177.

5

The Area of Social Property

The development of a dominant (or "hegemonic") public sector in Chile was regarded by the Allende regime as utterly central to the accomplishment of its broader objectives, and rightly so. For if socialism was to have any meaning, at least in the Marxian sense of the term, then the Chilean state would have to acquire ownership or control of the principal means of production. This projected transformation was crucial in another sense as well: it occupied that common tactical ground where the government's major economic, political, and ideological goals converged. That is, it was anticipated that the profits of mining and manufacturing, banking and insurance, transport and energy, formerly remitted to private hands at home or abroad, henceforth would be placed at the disposal of the state, which in turn would utilize them to generate self-sustained economic growth, full employment, and a higher standard of living for Chileans.[1] Such a happy eventuality presumably would broaden the government's base of popular support, deliver a decisive electoral majority, and permit President Allende to convoke a plebiscite. This would permit him to widen still further the discretionary power of his government, consolidating definitively what had been achieved. Perhaps most important of all, this process, taken as a whole, would facilitate a peaceful, legal transition to socialism within a democratic framework. Thus would be consummated the dream which had evaded with equal persistence Marx and Engels, Bernstein and Bebel, Luxemburg and Jaurès, and their triumphant successors in Moscow and Peking, Pyongyang and Hanoi, Warsaw and Havana.

That a small, remote, semi-industrialized South American country should be called upon to realize an almost milennarian dream seems in retrospect remarkable, to say the very least. Yet President Allende himself saw nothing particularly improbable about the prospect. As he declared in his First Annual Message to Congress on May 21, 1971:

> our revolutionary path is the pluralist path, anticipated by the classic theorists of Marxism but which has never before become a concrete fact. Social philosophers have always supposed that the first to put it into practice would be the more developed nations, probably Italy or France, with their powerful Marxist working-class parties.

> However, once more history has broken with past patterns. The opportunity has arisen to build a new model of society, not just where, in theory, it was to be expected, but where concrete conditions have arisen which favored its emergence. Chile is today the first nation in the world called upon to set up the second model for transition to a socialist society.[2]

But still, why Chile? Because, apparently, it uniquely possessed those "concrete conditions" outlined by Friedrich Engels in the final phase of his life for an evolutionary socialist transformation—a strong labor movement operating in a vigorous democratic political culture. In his First Annual Message Allende specifically made reference to those assets, as well as to the constitutional tradition of the nation's armed forces. And it was known, of course, that Chile's industrial working class was preponderantly loyal to Marxist parties. Allende omitted mention of two other elements which might have been marshalled in support of his view: the relatively high (for Latin America) level of economic development, and the prior existence of a public sector which, though far from dominant, had already played a catalyzing role in Chile's early emergence as an industrializing South American nation, and whose importance had grown in the Christian Democratic period.

All of this did not add up to a consensus on behalf of socialism, and Allende's people knew it. However, they expected, through a policy of social alliances, to widen support for a more thoroughgoing reshaping of the economy. For some years, conventional wisdom had held that the nation's wealth—particularly in banking and industry—was dominated by a handful of economic "supergroups," controlled in turn by an interlocking network of powerful families (or "clans," as they were often pejoratively labelled). In 1961 economist Ricardo Lagos Escobar had published a study (*La concentración del poder económico*), many times reprinted, which through extensive use of statistical materials, had established to the satisfaction of many the truth of this assertion. Echoes of Lagos' book resounded in the 1970 Popular Unity electoral program, which made specific reference to "150 firms," who, it held, "monopolistically controlled the entire market, received most of the assistance from the state, and most of the bank credit, and exploited the rest of the country's businessmen by selling them raw materials at high prices while buying their output at low prices." These 150 constituted nothing more than the apex of a huge pyramid, whose full dimension the program measured as some 30,500 firms (including artisanal establishments). The same document held out hope to the vast majority of Chilean entrepreneurs that their interests would be safeguarded—indeed, enhanced—in the new dispensation. It promised the "non-monopolistic sector" additional credit, technical assistance, and more benevolent tax and tariff structures, "enabling [its members] to fulfull the important role which they play in the national economy."[3]

The sharp distinction between "monopolistic" and "non-monopolistic" enterprises—between a sharply peaking summit and a sprawling base—was to find its institutional expression under Allende in the tripartite division of the Chilean economy. A dominant public sector, dominated by the Area of Social Property, would acquire ownership of the nation's mines, banks, insurance companies, foreign trade, large distribution, and "strategic industrial monopolies" (defined as transportation, communications, oil, iron and steel). A privately-owned sector, the Area of Private Property, would remain numerically superior, although it would be subordinated to the Social Area for purposes of planning. Finally, an Area of Mixed Property would be constituted largely out of enterprises in which the government preferred control rather than outright ownership. These were largely firms which functioned as subsidiaries of foreign concerns, employing highly sophisticated technology or requiring access to scarce raw materials or processes. In these enterprises, which were actually few in number, the government would acquire a controlling majority of the stock, but—in exchange for continued participation under new rules—would permit regular repatriation of profits to the parent company.[4]

The separation of industrial firms into three areas was intended to turn the highly asymmetrical pattern of ownership to Popular Unity's advantage. Assuming that the concentration of economic power in Chile was as great as the Marxist parties (and many others) believed, the political consequences of expropriation would be quite limited. "We have no fear that [once deprived of their holdings], the big bourgeoisie will make a comeback," MAPU Secretary-General Rodrigo Ambrosio confidently declared in the final days of 1970. "For in the measure . . . that the dominant economic area passes into the hands of the State, the bakers, the shopkeepers, the garage owners, the haberdashers, the small farmers, will not be able to turn the clock back."[5] Nor, if Popular Unity's program was believed, would they wish to. For apart from the presumed benefits of a new economic policy, the petty bourgeoisie would be liberated from the influence of the "monopolies" on a more diffuse ideological level. Deprived of its economic base, grand capital, domestic and foreign, would presumably lose its capacity—through the loss of access to advertising, among other things—to influence opinion through the press and the electronic media.

However, the transfer of large-scale industry to the state was not merely a negative exercise intended to punish and disarm the government's most powerful political opponents. Extravagant hopes were placed in the Area of Social Property, as if the mere possession of the "commanding heights" of the economy would provide keys for the resolution of all the ills which afflicted Chilean society. As one shrewd observer has written, Allende's planners conceived of the Chilean economy as a "mechanism highly amenable to control and reorientation. From the command center of the Area of Social

Property one could do practically everything,'' they presumed, from reducing frauds in foreign trade to improving tax collection; from facilitating the redistribution of credit to increasing production; from diminishing inflationary pressures to relieving monetary shortages. It was even thought that control of this sector would "moderate the wage demands of the workers."[6]

On paper—it must be admitted—Popular Unity's plans for the Area of Social Property sounded plausible enough. What the Chilean public (and for that matter, even ordinary supporters of the government) could not know in 1970 was the degree to which the whole concept was but a fragile mask covering critical differences of view within the victorious coalition. After a honeymoon period which lasted for most of Allende's first year, those differences—over methods of acquisition of industrial properties, over the proper boundaries of the public sector, over the relationship between Social Property enterprises and the industrial labor force, over the internal organization and management of the "reformed" firms themselves, and finally, over the relationship of the Area of Social Property to the economy as a whole—surfaced with a virulence which could not be wished away. The failure to resolve them introduced tensions within the government, and between the government and its opponents, which eventually proved fatal to the regime and to its stated aspiration to introduce a "second model for transition to a socialist society."

The Formation of the Area of Social Property

Since so much was made—by President Allende and others—of the opportunities offered by the Chilean institutional context for a legal transition to socialism, it seems appropriate to review the nature of the devices which were available.

The first was the prerogative of any government to expropriate foreign property. By 1970, international law and practice generally recognized this right, although the standards of compensation were not very clearly defined. Traditionally, such matters were left to whatever agreement could be reached by the affected parties, and sometimes also by their respective governments. Negotiations over compensation typically extended over rather long periods of time—particularly where minerals and hydrocarbons were concerned—and their outcome often responded as much to consideration of future investment policies as to the abstract rights of the expropriated parties or the hypothetical value of their properties. In the case of Chile, the principal locus of foreign investment was the copper industry, whose overarching importance requires separate treatment elsewhere in this book. However, it is worth noting here that in nationalizing American holdings in this industry, Allende chose not to rely upon the broader norms of international law, but specifically sought (and obtained) from the Chilean Congress a constitutional amendment which empowered him to proceed. While the copper companies themselves (and the United States government) did not accept the Chilean position on the matter of compensation, their grievances found virtually no resonance within the Chilean polity or within the local court system. In short, having obtained specific legislation, Allende's right to expropriate copper was not in doubt, and therefore did not become a domestic political issue.

The matter became more complicated, however, when the Popular Unity government turned to *Chilean* industrial and financial holdings. The state could, of course, purchase any firm outright—provided it could come up with the money to pay for it, and provided, also, that the owners wished to sell (or could be persuaded to wish to sell). Beyond this, the legal options rapidly narrowed. Article 10 of the Chilean Constitution countenanced expropriation "when the interests of the national community so require, [of] natural resources, productive resources, or other elements declared to be of preëminent importance to the economic, social, and cultural life of the country," but outlined with exceptional clarity the limits which such procedures were obligated to respect:

> No one [the same article went on the say] can be deprived of his property save by virtue of a general or special law which authorizes the expropriation for reasons of public utility or social interest, as defined by the legislation author.
>
> The expropriated party will always have the right to compensation, whose amount and conditions of payment will be fairly determined, taking into account the interests of both the community at large and that of the expropriated parties. The law will determine the norms for fixing the indemnification, the tribunal which will hear appeals concerning the amount of compensation, which in every case will adjudicate in conformity with the law, the form of liquidating this obligation, and the opportunity and manner in which the expropriating agency will take material possession of the expropriated property.[7]

Nearly half a century of judicial interpretation left little doubt that this document required vast circumspection in the treatment of private property. In the 1960s, it severely constrained efforts at land reform, until the Frei administration succeeded in obtaining an amendment of its own design in order to broaden the criteria for expropriation and loosen the requirements for compensation. However, the Christian Democratic amendment applied exclusively to rural holdings; it was only when this much was made explicit that the parliamentary representatives of the Right were persuaded to vote for it.[8]

Thus, firms which the Popular Unity government did not wish to (or could not) purchase outright could not easily be expropriated under Article 10—again, in the absence of specific legislation, and even then, only when the state was willing to offer prompt and effective compensation. However, searching through the maze of legal precedents, Allende's strategists uncovered an almost forgotten decree-law, Number 520 of August 30, 1932 (never subsequently repealed) which could serve as an instrument for the ready acquistion of industrial properties.[9] Specifically, it enabled the president to "requistion" temporarily industries and businesses which produced or distributed articles "of basic necessity" in the event that they ceased production, failed to produce articles "of primary necessity" contracted for by the government, or "unjustifiably" produced deficiencies in supply. "Requisitioned" industries were subject to attachment (*incautación*) of equipment and installations, and in such cases their management and directorate were replaced by a delegate (*interventor*) appointed by the Department of Industry and Commerce of the Ministry of Economics.

The same decree-law permitted the expropriation of firms for similar reasons, but in such cases full payment in cash was required for the property seized, and approval of a government board of legal advisers. (In other words, it followed very closely the guidelines for expropriation outlined in Article 10 of the Constitution.) Significantly, the section of Decree-Law 520 dealing with expropriation was not much used during the Allende period; only seven firms were nationalized under this clause, probably because of the high costs involved.[10]

The president could also take over industrial plants by recurring to various legal dispositions which provided that, in case of labor conflict in enterprises producing articles of prime necessity, the authorities were empowered to name a civilian or military interventor to facilitate resumption of production and normalization of conditions within the enterprise. During the final years of Christian Democracy, these provisions were somewhat amplified. Workers in any plant paralyzed by labor conflict could request intervention. The procedure called for a vote by an absolute majority of workers through secret ballot, in the presence of a labor inspector.[11]

Two points emerge from this analysis. One, that the Allende regime generally chose not to avail itself of the existing provisions of the law which permitted expropriation, because (a) they required specific enabling legislation, which the government judged impossible to obtain from Congress, and (b) they required effective payment for expropriated properties, which Popular Unity could not (or would not) countenance. Two, that the Allende government therefore recurred to legal expedients which indisputably allowed the temporary takeover of factories (through requisition or intervention), *but not the transfer of ownership*. "On this latter point," one Chilean legal scholar has explained, "there was never any difference of opinion between the opposition and the government . . . . What occurred in practice was that requisitions were very carelessly defined from a legal point of view, such that, having established their temporary nature, the law did not indicate the maximum period of time allowed" them. The same applied to interventions presumably intended to resolve labor disputes. "The powers of the interventor were uniquely and exclusively limited to those acts which had as their objective the solution of the labor conflict . . . Intervention was . . . an essentially transitory measure . . . in no case destined to transfer property from private hands to those of the state.[12] In this distinction lay the seeds of a very serious legal and institutional conflict.

The Course of Acquisition: Purchase

During the first months of the new regime, the potential for controversy was minimized by following the path of least resistance—purchasing firms outright. Several factors encouraged this course. The government had inherited a large fund of foreign exchange which could be drawn upon to pay indemnities. Many well-to-do Chileans (as well as some foreign investors) imagined that the end had come, and in a mood of panic and despair, rushed to sell their holdings while there was still a willingness to pay for them, even at a fraction of their true worth. For example, the powerful Edwards family, one of the wealthiest in Chile, fled the country during the first days of Allende's presidency, and began negotiations (subsequently broken off) for the sale of their properties, which included *El Mercurio*, the nation's most prestigious newspaper. Finally, while the government could not technically compel anyone to sell who did not wish to, it could bring considerable pressure to bear through its broader powers in the area of economic policy.

A prime example was the banking system. On December 30, 1970, President Allende announced on nationwide radio and television his intention of acquiring ownership of the nation's nearly two dozen financial institutions. On that occasion he promised that a bill would soon be sent to Congress to obtain the necessary financial authorization. In the meanwhile, during the next 40 days (later extended to an indefinite period), the government would purchase shares of any stockholder who wished to sell, on a sliding scale of compensation which rose in inverse proportion to the value of his holdings. As things happened, however, the promised legislation never materialized. Instead, Allende veered along a more circuitous route. In the same address on December 30, the president announced that he would exercise his prerogative to reduce interest rates from 44 to 31 percent, lower still "for certain economic activities and some businesses."[13] What declining profitability could not be accomplished through lower interest rates, massive withdrawals by government agencies could; in February 1971, the State Development Corporation—surely one of the largest public depositors—removed its holdings from private banks. The forced departure of foreign concerns—First National City Bank of New York, the Bank of Brazil, Bank of London and South America, Bank of America, and the French and Italian Bank of South America—further undermined the Chilean financial structure, for these were the sources from which local houses obtained short term lines of credit, reported to sometimes amount to as much as $250 million at a time.[14] That the Popular Unity government succeeded in making private banking an unattractive proposition (and therefore, providing strong incentive for stockholders to liquidate their shares) cannot be doubted. In 1971, the newly-nationalized banking system—consisting of ten acquisitions plus the Central Bank and the State Bank—showed whopping financial losses.[15] However, Allende's political purposes had been achieved; by March 1972, only three banks in Chile remained in private hands, and the state possessed a virtual monopoly of credit.

The government was also able to obtain controlling interest in several large foreign firms—notably, subsidiaries of Radio Corporation of America and General Tire (in which the government was already a partner), and concerns producing chemicals, ceramics, glass, copper products, and refined sugar. The two locally-owned shipping enterprises—Compañía Interoceánica de Navigación and the Compañía Sudamericana de Vapores—were persuaded to sell out to the state, the latter only after it became clear that no alternative existed.[16]

Efforts to acquire a majority of the stock of the Compañía General de Papel y Cartones, S.A., were less successful. This particular case was replete with political significance: the company was controlled by the Alessandri family, and attempts to nationalize it were seen (quite rightly) as a vindictive swipe against a defeated opponent, who happened also to be the leader of the country's conservative political community. More to the point, as one of the two national concerns manufacturing paper and newsprint (the other already government-owned), the absorption of the Alessandri firm would have given Popular Unity the means to impose a tight monopoly over printed matter. This in turn would violate the spirit (and very probably the letter) of the Statute of Democratic Guarantees, to which Allende had solemnly subscribed in order to obtain Christian Democratic support during the congressional deliberations over the outcome of the 1970 elections.

There were few illusions as to what was at stake here, and the opposition made the most of its opportunities. A National Freedom Fund was successfully established to outbid the state for the shares of any stockholder who wished to sell, and the government was eventually forced to abandon its plans. Efforts to acquire the Alessandri paper enterprise are also of interest for what additional details they afford concerning the process by which reluctant industrialists were persuaded to cooperate with the government's plan to buy their properties. Through its price-control mechanism, the Allende regime decreed increases for raw materials used to manufacture paper, but, at the same time, it required a freeze on the cost of the finished product—"a patent effort to bankrupt the company."[17] This tactic was not technically illegal, and produced favorable results for Popular Unity in a number of other concerns, where low (or disappearing) profit margins drove stock prices down, and made the purchase of shares far less expensive than would otherwise have been the case. In one other instance, somewhat similar to the Alessandri affair, the Zig-Zag publishing complex, which comprised a chain of popular magazines, including a prominent opposition weekly, a book publishing house, and a network of newsstands throughout Chile, was effectively bankrupted by huge wage increases decreed after a prolonged strike by the Communist-controlled Printers Union.[18] Purchased by the government in its nearly moribund condition, it became the basis for a new state publishing house.

In cases involving purchase, the government did not ask for budgetary appropriations from Congress. Therefore, while the pressures brought to bear upon industrialists skirted the bare edge of legality, it was arguable whether indeed President Allende had ever possessed the authority to make such use of public monies in the first place. This point might have become the axis of judicial controversy over the expansion of the public sector, were it not for a decisive shift by government forces to other methods by late 1971 and early 1972.

The Course of Acquisition: Requisition and Intervention

The vast majority of firms which passed under the control of the state during that Popular Unity period were seized under the provisions of Decree-Law 520 ("requisition"), or, to a lesser extent, under existing legislation intended to resolve labor disputes ("intervention"). The wording of the former is strongly indicative of the historical context in which it was drafted, namely, the depths of the Great Depression, when factories all over the world were involuntarily closing their doors. Intended as a temporary expedient to resume the production of articles of prime necessity, it nonetheless armed Allende with an instrument to confront slowdowns of any sort, or (as things later developed) to deal with employer lockouts.

Leaving the latter aside for the moment, it is obvious that what constituted a failure to produce articles of prime necessity depended wholly upon one's political frame of reference. Since several hundred cases were involved, most of them imperfectly documented, it simply is not possible to say with any assurance how many factory requisitions were justified under the terms of Decree-Law 520. Many plants were seized on the pretext of employer "sabotage," "investment strikes" (e.g., failure to make new investments), or withdrawal of liquid assets—charges which may or may not have been accurate, but which in the worst of cases afforded no legal grounds for expropriation. Given the wage-price scissors imposed by the government in 1971, whose effect was to reduce (or even abolish) the profitability of individual enterprises, the failure of employers to increase or even maintain production could have been nothing more than a rational response to the laws of the market and of economic incentive.[19] Likewise in this context, genuine labor disputes involving wage and working conditions, and those artificially ignited for the sole purpose of provoking a government take-over (intervention), became indistinct.

Much evidence has come to light—both during and after the Allende regime— pointing to requisition and intervention as part of a coherent strategy rather than the reaction of a beleaguered government faced with an uncooperative industrial class. In April 1972, *El Mercurio* ran over several days' time an internal Popular Unity government article which outlined in considerable detail methods recommended to achieve the nationalization of large enterprises. Special emphasis was placed on labor agitation to create a situation requiring intervention, and the economic "asphyxiation" of enterprises through the purposeful application of price controls. Economics Minister Pedro Vuskovic immediately claimed that the document was a fabrication, but was soon embarrassed by the admission by MAPU Secretary-General Ambrosio that it was the draft of a document produced by his party's Industrial Commission, two of whose members were high-ranking functionaries of the economic team, including Vuskovic's most immediate subordinate, Undersecretary of Economics Oscar Garretón. The document itself—purged of some of its more revealing references ("labor agitation," "economic asphyxiation of enterprises")—was actually published by the MAPU some months later. Further, in October 1972, the Socialist party journal *La Aurora de Chile* even allowed itself to fret publicly at the failure of workers—in this case, in two large sugar refineries—to "mobilize to demand requisition."[20]

One MAPU trade union organizer in Santiago and Valparaíso, interviewed in European exile since the coup, has provided remarkably specific information on how these incidents were staged.

> Taking a particular area [he relates], we'd find out which factories had been involved in the most [labor] disputes, which were the best organized politically, and which were reducing or even sabotaging production. On this basis, we'd select one for an agitational program.
>
> Activists would distribute pamphlets and bulletins throughout the area, especially at factory gates. This made other workers aware of the issue. Meanwhile, the party [MAPU] would strengthen contacts inside the factory, raising the possibilities of the workers requesting intervention and especially expropriation. These projects had to be carefully planned. Spontaneity meant the risk of serious setbacks . . .
>
> So the workers took the initiative . . . They demanded a rise [in wages] which wasn't given, then occupied the factory in order to get it expropriated.[21]

Nonetheless, the precise relationship between worker occupation of plants and their requisition by the government cannot be stated simply. In some cases, the occupiers were clearly responding to directions from above, particularly in some of the older industries.[22] Here the regime sought both to create a pretext for acquisition, while at the same time posing as a responsible authority striving to canalize or even contain revolutionary effervesence. In others, the initiative was taken by militants of the Popular Unity parties, without the approval (or perhaps even the prior knowledge) of the government, which made it appear as if Allende was being challenged by a "revolution from below."[23]

Behind these insurrectionary appearances, however, lay not the industrial working classes as such, but contending forces on the Left for the control of the labor movement, and by indirection, of the political process itself. Prototypically, these were leaders who represented the more "advanced" elements of Popular Unity—MAPU, the Izquierda Cristiana, or the left wing of the Socialist party. Often initiating these actions, or assisting in their organization, were members of the labor wing of the MIR, the Frente de Trabajadores Revolucionarios (FTR). "Spontaneous" factory seizures (that is, occupations unplanned by the government) had the potential of embarrassing the regime, and also saddling it with plants it did not need or want, but since the method itself was so useful in expanding the public sector, Allende could not easily repudiate it whole cloth. Difficulties later arose within Popular Unity over the excessively casual recourse to this tactic, but at the beginning, at least, the government was apparently satisfied to rely upon agitation to acquire enterprises, even if this spilled over into sectors not originally contemplated for inclusion within the area of Social Property.

Quantitative and Qualitative Growth, 1971–1973

The disjointed fashion in which firms were brought into the public sector had some peculiar consequences. In the first place, it was never possible to say exactly how many enterprises had actually been incorporated. Table 5.1 lists some estimates, arranged chronologically, but does not exhaust the possibilities.

These variations warrant some explanation. The regime resisted defining the Area of Social Property in numerical terms; or, more precisely, its definition changed several times, but was never established once and for all. Further, some enterprises, seized by their workers, became the responsibility of the public sector, but were never formally annexed to the Area of Social Property, and therefore never were officially acknowledged as having passed under government control. There were "waves" of occupations, followed by lesser countercycles in which some firms were returned to their owners. Periods of particularly intense factory occupations (not always, however, completely reflected in the figures in the table) seem to have been May–June

TABLE 5.1
Estimates of Numbers of Firms in the Public Sector

Date	Estimate	Source
September 1970	43	[Owned by state at time of Allende's election]
September 1971	187	Rexford Hudson [1]
December 1971	150	Barbara Stallings [2]
May 1972	263	SOFOFA [3]
June 1972	264	*El Mercurio*, June 22, 1972
Mid-1972	500	Landsberger and McDaniel [4]
October 1972	211	Barbara Stallings [5]
December 1972	202	Pedro Vuskovic [6]
	240	Instituto de Economía y Planificación [7]
February 1973	250	*The Economist*, February 24, 1973
May 1973	285	Pedro Vuskovic [6]
June 1973	526	Paul Sigmund [8]
September 1973	335	Junta estimate [9]

Additional Source Notes: [1] "The Role of Constitutional Conflict over Nationalization in the Downfall of Salvador Allende," *Inter-American Economic Affairs*, XXXI, 4 (1978), p. 64; [2] *Class Conflict and Economic Development in Chile, 1958–1973* (Stanford, 1978), pp. 131–132; [3] Sociedad de Fomento Fabril, a private interest group representing Chilean industry; [4] "Hypermobilization in Chile, 1970–73," *World Politics*, XXVIII, 4 (1976), p. 327; [5] *Class Conflict . . .*, pp. 156–157; [6] *Las Noticias de la Ultima Hora* (Santiago), June 7, 1973; [7] *La economía chilena en el año 1972* (Santiago, 1973), pp. 96–98, 135; [8] *The Overthrow of Allende and the Politics of Chile, 1964–76* (Pittsburgh, 1977), p. 215; [9] República de Chile, *Un año de reconstrucción* (Santiago, 1974).

1972, when the government began to encounter serious economic and political difficulties;[24] October 1972, during a general strike of the opposition, characterized (among other things) by widespread lockouts; and June 1973, when the regime was faced with an abortive military coup. This would account for the unusually high figure of Landsberger and McDaniel (Table 5.1).

These fluctuating but generally rising statistics also chart a gradual change in the role assigned to the public sector. Initially, the acquisition of enterprises was intended to serve economic ends, with attendant (and obviously much desired) political consequences to follow shortly. However, by mid-1972 the priorities seem to have been largely reversed. Factories were henceforth occupied as part of a political strategy to disarm or at least threaten the industrial bourgeoisie, which was by then seen (not unnaturally) as the mainstay of the opposition. Thus, for example, President Allende's appeal to workers to occupy their factories during the crisis of June 1973. At a somewhat more sophisticated level, the rapid expansion of government control over industry was expected to undercut the alarming advances which the opposition forces (particularly Christian Democrats) were making within the labor movement by mid-1972. (Traditionally in Chile, as elsewhere in Latin America, employees of public enterprises found it well advised to vote for the party in power.) Finally, some of the more leftward elements of Popular Unity (as well as the MIR) looked upon factory occupations as preliminary exercises in the creation of a parallel state. This concept, with its strong anarcho-syndicalist associations, held the economic logic of such acts to be essentially irrelevant to the broader quest for power.

Second, by countenancing the use of quasi-legal methods of acquisition, control of which was not always possible, the government was faced with a public sector whose configuration only partially conformed to its objectives. That is, although after December 1971 the *number* of enterprises formally or informally incorporated into the Area of Social Property never fell below 150—the figure mentioned in Allende's 1970 campaign program—*the actual industries seized* did not fully coincide with those alleged to "monopolistically [control] the entire market." "As a result," one high-ranking economic functionary has recalled, "many enterprises originally planned for inclusion remained under the control of monopoly capital." He complains, for example, that by mid-1972 "only 7 of . . . 90 enterprises originally planned for the social sector had become state property. [These were in fact purchased outright.] Another 29 had been requisitioned or intervened. Yet," he points out, "113 firms not on the list [of 90] had been requisitioned or intervened. As late as July 1973, 32 of the 90 were still in private hands. Of these, 22 were industrial firms, and the value of their production alone was equal to the total production of all the enterprises which had been requisitioned or intervened."[25]

The survival of important salients of private enterprise to the very end of the regime was obviously of political significance, if only for the financial base which such corporate entities represented for the opposition. These islands of capitalism—however prominent on the horizon—were not, however, themselves large enough to relieve the government of responsibility for an enormous portion of the industrial economy. That is, the sheer number—if not always the economic magnitude—of plants seized and held by the forces of Popular Unity made the performance of the public sector an unavoidable determinant of the government's overall economic success.

The Public Sector Under Allende

Long before the elections of 1970, the state was recognized as an important, and in some ways even critical force in Chilean economic life. Beginning in the final years of the nineteenth century, and followed by a particularly intense period in the 1930s, it had enlarged its patrimony to include the nation's railroads, its urban transportation facilities, most electric power outside the Santiago-Valparaíso metropolitan region, petroleum exploitation and refining, and one of the country's two woodpulp and paper enterprises. It either owned or controlled companies producing steel, chemicals, sugar, light

metals, fertilizers, fishmeal, petrochemicals, electronic equipment, and computers. During the Christian Democratic years, the tendency towards public
ownership was considerably strengthened, among other things, through the
acquisition of the majority of shares in the principal mining enterprises.

This did not make Chile a socialist state—most major industrial activities
before 1970 remained in private hands—but it did point to a firmly-grounded
tradition of public ownership, and perhaps more important still, a commitment to industrialization through public rather than private initiative. For in
the three decades prior to the advent of Popular Unity, the Chilean state had
also enlarged its role as investor-initiator of a wide variety of projects, reaching a new plateau in the development-conscious 1960s. Thus, for example,
between 1961 and 1969, direct public investment in physical capital (between
7 to 9 percent of GDP) expanded at an annual rate of 6.3 percent, and
"accounted for at least 50 percent of the gross capital formation since 1950."
If indirect public investment was added, "the share of total public investment
in gross domestic capital formation [rose] from 46.6 percent in 1961 to 74.8
percent in 1969."[26] This explains why Allende's minister of mines was not
reluctant to describe the country Popular Unity inherited in 1970 as "already
the nation in Latin America (excluding Cuba) where the state had the greatest
participation in economic activity."[27] It also accounts for some of the optimism with which Allende's economists contemplated the expansion of the
public sector. If this was what it could do within the presumed confines of
capitalism, "dependency," and "imperialism," what miracles were not to be
expected under a more comprehensive and decisively socialist framework?

The lynchpin of the pre-Allende public sector was the Chilean State Development Corporation, more commonly known by its Spanish acronymn
CORFO. Founded in 1939 by the Popular Front government to finance reconstruction of earthquake-devastated areas, the Development Corporation
quickly became a catalyst for import-substituting industrialization. Between
1940 and 1970 it served as a financial agency responsible for the development
of basic industries in Chile, particularly those requiring heavy outlays for
machinery and sophisticated technology. It extended credit both for working
and investment capital; it guaranteed foreign loans to domestic enterprises; it
participated in the equity of both public and private enterprises; it established
artifically low interest rates, favorable terms of amortization, and so forth.
One economist described the corporation as a "sui generis investment bank,"
differing from its counterparts elsewhere in that it operated "as a nonprofit
organization, . . . [dispersing] its vast resources without applying the traditional rules of profit-motivated investment banks." Further, it did not float its
own liabilities, create species, or accept deposits. Instead, it obtained its
yearly capital from government contributions, foreign or domestic loans, and
income derived from its own activities.[28]

The role of the Development Corporation in the Chilean economy was always a point of controversy, since it not only financed new public enterprises, but made loans to ongoing private concerns, and also "rescued" (absorbed) those on the verge of bankruptcy. Further, it was often said to divest itself of public enterprises once they became profitable. In other words, many saw CORFO as largely an instrument of state capitalism, utilizing government monies to advance the private sector at the expense of the public.[29] However, without the Development Corporation there would have been no significant public sector in Chile, and certainly none so heavily centered in vital areas of production and technology such as steel, chemicals, and computers. Probably the most important legacy of this particular critique was the conviction that both the Development Corporation and the public sector would function more effectively if loans were channeled exclusively to government enterprises, as in fact occurred after 1970.

On paper, the record of state-as-investor and state-as-initiator of new and basic industries appeared to be a resounding success. That is, by 1970, the range of products elaborated within the country had increased by quantum amounts over 1940. However, import-substitution industrialization, in Chile as elsewhere in the Third World, led to neglect of traditional exports and the curious reversal of trade patterns, wherein items formerly produced at home (foodstuffs and some producer durables) were now imported, often at the cost of increasing amounts of scarce foreign exchange.[30]

Even more to the point, the Development Corporation was never placed on a firm financial footing, a fact which was hidden from the Chilean public for thirty years by clever accounting procedures. State contributions to CORFO were supposed to come from both general revenues, and taxes on foreign-owned copper-mining concerns. In practice, however, in the early years the Corporation's activities were almost exclusively financed by levies on American copper companies (although only a minority of these revenues were actually transferred to the Development Corporation.)

After World War II, CORFO began to draw upon another source—foreign loans, particularly from the United States, or from U.S.-dominated multilateral lending agencies. The Development Corporation was supposed to operate as a quasi-neutral agency, mediating between foreign financial institutions and national enterprises. In fact, however, it habitually converted the hard currency it received from the U.S. and other Western credit sources into domestic soft loans. Without escalator clauses to compensate for Chile's rampant inflation, "only a fraction of the real value of these loans [had] ever been repaid by the recipient enterprises."[31] Even after dollar clauses were introduced into agreements after 1960, effective repayment was rarely insisted upon. In short, since inflation tended to shrink drastically the true value of CORFO's loans for repayment purposes, the recipient enterprises could al-

TABLE 5.2
Financial Balances of Public Sector Enterprises Owned Before 1970
in the Period 1971–1973
Expressed as a Percentage of Expenditure of GDP

1971	1972	1973
(–)4.3	(–)5.4	(–)8.4

Source: Alberto Martínez, "The Industrial Sector: Areas of Social and Mixed Property in Chile," in S. Sideri, ed., *Chile, 1970–73: Economic Development and Its International Setting* (The Hague, 1979), p. 280.

ways show a successful record of operation. Meanwhile, the deficits (representing hard currency obligations overseas) were quietly transferred to the Chilean state in the form of a burgeoning national debt.[32]

Such lending procedures meant that recipients of CORFO loans were liberated from conventional demonstrations of creditworthiness, and, whether public or private enterprises, were able to operate essentially without much concern for normal standards of profitability. Insofar as the public sector was concerned, the Chilean experience was, of course, hardly unique: in many Western countries, notably Italy and the United Kingdom, state enterprises were long recognized to be money-losing propositions, and subsidized out of general revenues or taxes levied on the private sector. What was distinctive about the Chilean case was the failure to recognize frankly that the public sector could operate in the black as long—but only as long—as two conditions were present: (1) a profitable mining sector capable of generating a fairly high level of tax revenues, and (2) a ready and continuing source of hard currency loans to permit the Development Corporation to continue its politically convenient credit practices. When both of these conditions disappeared after 1971, the deficits of the public sector could no longer be hidden from view.

For reasons already indicated, it is difficult to establish the precise dimensions of the public sector under Popular Unity, and therefore, the figures for its performance. However, what data we do have strongly suggest that moderate losses before 1970 simply increased by leaps and bounds in the three subsequent years. Table 5.2 illustrates what happened to the "old" (pre-Allende) public sector enterprises from 1971–1973.

Particularly large losses were sustained by the National Electric Company (ENDESA), the Agricultural Marketing Enterprise (ECA), and the Chilean Chemical Company (SOQUIMICH); the all-important copper mines, reorganized as a state monopoly (CODELCO) in 1971, just barely broke even in 1972 and 1973. When consolidated with the "new" state industries (that is, firms incorporated into the Area of Social Property), the figures are equally unimpressive. Expressed in the same terms as Table 5.2, the indices for 1972 and 1973 are (-)4.7 and (-)6.2, respectively.[33] To state the matter more concretely, in 1972 the Social Property enterprises showed a deficit of 22 billion escudos, approximately 60 percent of the revenues collected that year. By mid-1973, Pedro Vuskovic, now vice-president of the Development Corporation, was projecting the losses of the Area of Social Property to be *nine times* what they had been in 1972, "almost double the total revenues that the State would collect during the entire year."[34] Clearly, something more than an extension of previous financial practices was afflicting the public sector in Allende's Chile.

The Labor Movement and the Public Sector: An Uneasy Partnership

The failure of the Social Property enterprises to turn a profit derived in large part from an inability to fully harness the Chilean labor movement to the government's overall economic objectives. At first glance, this seems paradoxical: here, after all, was a Marxist regime whose principal base was an industrial working class loyal to Communist and Socialist trade unions. However, party identification was one thing, ideology and practice quite another. In the early days of the Chilean labor movement, this disjunction did not exist, since unions were illegal and there was no apparent way of satisfying even modest economic goals through total structural change. The introduction of a comprehensive labor code in 1924 altered this situation by recognizing—in however limited a fashion—the right of labor to pursue narrowly economic objectives within the existing political structure.[35] Thereafter, the persistence of labor support for Marxist parties arose less out of an unsullied commitment to revolutionary change, than to the conviction (often ratified by concrete experience), that in the limited universe of economic and political choices, only the Communists and Socialists could afford to advocate unlimited "revindicationist" (bread-and-butter) gains for labor. Put another way, the close relationship between the labor movement and the Marxist parties was sustained by mutual pragmatic needs—that of the former to advocate its economic interests at the centers of power (Congress, the Labor Ministry, the courts), that of the latter for a constituency, once they opted in the mid-1930s to play Chilean politics by the traditional rules of the game.[36]

Repeated surveys carried out during during the decade prior to Allende's assumption of power confirmed the fundamentally incrementalist (as opposed to revolutionary) outlook of industrial labor in Chile, and at all levels. Perhaps not surprisingly, as one descended from general secretary through shop steward to the worker on the line, the ideological profile of Marxist affiliation became increasingly indistinct.[37] But even when one reascended to the apex, "the first overriding concern" of labor leaders remained that of "obtaining economic betterment" for their membership.[38] This did not mean that the

Marxist trade unions in Chile did not take their "maximum" programs seriously, but rather, that these were subordinated to second, third, or even fourth place in the hierarchy of organizational commitments.[39]

As long as the Marxist parties remained in opposition, the anomaly of an essentially moderate labor movement marching under revolutionary banners presented no particular problems. Within Communism and Socialism proper, "ideologists" and "pragmatists" could coexist more or less comfortably, debating a future which was, after all, problematical. Those who believed that revindicationist objectives should dominate labor activity simply did what came naturally, while even those who favored more revolutionary uses of the union movement could regard day-to-day economic struggles as politically instructive, and useful in preparing the working class for some final, definitive confrontation.

Once Allende was elected, however, resolution of this fundamental contradiction could be postponed no longer. Had Popular Unity come to power through a coup or foreign invasion, it could have imposed that model of industrial relations which prevails in all socialist countries, in which labor unions act as collaborators, rather than adversaries, of management. However, the *sui generis* nature of the Allende regime made this impossible. Still pursuing a majority at the polls, Popular Unity could not afford to disavow the dominant revindicationist thrust of labor activity, whether the management toward which it was directed was private or public. Moreover, faced with an increasing challenge within the labor movement both to its left and to its right, the government found it difficult to impose a policy of wage restraints.[40] Consequently, the one fundamental need of the regime in the industrial sector—to increase production at minimal cost—worked against the other, equally basic requirement in the political arena: the need to retain and even expand its support within the industrial working class.

In spite of ritual reaffirmations that the gap between Marxist labor, on one hand, and socialist management on the other, could be bridged by careful negotiations and "political education,"[41] the trade union movement as a whole continued to view industrial relations in conflictive terms. Appeals to win the "battle of production" after 1971 were greeted with cynicism and disbelief, partly because the numerical majority of firms remained in private hands, but partly, too, because this constituted so abrupt a reversal of the historic Marxist critique of supply-side economics. Further, far from inaugurating an era of industrial peace, the advent of Popular Unity was the cue for an unprecedented wave of strikes, surpassing even the record figures for the late Frei years, the last of which is included in Table 5.3.

Particularly striking was the large and increasing number of stoppages in public sector enterprises. The ratio of strikes in such firms "increased [between 1971 and 1972] from 12 to 25 percent; the number of workers went up

TABLE 5.3
Aspects of Industrial Strife in Chile, 1970–1973

	1970	1971	1972	1973
Number of Strikes	1,819	2,696	3,325	2,050
Number of works involved	656,170	298,677	393,954	711,028
Working days lost	2,814,517	1,387,505	1,678,124	2,503,356

Source: James W. Wilkie and Peter Reich, eds., *Statistical Abstract of Latin America, 1977* (Los Angeles, 1977), Table 1407.

to 31 percent, i.e., one out of every three striking workers [in 1972] was employed in the public sector."[42] Notable for their negative impact upon the economy as a whole were walkouts in the nationalized copper mines. According to one study produced by Popular Unity economists at the University of Chile, during 1972 one out of two miners went out on strike, and in 1973, this most vital of Chilean industries was crippled by a stoppage lasting 74 days and inflicting upon the public sector an estimated loss of $70 million.[43] There was also an increase in the number of short or "wildcat" strikes, prototypically (but not exclusively) fomented by the ultra-Left. As early as March 1971, President Allende was urging workers "not to ask for salaries higher than the possibilities warranted by their firms,"[44] and at the Sixth Congress of the CUT in December, federation vice-president Edgardo Rojas (Communist) took note of what he called "frankly provocative and divisionist expressions by some declassed elements," which he labelled "objectively counter-revolutionary."[45]

It was perhaps predictable that in a political coalition whose ultimate shape was still undefined, there would be some jostling among rival groups. Thus, newer elements on the left sought to outbid the Communists and Socialists for support among industrial workers. More ironic, however, was the way in which the government's discomfort was aggravated by activities of the opposition, which (again, in a remarkable reversal of roles) now urged upon workers the most extensive revindicationist goals. This was true not only of the Christian Democrats, who after all had a labor movement of their own, but also of such astringently conservative forces as the National party.

Locked into a pattern of adversary relations with management which could not easily be discarded after nearly a half-century of practice, and beset of unprecedented waves of inflation, the working class as a whole took little note of the government's dilemma. "All trade unionists I interviewed throughout Chile [during the Allende years] maintained that unions should be autonomous and have the right to strike," one American Marxist reported. "One Socialist leader stated that the day they lost the right to strike, he would stop supporting the government."[46] There was no end to strikes, nor did the government forfeit much support from its traditional bastions. However, its capacity to retain the loyalty of most industrial workers derived less from a shared vision of the good society (and how to arrive at it) than from a hard-nosed and by no means inaccurate judgement on the part of labor— pinned between the fires of the ultra-Left on one hand, and those of the combined Center and Right on the other—that the Allende regime had no choice but to accede to its demands.[47]

Management and "Workers' Participation"

The government's problems with labor were compounded by its inability to forge a successful policy of socialist management. As one economic functionary reported in early 1972, there was "no immediate and automatic substitution of capitalist rationality in the enterprises transferred to the social property sector by a new socialist one."[48] For obvious reasons, however, the old system could not be allowed to remain intact, either. Instead, what emerged was a curious hybrid, whose elements often worked at cross-purposes.

At the level of macroeconomic planning, there was a distinct failure to integrate the Social Property enterprises, partly because of the haphazard fashion in which they were acquired, but also because workers who seized a plant were often loath to subordinate it to ODEPLAN, CORFO, or other government agencies.[49] Wage and price policies, dictated at the Economics Ministry, often caused distortions when applied at the factory level. One European economist found that the costs of labor and materials "were subject to steep and sudden change . . . . When, during 1972, the government began to allow large price rises, these were conceded reluctantly and after long delay. Some foodstuffs, manufactures, or services might be held at 10 escudos for six months, so that production began to be carried on at a loss, and then suddenly the price was raised to 26 escudos, resulting in a profit for a few months until costs once again surpassed the authorized selling price."[50] "Sometimes," confessed the same economic functionary quoted above, "workers [were] keen to get higher prices for their products, or [disliked] producing products which [were] not so profitable." The result, he said, was that "enterprises often [received] conflicting instructions."[51]

Within intervened or requisitioned factories, top management was replaced or superseded by a government official (interventor), or—in particularly large ministries— by a committee designated by the Economics Ministry. These functionaries were political appointees, more often than not with no experience in the particular industry, or, on occasion, in any other.[52] When the size of the enterprise required a collective executive, the composition of this body was determined by a system of quotas derived from the mathematical proportions representing the electoral strength of each party within the Popular Unity coalition. Given the ideological differences which divided these elements from one another—particularly the Communists, Radicals, and moderate Socialists from the far and farthest Left—a coherent policy of management was difficult to shape, much less apply. The same quota system determined the appointment of personnel at the ministries, at ODEPLAN, and in the Development Corporation, so that the lines of conflict ran not only horizontally, but vertically as well.[53]

The introduction of socialist management into several hundred industrial plants was also accompanied by something of a cultural revolution—the backwash of several decades of left-wing populist preachments, dispensed by the Marxist parties, their labor movement, and to some extent, by the Christian Democrats themselves. Its operative features were, in the words of one critic, "contempt for intelligence and the practical problems of economics . . . [underestimating] the problems of initiative and administration, and in fact [regarding] one part of the higher technical staff [of a plant] as parasites, and practically all of its [managerial and technical] components as easily replaceable."[54] Two experts on Latin American labor relations have pointed out that Chilean industry was already suffering a breakdown of authority during the two or three years prior to the election of Allende, but they emphasize the superabundance, after 1970, of

> accusations—which could be proved by examples, but not systematic statistics . . . that many engineers and managers had been dismissed after takeovers, not only at the insistence of government-appointed managers, but of workers. Indeed, there was said to be a general climate of outright insubordination, hostility, and aggressiveness against educated persons, especially those in authority, in part explicitly encouraged by extreme left political groups.[55]

These grievances could not have been wholly imaginary, since they have been indirectly confirmed from certifiably pro-Allende sources. At the IDS-ODEPLAN conference, members of the economic team frankly admitted frequent "management difficulties" arising out of government attempts to impose technocrats—as opposed to labor militants—as interventors of requisitioned enterprises.

> One union group [the conference was informed] had explained that in their industry, workers' representatives preferred to cooperate with a worker as interventor or director, rather than with a professional man, however highly qualified and politically motivated he was. However, owing to the inherent educational limitations in a workers' background, it was not easy for him to acquire the knowledge necessary for fixing sales and purchasing policies, or for giving effective production directives.

An expedient which reportedly was applied with some success in one of the largest plants, was the appointment of a figurehead worker-interventor, with real power entrusted to a technical staff of CORFO delegates ("advisers").

"However," they recounted—apparently without irony—"it was important the advisors should carry out this function without antagonizing the [workers' representatives] or abrogate to themselves authority, such as that [the latter] felt that it was not taking the final decision itself."[56] How well such compromises worked elsewhere (when and if they were applied) cannot be stated; however, even where party men were permitted to exercise full authority as directors of Social Property enterprises, there was no necessary end to conflict with the work force. One Socialist party document which surfaced in March 1972, even recited the familiar complaint of disillusioned revolutionaries of every time and circumstance—that the new class of interventors received excessively large salaries, and drove around in company cars "just like capitalists."[57]

To close the gap between labor and capital in the Social Property enterprises, the government drafted plans for a parallel system of management, widely advertised as "workers' participation." On a practical level, the new structures were intended to persuade labor to act "responsibly" toward public management;[58] no less important, on a strictly ideological plane, these bodies were expected to rescue Chile from all those "bureaucratic deformations" into which every socialist experiment since 1917 had unfailingly fallen.[59]

The rules for this new system of industrial relations were set forth in *Basic Norms for Participation for Workers in the Administration of Enterprises in the Area of Social and Mixed Property*, a charter produced by a government-CUT working group in mid-1971. Like all such products of Popular Unity, this document was really a treaty between warring forces rather than a blueprint for action—in this case, between the rigidly hierarchical concept of authority inherent in the Communist tradition of "democratic centralism," and the libertarian and populist notions which informed all of the other parties of the governing coalition. In theory, the *Basic Norms* reposed all the power in a given factory in its labor force, sitting as a sort of committee-of-the-whole ("workers' assembly"). From this body were hived off workers' delegations and representatives of the labor force at all levels of authority, including the enterprise Board of Directors. When these structures were placed next to, or superimposed upon, preexisting forms of factory organization, the result, according to one sympathetic foreign observer who reported to the IDS-ODEPLAN conference, was

> very complex and almost baroque. Fifty separate committees, often with overlapping membership, were to be set up in various shops, sections, and departments of an enterprise [in this case] of about 1,000 workers.
>
> Although an elaborate hierarchical structure existed on paper, it was not clear if there was to be any real hierarchical relationship between the committees. At

the top there was the administrative committee, and below the coordinating committee, both with responsibilities for the whole enterprise; in the absence of further details about their respective roles, the scheme was not at all clear.[60]

Whatever other controversies remain, there is a remarkable unanimity of view that "workers' participation" in Chile never operated the way it was supposed to.[61] According to one estimate, by the event of the regime the relevant organs of participation were fully operative in only thirty-five enterprises, very roughly ten percent of the firms incorporated into the public sector.[62] An important source of resistance was the trade union movement itself, whose leaders—excluded under the *Basic Norms* from sitting on the plant executive committee—"feared a displacement of their traditional functions."[63]

Even more striking was a lack of enthusiastic response from the industrial working class itself. "Paradoxically, the groups with the longest experience of class struggle and the longest tradition of class organization under leftist leadership were the ones least interested in participating in decision making within the nationalized firms," one investigator found. Typical of the more established elements of the labor movement were workers of a large textile plant he surveyed. There, many skilled workers and a few highly motivated shop stewards appeared capable of embracing a larger view of the process. But the unskilled, while reportedly sympathetic, were generally unclear as to what "participation" meant. Lower management was sharply divided: in favor, suspicious, or flatly opposed.[64]

It is far more difficult to say what effect "participation"—or lack of it—had upon the actual performance of individual plants. Since the issue is so laden with ideological baggage, survivors tend to recount their experiences wholly in terms of their particular world view. One Communist interventor (who, likes his confreres, strongly preferred "consultation" to participation) credits the success of his enterprise to the preservation of conventional administrative norms.[65] In contrast, advocates of the participatory model (in this case, a Socialist) attribute increased production to a sudden wealth of input from the assembly line.[66] More typically, the "radicals" and their many foreign sympathizers) are forced to explain systemic failures—unfulfilled production targets, enterprise losses, or an excess of strikes. This they do by pointing to the persistence of traditional management practices ("paternalism,"[67] or "the gradual bureaucratization of the new structures"[68]). In other words, if structural change failed to increase productivity, it must not have been drastic enough. To the extent to which workers' participation was supposed to stem the vigorous revindicationist tradition of the Chilean labor movement, however, there can be no question that it failed to achieve its purpose.

It is very possible that the participation structures introduced by Popular Unity had precisely the opposite of their intended effort. Rivalries within the

Left, heretofore confined to union elections, were often displaced to the parallel organs of management. Having failed to make serious inroads into the Communist-Socialist-dominated CUT, the newer parties (MAPU, Izquierda Cristiana, above all the MIR) could nonetheless hope to capture the factory councils and workers' assemblies.[69] The conflictive theater of labor relations in Chile thus witnessed a new and hitherto unforseen spectacle: management and unions *both* confronted by a third force, pursuing the same tactics as those formerly employed by the CUT in the pre-Allende period, and bidding for support of the rank-and-file by staking out the most "advanced" positions.

In this way, participation structures became something of a sorcerer's apprentice. "Instead of the kind of controlled mobilization that a successful system might have represented," two political scientists remark, "the UP was increasingly faced with an uncontrolled mobilization, which it clearly did not want: a widespread refusal to obey any kind of institutionalized and previous legitimate authority, and a rise of "indiscipline'."[70] A high-ranking member of the economic team, not normally given to excesses of critical self-examination, nonetheless concurs, at least to the extent of characterizing workers' participation as a "double edged" sword. "On one hand," he writes, "there was a considerable increase in the initiative taken by the workers in all fields . . . On the other . . there is evidence of a certain amount of labor disorder: absenteeism, unjustified work stoppages, and failure to perform the allotted tasks."[71]

Industrial Performance: Productivity and Profitability

The regime's own social, economic and foreign policies also contributed—indirectly, but very materially—to a negative environment for Chilean industry. Its deliberate promotion of social polarization created a situation where, we are told, "in order to counteract the right-wing offensives," workers had to "spend much of their time in demonstrations, meetings, and political activity, much of which cut down on working time."[72] The existence of a ubiquitous black market—the fruit of an unrealistic pricing policy and its attendant shortages—added an incentive for laborers to absent themselves from their plants, either to queue up for scarce commodities, or even to engage in a bit of clandestine trade on their own, particularly if theirs was an industry in which wages were partly dispensed in kind.[73]

Further, spending policies which led to a moratorium of payments on the foreign debt as early as November 1971 and a refusal of compensation to the expropriated copper companies, seriously undermined Chile's creditworthiness, translated in time into shortages of spare parts, certain essential raw materials, and cash flows of various sorts.[74]

TABLE 5.4
Estimates of Industrial Production, 1970–1973

Estimator	1970	1971	1972	1973
INE	(–)0.3	+ 14.7	+ 2.8	(–)4.3
SOFOFA	n/a	+ 10.8	+ 2.5	(–)6.5

Sources: Instituto Nacional de Estadísticas (INE); Sociedad de Fomento Fabril (SOFOFA).

It is far easier to identify these factors, however, than to weigh their actual importance. For example, insofar as production is concerned, the figures from both government and opposition sources agree that there was no serious drop until 1973.

It is not clear—nor can it be made so—how much the decline in 1973 was due to a shortage of spare parts, particularly when the figures aggregate other data, such as the number of work days lost through strikes, which rose 150 percent over the previous year (Table 5.3).[75] However, it seems probable that the spare parts problem was aggravated unnecessarily. A wide variety of sources repeatedly cite poor maintenance of existing equipment, a common affliction in societies (of what ideological coloration) which experience a sudden collapse of traditional authority.[76] In addition, the regime's economic planners employed the concept of "idle capacity" without much precision or care, as if it were possible to measure accurately what in more advanced industrial societies (with far better statistical material than Chile) has proven extremely elusive.[77] There was a tendency to define idle capacity in social rather than economic terms, e.g., how much the regime *wanted* to produce (or Chileans to consume) rather than how much its plant and labor force was really capable of turning out.[78] The net result must have been rather hard on the machinery. Thus, a Swedish Marxist resident in Chile during the period records that to travel within the country "was indeed expensive, and to obtain tickets correspondingly difficult. Within the capital demands for fares increased tremendously; employment was high, and many a worker could for the first time afford to take the bus to the factory." But, he adds, as a consequence, "part of the local transporation system almost broke down, and traffic congestion in greater Santiago reached new heights of absurdity."[79]

In any event, the problem of the Social Property industries was less one of gross production than of profitability. Apart from their vulnerability to heavy wage demands from organized labor, the public enterprises were forced to carry the burden of the regime's full employment policies. While the artificial boom of 1971 subsided in 1972, and the indicators registered a perceptible drop in 1973, employment figures continued to rise (Table 5.5); it simply cannot be assumed that—given the general business environment—that the

TABLE 5.5
Employment and Population in Chile

Year	Employed Population (in thousands of persons)	Unemployed	Rate of Employment (percentage)
1970	2,770.1	180.0	6.1
1971	2,906.1	114.8	3.8
1972	2,998.9	95.9	3.1
1973§	3,015.6	152.0	4.8

§Employment figures for 1973 are considerably lower than they otherwise would have been, since they encompass the months of September-December (after the coup), during which there were massive dismissals.

Source: Planning Office, Latin American Demographic Center.

newly-employed were finding work in private industry. Rather, public sector enterprises continued to hire, causing a decline in unit productivity—that is, more workers were paid to produce the same amount (or, in 1973, substantially less).

The Social Property industries also suffered from the same price controls which forced many private firms to operate at a loss. Perhaps indeed the public sector fared even worse, since the greatest impact of losses imposed by controls reportedly fell upon "those traditional state enterprises which were using the most widely-utilized inputs (electricity, fuel, and others), and consequently, influencing the greatest number of prices." Caught between the need to maintain and expand its political base by increasing employment and holding consumer prices down, and pressures to reduce deficits in the public sector industries, the government allowed itself to be pushed along the path of least resistance—that of continuing to run the latter in the red. There was a certain short-term political logic to this option, but it transformed the Area of Social Property from its original economic purpose—"accumulating surpluses"—to something quite different, namely, "distributing resources."[80]

Political Conflict, 1970–1973

The economic problems provoked by the rapid expansion of the public sector were matched by an increasingly acute political and constitutional conflict. Two points were at issue: one, the legality of individual plant requisitions and interventions; the other, the definition (size) of the Area of Social Property.

The first was fought out largely in the courts and with a quasi-judicial body known in Chile as the Office of the Comptroller-General of the Republic (*Contraloria General de la República*).[81] Here Popular Unity was operating on distinctly disadvantageous grounds, since, as noted earlier, almost all of the Social Property enterprises had been seized under Decree-Law 520 or existing labor legislation, neither of which permitted the actual transfer of ownership.

Between August and December 1971, the Comptroller-General declared invalid the requisition of eight major enterprises, a practice which he would repeat many times thereafter. Then, in January 1972, the first of an extended series of court decisions overturned a presidential decree authorizing the acquisition of the Yarur textile mills, one of the largest firms affected by what were in effect *de facto* expropriations. In April, the judiciary took up the apparently spontaneous seizures (*tomas*) of several factories by their workers, and found these lacking even the flimsy legal underpinnings afforded by Decree-Law 520. In cases of the first sort, the regime typically accused the courts of infringing upon the prerogatives of the executive branch, and in that of the second, steadfastly refused to provide the physical force necessary to dislodge the occupiers. By late 1972 relations between the president and the Supreme Court had all but broken down, with the president insisting upon the inviolability of his decree, and the court just as firmly reminding him of the limitations of existing law.[82] Even Allende's chief legal advisor and the architect of the strategy to acquire industrial properties through intervention and requisition, could not help wondering aloud "whether it is still possible to think that revolutionary changes can be made lawfully."[83]

The obvious way out of this impasse was to seek specific legislation from Congress authorizing the creation of an Area of Social Property. The government put off doing this until the Christian Democrats seized the initiative and sponsored a bill of their own. The proposal in question was introduced into the Senate on October 14, 1971, by two Christian Democratic members, Juan Hamilton and Renán Fuentealba, in the form of an amendment to the Chilean Constitution.

The Hamilton-Fuentealba bill, better known as the Three Areas Amendment, (1) defined the enterprises that the government could control directly (the social sector), those it could operate in conjunction with private enterprise (the mixed area), and those which would forever remain in the private sector; (2) required separate legislation for the expropriation of each individual enterprise; (3) annulled Decree-Law 520, sources of much of the pending litigation in the courts and of the conflict between the president and the comptroller-general; (4) declared illegal all expropriations carried out after the date the bill was first introduced into Congress; (5) displaced the government's idea of a state-controlled Area of Social Property with self-managed businesses in all sectors, based on what was purported to be the Yugoslav model.

It is not difficult to see why the Popular Unity leadership had no taste for this particular piece of legislation. Apart from imposing an indefinite moratorium on *de facto* expropriations, it forced the government to justify before Congress the acquisition of companies on an enterprise-by-enterprise basis. Allende's coordinator of the Development Corporation has claimed that under this latter arrangement, "even had the government enjoyed the collaboration of Congress, it would have required at least twelve years for bills representing planned nationalizations to complete their path through Congress."[84] If this is so, then the only recourse for expeditious formation of the Area of Social Property was to convoke a plebiscite. On repeated occasions in the course of debate over nationalizations, this was precisely what the congressional opposition challenged President Allende to do, and what—just as repeatedly—he opted not to do. Therefore, by his own choice, the locus of conflict remained in Congress—dominated, to the very end of his regime, by the forces of the opposition.

The Three Areas Amendment was passed by the Senate on November 18, and by the Chamber of Deputies on December 21, 1971. It was sent to President Allende for signature after Congress reconvened following the (Chilean) summer recess in late February, 1972, and vetoed by the chief executive a month thereafter. On July 7, the Senate overruled by simple majority most of the 33 objections upon which Allende based his veto, and forwarded the bill to the Chamber of Deputies, which, after much deliberation and many negotiations, eventually ratified the decision of the Upper House by a vote of 60 to 24, taken nearly a year later on April 25, 1973.

The President then appealed to the Constitutional Tribunal to rule on the question of whether a simple majority (as opposed to a two-thirds vote) was sufficient to override a presidential veto.[85] On May 30, the Tribunal declared itself incompetent to rule on the issue on the somewhat casuistical grounds that Article 78(b), letter (a) of the 1970 reform to which it owed its existence as a judicial body, did not specifically empower it to rule on Constitutional amendments, only on ordinary legislation. Apparently, then, the President's veto stood.[86] But—and here, the crucial point—to have buried the Three Areas Amendment still did not provide the government with the power to expropriate industrial properties, or relieve it from the obligation to cooperate with the courts and the comptroller-general in the matter of factory occupations.

On October 19, 1971, a few days after Hamilton and Fuentealba introduced their Three Areas Amendment into the Senate, the president sent Congress a bill of his own, drafted by Communist party chief (and Senator) Luis Corvalán. Oddly enough, although Popular Unity came to power on a platform explicitly promising the establishment of the foundations of socialist society, and had been in office for nearly a year, this was the first time that it allowed itself to state numerically the intended dimensions of the Social Property area.[87]

The Corvalán bill identified 150 "strategic" industries which it requested the authority to nationalize. Nonetheless, nothing in the proposed legislation indicated what would happen to intervened or requisitioned plants which did not figure on the list, of which there were by that time several score. When the opposition majority in Congress rejected the Corvalán bill, the government in January 1972, produced a reduced list of 90 firms which it proposed to acquire instead. However, from now on the government estimates of what it wanted where constantly being revised—and invariably upward. On February 7, 1972, while his "list of 90" was being considered by Congress, Allende told an audience in Concepción that in the coming year (1973) he proposed to nationalize "another 120 industries."[88] On May 1, the President mentioned yet another figure—this time, 181 firms. The October strike of 1972 confused the matter still further, by adding those plants acquired through worker occupation.

In an attempt to regularize the situation, the regime submitted in January 1973 the so-called Millas-Prats bill, "which requested congressional approval for the expropriation of 49 firms on the list of 90 which had been intervened or requisitioned during the October strike, and the [additional] power to expropriate any 'strategic' enterprise."[89] The fate of another 123 firms occupied by workers and managed by the state or factory committees was to be determined by a Commission of Special Cases chaired by the Minister of Labor, which was empowered to return them to their former owners if found by the commission not to be of "strategic character for national industry."[90]

Before Congress could act upon the new bill, however, on March 4, 1973, Allende suddenly amended it to include "an additional 44 enterprises to be expropriated (for a total of 93) and to further extend his takeover powers. He also issued an insistence decree [which overruled the findings of the comptroller-general] which made 'official' the takeover of 40 companies."[91] Although this was the last time the regime identified the desired boundaries of the Area of Social Property, by comparing Table 5.6 (below) with Table 5.1, it is clear that what the government said it wanted and what it actually took were almost never the same.

Behind the constantly shifting estimates lay a serious division within Popular Unity itself. According to one knowledgeable internal source, the relevant differences actually predated the regime itself, and turned on "the general definition of the character of the Chilean revolution and of the tasks thus suggested for the people's [Allende's] government." From the very beginning, the Communists apparently favored an "anti-imperialist, anti-

TABLE 5.6
Definition of the Area of Social Property

Date	Place	Size
1970	UP Electoral Program	Not stated numerically, but defined as industries which "as a rule . . . have a strong influence on the nation's social and economic development."
October 1971	Corvalán-authored bill sent to Congress by Allende	150 "strategic" enterprises
January 1972	Executive announcement	90 enterprises
February 1971	Allende's speech in Concepción	Another 121 enterprises
January 1973	Millas—Prats bill	49 firms on the "list of 90" intervened during the October strike, plus the power to expropriate (unspecified) "strategic" enterprises
May 1973	Millas-Prats bill as amended by Allende	44 additional enterprises
	Decree of insistence	40 more companies

Source: "The Popular Unity's Programme," in J. Ann Zammit, ed., *The Chilean Road to Socialism* (Brighton, Sussex, 1973), p. 266; Rexford A. Hudson, "The Role of Congressional Conflict over Nationalizaion in the Downfall of Salvador Allende," *Inter-American Economic Affairs*, XXXI, 4 (1978), pp. 63–80.

monopolist" government which would lay the foundations for a (vaguely defined) future "transition to socialism," while the Socialists and other elements of the Left held, in contrast, that "the initiation of socialism [should] be a task for this government and not simply an historical perspective.[92] When applied to the construction of the Area of Social Property, these apparently theoretical divergences had some remarkably concrete political and economic consequences. Roughly speaking, the Communists advocated capturing the "commanding heights" of the economy and isolating "monopoly capital"— as reflected in the 1970 Popular Unity electoral program, for which they were very largely responsible. For the Socialists and their allies on the Left and ultra-Left (MAPU, Izquierda Cristiana, and MIR), the boundaries of the capitalist system could not be so neatly traced; in their view, in fact, to divide enterprises into "monopolistic" and "nonmonopolistic" categories was "a false distinction."

> We stressed [one MAPU militant recalls] that the prospect of socialism divides loyalties along class lines—that the bourgeoisie as a whole would resist, which meant a need for popular power, working class organizations within the shell of the bourgeois state.[93]

Edward Boorstein reflects the frustrations and despair which comments such as these provoked within the leadership of the Communist party:

Some UP people seemed to think that the destruction of the material base of the ruling class would by itself solve the problem of power in Chile. By creating a state sector and destroying the material base, one was setting up a new "alternative" power which would somehow take over from the old power.

I have never read or heard a clear explanation of how the transfer of power would come about, or how destroying the material base would solve the problem of the armed forces of the bourgeois state.[94]

To add to the confusion, there was, one government economist reports,

a lack of clear criterion for determining what was meant by monopolistic or strategic activities, and the subsequent attempts to find definitions caused much dissent within the UP . . .

From a strictly political viewpoint, it was necessary to establish the dividing line between enemies and possible allies, or at least, sectors which could be neutralized . . .

The activities of power groups, from a strictly technical point of view, extended to the monopolistic and oligarchic areas as well as those areas where a certain degree of competition existed. Therefore, an additional criterion was regarded in order to fix a general demarcation line.[95]

These remarks go far to explain why President Allende preferred to postpone the exact definition of the Area of Social Property as long as humanly possible. Even when forced to do so in the face of a Christian Democratic alternative (the Three Areas Amendment), the President's blueprint was forever undergoing modification brought about by the visible manifestation of internal coalition pressures, the force of events themselves, and the shifting evaluations of his advisers as to what constituted the most opportune mix of tactical and economic considerations. By mid-1972 it was obvious that some sort of compromise with the Christian Democrats was necessary if any legislated solution was to be found. In June, a series of talks were initiated by Christian Democratic party president Renán Fuentealba and Minister of Justice Jorge Tapia Valdés. Within fifteen days these negotiations had broken down irretrievably. The subsequently published correspondence between the two principals leaves no doubt that Allende's representative simply was not in a position to make any meaningful concessions, particularly in those areas dealing with the discretionary powers of the executive.[96]

By late 1972 the picture had become more complicated still by the increasing practice of requisitioning plants for purely political reasons, particularly at crisis-points in the life of the regime (October 1972; June 1973). It was easier to invite workers to seize control of their factories than to know what to do when the emergency had passed. While the comptroller-general continually reminded President Allende that Decree-Law 520 did not authorize expropriations, even in a *de facto* fashion, leaders of his own party warned him not to take a single step backwards. Thus, when the government was wavering on the eve of the 1973 congressional elections over the return of factories requisitioned during the October strike, Senator Carlos Altamirano stated that

> as Socialists we have a clear and categorical position on this. We believe that no occupied enterprise should revert to its former owners; this applies not only to the strategic, monopoly enterprises, but also to the smaller ones which have passed over to the social sector of the economy as the result of being abandoned by their owners or attempts by the latter to paralyze them.[97]

This left Allende with no clear political alternative except to go into elections hoping to win a decisive majority in parliament, which in turn would give him unlimited authority to reorganize the Chilean economy. When this did not materialize, the regime entered into its final crisis.

Summary and Conclusions

The "second model" for the transition to socialism outlined by President Allende in his First Message to Congress presupposed the existence of two indispensable elements: one, in an institutional order sufficiently flexible to admit legislation of substantial changes in the system of property relations; and two, a decisive majority—a consensus, if one will—in favor of those changes, as expressed through the appropriate representative organs. There is little doubt that Popular Unity inherited the first, but it is equally obvious that it never managed to acquire the second. In spite of repeated charges that Congress no longer reflected Chilean opinion (since most of its members had been elected before 1970), and that a substantial shift was evident in the combined percentages of Allende and Tomic (the "ideological majority" thesis), it is revealing to note that the regime never reposed sufficient faith in its own propaganda to try its propositions out by calling a plebiscite. Very probably Allende recognized from the start that there was no majority for socialism in Chile, but believed that through clever manipulation of the political and economic resources readily available to any Chilean chief executive, such a majority could be coaxed into existence.

This led him to attempt to introduce socialism through the back door by administrative and quasi-legal devices. In the early months of the regime, this strategy appeared deceptively simple. In the atmosphere of panic which prevailed among the ranks of the Chilean wealthy following the 1970 elections, more than one industrialist was willing to cut his losses and sell his properties the regime for whatever he could get for them, and those not so convinced could often be persuaded through the imposition of arbitrary wage raises and price controls. When the government began to meet with some resistance to these tactics (or when, in the judgment of some of its more "advanced" elements, matters were not moving quickly enough), it recurred to Decree-Law 520 or to labor legislation which allowed the (temporary) requisition or intervention of industrial enterprises.

These measures clearly afforded only short-term relief, but with the expected profits of the requisitioned enterprises, combined with the economic boom generated by the government's 1971 expansionary policies, it was possible to anticipate that a majority for socialism could be bought—and secured as well—through a plebiscite which would forever alter Chile's political institutions. All of this was to be accomplished before the government had to face up to the legal consequences of its confiscatory acts.

Perhaps at one particular point in the life of the regime this tactic might have worked although when such a decision should have been taken has provoked much subsequent debate. The most commonly mentioned date is April 1971, immediately following the national municipal elections, in which Popular Unity received slightly more that 50 percent of the vote. Yet even then, Allende's own party felt insufficiently sure of the results to urge postponement—permanently, as events were to prove.[98]

Whether or not April 1971, was a unique opportunity irretrievably lost, from then on the prospects for a popular vote in favor of a new economic and political system sharply declined. In large part this was due to the disappointing performance of the Area of Social Property. Apparently ignorant of the fact that public sector enterprises in Chile had traditionally run at a loss, Popular Unity simply assumed that the profits of newly-nationalized firms would finance continued economic expansion, and also the regime's ambitious social welfare program. Instead of generating surpluses, however, most of these firms lost money; as the number of firms requisitioned and intervened rose, so too, and often in a geometrical fashion, did the deficits. To cover these losses, the regime printed more paper money, even though the lavish emissions of the Central Bank pushed inflation to unprecedented heights. This in turn undermined the popularity of the regime with the electorate generally, and therefore made the convocation of a plebiscite all the more inadvisable.

Theoretically, Popular Unity could reduce its deficits by raising the price of products turned out by the Social Property enterprises, or even return unprofitable firms to their owners. In fact, however, neither of these measures were considered politically feasible. To increase prices to the level of profitability flew in the face of the need to retain and expand the government's following among low-income consumer,[99] while a wholesale return of requisitioned plants (apart from the ideological embarrassment and the threat of a rebellion on the farthest Left), would lead to massive dismissals of workers hired largely to satisfy political, rather than economic criteria.

These contradictions were aggravated by broader political problems. The Area of Social Property was the source of endless theoretical squabbles on the

Left—over the intended size of the public sector, its proper role, the use of its resources, even whether it was necessary for public enterprises to show a profit at all. One economist speculates that the reason why so many functionaries of Popular Unity favored the indiscriminate expansion of the public sector was that they imagined that in this way the captured enterprises would be "withdrawn from the market and the 'law of value'."[100] Others point to the narrowly political goals of confiscation—either to destroy the economic base of the bourgeoisie, or to capture more votes through the attachment of more workers to government-run enterprises.

If the seizure of industrial firms introduced elements of dissention and difficulty among the government and its friends, it acted as a remarkable unifying agent among the forces of the opposition. The process by which this took place, however, does not appear to be very well understood by Allende's people even now, many writing from their places of exile with the benefit of hindsight. The accession of more conservative elements to the control of the Christian Democratic party in 1972—replacing a more leftist, "communitarian" leadership—is often described by veterans of Popular Unity as if it were nothing more than a change in the weather.[101] Yet, ironically, employing strictly Marxian categories of analysis, it is easy to interpret this development in terms of a massive shift of that party's base. Clearly, the haphazard fashion in which nationalization of industry proceeded, the constant refusal to define once and for all the boundaries of the Social Property area, and the reluctance (or even inability) to return firms which by no stretch of the imagination could figure on any list of "monopolistic" or "strategic" enterprises, struck fear into the hearts of the Chilean middle class. It was this fear—by no means wholly irrational—which provoked the October strike, (an event precipitated by a perceived attempt to nationalize the trucking industry, in Chile the small business operation par excellence) as well as a chain of subsequent political and economic difficulties. And what was true for the Christian Democrats was more valid still for the Radical party, the quintessential expression of the provincial petty-bourgeoisie, which left the Popular Unity coalition and crossed over to the opposition after President Allende vetoed the Three Areas Amendment in April 1972.

If one moves from the level of political parties to the specific groups whose interests they aggregated, this point becomes even clearer. During the first months of 1971, Economics Minister Vuskovic convened a series of meetings with representatives of Chilean industry.

> It could be seen in these meetings [one of Vuskovic's aides recalls] that the majority of entrepreneurs were from medium-sized sectors rather than from monopolistic groups. The general trend at these meetings was that the entrepreneurs demanded the formulation of guarantees which would be offered to the medium-sized entrepreneurs.[102]

On the face of it, this demand was not particularly remarkable, indeed, was eminently in accord with Popular Unity's electoral program, which had gone as far as to hold out the hope of a tactical alliance with these groups. Yet those precious guarantees were never given. While the disorganized fashion in which the government went about creating the Area of Social Property provoked an acute sense of psychological and political insecurity among small and medium-sized entrepreneurs, the failure of the public sector enterprises to turn a profit also inflicted concrete economic damage on these potential allies. The more favorable access to credit which they had been promised in 1970 quickly evaporated after 1971, when every spare escudo had to be diverted to cover the massive and growing losses of the nationalized firms.[103]

Lacking access to short lines of credit—a virtual government monopoly after Allende's first year—small businessmen found it difficult to acquire spare parts and raw materials, and were often forced to shut down operations until the missing elements could be located, usually in a vigorous black market.[104] The policies of increasing wages and holding prices constant undermined or erased the profits of public and private industries alike, but while the former could cover their losses with emissions from the Central Bank or soft loans from the Development Corporation, no such safety nets existed for the "non-monopolistic" private entrepreneur.

The failure of the Area of Social Property to operate the way it was intended thus constitutes a principal cause, perhaps indeed *the* principal cause, of Allende's downfall. By failing to win over or even neutralize the constituencies of the Center and Center-Left, Popular Unity could not hope to construct the "second model" of which the President so eloquently spoke.

The price of Allende's failure, however, was not merely abandonment of the prospect of a legal "transition to socialism," but the very survival of the regime itself. For the Area of Social Property was not created in a political vacuum. By late 1972 it was clear that Chile was suffering from an acute institutional crisis. The president could intervene and requisition industrial enterprises, but he could not legally expropriate them; according to the courts and the comptroller-general, he could not even hold them for an indefinite period. The one body capable of giving him that authority—and the Congress—refused to do so. The only recourse which remained was a direct appeal to the people, an expedient which Allende chose for reasons of his own not to employ.

Instead, to break the stalemate, the president turned to the Chilean military. In November 1972, Army Commander General Carlos Prats assumed the Interior Ministry, while two other flag officers accepted the portfolios of civilian departments. In exchange for these stabilizing actions, however, the military extracted from President Allende a promise to reach an agreement with the Christian Democrats and with Congress on the matter of the Three Areas Amendment, or to call a plebiscite upon it.

In effect, Allende could do neither, but in an environment of strikes and hyperinflation, it was no longer possible to temporize. The knot was broken on September 11, 1973, when many of the same generals whom the president had used so successfully turned against him, and shattered the precarious legal and political balance upon which Popular Unity had reposed from the very start.[105]

Notes

1. Luis Figueroa, "Participation under the Popular Unity Government," in Zammit, ed., *The Chilean Road to Socialism*, pp. 187–88, and José Ibarra, "Some Aspects of the Popular Unity's Development Model," in ibid., p. 61.
2. *Chile's Road to Socialism*, tr. J. Darling, (Harmondsworth, Middlesex, 1973), p. 140.
3. "The Popular Unity's Programme," in Zammit, *The Chilean Road to Socialism*, pp. 266–267.
4. Alberto Martinez, "The Industrial Sector: Areas of Social and Mixed Property in Chile," in Sandro Sideri, ed., *Chile, 1970–73: Economic Development and Its International Setting* (The Hague, 1979), pp. 228, 236.
5. *Documents on the Chilean Road to Socialism* (Philadelphia, 1977). Vols. 1–2, pp. 23–24.
6. Genaro Arriagada Herrera, *De la via chilena a la via insurrecional* (Santiago, 1974), pp. 107–108.
7. *Constitución política de la República de Chile* [Texto actualizado al 31 de mayo de 1973. Edición revisada y puesta al día por Francisco Cumplido C. y Cecilia Medina Q.] (Santiago, 1973), pp. 15–16.
8. Kaufman, *The Politics of Land Reform*, pp. 166–177.
9. A veteran student of Chilean politics and jurisprudence has defined decree-laws as "act[s] of the executive by which legislation is enacted without authorization by delegation and in clear usurpation of the powers." He goes on to explain that "in Chile, numerous [decree-laws] have been issued by various de facto governments since the adoption of the Constitution of 1925, giving rise to difficult juridical questions . . . However, the Supreme Court has ruled that 'during the period of the military governments of 1924 and 1925, in which no legislative organ existed, the courts applied decree-laws and accepted them without restrictions as obligatory and efficacious norms, emanating from the only authority in effective control of the government.' Since 1932," he continues, "the Supreme Court has maintained this view in numerous decisions, recognizing that presidential orders in times of constitutional abnormality were as valid as any other laws, and accepting executive legislation by decree as a *fait accompli.*" Federico Gil, *The Political System of Chile* (Boston, 1966), p.100. Acceptance of the validity of *past* decree-laws did not, however, enable Presidents to recur to this expedient whenever they wished, since the logic of the Supreme Court's findings required the absence of a legislative body. Congress was continually in session throughout Allende's presidency.
10. Paul Sigmund, *The Overthrow of Allende and the Politics of Chile, 1964–76* (Pittsburgh, Pa., 1977), p. 33; Arriagada, *De la via chilena*, p. 139.
11. Arriagada, *De la via chilena,* p. 139.
12. Ibid., pp. 138–139.

13. Allende, "The Nationalization of the Banks," in *Chile's Road to Socialism,* p. 84. As an official of First National City Bank of New York later explained to Senate investigators, "We had great difficulty in the face of certain governmental measures" taken during the period between Allende's inauguration and the point at which the government decided to nationalize the bank's holdings. "For example," he explained, "interest rates on loans were ordered to be dropped substantially at a time when banks were required to give 40 percent across-the-board salary increases to their entire staffs." Furthermore, "permanent inspectors from the superintendent of banks were assigned to each bank and all operations were scrutinized on a daily basis. Later, important foreign exchange operations were assigned exclusively to government-owned banks; this further reduced income to our bank, which had been heavily engaged in foreign exchange and related transactions." Subcommittee on Multinational Corporations of the Committee on Foreign Relations, U.S. Senate (93rd Congress, 2nd Sess.), *Multinational Corporations and United States Foreign Policy* (Washington, D.C., 1973) Part 1, p. 346.
14. Robert Alexander, *The Tragedy of Chile* (Westport, Conn., 1978), p. 152.
15. Markos J. Mamalakis, *The Growth and Structure of the Chilean Economy* (New Haven, 1976), p. 255.
16. Alexander, *The Tragedy of Chile,* p. 152.
17. Sigmund, *The Overthrow of Allende,* p. 157.
18. Arriagada, *De la via chilena,* p. 213n.
19. Of course, factory owners did not proceed upon purely economic grounds alone; they were being told by spokesmen for the government on an almost daily basis that their liquidation as a class was but a matter of time. The point, however, is that even in the absence of such unambiquous warnings, their conduct would have made sense strictly in economic terms.
20. Arriagada, *De la via chilena,* p. 213n.
21. Colin Henfrey and Bernardo Sorj [eds.], *Chilean Voices: Activists Describe Their Experiences of the Popular Unity Period* (Hassox, Sussex, 1977), pp. 45–46.
22. In the textile industry, the government did not even attempt to dissimulate its role. The seizure of the eight largest textile mills by their workers in May, 1971, came within hours of a speech by Economics Minister Pedro Vuskovic declaring these firms "monopolies" which would, as a matter of state policy, be incorporated into the Area of Social Property. The following day, the Minister toured the occupied plants to congratulate their workers on their revolutionary resolve. In the midst of a festival atmosphere, Vuskovic even declared that the Economics Ministry would "issue orders for requisition [in the future] if industries continue to be paralyzed " *(sic).* Arriagada, *De la via chilena,* p. 149.
23. This is the point of view developed in Michel Raptis, *Revolution and Counter-Revolution in Chile: A Dossier on Workers' Participation in the Revolutionary Process,* tr. John Simmonds, (New York, 1974), and also in Peter Winn, *Weavers of Revolution* (New York, 1986), pp. 159–196, which provide a vivid account of the manipulative techniques of the Socialist and MAPU parties at the factory level. Thus, many workers at the Yarur textile mill who supported their unions' "impossible" demands in April 1971, were artfully misled. As one woman, a MAPU sympathizer, later declared, "in voting to strike I had no idea that we were [provoking] government intervention in the factory" (p. 177).

President Allende himself saw through the ruse and opposed the action, but was finally forced to come around when Vuskovic and his deputy Garretón threatened to resign if the government did not ratify what was represented as the action of the "workers."

24. Ian Roxborough, "Reversing the Revolution: The Chilean Opposition to Allende," in Philip O'Brien, ed., *Allende's Chile* (New York, 1976), p. 202.

25. Pío García, "The Social Property Sector: Its Political Impact," in Federico G. Gil, Henry Landsberger, and Ricardo Lagos Escobar, eds., *Chile, 1970–73: Lessons of the Socialist Years,* tr. John S. Gilitz, (Philadelphia, 1979), 173, 175.

26. Markos J. Mamalakis, *The Chilean Economy* (New Haven, 1976), p. 279.

27. Sergio Bitar, qu. in Arriagada, *De la via chilena,* pp. 47–48.

28. Mamalakis, *The Chilean Economy,* pp. 295–296.

29. Oscar Guillermo Garretón, "Some Preliminary Facts about the Management and Organization of the Industrial Sector," in Zammit, *The Chilean Road to Socialism,* pp. 64–65.

30. Mamalakis, *The Chilean Economy,* pp. 311–312.

31. Ibid., p. 300

32. Ibid., pp. 253–256, 301–304.

33. Martínez, "The Industrial Sector," p. 270, and balances supplied by the Empresa Ferrocarriles del Estado, ENDESA, SOQUIMICH, and the Ministry of Finance.

34. Arriagada, *De la via chilena,* p. 236.

35. Julio S. Valenzuela, "The Chilean Labor Movement: The Institutionalization of Conflict," in A. and J. S. Valenzuela, eds., *Chile, Politics and Society,* pp. 157–158.

36. Ibid., pp. 162–163.

37. Ibid., p. 158; James Petras, "Nationalization, Socioeconomic Change, and Popular Participation," in ibid., pp. 181–182.

38. Valenzuela, "The Chilean Labor Movement . . .," pp. 142–144.

39. Ibid., Henry A. Landsberger, "The Labor Elite: Is It Revolutionary?", in Seymour Martin Lipset and Aldo Solari, eds., *Elites in Latin America* (New York, 1967), pp. 264, 271–277; Henry A. Landsberger, Manuel Barrera, and Abel Toro, "The Chilean Labor Union Leader: A Preliminary Report on His Background and Attitudes," *Industrial and Labor Relations Review,* XVII, 3 (1964), pp. 399–420; Henry A. Landsberger and Tim McDaniel, "Hypermobilization in Chile, 1970–73," *World Politics,* XXVIII, 4 (1976), pp. 503–504, 510–514.

40. Joan E. Garcés, "The Popular Unity Government's Workers' Participation Model: Some Conditioning Factors," in Zammit, *The Chilean Road to Socialism,* p. 183; and "Discussion on Social Consciousness and Socialist Commitment," in ibid., p. 218.

41. See the comments of CUT Secretary-General Luis Figueroa in "Discussion on the Question of Participation," in ibid., pp. 200–201.

42. Arriagada, *De la via chilena,* p. 220.

43. Sobel, *Chile and Allende,* p. 129.

44. Landsberger and McDaniel, "Hypermobilization . . . ," p. 524.

45. Quoted in Alexander, *The Tragedy of Chile,* p. 195.

46. Petras, "Nationalization . . . ," p. 199n.

47. Valenzuela, "The Chilean Labor Movement. . . .," p. 164.

48. Garretón, "Some Preliminary Facts . . .," p. 67.

49. Alexander, *The Tragedy of Chile,* pp. 191–192.

50. Alec Nove, "The Political Economy of the Allende Regime," in O'Brien, *Allende's Chile,* p. 64.

51. Garretón, "Some Preliminary Facts . . .," p. 67.

52. There seem to have been a fair number of practicing physicians appointed to preside over industrial operations, perhaps because of the shortage of other politically reliable professionals, or because this was Allende's own profession, and he was in a position to know many Socialist doctors—surely, for North Americans, an inconceivably exotic species. One was assigned as interventor of the Disputada de las Condes copper mine, where he proved a disaster. "But I understand that, withal, he was an excellent physician," one of the resident engineers dryly remarked when I interviewed him in 1980. For some of the difficulties facing interventors, told from a Communist point of view, see Henry and Sorj, *Chilean Voices,* p.33.

53. Ian Roxborough, et al., *Chile: The State and Revolution* (New York, 1977), p. 96. See also Jorge Tapia Valdés, "The Viability and Failure of the Chilean Road to Socialism," in Gil et al., *Chile at the Turning Point,* p. 304, and Jorge Tapia Videla, "The Difficult Road to Socialism: The Chilean Case from a Historical Perspective," in ibid., p. 36.

54. Arriagada, *De la via chilena,* pp. 111–113.

55. Landsberger and McDaniel, "Hypermobilization . . .," p. 520.

56. "Discussion on the Question of Participation," in Zammit, *The Chilean Road to Socialism,* pp. 198–199.

57. *The New York Times,* March 17, 1972.

58. Patricia Santa Lucia (pseud.), "The Industrial Working Class and the Struggle for Power in Chile," in O'Brien, *Allende's Chile,* p. 136.

59. "Discussion on the Question of Participation," in Zammit, *The Chilean Road to Socialism,* pp. 197–198.

60. Ibid., p. 199.

61. Landsberger and McDaniel, "Hypermobilization . . .," p. 528, cites a number of critical evaluations from UP functionaries; see also Martínez, "The Industrial Sector . . .," pp. 249–250, and Francisco Zapata, "The Chilean Labor Movement under Salvador Allende, 1970–73," *Latin American Perspectives,* III, 1 (1976).

62. Barbara Stallings and Andrew Zimbalist, "Showdown in Chile," in Paul Sweedy and Harry Magdoff, eds., *Revolution and Counter-Revolution in Chile,* p. 131.

63. Valenzuela, "The Chilean Labor Movement . . .," p. 136.

64. Petras, "Nationalization . . .," pp. 184–85, 195.

65. Henry and Sorj, *Chilean Voices,* p. 36.

66. Ibid., pp. 58–59.

67. James and Eva Cockcroft, quoted in Alexander, *The Tragedy of Chile,* p. 203.

68. Petras, "Nationalization . . .," p. 187; see also Henry and Sorj, *Chilean Voices,* pp. 49–50.

69. Arriagada, *De la via chilena,* pp. 217–218, summarizes the findings of two pro-Allende sociologists, Fernando Castillo and Jorge Larrain.

70. Landsberger and McDaniel, "Hypermobilization . . .," p. 529.

71. Martínez, "The Industrial Sector . . .," p. 249.

72. Roxborough, *Chile, The State and Revolution,* loc. cit.

73. Landsberger and McDaniel, "Hypermobilization . . .," p. 525, cite the case of the SUMAR textile plant; see also Arriagada, *De la via chilena,* pp. 235–236.

74. Barbara Stallings, *Class Conflict and Economic Development in Chile, 1955–1973* (Stanford, 1978), p. 134; Martínez, "The Industrial Sector . . .," p. 250.
75. Further, the figures combine the performance of both public and private enterprises, even though very different sorts of constraints were involved. Private firms found it difficult to obtain spare parts because of the regime's foreign exchange policies, rather than its deteriorating creditworthiness. (See Chapter Three.)
76. Landsberger and McDaniel, "Hypermobilization . . .," pp. 529–530.
77. For an exposé of the UP point of view, see Martínez, "The Industrial Sector . . .," pp. 225–255; for some idea of the theoretical and econometric difficulties of measuring idle capacity in major industrial countries, see Federal Reserve Bank of St. Louis, *Rates of Change in Economic Data for Ten Industrial Countries* (St. Louis, 1977).
78. Insofar as the labor force is concerned, there does not seem to have been much idle capacity left by the beginning of 1973, since by then the regime was very close to reaching its goal of full employment.
79. Stefan de Vylder, *Allende's Chile: The Political Economy of the Rise and Fall of Unidad Popular* (Cambridge, England, 1974), p. 97.
80. Martínez, "The Industrial Sector . . .," p. 241.
81. This autonomous agency, createed in 1927, was charged with the supervision of government fiscal policy. However, it was also "vested with a significant power that permits it to exert effective control over the executive, [inasmuch as] it takes cognisance of executive decrees and pronounces upon their legality, if necessary returning them for reconsideration by the executive within twenty days of the time in which they are received." Decrees which the Contraloria refused to register could nonetheless be promulgated by what was known as a "decree of insistence," provided the President was able to obtain the counter-signature of every member of his cabinet. In such cases, the Comptroller-General would then refer the relevant information to the Chamber of Deputies, which would then "initiate proceedings against the executive if it so wishe[d]."

    Chilean Presidents in the years prior to Allende found it expedient to limit their use of "decrees of insistence," such that one authority wrote in 1966 that such recourse was "now limited to those decrees which deal with expenditures authorized by laws, and then only if there is no usurpation of powers belonging to other branches of government."

    The Comptroller-General was appointed by the President with the consent of the Senate for a lifetime term, and the independence of this functionary was further enhanced by his ability to appoint his own deputy and other key personnel of the agency.

    In view of the subsequent attacks upon this agency by Popular Unity, it might be useful to conclude with an evaluation by the authority cited above, written long before the powers of the contraloría were questioned in the name of socialist notions of legality. "The mere fact that such an institution exists in the first place speaks highly for the country's traditional respect for legality. What is more, the Contraloria has not encountered any serious interference with its work from the chief executive in its thirty years of existence . . . . Far from being merely an auditing agency, the Contraloria is an alert custodian of legality, and a vigorous and effective instrument capable of curbing, if necessary, the excesses of a President constitutionally endowed with a great deal of power." Gil, *The Political System of Chile*, pp. 97–99.

82. Arriagada, *De la via chilena*, pp. 180–83, 251–257.
83. Eduardo Novoa, "The Constitutional and Legal Aspects of the Popular Unity Government's Policy," in Zammit, *The Chilean Road to Socialism*, pp. 29–30.
84. García, "The Social Property Sector . . .," p. 175.
85. Here is how a pre-1970 political science text deals with this subject: "The President may . . . veto the laws that Congress submits for his signature. The Constitution provides specifically for the item veto for all legislation . . . The presidential veto is only suspensive, and the Congress may enact legislation rejected by the President if it then is approved by a two-thirds majority of the members present." Gil, *The Political System of Chile*, p. 103.
86. Rexford A. Hudson, "The Role of Constitutional Conflict Over Nationalization in the Downfall of Salvador Allende," *Inter-American Economic Affairs*, XXXI, 4 (1978), pp. 66–71.
87. Part of the confusion arose from the fact that the 1970 Popular Unity electoral platform made reference to "just 150 firms," which it claimed, "monopolistically controlled the entire market." However, it did not commit itself to the nationalization of that number, but rather, defined the new Area of Social Property in very much broader terms.
88. Sobel, *Chile and Allende*, p. 78.
89. Hudson, "The Role of Constitutional Conflict . . .," pp. 70–71.
90. Alain Joxe, "The Chilean Armed Forces and the Making of the Coup," in O'Brien, *Allende's Chile*, pp. 266–267.
91. Hudson, "The Role of the Constitutional Conflict . . .," pp. 70–71
92. García, "The Social Property Sector . . .," pp. 162–163, quotes various party documents.
93. Henfry and Sorj, *Chilean Voices*, p. 44.
94. Boorstein, *Allende's Chile* (New York, 1977), p. 129.
95. Martínez, "The Industrial Sector . . .," p. 230–231.
96. Arriagada, *De la via chilena*, pp. 184–189.
97. Quoted in Raptis, *Revolution and Counter-Revolution in Chile*, pp. 73–74.
98. García, "The Social Property Sector . . .," p. 172.
99. Martínez, "The Industrial Sector . . . ," pp. 244–245.
100. Nove, "The Political Economy of the Allende Regime," pp. 65–66.
101. For example, see Martinez, "The Industrial Sector . . .," pp. 237–238.
102. Ibid., p. 256n.
103. Mamalakis, *The Chilean Economy*, pp. 235–236, 241.
104. Arriagada, *De la via chilena*, pp. 231–232.
105. Hudson, "The Role of the Constitutional Conflict . . .," pp. 78–79.

6

The Copper Question

Copper has played so crucial a role in the development of modern Chile that the industry and the public issues it has raised require a chapter apart. A few statistics will illustrate why. In the twenty-five years prior to Allende's election (1945–1970), the value extracted by the two major producers alone accounted for anywhere between seven and twenty percent of the gross national product. Copper exports provided between thirty and eighty percent of the country's total hard currency earnings. And taxes imposed upon the copper industry at various points, between ten and twenty percent of all government revenues.[1] Put simply, no decision that any Chilean could make, from the President of the Republic on down, was as likely to influence the fortunes of the nation as much as the production figures at the mines and the movement of copper prices in the international marketplace. The fact that until the 1960s the major mining enterprises were wholly-owned subsidiaries of two North American corporations, Anaconda and Kennecott, meant that any controversies arising out of copper policy invariably intersected the lines of U.S.–Chilean relations.

Not surprisingly, the desire to wrest control of the industry from the hands of foreigners constitutes, if not the major theme of twentieth-century Chilean political history, certainly one of its contrapuntal motifs. It was merely left to Popular Unity to gather up all the separate elements of frustration and nationalist resentment, expropriate the companies, and push the Chilean state into a new economic role from which even Allende's successors have not chosen to withdraw.

Foreign Involvement in Chilean Copper

Although all of the great Chilean mines have been brought on line since 1914, the extraction of this red metal predates the Spanish conquest, and actually constitutes one of the country's oldest economic activities. The discovery of the Tamaya mines in 1833 propelled Chile into the rank of world's leading producer, a distinction it retained until 1876, when it accounted for 62 percent of global output. Thereafter, however, its decline was far more rapid than its rise; exhaustion of the richest veins, and the (then) technological impossibility of utilizing the remainder, reduced Chile to the role of marginal producer "to more efficient, larger-scale, and lower-cost suppliers," notably Spain and the United States.[2] The unsettling economic and social prospects which this development would normally portend were avoided, however, by the fortuitous outcome of the War of the Pacific (1879–1883), in which Chile wrested from its two northern neighbors some of the most valuable deposits of natural nitrates to be found anywhere in the world.

The nitrate bonanza underwrote the longest economic boom in Chilean history, embracing the final quarter of the nineteenth century and the first two decades of the twentieth. Thereafter, the industry sustained two grevious, and ultimately fatal, assaults—the introduction of synthetics developed by the Germans during World War I, and the world economic crisis of 1929–30. Even during the halcyon days of this curious product, however, a small copper industry continued to operate beside it under Chilean ownership and management, although by 1900 foreigners had taken over international marketing. But the declining fortunes of nitrates, combined with developments in the world economy, in mining engineering, and what might be called mineral entrepreneurship, eventually converged to facilitate the entry into Chilean copper, and ultimately the dominance, of capital from the United States.

The process was gradual, but once it gathered force, it was irresistible. It began far from Chile—in Europe and the United States, with the introduction of electric power and the development of the automobile, which in turn increased the demand for copper by geometric proportions. Mining engineers and geologists fanned out across the globe in search of new sources of the metal, and by the eve of World War I, both European and North American consortia had begun to survey Chilean ore bodies to see whether they justified large-scale investment. Apart from her past record as a major producer, Chile inspired interest on two specific counts. One was the demonstration by two "conspicuously successful" English companies operating there that "sustained investment in copper mines, with vertical integration of the industry to include smelting, could be profitable over a long period." And the other was a revolution in copper technology which suddenly made it economically worthwhile to work "low-grade porphyry ores, employing highly capital-intensive techniques of extraction, concentration, and smelting."[3]

The first North American entrepreneur to apply these new techniques in Chile was William Braden, an engineer who in 1904 acquired from its Chilean owners a massive ore body about 100 miles southeast of Santiago known as El Teniente (see Map). Within four years Braden found it necessary to sell out

SOUTH
AMERICA

Area of map

Pacific Ocean

Atlantic Ocean

CHILE

PERU

Arica

MOCHA

Pisaqua

CERRO COLORADO

IQUIQUE

● *SAGASCA*

BOLIVIA

TARAPACA

QUEBRADA BLANCA

■ *EL ABRA*

PAMPA NORTE

Tocopilia

CHUQUICAMATA

EXOTICA

Ocean

● *MANTOS BLANCOS*

ANTOFAGASTA

ANTOFAGASTA

CHILE
COPPER MINING SECTOR

■ GRAN MINERIA

● MEDIANA MINERIA

▲ ENAMI SMELTERS

■ KNOWN ORE BODIES

- - - - - PROVINCIAL BOUNDARIES

—·—·— INTERNATIONAL BOUNDARIES

Taltal

Borquito

■ *EL SALVADOR*

▲ *PAIPOTE*

Copiapo ●

ATACAMA

Pacific

Vallenar ●

ARGENTINA

La Serena ●
Andacollo ● *ANDACOLLO*

PELAMBRES

COQUIMBO

Illapel ●

ACONCAGUA

VENTANAS ▲ *CHAGRES*
VALPARISO

VALPARISO

San Antonio ●

SANTIAGO

▲ *ANDINA*

● *DISPUTADA*

⊙ SANTIAGO

EL TENIENTE

COLCHAGUA - - - **O'HIGGINS**

to the Guggenheims; in 1915, they, too, chose to transfer the property, this time to the Kennecott Copper Company, who remained the sole owner until 1965, when it sold a 51 percent interest to the Chilean state. As part of Kennecott's international minerals empire, El Teniente became the largest underground copper mine in the world, eventually yielding an output of 145,000 metric tons annually.

A holding of similar importance was acquired by the Chile Exploration Company in the desert wastes of the northern province of Atacama in 1915. This property, known as Chuquiquimata, was sold in 1923 to the Anaconda Corporation, who in turn developed it into the world's largest open pit copper mine. In 1927 Anaconda opened a new mine on its own, at Potrerillos, several hundred miles southeast of Chuquiquimata. When Potrerillos began to show definitive signs of depletion in the early 1950s, Anaconda replaced it with a new mine, El Salvador, several miles away.

The acquisition and development of these ore bodies by Anaconda and Kennecott over two decades completely transformed the entire nature of the Chilean mining industry. Chile once again became a major copper producer; between 1906 and 1929, its output increased tenfold, and by 1945 it accounted for slightly more than 20 percent of Free World output. However, the price paid for this was frank denationalization of what had once been a uniquely Chilean industry. Whereas in 1876, the last good year of low-technology vein mining, Chileans owned 90 percent of their domestic copper and resources, as early as 1918 the figure had dropped to four percent. A few Chileans remained active in small-scale operations which in the late 1930s accounted for about five percent of production (in wartime, slightly higher), but copper in Chile—"big copper" (gran minería)[4]—remained synonymous with Anaconda and Kennecott. At the time of Allende's election, three mines—Chuquiquimata, El Salvador, and El Teniente—were responsible for approximately 80 percent of the country's total output, and two new mines brought on line by the American concerns shortly thereafter raised the percentage to 85.

The gradual predominance of foreign capital in Chilean copper was implicit in the very conditions necessary to extract, process, and bring it to market. As late as the the 1950s, 99 pounds of overburden and ore had to be removed to obtain a pound of pure copper,[5] and the need to convey the product from remote districts of the Atacama desert or the Andes required the separate construction of railroads, storage depots, and other transportation facilities, as well as waterworks and power-generating plants.

Further, since most of the ore bodies were located in unsettled areas, the companies had to create entire towns where none had existed before, complete with schools, stores, and hospitals. A new mine thus required both heavy capital commitments and a relatively long gestation period before the ores were brought on line. A typical mining and smelting complex capable of producing relatively low-grade ores on a massive scale required a minimum investment of $100 million, and an average of four to six years to bring on line. (The same period was required to increase substantially the productivity of an existing operation.)[6] Potrerillos, for example, took ten years of work before it could be opened in 1927; Chuquiquimata required only two (1913–1915), but this was five years and $100 million after the purchase of the original property by the Guggenheims. All of the earnings of Kennecott's El Teniente during its formative stage of development, that is, from 1906 to 1927, were reinvested, and shareholders during this period received no dividends whatever.

These heavy capital commitments were clearly worthwhile, for Chile was known to possess a reserve of 100 million tons of copper of a highly uniform grade. What was required was initiative, courage, and a capacity to wait. Some Chileans of wealth and imagination were early partners in the new, technologically sophisticated enterprises, but withdrew almost immediately when it became clear that the gestation period was considerably longer than other economic activities.[7] As late as 1965, when Kennecott sought to recruit a syndicate of wealthy Chileans to buy substantial shares of its stock, none were forthcoming; "Chileanization" of copper would thus have been impossible had not the Chilean government been willing to act as the new majority stockholder.[8]

The financial rewards to the companies for their vision, industry, capacity to marshal resources, willingness to take risks and to wait, were quite simply astronomical, all the more so since during their formative years the Chilean state still imposed its major tax burden on the nitrate industry. Before 1925 levies on copper were negligent to the point of invisibility; between 1913 and 1924, for example, Braden Copper paid taxes representing less than one percent of the total value of its production.[9] However, the government began

TABLE 6.1
American Investment in Chilean Copper

Enterprise (Mine)	Brought on Line	Parent Corporation
Chile Exploration Co.		
(Chuquiquimata)	1915	Anaconda
Andes Copper Mining Co.		
(Potrerillos)	1927	
(El Salvador)	1957	Anaconda
Braden Copper Co.		
(El Teniente)	1912	Kennecott
Cía. Minera Andina, S.A.		
(Río Blanco)	1970	Cerro de Pasco
Cía. Minera Exótica, S.A.		
(Exótica)	1970	Anaconda

to shift its fiscal concerns to copper in 1925, at the suggestion of an economic mission from, of all places, the United States. That year was also the first in which the companies began to contribute to a system of compulsory social security established by the Labor Code of 1924.

Between 1925 and 1970, the general trend of Chilean fiscal policy was to appropriate an ever-larger portion of the companies' profits. This was accomplished through income taxes and royalties, as well as a variety of other devices, ranging from a discriminatory exchange rate, to customs duties, social security contributions, licensing fees, and non-recurring payments for special projects.[10] By one calculation, between 1930 and 1960 the share of the Chilean state in the returns of the industry grew at roughly three times the rate of the companies' profits.[11] The most conservative estimates, such as reflected in Table 6.2, suggest that if total operating expenditures (including, presumably, wages and salaries as well as local purchases) are taken into account, by 1970 Chile had recaptured three-fourths of the value of its copper production, the figure was even higher, in all likelihood exceeding 80 percent.[12]

The movement toward a significant increase of the tax load on the companies began after the collapse of nitrates in 1930, and gathered additional momentum with the advent of the Popular Front government in 1938. By the early 1940s copper taxes had come to constitute what they would long remain—the most important single source of government revenues. Although after 1939 a portion was specifically earmarked for investment in capital goods, in subsequent years the greater part was devoted to service and amortization payments of the public sector, imports of foodstuffs and other consumer goods, occasionally the wages and salaries of public employees (including the military), or deficits of government enterprises. (For example, in 1960–1964 the deficits of the State Railroads absorbed between 60 to 80 percent of all copper royalties.)[13]

There is no question that copper itself made less of a contribution to Chilean economic development during these years than might otherwise have been the case, although before 1970 discussion of this issue tended to focus on the alleged failings of those who produced the surplus (e.g., the companies) rather than those who received and allocated it (e.g., successive Chilean governments). If one restricted oneself to the figures, there was certainly no apparent reason for Chilean dissatisfaction. While the copper income of the Chilean state fluctuated (at times widely) over the 40-year period after 1930, if one deducted from the total of production all domestic expenditures of the companies (taxes, wages, etc.), it was not difficult to show that, enormous as were the earnings of Anaconda and Kennecott, the Chilean state came out slightly ahead of the companies. Specifically, while $1.682 billion was repatriated in the form of profits between 1930 and 1964, when juxtaposed against $2 billion induced capital inflows (not to mention taxes and wages),

TABLE 6.2
Chile's Retained Share of the CIF Value of Copper Production 1925–1970
(expressed in percentages)

Year(s)	Fiscal Revenues	Exchange Rate Differential	Local Operating Expenditures	Total
1925	4.9	n/a	33.1	38.1
1935	8.2	*	24.8	33.0
1945	16.9	*	41.2	58.0
1950–54 (average)	33.6	17.3	21.0	71.9
1955–59 (average)	32.5	2.1	25.3	59.9
1960–64 (average	25.9	1.5	35.2	62.6
1964–69 (average)	35.2	1.0	32.0	68.2
1970	39.5	0.7	35.4	75.6

* = annual average

Source: World Bank, *Chile: An Economy in Transition*, (Washington, D.C., 1980), p. 19.

the balance remained positive for Chile. The figures were even better for the boom period 1965-70, which coincided with (and unquestionably encouraged) an increasingly stringent Christian Democratic tax policy, during which Chile managed to retain some $2.986 of $3.629 billion in returns, slightly more than 80 percent.[14]

It would seem, then, that although Chile allowed ownership of its major copper resources to pass into foreign hands, in a longer view the economic benefits of alienation outweighed the costs, and increasingly so over time. This was not, however, what many Chileans thought, and by 1964 their number had increased to the point that both candidates in the presidential election of that year were promising some form of nationalization of the industry. Thus the figures alone are not enough to understand the course of copper policy; alongside them must be placed Chilean attitudes, perceptions, and responses to foreign investment, to the companies, and to the policies of the United States government.

The Rise of Copper Nationalism, 1920–1964

The Chilean critique of the copper companies has varied considerably over time, and ranged in intensity from mere uneasiness to calls for vindictive retribution. There is no way of arranging the bill of indictment in a perfectly logical order, particularly when some of the charges raised against the companies cancel each other out. One theme common to all, however, is the inherent danger and liability to a small nation when its major resource is controlled by outsiders. The first publicists to raise this issue—by no means men of the Left—drew most of their evidence by extrapolating from the experience of nitrates, since by the time the first American copper enterprises were beginning to come on line in the early 1920s, it was clear that the greater part of the resource surpluses generated by the previous mining boom had left the country.

Beyond this, the attack dispersed over a wide terrain, as did the implications for policy. The United States was accused of trying to deplete Chilean holdings to conserve its home reserves; later, some of the same critics reversed their terms, and complained that Chilean facilities were being neglected and allowed to fall behind the American mines in productivity. Others deplored the decline of smaller Chilean copper mines as a consequence of the emphasis on mass production of low-grade ores. Some of the charges levied against the companies have been heard wherever foreign investment in mining has been found: that working conditions in the mines themselves were inhuman; that discriminatory pay practices (''the gold roll'') renumerated foreign engineers and supervisors at a far higher rate than nationals, that various governments were bribed or pressured (or both) into suppressing strikes and other labor difficulties.[15]

The growing imposition of income taxes and other levies on copper in the early 1930s apparently obeyed a logic of its own: the drastic need of the government for revenues, rather than a desire to punish the companies.[16] But by the end of the decade fiscal expediency and nationalist sentiment had converged; thus, the special tax on copper that established the Development Corporation in 1939 coincided with a decision to construct a nationally owned copper smelter and a national steel industry.[17]

The entry of the United States into World War II further sealed the alliance between these two trends in Chilean domestic politics. During that conflict, export prices for Chilean copper were fixed by Allied governments at 12 cents a pound, a figure far below the market price which wartime demands would presumably generate. Thereafter it was widely held by copper nationalists in Chile (and not only by them), that as a consequence of U.S. price fixing in wartime, the country had foregone as much as $500 million in revenue. During the Korean War, a similar imposition from Washington (this time, without even bothering to consult the Chilean government), led to a chorus of complaint from all ends of the political spectrum. At the time, a difference of one cent a pound in the price of copper translated into U.S. $10 million in government revenues (three percent of all fiscal receipts).[18] The matter was rendered all the more serious by a general decline in Chile's terms of trade during this period. As one sympathetic American commentator put it, ''Chile was being denied full enjoyment of the boom side of the business cycle in the developed countries, while having the recession side of the cycle exported with exaggeration.'' Given the broad dependence of Chile's government on copper revenues for a wide range of development and social programs, he concludes, it was perhaps understandable that many perceived an intentional design "to frustrate Chilean efforts to build its own industrial base, provide for its own national welfare, and promote the broad process of development."[19]

Throughout the 1950s and early 1960s a wave of copper nationalism generated by wartime price controls gathered additional force. As Chile's share of the world market dropped, much of the critical focus shifted to the failure of the companies to expand existing facilities and output. The refusal of Anaconda and Kennecott (under pressure from the U.S. government) to sell to the Eastern bloc countries, or even to unreliable intermediaries, led to Chilean calls for a national sales monopoly. The continued profitability of the mines, juxtaposed against the absence of new investment, led to charges of exploitation; it was increasingly argued that the country was suffering because company profits were "too high," and that they were too high because of the "monopolistic" nature of the industry.[20] Finally, against the background of a long period of post war economic stagnation, it was perhaps inevitable that copper became the centerpiece of a Chilean version of dependency theory — that explanation of underdevelopment which attributes all ills to the leakage of resources of "monopolistic" foreign capital. Thus the quest for an increasing share in the returns of foreign enterprise eventually became a movement to recuperate ownership of the mines as the first step towards economic independence and self-sustained development.

The World Copper Industry: Some Realities

Much of the conflict between Chile and the companies is easier to understand within the larger context of the international metals market. The principal difficulty under which copper mining concerns have labored throughout the present century has been the inability to achieve oligopoly, which in turn would arm them with the capacity to dictate prices. In fact, since 1900, seven major attempts to form an international cartel have failed. The reasons are many. They include the continuing discovery of new sources, including increased technological capacity to mine low-grade ores; subsidies by major governments (the United States, Germany, Japan) to expand production, especially during wartime; increasing investment in small copper mines; the entry of non-copper mining concerns into the red metal as part of a general movement towards diversification. In effect, a major study concludes, "copper deposits have not been scarce enough, nor the technology of extraction esoteric enough, to permit effective control of prices or production." Consequently, "there has been a steady dilution in the international oligopoly at the production stage, and a long-term downward trend in prices."[21]

Probably the single most important depressant of copper prices has been the development of aluminum as a viable substitution shortly before World War

II. So great has been the threat of substitution, in fact, that the companies have found it expedient to accept government-imposed price controls in wartime rather than risk engineering conversions which would represent a permanent loss of market. In subsequent years, they have felt pressured to diversify into competition; hence, world production figures for aluminum increased by 100 percent between 1946 and 1965, in contrast to a 20 percent increase in copper for the same period. The Vietnam War abruptly reversed the long-term trend in copper price declines for approximately five years; then, in 1971, the charts resumed their accustomed configuration. Both these developments were of great moment for Chilean politics.

The failure to achieve oligopoly and the emergence of a major substitute have not only caused a steady erosion in world copper prices, but in the rates of profit for the companies. This is an important point, because it establishes that the principal beneficiaries of this development have been the consumers; the losses have been shared alike by the primary producers and the host countries where they operate. What the Chileans failed to see (perhaps because the companies never persuasively explained it to them) was that although the division of the final proceeds could legitimately engender controversy, in the matter of prices, the interest of the foreign producer and the host country was virtually the same. This was so notwithstanding the perennial allegations of copper nationalists that the companies kept prices "artificially low" to collect their profits downstream, at the fabrication stage. After examining these charges in exhaustive detail, the study cited above confirms that "the bulk of the profits produced in the international copper industry [throughout this period] continued to be taken by necessity at the production stage."[22] The discrepancy between world market realities and Chilean perceptions led increasingly to an emphasis upon recovering control of copper resources by a wide range of legal devices which were necessarily confined to Chile itself, and therefore limited in their ultimate effects.

Chilean Copper Policies, 1946–1955

In the post-war period Chilean copper policy fluctuated rather abruptly between two attempts to appropriate an increasing portion of the companies' profits, and one short-lived effort to coax an increase in foreign investment through greater tax incentives. The failure of both courses to yield a satisfactory result is the necessary background to the "Chileanization" agreements struck with the Christian Democrats between 1965 and 1969.

The Period of "Onerous Taxation," 1946–1954. This period was marked by the imposition of twenty-five different modifications to existing agreements with the companies, all intended to increase Chile's share of revenues from major mining operations. These included new income taxes, an increas-

ingly discriminatory exchange rate, import duties, low depreciation allowances, and ad hoc assessments for special projects. After May 1952 (and to
1955), the government took over international marketing, and imposed a
special "overprice tax" which permitted it to retain the proceeds on all sales
above 24.5 cents a pound. Particularly important was a drastic increase in the
foreign exchange penalty. First instituted in the early 1930s, this required the
companies to surrender dollars to be spent in Chile on labor, services, and
materials ("legal costs") at a fixed, overvalued rate of exchange. By the early
1950s, the value of this penalty was equivalent to 17 percent of the gross value
of production.[23]

There is no doubt that in the short run the combination of direct taxes and
"legal costs" of production accomplished their purpose, for during the period
1945–1955 revenues from the former rose from $18.1 to $121 million, to
which receipts from the latter added by the end of the period another $59.6
million.[24] Again, if the goal of this policy was to reduce the profit margins of
the companies, this, too, was achieved; in 1940, Anaconda and Kennecott had
repatriated $68.6 million; by 1953, the figure had fallen to $10.5.[25] The
decline reflected the choice of the Chilean government to increase its share of
what copper was produced, rather than to encourage an increase in output,
from which a larger aggregate figure (but smaller percentage) could be retained.

In this anomaly lay the difficulty of long-term application of "onerous"
(and even, in some commentaries, "confiscatory") taxation. As profits declined, so, too, did the interest of the companies in making new investments.
Instead, they turned to marginal mines in the United States, now suddenly
rendered more attractive by nothing more than Chilean fiscal policy. Net
disinvestment occurred in the Chilean copper industry between 1950 and
1954—and this, in spite of the addition of a sulphite treatment plant at Chuquiquimata at a cost of $130 million. What was perhaps more important was
a decline in both output (-31 percent between 1943–1945 and 1953–54), and
in Chile's share of the world market (from 19 to 13 percent between 1946 and
1953). From a producer second only to the United States, Chile fell behind
Northern Rhodesia. More ironic still, the heavy foreign exchange penalty
made it increasingly prohibitive to buy locally, so that the companies found
themselves compelled to acquire elsewhere materials formerly purchased from
Chilean factories; likewise, the same constraints led them to reduce their work
force by one-third through the introduction of labor-saving technology. Thus
what began as an attempt to appropriate the lion's share of copper, ended by
actually reducing the size of the tax base from which revenues were obtained.[26]

A similar outcome—for different reasons—attended the national sales monopoly imposed in 1952 in response to U.S. attempts to establish a copper
price ceiling during the Korean War. For a brief moment, while international

demand soared to new heights, the Chilean government was able to sell the output of Anaconda and Kennecott at nearly double the price fixed by Washington. The "new" customers of this monopoly, however, were not actually new at all; they were purchasers who normally maintained a close relationship with major producers, and who recurred to the open market only in periods of scarcity. Once the Korean War ended and demand slackened, these same parties abandoned their marginal source ("independent producers"). At the same time, the United States government released a large portion of its strategic reserves, causing a sharp drop in world prices. Chile was left in 1953 with a stockpile of 100,000 tons of unsold metal. If the policy of "onerous taxation" had thus proven that Chile did not possess the leverage to force the companies to reinvest in the context of sharply declining profit rates, the sales monopoly revealed that her share of the copper market was not large enough—save in exceptional circumstances—to dictate the international price.[27]

The New Treatment Law (1955–1960). The cumulative failure of "onerous taxation" led to a sharp (if brief) reversal of Chilean copper policy in an attempt to lure the companies into expanding production and enhancing the country's refining capacity. What was sought, in effect, was a replacement for Anaconda's Potrerillos mine, now approaching depletion, and a shift in the bulk of refining operations from the United States to Chile itself, partly with a view to equipping the country to export directly to Western Europe. In exchange, the Chilean government was prepared to meet virtually all of the companies' demands, embodied in Law 11.828 of May 1955, more commonly known as the New Treatment Law.

This new regime abolished the national sales monopoly, the foreign exchange penalty, and all import duties on new equipment. In addition, the companies received a special accelerated rate of depreciation on new investment and liberal expensing allowances for mine development. Particularly significant were the new tax incentives. The basic rate was reduced to 50 percent, with an additional 25 percent surtax which would decline progressively as production increased, and would disappear altogether when a given base was doubled.[28]

The New Treatment Law did deliver some of the things which its proponents, both Chilean and foreign, had promised. There was an increase in investment, as Anaconda expended $118 million to bring on line a new mine, El Salvador, to replace Potrerillos; at the same time, an additional $60 million was invested to expand the output of Chuquiquimata. Two new ore bodies were discovered; one would become the Exótica mine (an Anaconda property) and the other, the Río Blanco (a project of the Cerro Corporation, a newcomer to Chile). Significantly, the Exótica deposit, consisting of 150 million tons of copper of recoverable content of about 1.4 percent, was located by hitherto unknown "geological, geophysical, and geochemical techniques."[29] Chilean output expanded by 55 percent between 1954 and 1959. The removal of the discriminatory exchange rate led to an increase both in employment in the mines themselves and in local procurement of equipment and supplies.

From the companies' point of view, the outcome of the New Treatment Law could not have been more satisfactory: profits for Anaconda and Kennecott nearly doubled between 1955 and 1959 in comparison with the previous four-year period, and their Chilean operations suddenly became two to three times more remunerative than their investments elsewhere. For the Chilean government and public, however, the results of the new policy were profoundly, even bitterly, disappointing. Income from mining (in both taxes and local contributions of foreign exchange), which had averaged $163 million per year between 1950 and 1955, rose to an annual average of nearly $205 million from 1956–59, in other words, an increase of slightly less than 25 percent.[30] Further, those increases were due less to a growth in production (Chile only increased its share of the world market by one percentage point) than to recovery of copper prices, which had been depressed during the final years of "onerous taxation." Chileans preferred to make "the simple calculation of higher prices times the huge increases in production that they had expected after 1955 (but which never materialized), than to make the sad calculation of high prices times the weak sales of 1952–53 if they had not passed any legislation."[31] In other works, instead of comparing the increase in net revenues, Chileans continued to worry more about the profit rate of the companies than the aggregate dollar contribution of copper to the national economy. Nonetheless, there was legitimate cause for concern, since the results of the New Treatment Law fell so far short of the expectations which both the companies and their local allies had raised.

What had happened to frustrate those expectations? The answer is enormously complex. In the first place, just as Chile alone could not force the companies to invest under disadvantageous circumstances, neither could it necessarily expect them—in the absence of other constraints—to respond to purely local incentives for investment, given their involvement in a worldwide system of production and marketing. Or, as Theodore Moran has put it, the specific pattern of incentives offered by the New Treatment Law would have worked only "from the perspective of a single firm producing a single product under conditions of perfect competition."[32] This description hardly fits Anaconda or Kennecott; in fact, with the windfall profits earned in Chile during this period, the companies invested more heavily in the United States, and even began diversifying into aluminum! Thus, copper nationalism, thrown on the defense in Chile during the doldrum years 1953–54, was revivified with a whole new set of arguments and a larger, more receptive constituency.

Second, the agreements with the companies were drafted, it can now be seen, with insufficient care. Trusting blindly in the laws of classical economics, the Chilean authors of the New Treatment Law failed to specify a numerical amount they wished invested. In addition, the base figures used to calculate the relationship between production and taxes were too low, that is, 95 percent of the average output of each firm for 1949–1953, a period of decline. Thus, an increase of 100 percent over the "production base" (which would have eliminated the surtax entirely) would require an output still less than the average figure during World War II. Put another way, simply by increasing unused capacity, the companies could escape the need to sink new investments, yet eliminate 25 percent of their potential tax burden.[33]

Third, the New Treatment demonstrated that there was no necessary and direct relationship between changing rates of taxation, productivity, and investments. "It is apparent," Clark W. Reynolds has written in a classic study of the Chilean industry, "that reinvestment takes place less as a function of improvement in earnings (through a lower incidence of taxation) than as a function of the wearing out of assets or depletion of reserves in existing mines, and the need for exploration and development of new ore prospects."[34] What this meant was that while punitive taxation was certain to stifle investment, a more benevolent fiscal regime in and of itself could not guarantee new capital commitments. On the other hand, without the New Treatment legislation itself, Anaconda would not have opened El Salvador to replace Potrerillos, or expanded Chuquiquimata and without these initiatives, Chilean copper revenues in the second half of the 1950s would have been significantly, even disastrously, lower than they were.[35]

Fourth, it is just possible that the New Treatment legislation was not given long enough to justify itself. It is now known that additional plans by Anaconda and Kennecott for expansion were on the boards in the late 1950s, but a high rate of inflation in Chile, a new drop in world copper prices after 1956, and the elections of 1958 (in which Allende, in his first—nearly successful—presidential bid was committed to nationalization of the industry in the event of his triumph) all conspired to delay these projects long enough to separate them in the public mind, once they were finally unveiled, from the legislation to which they owed their inception.

The Return to Punitive Taxation, 1961–1965. The failure of the New Treatment Law to live up to Chilean expectations led to a period of sharply declining political fortunes for the companies. Even President Jorge Alessandri (1958–1964), himself an outspoken defender of free enterprise and foreign investment, could not resist the gathering forces of hostility and retribution. In 1961, Christian Democratic Senator Radomiro Tomic, in a famous speech, "The Copper Belongs to Chile," stated the case for copper nationalism with renewed vehemence (enriched by statistics); his criticisms—though not all of his proposals—were echoed by his colleague Senator Eduardo Frei. At the

TABLE 6.3
Evolution of Chilean Copper Policies, 1906–1973

1906–1924	Laissez-faire
1925–1931	Income tax on Gran Minería
1932–1937	Foreign exchange control and discriminatory exchange rate on copper, continued to 1955
1938–1949	Tax increases and World War II price controls
1950–1955	Government intervention in copper marketing; surtax on copper; temporary price control during the Korean War
1955–1960	New Treatment copper law, tax incentives, unitary exchange rate, "Buy Local" policy establishment of the Copper Department
1961–1965	Restoration of discriminatory exchange rate on copper
1965–1970	"Chileanization" program: expansion of production facilities to double output; new tax incentives for foreign participation; transformation of the Copper Department into the Copper Corporation (CODELCO); acquisition by the latter of a majority of stock in Kennecott Chilean operations; "pacted nationalization" of Anaconda properties (1969)
1970–1973	Full nationalization of copper, including expropriation of remaining Kennecott and Anaconda properties

Source: Adapted and expanded from Clark W. Reynolds, "Development Problems of an Export Economy: Chile and Copper," in Markos J. Mamalakis and Clark W. Reynolds, *Essays on the Chilean Economy* (Homewood, Ill. 1965).

same time, the Alliance for Progress and pressures from Washington for tax and land reforms, introduced a schism between the United States and its traditional friends in Chile, the Liberals and Conservatives. By the end of that year the companies discovered themselves bereft of defenders even in the traditionally congenial territory of the Chilean Right.[36]

The results were not long in coming. In January 1962, faced with the financial burden of a massive earthquake, the Alessandri administration reintroduced the exchange penalty for copper operations. When later in that year Kennecott, Anaconda, and now Cerro approached the government with expansion plans representing potential investments of, respectively, $200 million for El Teniente, $100 million for El Salvador and Chuquiquimata, and $75 million to bring Río Blanco on line, Alessandri felt unable to offer a long-term tax guarantee, or assurances that certain provisions of the New Treatment Law would not be removed or altered. The companies then turned to expanding their operations elsewhere. Investment in Chile fell to an average level of $16.5 million a year (1961–1965), less than half the mean value

($41.6 million a year) of the previous four-year period. And to judge by the presidential platforms of both Frei and Allende, some form of nationalization was virtually inevitable in the life of the next administration.

Chileanization Under Frei, 1964–1970

During his presidential campaign in 1964, the Christian Democratic candidate spoke repeatedly of the need for a new start in copper policy. On one hand, he promised to exact definite commitments from the American companies for substantial increases in production; on the other, he pledged to seek some form of joint ownership on the part of the Chilean state. In time these notions congealed into a full-fledged program whose objections were (1) to double Chilean output, which would restore to the country its nineteenth-century distinction of being the world's largest copper producer, (2) to expand refining capacity to cover the major portion of extracted ores, and (3) to vest the Chilean state with substantial shares in the major enterprises, and to enable it to participate in the international marketing of the product.

Frei's copper program received a strong initial impetus shortly after his election when Kennecott, sensing that the time had come for a fundamental change in its relations with Chile, suddenly offered to sell 51 percent of the equity of Braden Copper to the Chilean state. At the same time, it proposed to expand production at El Teniente by about one-half, and to make major improvements in worker housing at the site of the mine itself. It also offered to help Chile arrange the financing, and agreed to manage the new joint venture for ten years (or longer, if the Chileans so desired). It also stood ready to supervise completion of the expansion project, and the marketing of its output.

In exchange, Kennecott asked for compensation amounting to more than twice the book value of 51 percent of its property, and a reassessment of its remaining assets at a still more favorable rate. It also requested an immediate tax reduction on its (now) diminished share of returns, and a formal 20-year guarantee against expropriation. Beyond this, the company went to extraordinary lengths to protect what remained of its Chilean assets. It insured the sale of its equity ($80 million) with the Overseas Private Investment Corporation (OPIC), a newly-established agency of the U.S. government initially funded by Congress to cushion American investors from some of the more egregious risks of operating abroad. This meant that in the event of precipitous expropriation, the United States government would automatically become a party to the litigation. Kennecott also demanded that the sale amount and repayment of U.S. loans for expansion be unconditionally guaranteed by the Chilean state and made subject to the laws of New York State.[37] To expand the range of assurances, Kennecott then wrote $45 million worth of contracts with European and Asian consortia, selling the "factoring" rights to Italian and Japanese banks. This made any default in effect subject to legal sanctions around the globe.

The financing which Kennecott arranged for the expansion program was perhaps the most controversial aspect of the agreement. Of the $230 million required, $110 million was loaned to Chile by the U.S. Export-Import Bank. An additional $80 million, plus interest, representing Chilean payment for 51 percent in the new joint venture, was immediately loaned back to the company. The Chilean government also contributed an additional $27.5 million on its own account. Thus, Kennecott managed, while pulling back from formal ownership of its Chilean subsidiary, to increase the value and also the profitability of what remained. the contracts were written based on an exception of a world copper price of 29 cents a pound; when the Vietnam War sent the figure up to three times that amount, Kennecott and its Chilean partner divided among themselves what amounted to a bonanza.

Anaconda, whose Chilean operations comprised a far larger share of its world copper output, was reluctant to follow Kennecott's lead and relinquish legal sovereignty over its operations. Instead, it proposed to undertake on its own account to increase production in Chile by more than 200,000 metric tons a year.[38] To meet the rising Chilean demand for ownership, Anaconda did agree to sell the Chilean government for $3.75 million a 25 percent interest in the new Exótica mine which it proposed to open near Chuquiquimata. In return, Anaconda was promised a tax reduction from an effective rate of about 62 percent to 52 percent on returns from a substantially expanded output. At the same time, however, the company was required to surrender some previous benefits in the form of accelerated depreciation and rebates on refined copper. In contrast to Kennecott, then, Anaconda forewent considerable financial benefits in order to retain control of its Chilean operations, and also postponed recuperation of much of its investment until the later 1970s.

A third party to Frei's mining program was the Cerro Corporation, which had been surveying the country's ore bodies since the late 1950s, but only now regarded conditions as sufficiently opportune to make a firm commitment. Cerro proposed to open its first Chilean mine at Río Blanco, high in the mountains of Antofagasta Province. The capital cost of the project eventually came to $157 million, divided among the corporation itself (49.9 million); the Export-Import Bank (56.4 million); a consortium of Japanese customers ($32.1 million); and the Chilean government (18.6 million). Cerro retained 70 percent of the company's equity, while 30 percent passed to the Chilean government. In a fashion somewhat similar to Kennecott, but in contrast to Anaconda, the Chilean government guaranteed part of the loans of Eximbank and the Japanese.[39]

The new agreements also abolished the old Copper Department and in its place created the Chilean Copper Corporation (CODELCO), which became the government's shareholder in the new companies. The Copper Corporation was also designated to act as Chile's banker for the new joint ventures, receiving all of the dividends and paying out the interest and amortization due to foreign lenders. What was perhaps more important, the Copper Corporation was empowered to restore the sales monopoly if warranted by extraordinary conditions (defined as disturbances in the international market, wartime situations, or "any other circumstance which might be perilous to the national interest.")[40]

Results of Chileanization: Windfall Profits, Surtaxes, and "Pacted Nationalization"

The original Chileanization plans envisioned a six-year program involving an investment of slightly more than $600 million. Begun in 1967, by the end of Frei's term three years later, virtually the entire sum had been raised and expansion was actually moving ahead of schedule. It would be several more years before the full impact would be felt at the level of production and refining, a bounty bequeathed to Allende (and even more, to his successor). The most impressive results of Frei's copper policies, however, were in the area of revenues. Whereas taxes on copper in 1964 represented nearly $105 million, in 1969 they had more than doubled to $224 million. This sudden improvement in the profitability of mining was due to a sharp upturn in world prices as the result of prolonged strikes in the United States, and above all, the Vietnam War. Coupled with this change in market conditions was a bold decision to break with its traditional benchmark, the U.S. producer's price (f.o.b. New York), which was artificially low, and recur instead to the standard set by the London Metals Exchange ("the free market"). In effect, Chile was resuming the old sales monopoly of the Korean War years, but with far more remunerative results. However, because the mines were joint ventures, the Copper Corporation had to share its windfall with its American partners. To many copper nationalists, this seemed an intolerable situation, all the more so in the new context of greatly enhanced Chilean competence, knowledge, and expertise in the industry.[41] By 1969, under growing pressure from the Chilean political public, including important sectors of his own party, President Frei had no choice but to seek revision of the original twenty-year agreements.

The first adjustment came in June 1969, when Anaconda agreed to a plan which would sharply increase Chile's share of income from copper whenever the price rose above 40 cents a pound. A similar accord was reached with Kennecott in October. In effect, the revision made it possible under favorable world market conditions for Chile's total receipts from the major mining enterprises to increase from an average of 72.6 to 91.8 percent of their profits. In 1970, the first full year in which this innovation was applied, Chilean government revenues from the metal soared to $268 million. At the very time that the surtax was announced, President Frei asked Anaconda to follow Kennecott's example and submit to Chileanization. Strongly urged to accept the offer by the U.S. Embassy,[42] long since abandoned by its local conservative allies,[43] and privately assured by the Chilean president that "if he could not win a spectacular 'deal' with the company, he would be forced to introduce his own nationalization proposal into Congress,"[44] Anaconda finally assented to sell its properties under an arrangement subsequently known as "pacted nationalization."

The 1969 Anaconda accords effected the transfer of 51 percent of the equity of the Chuquiquimata and El Salvador mines through the exchange of $174 million in promissory notes, and a commitment by the Chilean government to purchase the remaining 49 percent sometime between 1973 and 1981. In the interim, Anaconda was granted a management and marketing contract amounting to one percent of sales. The value of the company's remaining equity would be adjusted on a scale which would descend over time; that is, the longer Anaconda retained its minority ownership, and therefore shared in the continued profits of the industry, the smaller would be the ultimate value of its properties for purposes of compensation.[45] As for the Chilean government, between the increased share of its revenues accruing from a majority ownership of equity and the new surtax, it would receive (assuming an average price of 50 cents a pound, and the mines operating at 90 percent of capacity) 85 percent of the gross profits of El Salvador and Chuquiquimata, compared with an average of 67.5 percent under the previous arrangement.[46]

Chileanization in Retrospect: Some Comments

At the time of Allende's election in 1970, most of the work of nationalizing the copper industry had been done for him, and with conspicuous success, The Chileanization arrangements devised by the Christian Democrats reflected the knowledge and negotiating skills accumulated over two generations— a careful calculus which both accurately measured the amount of incentive necessary to attract new investment for expansion, and dictated the precise moment at which the strategic advantage passed to the host country. This enabled the government to revise the initial profit-sharing arrangements sharply in its own favor. Further, while Chilean participation in the management of the industry and the marketing of its output grew by enormous strides, the new joint ventures could continue to draw upon the evolving technological expertise of the companies, and to benefit from their worldwide network of sales and supply.

Nonetheless, neither the left wing of Christian Democracy nor the Marxist parties themselves regarded the Chileanization agreements as satisfactory. Their principal objection was the terms of compensation, which both Tomic and Allende promised to drastically revise after the 1970 elections. Chilean dissatisfaction with Frei's copper policy was shared by a significant body of social scientists in the United States and Europe, who repeatedly alleged that Kennecott had not invested a single penny of its own money in the expansion program, and that the costs of compensation far outweighed whatever "psychic benefits" Chileans might derive from juridical ownership of 51 percent of equity.

One superficially persuasive study by British economist Keith Griffin, published in 1969 (and presumably read by many of Allende's people), purported to show that outright nationalization in 1964 would have cost Chileans less, since they could easily have paid the same amount in compensation out of the benefits made later in the decade, while bypassing the necessity of sharing the copper returns perceived in that period with their partners in joint venture.[47] The problem with this analysis, as Paul Sigmund has pointed out, is that it completely ignores the fund-raising capacities of the copper companies themselves, who, unlike the Chilean state alone, could coax enormous outlays of capital from the Export-Import Bank and other foreign private sources. It also treats access to the technology of Anaconda and Kennecott as of no economic value whatever, and overlooks the fact that the agreements *as written* made it possible for Chile to break with the companies' traditional marketing channels when it became more financially advantageous to do so.[48]

Another economist who subjected Griffin's econometric projections to some rigorous examination, found that in order for his model to work, the average price of copper would have to be 92 cents a pound with a mean production level of 634,000 metric tons for the combined El Salvador, Chuquiquimata, and El Teniente complexes. In the event, however, the average price between 1965 and 1970 on the London Metals Exchange was 61.1 cents a pound, and the mean production level in Chile was 523,000 metric tons.[49] Without the investment brought in during the Frei years to open Exótica and Río Blanco, the production figures for 1970 (and therefore the total for the Christian Democratic period) would have been slightly lower than this. The same economist points out that the superiority of the nationalization case also depended upon insuring that percentage increases in cost never exceeded percentage increases in price. "If the cost of production rises at an even slightly greater pace than price increases," he found, "the impact on receipts [will be] disastrous."[50] In this consisted precisely the failure of copper policy under Popular Unity.

Nationalization and Expropriation Under Allende, 1970-1973

With the victory of Allende, the full nationalization of copper became a matter of historic inevitability. This was so not merely because the new president had been so clearly identified with this position over his entire political career, but because few moments in Chilean history have been more propitious for the step which the new government proposed to take. The copper companies themselves had just completed a major expansion program and were not likely to sink new funds into Chile in the near future; copper prices were still inflated by the Vietnam War, and returns to the government had reached unprecedented levels. There was a pervasive sense—however inaccurate in some crucial details—that Chile was already running the industry with a minimum of foreign help; the system of internal political alliances upon which Anaconda and Kennecott once depended had virtually dissolved.[51]

Perhaps recognizing that here, at least, there was widespread public support for one of his innovations, President Allende saw no reason to deviate from strictly legal methods. On December 22, 1970, about six weeks after taking office, he sent Congress a bill to nationalize foreign interest in Chilean copper by amending Article 10 of the Chilean Constitution (subsequently, Law 17.450). The proposed amendment included a provision for compensation of the properties taken (excluding the ore bodies) on the basis of their book value as determined by the comptroller-general. Payment to the expropriated parties would take the form of 30-year bonds bearing an interest rate of at least three percent. Compensation was to be calculated on the basis of "original cost," less amortization and other deductions.

Some of the subordinate features of the bill were more fraught with conflictive possibilities than a cursory reading might at first suggest. The president was empowered—though not obligated—to deduct "excess profits" from the value of compensation. Further, the debts of the joint ventures guaranteed during the previous administration were not to be assumed by the new government unless, again, in the judgement of the sitting president (Allende), they had been invested "usefully." The comptroller-general's decision as to the book value of foreign investment was subject to appeal within 15 days before a five-man Special Copper Tribunal, established for this very purpose. Its membership was made up of two jurists and three government officials appointed by the president.[52]

The bill moved through Congress with unusual dispatch, and with minor modifications was passed by unanimous vote of both chambers on July 11, 1971. Five days later, it was signed into law by President Allende, closing an entire period of Chilean economic history.

Compensation and "Excess Profits"

On September 28, 1971, two weeks before the comptroller-general was to announce his findings on the book value of the American holdings, President Allende released his own figures on the "excess profits" to be deducted from the total. When the comptroller-general's report was subsequently released, the compensation due the companies was found to be inferior to the amount the president proposed to deduct. In fact, it appeared that, far from owing the companies any money, the latter were $145 million in arrears to the Chilean government! The consolidated positions of the president and the comptroller-general are presented in Table 6.4.

President Allende held that the legitimate percentage of return for the companies could not exceed 15 percent, and that his deductions were made to take this standard into account. Unfortunately, however, there has never been a generally-recognized criterion for "normal" repatriated profits in the mining industry. "As a rule of thumb, one economist has written, "it may be said that the rate of repatriation is less than normal when it falls below 20 percent of total profits and more than normal if it exceeds 50 percent."[53] Misunderstandings between investors and host countries often arise out of the fact that the former must average out their returns over a long period in order to compensate for the period of gestation, during which no returns are perceived. In one hypothetical case involving a mine in which a period of three years was required to bring an ore body on line, a 15 percent internal rate of return for

TABLE 6.4
Chilean Government Rulings on Compensation to American Mining Concerns (millions of dollars)

Enterprise (Company)	Book Value	Revaluation	Mineral Rights	Defective Assets	"Excess Profits"	Net Due
Chuquiquimata (Anaconda)	242.0	n/a	5.4	13.1	300	−76.5
El Salvador (Anaconda)	68.4	n/a	0.4	5.6	64	−1.6
Exótica (Anaconda)	14.8	n/a	0.25	4.55	—	+10.0
El Teniente (Kennecott)	318.8	198.6	0.2	20.5	410	−310.4
Río Blanco (Cerro de Pasco)	20.1	n/a	1.5	0.3	—	+18.3

Source: Comptroller General, Government of Chile, "Determination of the Compensation to the Nationalized Copper Enterprises, October, 11, 1971," American Society of International Law, *International Legal Materials*, 20, no. 6 (November, 1971); *Peruvian Times* (Lima), October 22, 1971, as presented in George Ingram, *Expropriation of U.S. Property in South America* (New York, 1974).

ten consecutive years required "annual after-tax profits as a percentage of capital expenditures [of] about 23 percent."[54] In the specific case of Chile, however, it should be emphasized that at no time in the history of the American companies' involvement were they ever asked to restrict their rate of profit to any given level; thus, whatever returns Anaconda and Kennecott might be shown to have perceived would not stand in violation of Chilean law nor of specific obligations undertaken with successive governments.[55] The concept of "excess profits" therefore is one which cannot be tested. In fact, there would be no point in exploring it further, were it not for the widespread criticisms of the companies' conduct in response to expropriation.

Any investigation of Allende's charges against the companies immediately runs up against the fact that even the most determined partisan of Popular Unity could not readily replicate the President's figures. This was so because the bases upon which "excess profits" were calculated were never actually revealed. To be sure, some reference was made to the Cartagena Agreement of the Andean Pact, which established a limit of 14 percent on the repatriated earnings of foreign investment; to certain precents in Chilean legislation establishing maximum profits on other (very different) types of foreign enterprises; and to a comparison of profits on copper operations in Chile and elsewhere. It was held that the rates of return in Chile for Anaconda and Kennecott exceeded two to three times those obtained by the companies elsewhere. However, no systematic breakdown was ever provided. Oddly enough, by limiting his deductions to the period after 1955, the president voluntarily relinquished evidence which would have strengthened his case, since those were precisely the years in which the comparison between the companies' earnings and their overall contribution to the Chilean economic was most radically asymmetric.[56]

Instead, Allende and his people launched a series of vague accusations against the companies' recent stewardship of their Chilean enterprises, as if the concept of "excess profits" had been devised as an excuse to fine them for past misconduct. It was said that production failed to reach the goals set by the Frei administration and the companies themselves. Anaconda and Kennecott were blamed for the rising costs of production, which reduced the profitability of the enterprises. The companies were further charged with sabotaging the mines and even purposely operating them at a loss. And again, reference was made to alleged minimal financial contribution in the expansion of the great enterprises themselves, as if there had been some unspoken obligation to use their own funds rather than creditworthiness with major public and private foreign lenders. The president's case against the companies was confirmed, Chileans were told, by the findings of two independent foreign teams of mining experts, one French, one Soviet, invited by his government to survey the properties immediately after nationalization. Both,

Allende claimed, had reported to him that Anaconda had been concerned only with short-term profits, while Kennecott's El Teniente mine had been found in a ruinous condition.[57]

If the deductions for "excess profits" rested on this bill of indictment alone, they would not stand in any objective court of review. For the facts were, that the expansion plans were drawn up by the companies' engineers under the surveillance of the Chilean government, and their execution was actually ahead of schedule at the time of the 1970 elections. Moreover, those plans were devised and implemented at a time when the companies had every expectation of participating in the profits of joint venture, that is, well beyond 1970. The profitability of the enterprises did decline somewhat in the late 1960s, but this was due to rising labor costs and a newly frozen exchange rate which passed those costs on to the companies. A combination of high world copper prices and generally sound management practices, however, maintained the enterprises in the black to the day of their expropriation. Particularly damaging to Allende's case was the subsequent discovery that the contents of the French and Soviet reports had been vastly misrepresented; the government had never published their texts in full. When El Mercurio came upon a copy of the French brief, which turned out to be generally full of praise for the companies (with mild criticism of certain details, the only sections which had previously been released to the press), the Communist daily El Siglo had no choice but to publish the less favorable Soviet report—less favorable, but by no means the harsh critique the government had made it out to be.[58]

How profitable had Chilean copper been to the companies between 1955 and 1970? In his address to the General Assembly of the United Nations in November 1972, President Allende claimed that Anaconda's realized return on its book value in Chile had averaged 21.5 percent a year, compared with returns of 3.6 percent on its properties elsewhere. For the same period, the president continued, Kennecott reaped an annual average of 52.8 percent of book value, even reaching "such incredible rates" as 106 percent in 1967, 113 percent in 1968, and 205 percent in 1969.[59] Estimates by American economists (none directly or indirectly connected with the companies) vary considerably, but all run at a fraction of the President's figures. Their findings appear in Table 6.5.

Since there is no generally accepted method of measuring the profitability of such enterprises, one cannot be certain which of these estimates is correct; perhaps none of them are. But unlike Allende's figures, they do at least have the virtue of resting upon open calculations openly arrived at. The fact that they run lower than the president's reflects (quite apart from political considerations of the moment), a historic Chilean reluctance to acknowledge the legitimacy of deductions from profitability of amortization and depreciation,

TABLE 6.5
Estimates of Net Profit Rate of Anaconda and Kennecott in Chile
(selected years)

Estimator	Period	Percent
Clark W. Reynolds [1]	(1956–1959)	9 *
John V. Sweeney [2]	(1955-1965)	11
Eric N. Baklanoff [3]	(1955-1970)	12.4
Theodore H. Moran [4]	(1955–1959)	20.4
	(1960–1964)	11.3
	(1956–1969)	21.6

* = "average net yield on net assets"
Sources: [1] "Development Problems of an Export Economy . . .," p. 312; [2] "An Economic analysis . . . of the Gran Minería," pp. 47–49; [3] Expropriation of U.S. Investments, pp. 91–94; [4] Multinational Corporations, p. 264.

and a tendency to forget altogether the obligations of a company to its capital stock.[60] Above all, the conflict over "excess profits" drew upon a rigid zero-sum concept tenaciously held by copper nationalists of all stripes over three generations: if the companies were making money, this was somehow bad for Chile, regardless of accumulating evidence to the contrary in the form of both increasing sums and an ever-larger share of copper profits perceived by the Chilean treasury.

Response of the Companies and the U.S. Government

At the time of expropriation, the nationalized enterprises were obligated to foreign creditors in the amount of $736 million. This figure included $182 million owed to the Export-Import Bank, $92.9 million to Kennecott for 51 percent of El Teniente's stock, $174.5 million to Anaconda for a similar share of Chuquiquimata and El Salvador. Prior to nationalization, Anaconda had received three of its semi-annual payments; on December 31, 1971, it was due to receive its fourth, some $11.9 million. Kennecott on the same date was due to receive its first installment of $5.8 million. On December 29, President Allende decreed that the payments would be suspended until the "usefulness" of the investments had been determined.

On February 2, 1972, Kennecott brought suit in the U.S. District Court in New York City against the bank accounts of nine Chilean government agencies operating in the United States, notably the Copper Corporation and the Development Corporation. On February 18, the judge agreed to freeze Chilean assets (which, in anticipation of the outcome, had been previously reduced to a minimum.) Less than two weeks later, Anaconda obtained a similar judgement from the same source. In response, the Chilean government suspended a shipment of copper consigned to Anaconda, and announced that it would not honor its promissory notes to the company. The Chileans suddenly chose to make the first payment to Kennecott on March 31, 1972, obligating the company to vacate its federal judgement; on June 6, the second installment was paid. The third was indefinitely postponed in the context of a moratorium on the Chilean foreign debt unilaterally declared in November. Anaconda's judgement in New York still stood, and remained in effect through the end of the Allende regime.

Meanwhile, the companies appealed the findings of the comptroller-general on book value and the president's determination of "excess profits" before the Special Copper Tribunal. At issue here was, above all, the value of the remaining 49 percent of their assets which had in effect been expropriated. The Copper Tribunal met and heard the briefs of Anaconda and Kennecott in August 1972, but—surprisingly—instead of actually passing judgement on the merits of the case, simply declared its incompetence to make a finding. In September, Kennecott's petition for a rehearing was turned down. Banned by the nationalization amendment from recurring to ordinary Chilean courts,[61] Kennecott saw no recourse but to begin legal actions in third countries.

In September 1971, the company successfully sought writs of attachment in French, Dutch, and Swedish courts against Chilean copper shipments, although a similar attempt in Germany several months later proved unsuccessful; at the time of Allende's overthrow a suit against three Italian concerns utilizing Chilean copper was still pending. The Popular Unity government had wisely honored Kennecott's advance sales contracts with European and Japanese factors, which effectively limited the scope of the company's legal reprisals. The court actions did, however, place in doubt the capacity of the copper shipments for which they had contracted, which may well have diverted some of Chile's business to other sources.

The refusal of the Chilean government to honor obligations assumed by the previous administration inevitably involved it in a serious dispute with the United States government. Quite apart from the fact that the United States has traditionally maintained—even more during periods of Republican ascendancy—that it has an obligation to protect the property of its nationals overseas (or failing that, to seek "prompt, adequate, and effective compensation")[62] several aspects of the copper controversy were bound to provoke a serious diplomatic rupture with Chile. The financing of the Kennecott joint venture had been partly provided by the U.S. Export-Import Bank, funded by the U.S. Congress. The insurance of the company's equity was held by OPIC, another semi-public agency. And recent legislation, particularly the Gonzalez Amendment (1972) required the U.S. government to take cognisance of the treatment of its investors abroad in its votes on the boards of multilateral lending agencies. Finally, the court judgements in New York were bound to affect Chile's capacity to resupply its industrial plant—including, needless to say, its copper mines—which restraint constitutes the centerpiece of the frequently-cited "invisible blockade."[63]

In this conflict neither the companies nor Chile scored much of a victory. Kennecott could not force the regime to meet its obligations, and eventually accepted an insurance settlement from OPIC inferior to its original claim; without insurance, Anaconda was led to strike a similar deal with the junta after Allende's fall.[64] On the other hand, Chileans quickly discovered that running the industry without links to the traditional centers of technology, marketing, and supply was far more costly than they had ever imagined. Thus political events in 1971–1973 unravelled a carefully-wrought arrangement arguably beneficial to both parties, and put in its place precisely its opposite.

The Copper Industry Under Popular Unity, 1971–1973

At the time of nationalization, the Allende government forecast savings of $92 million a year in repatriated profits and an additional $33 million in depreciation, even if the world price of copper hovered between 50 and 55 cents a pound.[65] Instead, there was a sudden, catastrophic drop in revenue from the industry. Table 6.6 provides a basis for comparison by including the two years preceding the advent of Popular Unity, and one year following its overthrow. Some of the decline, as the table illustrates, was due to a fall in world copper prices, coinciding with U.S. withdrawal from Vietnam. But it is obvious that the drop in revenues was far steeper than that of prices, and that Chilean returns rose far more slowly than prices when the latter began another sharp upturn in March 1973.

Nor was this turnabout wholly due to a fall in output. Table 6.7 establishes that while there was a drop in 1971 in all three of the major mines, in two of the three in 1971, *overall* production of the copper industry actually increased thanks to the entry of two new mines, Exótica and Río Blanco, in 1970. However, by including 1974, the same table shows that the expansion funded and largely carried out under the previous administration began to reach its fullest potential only after Allende's overthrow.

TABLE 6.6
Copper Prices and Chilean Government Revenues
from the Industry, 1969–1974

Year	Copper Prices*	Revenues Perceived**
1969	.67	223.9
1970	.64	267.9
1971	.49	39.1
1972	.48	25.7
1973	.80	19.2
1974	.90	190.6

* = London Metals Exchange, U.S. cents per pound
** = millions of dollars
Sources: Central Bank of Chile and Ministry of Finance, Budget Office.

TABLE 6.7
Large Mine Production by Mine, 1969–1974
(1,000 metric tons of fine copper)

Year	Chuquiquimata	Salvador	Teniente	Exotica	R. Blanco	Total
1969	283.4	77.1	179.9	—	—	540.4
1970	263.0	93.0	176.6	1.9	6.0	540.5
1971	250.2	84.9	147.3	35.3	53.6	571.3
1972	234.3	82.9	190.3	31.2	53.9	592.6
1973	265.3	84.0	178.1	31.8	56.1	615.3
1974	356.8	80.0	225.5	32.2	68.4	762.9

Source: CODELCO.

Tables 6.6 and 6.7 invite two additional comments. The virtual disappearance of profitability after 1971 suggests that the margin of successful operation of the mines was far closer to what President Allende thought the companies *should* observe (about 15 percent) than what he *said* they had actually perceived (on occasion, 200 percent). Otherwise, the errors of mismanagement and featherbedding to be recounted below would have been far less costly. In this the regime fell victim to its own propaganda; its margin for error was very slim indeed. Further, had the mines lived up to their new productive potential, some of the other leakages could have been significantly reduced. As one study points out, "with a price-cost differential of 15 cents per pound, an increase in output of only 10,000 tons yields a change in government revenues of $33 million, or nearly two percent of total central government income in 1974."[66]

Some of the problems of the copper industry strongly resembled those which afflicted other public sector enterprises during this period. There was, in the first place, a drop in unit productivity (Table 6.8), due largely to a drastic and (unwarranted) increase in the number of persons employed (Table 6.9). Many of those taken on made no measurable contribution to copper output, including an inflated office staff at the headquarters of the Copper Corporation in Santiago. Production costs were also raised by the addition to the payrolls of the mining communities themselves of whole new categories

TABLE 6.8
Labor Productivity at the Large Copper Mines, 1969–1973
(Average annual output per worker in metric tons of copper content)

Year	Total	Chuquiquimata*	Salvador	Río Blanco	Teniente
1969	23.5	33.8	16.3	n/a	18.2
1970	22.8	30.4	19.0	n/a	17.4
1971	21.9	30.5	16.6	45.9	14.0
1972	20.3	26.5	15.0	31.7	16.0
1973	19.5	27.4	14.1	27.7	14.3

*Includes Exótica
Source: CODELCO.

of employees—"sociologists and psychologists and public relations men," who, in the narrative of one veteran observer of the Latin American labor movement, "plunged into political work on behalf of Popular Unity or infantile rivalry among themselves."[67]

The profits of the nationalized enterprises were further depleted by a wave of what one labor leader sarcastically labelled "mineral tourism"—visits at Copper Corporation expense to mining areas by foreign sympathizers or political personalities of the government parties. At Chuquiquimata the crush of outsiders became so severe that the scarce billeting facilities proved inadequate, and an extra fleet of sedans had to be laid on—automobiles which, the same labor leader pointedly remarked, were used as much for sight-seeing and excursions to the beach as for anything else.[68]

In the mines, as elsewhere in the nationalized sectors of the economy, there was a serious breakdown in labor discipline, and damage to plant and equipment due to poor maintenance or none at all. President Allende himself on a visit to Chuquiquimata in 1971 complained publicly of "wildcat stoppages for pretty grievances" and "extra time spent at lunches, dinners and teabreaks and at the beginning and end of each work shift," which, he told miners, had cost the economy an estimated $36 million in that enterprises's output in 1970.[69] Above all there was the problem of politics. Both at the Copper Corporation offices in Santiago and at the oresites themselves, contending elements of Popular Unity, ensconced in the highest reaches of management according to the "quota system," were observed "watching and challenging each other with a high propensity to foul decision making."[70] The structures of "workers' participation," intended to run parallel to the trade unions, were often found verging at acute angles.[71] Authoritative decisions were difficult to reach, often impossible to implement.

Certain unique characteristics of the copper industry itself posed additional problems. The mines were located in bleak and isolated areas where extraordinary incentives had been necessary to attract and retain a qualified management and a disciplined, productive labor force. Over the years the presence

TABLE 6.9
Employment in the Large Mining Sector, 1969–1973
(average number of persons per year*)

Year	Number of Employees
1969	22,981
1970	23,697
1971	26,127
1972	29,169
1973	31,484

*Includes CODELCO offices in Santiago
Source: CODELCO.

of foreign engineers and supervisors gradually dwindled down to a tiny minority of the whole, with Chileans assuming practically all of the major posts (and after 1967, virtually all). But the system of privileges, including payment in foreign currency deposited in foreign banks, access to imported goods at company stores, comfortable (luxurious, by local standards) housing, and separate schools and medical facilities, all remained. Thus much of middle and higher-level management in the mines was wary of changes which would reduce their positions to the less favored categories of civil service. President Frei was brought up sharply by these apprehensions when he visited Chuquiquimata on the eve of "pacted nationalization." Those fears must have been shared by many blue collar workers as well, since the mining community as a whole voted for Alessandri in the presidential elections a few months later in contrast to the rest of the electorate in the (traditionally socialist) Antofagasta province.[72]

The victory of Allende transformed threat into reality. In November 1970, the new government cancelled the provision for payment in foreign currency; in March 1971, Congress established a new schedule of maximum salaries for government enterprises; between July and September a new cadre of interventors relieved the managers of the principal mines of their authority. The result was a massive exodus of technicians and supervisors, running in waves roughly congruent with the four events just mentioned.[73] By 1971, the unyielding edge of the government's generally egalitarian policies, followed by quarrels between technicians and politicos sent out from Santiago to run the mines, had cost Chile several hundred of its most qualified technicians in the industry.[74]

Adequate replacements for these people were not immediately forthcoming, in part because so few qualified personnel could meet the government's criteria for political reliability. At Chuquiquimata the new manager was a mining engineer of Communist affiliation who had, however, spent virtually his entire career at various desk jobs in Santiago. At El Teniente control of the crucial smelter fell into the hands of the Communist and Socialist parties each delegated, respectively, a lawyer and a former administrator for the State Technical University to run it, neither of whom had ever worked in a mine before. At lower levels, a departed supervisor or section chief was often succeeded by a worker far down the line of seniority or qualification, or even—in the astringent account of the labor leader cited above—by four or five. Having broken with the American companies, the nationalized enterprises could no longer rely upon the parent organizations for specialized technical advice. This was particularly serious because many of the production increases programmed under Chileanization were dependent upon new and complex production technologies, such as a pioneer oxygen-injection process at El Teniente for which a team of Chilean and American engineers had been specially trained. By 1971 the computer console installed to guide this operation was found "gathering dust," and production at the mine running far below capacity.[75]

Perhaps in no area were management deficiencies so obvious as in the acquisition of spare parts. At any one time approximately 130,000 different items had to be kept in inventory, most of U.S. origin. Immediately after expropriation, the government transferred procurement—the lines of which formerly ran from expert teams at the individual mines directly to North American suppliers—to Santiago, where an enormously complex process was suddenly thrust into the hands of inexperienced personnel. Less than a year later, the Copper Corporation had gone through three different procurement managers, and, in the face of Anaconda's attachment of Chilean government assets in New York, was forced into "the complicated business of ordering inexact replacements for U.S. machinery and parts" in Western Europe, Japan, and the Soviet Union. Failure to identify and maintain the most essential articles occasionally forced the government to recur to emergency reprovisioning by air, with attendant costs to the finished product.[76]

The special treatment that the government refused to grant management was at first extended to labor. In time, however, the ruling parties' own history as political brokers for the mining proletariat turned against them. For many years the Socialists and Communists had reaped considerable political capital from advancing maximalist wage demands against the American companies (or later, the joint ventures); with the transfer of ownership to the Chilean state under a regime of their own making, the Marxist parties were ultimately left with no choice but to moderate their previous stance, hoping that the unions could be persuaded to follow. How the workers themselves could be expected to respond was revealed rather ominously in a survey conducted at El Teniente shortly after nationalization. While the miners were found to favor Allende's act of recuperation, they understood it in narrow "economistic" rather than broad ideological terms, and had no intention, it appeared, of abandoning their adversary relationship with management. "I am in favor of nationalization of the mines—it will bring more work for everybody," one told the investigator, and American Marxist sociologist, "as long as we keep our social benefits and they arrange our collective bargaining contracts." Another added more pointedly, "We are the ones who produce for the country, therefore we should receive better salaries at the end of the year."[77]

During 1971 the potential for conflict between the miners and the government was minimized through ready accession to union demands. But in 1971, with the rate of inflation running far higher than the original projections and the fiscal competence of the government declining, the number of strikes in the industry nearly doubled (Table 6.10).

TABLE 6.10
Labor Stoppages in Mining, 1965–1973

Years	Number of Incidents	Man/Days Lost
1965–1970	122 (annual average)	n/a
1971	125	53,699
1972	248	93,835
1973	218	119,149

Source: Ministry of Finance, Budget Office.

A perceived lack of enthusiasm for these walkouts on the part of the Communist and Socialist union leadership suddenly breathed life into some unlikely political forces; at Chuquiquimata, control of both the blue- and white-collar unions passed from the government parties to the Union Socialist Party (USOPO), a tiny schismatic remnant of the Socialists which stood outside the ruling coalition. In trade union elections in February 1973, loyalties shifted once again—this time to the Christian Democrats, with only 26 percent of the vote cast for Popular Unity.[78]

The uneasy peace between the government and the miners' unions was finally shattered in April 1973, when the government, emboldened by its showing in the congressional elections the month before, decided for once to resist demands for additional increases by workers at El Teniente. In the ensuing strike, that mine was shut down for four months. Events took an unusually ugly turn in June when a delegation of miners marched into Santiago and clashed with both police and supporters of the government. A wave of strikes sympathetic to the miners swept Chuquiquimata and elsewhere, followed by a cycle of counter-strikes supportive of the government. When an agreement was at least reached on July 2, the country was estimated to have forfeited some $70 million in copper revenues.

The El Teniente strike vividly illustrated two dilemmas which, carried over from earlier times, could not readily be resolved through mere nationalization. One was the fact that the miners themselves, while "privileged" relative to the compensation offered to other Chilean laborers, still undertook work so uniquely dangerous, so difficult and indispensable to the national income as to be in a position to demand and obtain differential renumeration from management—whether private or public. And the other was that when the Marxist unions ceased to represent the most intransigent position in the collective bargaining process, they rapidly ceded the initiative to rival forces. By the same token, the parties of the Center and Right, who in the past had articulated more "moderate" views on the compensation of the work force, suddenly seized upon the miners' vindicationist demands with astounding— indeed, indecent—celerity. It was a cynical exercise, no doubt, with purely political goals in view, but no different in essence from what the Marxist parties themselves had done so often in the past. Against these persisting features, neither decades of formal affiliation with Communist and Socialist parties, nor intensive programs or "political education" by organisms of "workers participation" could prevail.

Concluding Remarks

Whatever one may think of the legality of Allende's act of expropriation, there can be no doubt that the definitive nationalization of the copper mines rested upon a broad national consensus. In the very short run, in fact, the president's decision cost him nothing and probably gained him a few votes. The problem was that once the deed was done, the regime was condemned to make nationalization a decisive success. This meant, quite simply, that Chile could not afford indifferent or diminishing output in the context of declining world prices for the metal. Other industries could be run at a loss as long as copper generated its accustomed returns, but if the mines ceased to be profitable to their new owner, the Chilean state, the effects would necessarily work themselves through the entire economic system, and eventually undermine whatever short-term political gains had been obtained.

All of this suggests that whatever price had to be paid to make the mines work—whether compensation to the American companies, preservation of special privileges for management, or differential wage scales for labor, or any combination of the three—was bound to cost less in the end than treating copper as just one more industry slated for expropriation. This sort of pragmatism was precluded from the very beginning, however, by the ideological nature of the regime, by rivalries between its contending elements and between it and forces to its left, by generations of nationalist preachments across the political spectrum, and the demonstrable (and tempting) success of Chileanization. The cumulative effect of all of these factors was to push President Allende in a direction toward which, in any case, he was disposed to go. Having so sharply disqualified President Frei's efforts toward "pacted nationalization," he could do no less. Therefore he had no choice but to accept the consequences.

Notes

1. Theodore H. Moran, *Multinational Corporations and the Politics of Dependence: Copper in Chile* (Princeton, N.J., 1974), p. 6; Herbert Lindow, "The Chilean Copper Mining Industry," U.S. Department of Commerce, Bureau of Foreign and Domestic Commerce, *Copper: Quarterly Industry Report*, Fourth Quarter, 1972 (Washington, D.C., 1972).
2. Clark W. Reynolds, "Development Problems of an Export Economy: The Case of Chile and Copper," in Markos J. Mamalakis and Clark W. Reynolds, *Essays on the Chilean Economy* (Homewood, Ill., 1965), p. 211.
3. Ibid., pp. 212, 214.

4. Chilean law eventually divided copper mines into three categories—Gran Minería (large-scale operations producing an annual output of more than 165 million pounds); Mediana Minería (80 enterprises producing less than 165 million pounds per year but with a capitalization of at least US $45,000); and Pequeña Mineria (several thousand small, highly labor-intense individual or group operations which concentrated on the exploitation of high-grade ores; these were the true successors to the earliest Chilean copper entrepreneurs).

5. Reynolds, "Development Problems of an Export Economy . . .," p. 261.

6. Ibid., 217.

7. Mamalakis, *Growth and Structure*, pp. 40-41; George M. Ingram, *Expropriation of U.S. Property in South America: Nationalization of Oil and Copper Companies in Peru, Bolivia and Chile* (New York, 1974), p. 220.

8. Eric N. Baklanoff, *Expropriation of U.S. Investments in Cuba, Mexico, and Chile* (New York, 1975), p. 85n.

9. John Vincent Sweeney, "An Economist Analysis of the Nationalization of the Gran Minería of Copper in Chile" (Unpublished Ph.D. diss., Catholic University of America, 1977), p. 13.

10. Ibid., pp. 95–96.

11. Reynolds, "Development Problems of an Export Economy . . .," pp. 316–317.

12. Norman Gall, "Copper is the Wage of Chile," American Universities *Fieldstaff Reports*, West Coast South American Series, XIX, 3 (1972), p. 2; Baklanoff, *Expropriation of U.S. Investments*, pp. 96–98; see also note 14, below.

13. Markos J. Mamalakis, "The Contribution of Copper to Chilean Economic Development, 1920–67: Profile of a Foreign-Owned Export Sector," in Raymond F. Mikesell, ed., *Foreign Investment in the Petroleum and Mineral Industries* (Baltimore, 1971), pp. 414–415.

14. Mamalakis, *Growth and Structure* . . ., pp. 223–224.

15. Ingram, *Expropriation of U.S. Property*, pp. 221–223.

16. Reynolds, "Development Problems of an Export Economy . . .," pp. 315–316.

17. Sweeney, "An Economic Analysis . . . of the Gran Minería," p. 17.

18. Moran, *Multinational Corporations, p. 58.*

19. Ibid., p. 63.

20. Ibid., p. 25.

21. Ibid., p. 30. This entire sub-section relies very heavily on this source.

22. Ibid., p. 44.

23. World Bank, *Chile*, p. 19. Between 1940 and 1954, the average returns to the government of Chile from "legal costs" of production were nearly double those of direct income taxes on the companies; after 1955, between that year and 1964 on the average they nearly replicated them. Mamalakis, "The Contribution of Copper . . .," Table 119.

24. Mamalakis, "The Contribution of Copper . . .," p. 400.

25. Ibid., loc. cit.

26. Sweeney. "An Economic Analysis . . of the Gran Minería," pp. 22–26; Baklanoff, *Expropriation of U.S. Investments*, p. 68; Reynolds, "Development Problem of an Export Economy . . .," p. 264; Moran, *Multinational Corporations*, pp. 90–93.

27. Balkanoff, *Expropriation of U.S. Investment*, p. 72.

28. Tacked onto the law by copper nationalists in Congress who objected to the entire concept of New Treatment was a provision establishing a copper department, to begin to compile records on the operations of the companies. The copper department later became the Chilean Corporation (CODELCO).
29. Baklanoff, *Expropriation of U.S. Investments*, p. 72.
30. Mamalakis, "Contribution of Copper," Table 119.
31. Moran, *Multinational Corporations*, p. 105.
32. Ibid., p. 96.
33. Sweeney, "An Economic Analysis . . . of the Gran Minería," p. 30; Paul E. Sigmund, *Multinationals in Latin America: The Politics of Nationalization* (Madison, 1980), pp. 137–138.
34. Reynolds, "Development Problems of an Export Economy . . .," p. 315.
35. Raymond F. Mikesell, "Conflict and Accommodation in Chilean Copper," in *Foreign Investment in the Petroleum and Mineral Industries*, p. 372.
36. Theodore H. Moran, "The Alliance for Progress and the Foreign Copper Companies and their Local Conservative Allies in Chile, 1955–1970," *Inter-American Economic Affairs*, XXV, 4 (1972), pp. 3–24.
37. This was so, evidently, because most of the operation involving procurement of equipment and parts by the Development Corporation, what subsequently became the Chilean Copper Corporation (CODELCO), and other public sectors agencies were channelled through the Chile Trading Office in New York. The New York connection with private international banking is too obvious to require comment.
38. The Kennecott agreement had committed the company to increase the ouptut of El Teniente from 180,000 metric tons per year to 280,000.
39. Moran, *Multinational Corporations*, pp. 133–137.
40. Sweeney, "An Economic Analysis . . . of the Gran Minería," pp. 41–42.
41. At the time the boards of the Chileanized companies were, of course, binational; the Copper Corporation itself had a team of experts such as had not existed at the time of the earlier sales monolopy; in the mines themselves, virtually all of the supervisors and managers were Chilean.
42. Sigmund, *Multinationals*, p. 145; Moran, "The Alliance for Progress . . .," p. 21.
43. Moran, "The Alliance for Progress . . .," p. 15.
44. Moran, *Multinational Corporations*, p. 213.
45. The formula was as follows: if the company sold its remaining assets in 1973, payment would amount to eight times the average earnings of that year; if in 1974, 1975, or 1976, the multiples would be reduced to 7.5, 7, and 6.5 respectively; after 1976, the multiple would be 6.
46. Sweeney, "An Economic Analysis . . . of the Gran Minería," p. 40.
47. Keith Griffin, *Underdevelopment in Spanish America* (London, 1969), passim.
48. Sigmund, *Multinationals*, p. 142.
49. Sweeney, "An Economic Analysis . . . of the Gran Minería," pp. 125–127. I have recalculated Sweeney's figures to restrict them to the years 1964–1970, since his own computations go back to 1956. My source was CODELCO statistics published by the World Bank.
50. Ibid., p. 121.
51. Moran, *Multinational Corporations*, pp. 126–127, and "The Alliance for Progress . . .," *supra*.

52. Sweeney, "An Economic Analysis . . . of the Gran Minería," pp. 45–47; Baklanoff, *Expropriation of U.S. Property*, pp. 89–90.
53. Mamalakis, "Contribution of Copper," p. 390.
54. Mikesell, "Conflict and Accommodation in Chilean Copper," pp. 187–188.
55. Two key Popular Unity officials admitted as much. Carlos Fortín, representative of the Copper Corporation in Great Britain, told a forum of the American Bar Association that the imposition of damages for "excess profits" was an "act of revison of formulas that were legal at the time which they were applied, but which with the perspective of time appeared as unconscionable to the national interest." Fortin went on to say that in his own mind the juridical basis for the deduction was not the illegality of the acts, but the "unjust enrichment" of the companies deriving from the acts themselves. President Allende's chief advisor, Eduardo Novoa, put the matter more cynically. In a book on the copper question published in 1971, he argued that deduction of excess profits retroactively would have been impossible in strict accordance with legal principles. It was therefore necessary, he wrote, to give priority to "reasons of social justice, and [therefore] close the road to possible judical claims for compensation on behalf of the companies." Both quoted in Eric N. Baklanoff, *Expropriation of U.S. Investments in Cuba, Mexico, and Chile* (New York, 1975), pp. 114–115 and 114n.
56. "The leakage of copper resource surpluses due to foreign ownership was most severe during the 1930–1940 laissez-faire period, when the surplus was at its minimum." Mamalakis, *Chilean Economy*, p. 277. Or perhaps Allende did not wish to illustrate through figures how the relationship had changed over time, to the benefit of Chile (if not always to the detriment of the companies).
57. Ingram, *Expropriation of U.S. Property*, pp. 276–277.
58. Ibid., pp. 277–280.
59. Ibid., p. 232.
60. Ibid., p. 232. Sweeney points out that deduction for "excess profits" of a magnitude proposed by President Allende would actually have reduced the earnings of the companies during the affected period to not 12 to 15 percent (the approved standard *post hoc*), but to "less than 5 percent annually on direct capital flow basis given historic investment, depreciation, and amortization levels." "An Economic Analysis . . . of Gran Minería," pp. 51–52.
61. President Allende's chief legal advisor, Eduardo Novoa, with characteristic candor, frankly conceded that this was necessary to liberate the Chilean state from the obligations assumed by the previous administration. It was important, he stressed, to make sure that "integral nationalization" was not "exposed to the interminable discussions before regular courts of justice." Quoted by Baklanoff, *Expropriation of U.S. Investments*, p. 87.
62. Roderick T. Groves, "Expropriations in Latin America: Some Observations," *Inter-American Economic Affairs*, XXIII, 23 (1969), pp. 47–66.
63. For a fuller discussion, see Nathaniel Davis, *The Last Two Years of Salvador Allende* (Ithaca, N.Y., 1985), pp. 25–26.
64. Cerro was not judged to have earned "excess profits" (which would, in any case, have been difficult considering that it began operations shortly before Allende's election) and eventually reached an amicable settlement over its properties.
65. Sigmund, *Multinationals*, p. 159.
66. Sweeney, "An Economic Analysis . . . of the Gran Minería," pp. 124–125.
67. Gall, "Copper is the Wage of Chile," p. 7.

68. "Ineficiencia, despilfarro, y sectarismo en Chuquiquimata," *El Mercurio* (Santiago), May 29, 1972. This story summarizes the comments of Senator Ramón Silva Ulloa of the Union Socialist Party (USOPO), leader of the strongest trade union organization at Chuquiquimata. I have purposely chosen not to draw upon a two-part series by Carlos A. Correa Iglesias "Chuquiquimata por dentro," *El Mercurio*, December 23–25, 1971, on the advice of Norman Gall, who regards it as a tendentious mix of fact and fiction.

69. Moran, *Multinational Corporations*, p. 250.

70. Ibid., pp. 251–252.

71. Francisco Zapata, "The Chilean Labor Movement under Salvador Allende," III, 1 (1976), pp. 85–96.

72. Gall, "Copper Is the Wage of Chile," p. 4.

73. Ingram, *Expropriations of U.S. Property*, pp. 277–280.

74. Gall, "Copper Is the Wage of Chile," p. 12. The offer of Kennecott and Anacondato find employment for these people outside of Chile has led to the frequent assertion that this, rather than Allende's policies, explains the massive resignations. The chronology of events does not support this interpretation, although obviously the offer must have had some effect. Each will weigh these matters according to his own lights (or ideological preference).

75. Ibid., pp. 6–7, 11–12; Moran, *Multinational Corporations*, p. 251; "Ineficiencia, despilfarro, y sectarismo . . . ."; Sweeney, "An Economic Analysis . . . of Gren Minería," p. 148. When in 1980 I asked an important Chilean mining engineer what efforts the Soviets had made to assist Allende with qualified personnel, he assured me that "little, if anything, was forthcoming from that quarter. Instead, the Russians occupied an entire floor of the Copper Corporation Building [in downtown Santiago], where they set themselves to studying the plans of the American machinery."

76. Gall, "Copper Is the Wage of Chile," pp. 9–10; Moran, *Multinational Corporations*, pp. 251–252; "Inefficienca, despilfarro, y sectarismo . . . ."

77. James Petras, "Nationalization, Socioeconomic Change, and Popular Participation," in A. and S. Valenzuela, eds., *Chile: Politics and Society* (New Brunswick, N.J., 1976), pp. 178–179.

78. Zapata, "The Chilean Labor Movement . . .," p. 91; Sigmund, *Multinationals*, p. 160.

7

The United States and Chile, 1970–1973

At the time of Allende's fall in September 1973, there was widespread presumption throughout Latin America and in much of Western Europe that the United States had been deeply, perhaps crucially, involved in the turn of events in Chile. This presumption fed not only on a general mood of anti-Americanism generated by the Vietnam War, or even on the accusation of Allende's collaborators after the coup, but also on release to the world press in March 1972 of documents stolen from the files of the International Telephone and Telegraph Company (ITT), one of the largest American corporate investors in Chile.

These documents appeared to reveal, among other things, the existence of a plot hatched by ITT in late 1970 that, with the assistance of the U.S. Central Intelligence Agency (CIA), would "plunge the Chilean economy into chaos and thus bring about a military uprising that would keep Allende out of power."[1] As subsequent materials were published on successive days by syndicated columnist Jack Anderson, the Chilean Congress voted on March 28 to appoint a commission of thirteen members to investigate the matter; in Washington the Subcommittee on Multinational Corporations of the Senate Foreign Relations Committee launched an investigation of its own but delayed publication of its findings until after the 1972 U.S. presidential election.[2]

More information on the U.S. role came to light a year after the coup as the result of a congressional indiscretion. In the spring of 1974, CIA director William E. Colby briefed the Intelligence Oversight Subcommittee of the House Armed Services Committee on Chilean operations. For some inexplicable reason, the stenographer did not observe the normal practice of stopping the transcription of testimony at points when security-sensitive matters were broached. Representative Michael Harrington of Massachusetts, a liberal Democrat with a strong interest in Chilean affairs, presumed upon his membership on the House Foreign Affairs Committee to read the classified testimony, although he was not permitted to take notes at the time. In a subsequent letter to his committee chairman, Representative Thomas B. Morgan of Pennsylvania, Harrington reported that Colby had revealed the expenditure of nearly $8 million by the Nixon administration for covert political operations in Chile during the Allende period; the purpose of these activities, the letter explained, was to "destabilize" the Popular Unity government.

The ink on this correspondence was hardly dry before copies had found their way to the editorial offices of the *New York Times* and the *Washington Post*, whose subsequent publication of it forced President Gerald R. Ford to acknowledge publicly in a televised news conference on September 16, 1974 that the sums in question had indeed been deployed in Chile. But President Ford categorically denied any U.S. role in the coup itself.

At about the same time, Seymour Hersh, chief investigative reporter for the *New York Times,* published a series of articles that purported to outline the way in which covert action funds had been spent in Chile. The article of September 20, for example, informed readers—in the credit of unnamed "intelligence sources"—that

> more than $7 million [was] authorized for clandestine CIA activities in Chile . . . in 1972 and 1973 to provide strike benefits and other means of support for anti-Allende strikers and workers . . . Among those heavily subsidized, the sources said, were organizers of a nationwide truck strike that lasted 26 days in the fall of 1972 . . . Direct subsidies, the sources said, were also provided for a strike of middle class shopkeepers and a tax strike, among others, that disrupted the capital city of Santiago in the summer of 1973.[3]

On September 24 Hersh followed this story with another, attributing to "an administration source with first-hand knowledge" the information that shortly after arriving in Chile in mid-1971 to succeed Edward M. Korry as U.S. ambassador there, Nathaniel Davis received a message from Washington "saying, in effect, 'from now on you may aid the opposition by any means possible.' " Yet "another source" is quoted as saying simply that the ambassador "had been told to 'get a little rougher.'" Finally, still one more unidentified source confirmed "Ambassador Davis' direct involvement."[4]

Such charges, particularly in the light of what had already been revealed in the ITT documents before Allende's fall, could not be ignored, and a lengthy congressional investigation followed. The body constituted to look into U.S. activities in Chile during the Allende period was formally designated the Senate Select Committee to Study Governmental Operations with Respect to Intelligence Operations, but it has become better known through the name of its chairman, Senator Frank Church of Idaho. The Church committee was eventually responsible for the publication of four important documents: the hearings on covert action in Chile (December 4–5, 1975); a committee print (that is, a staff report that summarized testimony and presented committee findings); an interim report on U.S. involvement in an abortive military coup in Chile in 1970; and a final report that supplemented and corrected several aspects of the interim report.[5] Somewhat parallel to the activities of the Church committee was a massive—and from a scholarly point of view, quite impressive—study of U.S.-Chilean relations during the Popular Unity period by the House Committee on Foreign Affairs, an investigation that actually began some months before the coup and continued for several weeks thereafter.[6] It is upon these documents—which are based on a review of CIA materials of the highest classification, National Security Council records, and other highly sensitive files—that all that is said to be known for certain about the U.S. role in Chile must rest. Therefore, the findings of these committees, particularly the Church committee, must be examined with extreme care to see whether they are in fact congruent with the charges that have been made against the U.S. government by those sympathetic to the Allende regime or, at any rate, philosophically opposed to covert action on the part of U.S. intelligence agencies.

The need to compare charges with documentation is all the more pressing because high officials of the U.S. government and distinguished members of the American intellectual community have accepted in varying degrees the responsibility for Allende's failure. The most egregious case occurred on March 8, 1977, when Brady Tyson, newly named U.S. representative to the United Nations Commission on Human Rights in Geneva, declared to that body that "our delegation would be less than candid and untrue to ourselves if we did not express our profoundest regrets for the role some government officials, agencies, and private groups played in the subversion of the previous democratically elected Chilean government that was overthrown by the coup of September 11, 1973." Although his statement was immediately disavowed by President Jimmy Carter, and Tyson was abruptly called home for "consultations," the delegate insisted that his statement was "in the spirit of the Carter government foreign policy as I understand it."[7] Three years later former Attorney General Ramsey Clark, attending a conference on alleged U.S. crimes against Iran in Tehran, cited the Chilean case as one other wrong for which the American people would yet have to atone.[8] And historian Barbara Tuchman probably summarized best the views of many in the literary and academic world when she wrote that "a vicious tyranny . . . has descended upon Chile, with the assistance of the United States . . . For the United States to interfere in the domestic affairs of a neighboring state in an attempt to thwart their legitimate operation is intolerable."[9]

Although a certain edge of partisanship can be detected in these comments (was not "Chile," after all, one more indictment in the bill of particulars against the disgraced Richard Nixon?) it was actually left to a Republican to

summarize most explosively the thesis of American guilt. In the midst of the
Church committee hearings, Senator Richard Schweiker of Pennsylvania burst
out in anger to former Ambassador Korry:

> I think your actions in Chile have proved the Communists right. The Commu-
> nists argued that we capitalists will never give Communists a chance to get
> elected through democratic means, and Socialists can never succeed in our kind
> of government because we would never let them. I never believed it and I didn't
> believe it until we come up here and say in essence that we'll overthrow the
> government, even if the chief of staff [of the Chilean Army] gets killed in the
> process, even if we have to buy all the newspapers, we'll stop them coming to
> power. We have proved Castro and the Communists right by our inept and
> stupid blundering in Chile, and that's my opinion. I have no more questions.
> [General applause][10]

It is of the greatest importance to both countries to examine critically the
thesis of American responsibility for Allende's failure. For Chile it can determine the degree to which the policies of Popular Unity were or were not
inherently self-destructive, and therefore whether they were well or poorly
conceived. For the United States the implications are even broader, for in the
wake of Allende's fall and subsequent revelations by congressional committees, new strains have been placed on the instruments of American foreign
policy, and , what is perhaps of greater moment, the United States as a society
seems to have lost the moral equipoise upon which its entire postwar foreign
policy long rested. If this drift in American mood is well founded in fact, then
obviously it is well advised. But it is vitally important to make sure that the
lessons of history are precisely those that history actually teaches. The case of
Chile offers a unique opportunity to find out.

American Interest in Chile

Let us begin by noting that the United States had been deeply involved in
Chile long before Allende's election. The motivation for that involvement,
though certainly not devoid of economic considerations, went considerably
beyond them. Chile was—in the words of Ambassador Korry—

> the most stable, tested, freest democracy in South America, a democracy which
> was of a totally different profile than any other country in Latin America . . .
> Democracy in Chile meant exactly what it meant in the United States. Even
> more: it meant an unfettered press. It meant a multipartied Congress. It meant
> an independent judiciary. It meant an apolitical army, an army that had never
> participated in politics.[11]

That the Ambassador may have spoke more warmly of Chilean institutions
than perhaps was fully warranted is irrelevant here, for his statement serves to

depict quite accurately how Chile was perceived by American policymakers. Precisely because it *was* seen in this light—as a mature and open arena for the competition of ideas and systems—it was selected as a "showcase" for the Alliance for Progress under President Kennedy. One result of this was the receipt of nearly $2 billion of aid (loans and grants) during the administrations of Presidents Jorge Alessandri and Eduardo Frei. This made Chile the largest per capita beneficiary of Alliance funds in the hemisphere. But in the context immediately following the Castro revolution in Cuba, it also burdened Chile with the obligation to prove the most advantageous hemispheric battlefield on which to meet the Cuban challenge to Western ideals.

This aspect of U.S. policy meshed with the darker side of Chilean politics. For if American officials could celebrate the openness and civility of the political process in Chile, they had ample reason to be troubled by its highly ideological environment and the active participation of two large, well-organized, and (particularly in the case of the Socialists) imaginatively led Marxist parties. The situation was in some ways analogous to that of Italy, and it was indeed Italy that provided the metaphor for U.S. covert action in Chile during the 1960s.[12] This much is clear from the memoirs of former CIA Director William Colby, who had designed and executed such a program in Western Europe during the first postwar decade. As defined by him, it included efforts to "strengthen the center democratic forces—parties, cooperatives, women's groups, etc.—against the leftist challenge."[13] In Chile this meant subsidies to a wide range of non-Marxist political organizations, publications, and labor unions, a practice that eventually ballooned to such proportions that it was frequently quipped in Washington and in U.S. embassy circles in Santiago—only half in jest—that an entire generation of Chilean public men and women had come to depend upon the CIA for maintenance of living standards to which they had, perforce, become accustomed.

The largest effort in the area of covert action made by the United States before Allende's assumption of power in 1970 took place in connection with the elections of 1964. On that occasion some $4 million was appropriated by the U.S. government in support of the electoral campaign of Frei, slightly more than half the victorious candidate's war chest, disbursed apparently without Frei's personal knowledge.[14] According to Colby, "In the subsequent years [that is, 1964–1970] at least that much money was . . . spent by the CIA to keep Frei and other democratic forces in power," largely through "direct propaganda and election activities."[15] Later agency evaluations found that Frei would probably have won the elections anyway, but the abundant subsidy covertly tendered to the Christian Democrats enabled them to secure a solid majority for their candidate rather than, as was more typical in Chile, a mere plurality.[16]

Two forms of covert activity contemplated during the Popular Unity period were clearly eschewed in 1964, however. On that occasion the CIA refused when asked to act as a conduit for contributions by American businessmen to anti-Allende electoral forces; the agency did, however, use one Chilean-based corporate executive to channel funds that were represented to be private, when in fact they were foreign and public.[17] Nor did the agency explore the possibilities of a military coup in the event of an Allende victory. In fact, in the weeks before the elections of 1964, both the CIA and the U.S. embassy strongly turned aside such suggestions which in a sense were dangled before them by some apprehensive Chilean military men.[18]

Whatever one may think about the propriety of these actions, they were "covert" in name only. The source of funding was obvious not only by its very magnitude but by the techniques employed, which were wholly evocative of an American campaign. These included "polling, voter registration, and get-out-the-vote drives."[19] As Ambassador Korry later recalled, during the period in 1967 when he was being briefed in Washington before taking up his post in Chile, "I was told, not asked, by well-known reporters of our leading media outlets, by Congressmen, Senators, and their staffs, of the very large United States role in the election of 1964 in Chile; that is, the large effort mounted covertly." If it was a secret, he added, for some years it had been one of the most poorly kept in Chile.[20]

Covert foreign funding of Chilean electoral campaigns had become such a way of life in the period just before the 1970 presidential contest that Ambassador Korry was approached for contributions by representatives of several potential candidates, including Frei's foreign minister, Gabriel Valdés, Radomiro Tomic, Alessandri, and even Allende—whose campaign manager demanded a cool million dollars. All these proposals were sharply rejected.[21] After the nomination process was completed, it was assumed that the United States would have no choice but to follow the by-then-established practice of providing massive financial support either to Alessandri or to Tomic. Instead, something quite different occurred— a lengthy series of delays, an eventual decision to support no particular candidate, and, finally, the allocation of sums estimated at between $425,000 and $1 million to fund a "spoiling" campaign, which would merely emphasize the dangers of a Popular Unity victory.[22] In addition, the CIA in Chile produced what is called "black propaganda," that is, materials apparently originated in the constituent parties of the Allende coalition, with a view of sowing dissension among them. In this connection, CIA funds were channeled to an unidentified small political group—presumably the schismatic Democratic Radicals—with a view to reducing the number of Radical votes for Allende.[23]

Although U.S. government policy did not lean to the support of a single candidate, the American business community in Chile not unnaturally preferred Alessandri, and as early as April 1970, a board of officers of various multinationals led by Chase Manhattan Board Chairman David Rockefeller began a series of representations in this sense to the State Department. Initially they offered to raise a common fund of their own—$500,000—to be dispersed by the CIA. When informed of this proposal, Ambassador Korry sent Washington what he has described as "a blistering cable of opposition." In addition, the ambassador found himself "subjected to the most intense, incessant pressures from the CIA and its Chilean allies (including Chilean-based U.S. business concerns) to have the United States commit its covert support to their candidate. I refused."[24]

Having failed to exact a decisive commitment to Alessandri from the Nixon administration, the multinationals were nonetheless offered by way of consolation the assistance of the CIA in locating channels through which funds could be covertly passed to his campaign. In effect, however, ITT was the sole recipient of these services. The CIA and officials of ITT in Chile worked together closely in this sense, and eventually "at least $350,000 was passed by ITT to [the Alessandri] campaign." A roughly equal sum was passed through Chilean channels by other American companies, but, according to the Church committee report, "the CIA learned of this funding but did not assist in it."[25]

Even if one accepts unhestitatingly the most inflated estimates of U.S. financial involvement in the 1970 elections, it is obvious that far less was spent on that occasion than in 1964. Nor do financial figures themselves fully account for electoral outcomes—in Chile or anywhere else. In any case, to evaluate their impact fully—in 1970, at least—one would have to know more about the countervailing efforts on Allende's behalf. On this, Henry Kissinger, then national security adviser to President Nixon, has simply stated that "throughout 1970 we received credible reports that substantial covert funds and assistance from Cuba and other Communist sources were being funnelled to Allende."[26] The Church commitee report refers to "CIA estimates" that "the Cubans provided about $350,000 to Allende's campaign, with the Soviets adding an additional undetermined amount."[27] In addition, one must somehow factor in this unexpected twist: in 1970 Allende gained a considerably smaller percentage of the popular vote than he had in 1964, when covert support for his opponent was nothing less than massive. Undoubtedly, the U.S. decision not to support a particular candidate dispersed energies and resources that had been more effectively marshaled six years before; further, in the opinion of CIA Director Colby, the decision to focus on a "spoiling campaign," though "certainly a cheaper . . . tactic, also proved to be ineffective."[28] But all of this only suggests that the Nixon administration might inadvertently have contributed to Allende's victory; it does not tell us for certain what the result would have been had the U.S. government become more actively involved in the campaign, as the American business community wished it to do.

Precisely why a Republican administration would remain so impervious to corporate appeals on matters Chilean is a very arresting question. The Church committee report speculates that the Nixon administration's putative "mature relationship" with Latin America— a deemphasis on aid and social reform— possessed a covert action corollary that likewise dictated a less vigorous involvement in the political process. In addition, the report suggests that the activities of the United States in 1964 had become too obvious to be really effective a second time.[29] Former CIA official Cord Meyer offers another, simpler answer: "Nixon tried to avoid fueling a fratricidal rivalry between the two non-Communist parties by denying funds to both of them."[30]

A somewhat more elaborate and presumably more authoritative explanation has emerged in the memoirs of Henry Kissinger, who cites three factors: Nixon's and his own preoccupation with "so many other crises," domestic and foreign; an incorrect estimate of the most likely outcome of the Chilean elections ("I knew too little about Chile to challenge the experts"); and bureaucratic infighting between the CIA and the National Security Council (NSC) on one hand and the Latin American Bureau of the Department of State on the other. The latter, according to Kissinger, disliked Alessandri for being "too old, in reality because he was considered insufficiently progressive."[31] So much was this the case, he insisted, that the bureau actually preferred the risk of an Allende presidency to outright support of Alessandri. In addition, Kissinger ruefully recounts, these people "chose at this moment [1969–70] to attack the very concept of covert support for foreign democratic parties which had for so long been a central feature of our Chilean effort." The resources for any attempt to block Popular Unity's access to power, these people argued, "should hereafter be found entirely *within* Chile." What this meant, Kissinger concludes, was the demoralization "of the very forces we wanted to encourage. . . . In a close election the resultant subtle change in the psychological balance could be decisive."[32] (That Kissinger believes this does not, of course, mean it was necessarily so. But it does provide some understanding of the force and motives at work within the U.S. foreign policy apparatus.)

In any event, the so-called 40 Committee of the NSC, the body charged with monitoring covert action overseas, met to consider the Chilean elections only four times—once in April 1969, when it deferred any decision; again in March and June 1970, when it authorized the sums for the "spoiling" campaign; and finally in August 1970, at which point it was decided that nothing further could be done. Given the need for presidential approval of all its decisions and the subsequent paperwork, Kissinger writes, it is unlikely that even the relatively small sums allocated reached Chile "before the second half of July. And then the Embassy was constrained by instructions that made their effective use almost impossible."[33]

These deliberations took place against the background of repeated polls that—until quite late in the day—reflected a substantial Alessandri lead. By the time Washington's perceptions of Alessandri's prospects began to match evolving Chilean realities, a massive covert effort "had been foreclosed without ever being discussed, first with the argument that a substantial program was unnecessary, and later because it was then too late." By early September Kissinger became convinced that he had been "maneuvered into a position incompatible with my convictions—and more important, those of Nixon."[34] Thus Chile went to the polls.

U.S. Attempts to Prevent Allende's Assumption of Power

Allende's tentative victory on September 4—actually, a plurality that waited upon what was in effect a congressional runoff—fell upon the Nixon administration with an impact all the more explosive for being unexpected. The president, in Kissinger's vivid recollection, was "beside himself," insisting on doing "something, *anything*, that would reverse the previous neglect." Now that it was nearly too late, "all agencies threw themselves into a frenzied reassessment." Since the Chilean Congress was scheduled to determine the new chief executive on October 24, "we were forced to improvise . . . with no real preparation. With time running out, our actions were inevitably frantic."[35]

On September 8 and 14, the 40 Committee met to shape a response to the prospect of an Allende presidency. That effort eventually ran parallel to—and at several points intersected—another that had been germinating for some months in the Washington, New York, and Santiago offices of ITT. For reasons of both chronology and clarity, the activities of ITT are discussed here first.

Activities of ITT and the CIA

The Chilean elections were discussed at some length at the spring 1970 meeting of ITT's board of directors. At that meeting, there was a consensus that, as things then stood, Allende would win the popular election. In view of the company's large stake in Chile—which included a majority share in the national telephone company and two major hotels—this matter could not be viewed with equanimity. Hence board member John McCone, a former director of the CIA, was instructed to seek out the agency's chief, Richard Helms, to inquire what plans were under way to assist either Alessandri or Tomic. At their subsequent encounter, Helms informed McCone that the 40

Committee had already decided not to undertake a major covert effort; something would be done within the existing budget, he said—alluding, apparently, to the "spoiling" operation—but no additional funds were to be authorized for other covert purposes.

McCone then informed ITT chairman Harold Geneen of his conversation, but, to blunt its edge of disappointment, arranged with Helms for a meeting in Washington on July 16, 1970 between Geneen and William V. Broe, chief of clandestine services at the Western Hemisphere Division of the CIA. It was at this meeting, according to Broe's later testimony, that Geneen offered to raise an election fund of "substantial size" for Alessandri, to be channeled through the CIA. Broe turned aside the offer, which, he said, was inappropriate in view of U.S. policy—that is, not to support any particular candidate in the election.[36] As noted, however, the CIA subsequently agreed to assist ITT in identifying channels whereby corporate funds could be covertly passed to Alessandri. A second conduit was opened for ITT to the National party through the good offices of the station in Santiago, and representatives of the company and the agency in Chile met often to coordinate their work in the months before the elections.[37]

In the period after September 4 and up to the congressional runoff on October 24, ITT continued to be extremely active in exploring ways to forestall an Allende presidency. The most apparent opening was to persuade the Chilean Congress to confirm Alessandri rather than Allende. The former had, after all, won nearly as many popular votes as the victor, and if he could enlist a significant portion of the Christian Democratic representation in Congress, he could obtain the presidency. As conceived by ITT operatives and emissaries of Alessandri, and reported in a confidential cable from ITT's Santiago office on September 17, once confirmed by Congress, Alessandri would immediately resign. This would permit new elections, in which President Frei would then be eligible to succeed himself.[38] Although this was legal in the very narrow sense, it flew in the face of a well-established custom in Chile that the legislature confirms as president whoever receives a plurality of the popular vote; to break that precedent—with its attendant risks to the nation's political and institutional fabric—would require some additional persuasion.

To this end, at the September 9 ITT board meeting in New York, Geneen told McCone that the company was prepared to put $1 million "in support of any plan that [would bring] about a coalition of the opposition"—presumably a series of bribes to Christian Democratic congressmen. McCone then met with Kissinger and Helms to transmit the offer, but since Kissinger's office did not get in touch with him subsequently, he assumed that the tender had been rejected.[39] Meanwhile Jack Neal, director of international relations for ITT's Washington office, approached a member of Kissinger's staff and also the office of Charles A. Meyer, assistant secretary of state for inter-American relations. Although some reference was made in these conversations to a "sum in seven figures," their burden seems to have been less an offer of financial assistance than an appeal to the Nixon administration to remain neutral "in the event other attempts were made to 'save the situation' in Chile."[40]

In the final days of September there was a sudden shift in ITT tactics. A report from Santiago on the twenty-ninth cast considerable doubt on whether the "Alessandri gambit" would work, since "the prevailing sentiment among the PDC [that is, Christian Democratic congressmen who had presumably been individually canvassed] is said to favor Allende." These men would change their minds only if Chile seemed about to suffer an "economic collapse."

> The pressure resulting from economic chaos could force a major segment of the Christian Democratic party to reconsider their stance . . . It will become apparent, for instance, that there's no confidence among the business community in Allende's future policies and that the health of the nation is at stake. More important, massive unemployment and unrest might produce enough violence to force the military to move.[41]

The same day Broe met in New York with Edward J. Gerrity, senior vice-president of ITT, at the behest of his chief, Helms. It was apparent that some change of heart had occurred at the highest levels of the U.S. government, since it was now the CIA that was soliciting the help of the company. In New York Broe presented Gerrity with a plan following an identical logic, but fleshing out considerable detail what was already on its way in barest outline from the company's Chilean operatives. Specifically, he suggested that (1) American banks should not renew Chilean credits or should delay in doing so, (2) American companies should impose calculated delays on liquid advances, deliveries, and shipment of spare parts, (3) pressure should be applied to already foundering savings and loan institutions, and (4) all technical help should be withdrawn and no technical assistance promised in the future. Broe went so far as to suggest that companies in a position to do so should shut down their Chilean operations altogether. He then handed Gerrity a list of companies and suggested that ITT approach them in this sense.[42]

When he reported back to Geneen, Gerrity expressed serious doubts that the plan would work, an opinion later seconded by McCone.[43] In any case, there were no takers among other multinationals or major financial institutions. This was foreshadowed at the September 29 meeting, when Broe told Gerrity that "of all the companies involved [that is, companies with investments in Chile] *ours alone* had been responsible and understood the problem."[44] On October 9, after some soundings had apparently taken place, Charles Merriam, ITT's executive representative for international trade, was complaining in a memorandum to McCone that practically no progress has been made in trying to get American business to cooperate in some way to bring on economic chaos. General Motors and Ford, for example, say that they have too much inventory on hand in Chile to take any chances, and they keep hoping everything will work out right. Also, the Bank of America has agreed to close its doors in Santiago but each day keeps postponing the inevitable. According to my source, we must continue to keep the pressure on business.[45]

American banks proved particularly unreceptive to these appeals. Their executives, subpoenaed by the Senate Subcommittee on Multinational Corporations, or interviewed by its staff, categorically denied having been approached at this time by the CIA, ITT, or Chilean nationals. While strictly speaking this may not be true, the subcommittee itself could find "no evidence of [their] involvement . . . in a plan to block President Allende's election [either by the Congress] or in a concerted effort to weaken him by creating 'financial chaos.' "[46] Contrary to the Bank of America's promise to ITT, it did not "close its doors in Santiago."[47] Further, during this period, Manufacturers' Hanover Trust actually *increased* slightly its lines of credit to Chile,[48] as did the First National City Bank of New York; what makes the latter case particularly interesting is that the borrowers were Chilean government agencies rather than private individuals or firms.[49] Thus, for all the cable time, telephone calls, meetings, and lunches, and in spite of the undeniably dramatic flavor of the discussions, *in an operational sense no joint ITT-CIA plan to bribe the Congress or unleash a financial crisis ever existed.*[50]

Although it runs slightly ahead of the story, something should be appended here concerning ITT's activities after Allende's inauguration. In early 1971 Merriam invited Washington representatives of major U.S. corporate investors in Chile to form an ad hoc committee to coordinate their responses to the new government. The first meeting—one of several—took place in January, attended by personnel from Anaconda, Kennecott, Ralston Purina, Bank of America, Pfizer Chemical, and W. R. Grace.

The purpose of this committee, summarized in a minute prepared by Ronald Raddatz, the Bank of America representative, was to apply "pressure on the [U.S.] government, wherever possible, to make it clear that a Chilean takeover [of American properties] would not be tolerated without serious repercussions following."[51] This pressure, Merriam later testified, was expected to convince the U.S. government of the desirability of blocking loans to Chile by multilateral credit institutions such as the World Bank and the Inter-American Development Bank; this presumably would confront Allende with an early prospect of economic collapse and persuade him to become more disposed to negotiate with ITT on terms more favorable to the company than had been anticipated.[52]

Apparently the Anaconda Corporation shared the notion that this was the best way to proceed against the new Chilean government.[53] It quickly became clear, however, that other companies were moving to cut their losses, strike the best deal with Allende they could manage, or collect their insurance from the Overseas Private Investment Corporation. For example, Ralston Purina's Washington representative, William C. Foster, attended only the first meeting of the ad hoc committee; thereafter he was forbidden by his superiors to continue. The president of Ralston Purina gratuitously added his opposition to the "basic approach suggested," although Foster understood the purpose of the committee to be not the coordination of economic warfare but stiffening the resolve of the U.S. government,[54] which was seen by committee members as far too conciliatory toward expropriating Latin American governments.[55] As for Kennecott, after attending two meetings of the committee, its representative Lyle Mercer concluded that "there was no particular value to us for continued participation."[56] The Bank of America representative likewise withdrew after the second meeting.[57]

Abandoned by three of the seven original members of the committee, ITT persisted in lobbying the Nixon administration on its own. In late September 1971—now facing imminent expropriation—company representatives called upon Assistant Secretary Meyer and argued for an embargo of Chilean copper, combined with an immediate cut-off of all U.S. economic assistance. These proposals met with tepid response; Secretary Meyer reminded his visitors that, after all, a copper embargo would be tantamount to "an act of war."[58] A few days later Merriam submitted a detailed 18-point plan, which was designed to prevent Allende from getting through the allegedly "crucial" next six months, to Peter G. Peterson, Nixon's White House aide for international economic affairs. Among other things, the plan called for an embargo on all Chilean exports to the United States, not just copper, and delay or embargo of key U.S. exports to Chile, perhaps even extending to fuels destined for the Chilean armed forces. The plan also contained a covert political action component of grandiose proportions, including subversion of ("developing contacts with") the Chilean military, judiciary, and civil service, as well as coordinated diplomatic efforts with other foreign governments to isolate and pressure Allende.[59]

Peterson later testified that he did not take the ITT program seriously, but more to the point, he added, "If one reads what actually came out of [the] policy work on January 19, 1972, there is certainly no relationship that I can see between the recommendations of ITT and the administration's decision."[60] The "policy work" to which he referred was an NSC study commissioned in June 1971, to examine the probable economic and foreign policy aspects of Chilean expropriations of American property. The "decision" refers to a Presidential policy directive which conditioned future economic benefits to

Chile upon "reasonable steps to provide adequate compensation" for expropriated property. Indeed, the only area where the ITT memorandum and the Nixon directive clearly overlapped was in the matter of U.S. votes at the multilateral development banks. (See below).

On October 21, 1971, the major U.S. companies involved in Chile met with Secretary of State William Rogers, Jr. On that occasion ITT—once again in the lead—submitted to the Secretary its "White Paper on Chile," an abbreviated version of the 18-point economic warfare plan offered three weeks before to Peterson. The reaction at the meeting was mixed, both on the part of Rogers and the other company representatives present. The secretary emphasized the minimal leverage possessed by the United States over Chile, and his "only positive statements," the ITT minute noted, were a promise to speak out publicly against expropriations, and—if the appeals of the American copper companies were denied[61]—to invoke the Hickenlopper Amendment.[62] (In fact, however, the latter was never invoked against Chile.) The ITT minute concluded that Secretary Rogers was "pretty much going along with the . . . soft-line, low profile policy for Latin America" of Assistant Secretary Meyer, obviously not much to the company's taste.[63]

Having failed to organize a united front of American business concerns in Chile, and eliciting a minimal response from the Nixon administration, ITT turned from its plans for economic disruption to the serious pursuit of a negotiated settlement with the Chilean government. These talks had actually begun at the same time as the action just described, but apparently as a mere pro forma exercise while more adventurous strategies were explored. Having failed at the latter, the company was left with no choice but to behave responsibly and hope for the best.

Nixon, the CIA, and the Schneider Debacle: Tracks I and II

The sudden approach of the CIA to ITT on September 29 was a partial result of two meetings of the 40 Committee on September 8 and 14, 1970, whose purpose was to plot a response to the fact of Allende's electoral victory. These deliberations led to a decision to unleash a program of covert political activity to deny Allende the presidency through constitutional means (that is, some variant of the "Alessandri gambit"). The day after the second of these two conclaves, however, President Nixon summoned CIA Director Helms to his office, and in the presence of Kissinger and Attorney General John Mitchell issued secret instructions to organize a military coup in Chile to forestall a Popular Unity government. So secret, indeed, were these orders that they were kept not only from the State Department and Ambassador Korry, but even from the 40 Committee itself. To preserve cover, Helms was ordered to use a private reporting channel that would extend directly from the

CIA station chief in Santiago to Kissinger or his military deputy, Colonel Alexander Haig.[64] The Church committee subsequently labeled these two different approaches "Track I" and "Track II," respectively.[65]

To implement Track I, on September 14 the 40 Committee authorized Ambassador Korry to enlist Frei's aid in rounding up congressional support for the "Alessandri gambit." To this end, a $250,000 contingency fund was set aside to bribe wavering Christian Democrats legislators.[66] When these efforts met with no success, an alternative version of the scenario was devised, calling for what would essentially be a "preventive" military coup. Under this plan—which Kissinger attributes to Korry and assumes was "cleared by associates" of the Chilean president—key ministers of the outgoing government would resign and induce their colleagues to follow suit. Frei would then have the option of replacing them with military officers. "In other words," Kissinger explains, "Frei was to be given the means to trigger a constitutional crisis—designed, as in every other scheme [within Track I], to lead to another election so that the country could choose between Frei and Allende, between democracy and potential dictatorship." Here, however, Washington encountered additional difficulties:

> There was doubt about Frei's willingness to do this [either]. The principal obstacle, however, was perceived to be the Commander-in-Chief of the Army, General [René] Schneider, who took the position that the politicians having put Chile into this mess, it behooved them to extricate her. Another stumbling block was reported to be the fear of the Chilean military that if they acted they would be treated like the Greek junta—that is to say, deprived of military aid by the United States and harassed by the left globally.[67]

The 40 Committee then ordered Korry to meet with military leaders and assure them that they had nothing to fear from the United States on this score but that, conversely, inactivity would lead to what they most wished to avoid; and on September 29 pipeline shipments of military equipment were held up precisely to make this threat credible. At the same time, a propaganda campaign was mounted to convince Chileans, both civilian and military, of the economic ills that would befall the country in the event of a Marxist government. It was in this context, for example, that Ambassador Korry made his statement, much quoted subsequently, that in the event of an Allende accession the United States would not allow "a nut or a bolt" to reach Chile.[68]

On October 3–4, the Christian Democratic party assembled to consider, among other things, the attitude to be taken in the coming congressional balloting. On that occasion Frei made no attempt to persuade his followers to prevent Allende from assuming office. At the same time, it was clear to Washington that the military required additional pressure, and Korry was instructed to apply it.

What in effect was happening, as Kissinger has observed, was that Track

I and Track II were merging, though without the knowledge of some of the principal American and Chilean actors. Korry thought he was still working for a "constitutional" coup, although without Frei's cooperation, it is difficult to see how this scenario could be played out. Meanwhile, second-echelon elements of the same military who presumably would play a role in convoking new elections were being coaxed along a different path by the CIA. As the deadline date for the congressional runoff approached and the embassy's efforts proved increasingly fruitless, Nixon and Kissinger shifted emphasis— if not in intent, then by action and inaction—to an outright military coup.

The difficulties encountered along Track I paled into insignificance when compared with the obstacles faced by those who would implement Track II. Indeed, the latter could be mounted only over the loud and persistent objections of the intelligence community, who believe that conditions in Chile simply did not lend themselves to an adventure of this sort.[69] Nixon, whose respect for these people was not inordinately great in any case, waved their warnings aside. Thus, between September 15 and October 20, the CIA made twenty-one contacts with key military and police officers in Chile who were known to favor such action.[70]

Recruiting "assets," particularly on such short notice, proved an extremely daunting task, for U.S. policy during the Frei years had systematically discouraged coup plotting among the military. And as a result that policy—in the words of one intelligence professional—the CIA had "deliberately distanced itself from those officers who were inclined to think in those terms."[71] Eventually the CIA narrowed its search to two groups: one led by General Roberto Viaux, who had been forcibly retired after leading an unsuccessful military revolt in 1969, the other by General Camilo Valenzuela, commander of the Santiago military district. Both had qualities that recommended them to agency operatives. Viaux, whose adventure the year before was ostensibly a protest against the budgetary neglect of armed forces personnel, was a popular figure among career enlisted men and junior officers, and, since his retirement, a recognized figure in right-wing circles. As an active-duty officer in a key assignment, General Valenzuela was in contact with other senior military and naval figures and, what was more to the point, commander of the one garrison whose support was vital to success.[72]

Here again the obstacle was thought to be General Schneider. Failing to obtain Schneider's reassignment, the coup plotters decided to kidnap him and put him on a plane to Argentina. The CIA eventually decided in favor of the Valenzuela group; Kissinger says that Viaux and his associates were so informed on October 17;[73] the Church committee agrees.[74] The Valenzuela group carried out two abortive attempts, one on October 19 and one on the following day. One last effort was to be made on October 22. At 2 a.m. on the morning of that day, the CIA distributed to Valenzuela's men three submachine guns, some ammunition, tear gas grenades, and masks, all of which had entered Chile through the U.S. diplomatic pouch. Before this effort could actually be consummated, however, the Viaux group moved on its own. General Schneider's car was pushed off the road while he was being driven to work; the commander himself was shot and critically wounded when he reached for his pistol. The plotters fled, and the commander-in-chief died three days later in a Santiago military hospital.[75]

The Chilean military court that subsequently investigated the crime reported that General Schneider had been killed by handguns. These, in the findings of the Church committee, "were, in all probability, not those supplied by the CIA to the conspirators."[76] The committee also noted that an *unloaded* machine gun had been found at the site of the killing, but professed itself "unable to determine whether [it] was one of the three supplied by the CIA."[77]

The U.S. Role, November 1969–November 1970

If one assumes that the purpose of U.S. policy in Chile during the period under review was to prevent Allende's accession to power, one must confront the fact that virtually all American actions—whether by public or by private agencies—proved either irrelevant or counterproductive. The U.S. government's refusal to support a single candidate in the presidential campaign obviously inflicted no harm whatever on Allende's quest, and may even—if one accepts Kissinger's logic—have ensured his victory. Both the so-called spoiling campaign sponsored by the United States, and the more or less independent funding activities of U.S. corporations on behalf of Alessandri, seem to have had no decisive effect, at least in the direction desired.

In the period between election and inauguration, both ITT and the CIA, acting on instruction from President Nixon, explored various means of unleashing "economic chaos" in Chile, with a view either to convincing the Christian Democrats of the inadvisability of confirming Allende in the congressional balloting, or to persuading the Chilean military in effect to nullify the elections so as to restage them later as a two-way race. At the same time, $250,000 was set aside to win the concurrence of Christian Democrats deputies and senators, and military shipments to Chile were held up to convince the armed forces that failure to act in a way desired by the United States would have very serious consequences.

So much for U.S. intentions; the results were quite different. The CIA and ITT found it impossible to enlist other corporations and the banks in the plan to unleash "economic chaos." And although there was a high degree of economic uncertainty during the weeks between Allende's election and his inauguration, it arose out of preoccupations quite logical in their own terms, not as the result of an orchestrated campaign or concrete economic actions, which the Senate Subcommittee on Multinational Corporations was utterly unable to document. Even in the areas under its direct competence, the U.S. government betrayed a remarkable lack of bureaucratic coordination; even pipeline disbursements of nonmilitary aid to Chile continued unabated throughout this period.

Neither President Frei nor the Christian Democrats in Congress could be persuaded to play the role desired by Washington and the U.S. embassy in Santiago; consequently, the $250,000 that had been set aside *was never actually spent*.[78] The Chilean military could not be bribed negatively into sponsoring a coup, whether for new elections or some other purpose (Track I); when second-echelon figures in the armed forces were enlisted by the CIA to remove (not assassinate) General Schneider (Track II), a lack of control and discipline led to the precipitant events that climaxed in his death. The effect of the Schneider debacle was precisely the opposite of what was desired: it transformed the victim into a martyr of the "constitutionalist" traditions of the Chilean army; it encouraged other constitutionalist officers to support an orderly transfer of power to the new administration; and it discredited right-wing cabals both in the army and outside of it.[79] Two days after Schneider's death, the Congress met and with impressive dispatch confirmed Allende as the victor in the presidential contest.

ITT fared no better in its efforts. Shortly after Allende's inauguration, the company found itself subjected to the same treatment accorded to other large private economic concerns—the imposition of strict price controls combined with large mandated wage increases. In short order, the company began to experience serious cash flow problems.[80] Eventually the Chilean state took over the Chilean Telephone Company and offered to buy out ITT's local holdings for approximately $24 million. This was slightly more than one-eighth the company's own assessment of their book value, an appraisal that must have been closer to the truth, since it had been paying premiums to the Overseas Private Investment Corporation for properties worth over $108 million.[81] For some months negotiations between the company and the Chilean government dragged on with no visible result; the publication of the ITT documents by columnist Jack Anderson in March 1972 afforded the Allende regime a pretext to break off the talks. It was said—then and subsequently— that ITT deserved no better because of the role it had played in attempting to thwart Chile's democratic and constitutional processes. This argument would possess undeniable weight were it not for the fact that, by its own admission, the Chilean government had moved against the company's holdings in ignorance of the role that ITT had played in 1970 and early 1971.[82] Thus it cannot be doubted that even if ITT's conduct in Chile had conformed to the highest canons of corporate responsibility, it would have suffered precisely the same punitive and confiscatory treatment—as in the event it received.

U.S.—Chilean Economic Relations During the Allende Government

That Allende's accession to power was not regarded as welcome news by the United States requires no further documentation. There was, in the first place, a significant economic interest in Chile that was endangered by the new government. This included approximately half a billion dollars' worth of investment exposure, a large part of which was insured by the Overseas Private Investment Corporation—that is, ultimately, by the U.S. taxpayer.[83] At stake also were some crucial ideological and geopolitical issues—issues that, in the retrospective view of both former President Nixon and format Chilean Foreign Minister Clodomiro Almeyda, far overshadowed economic questions.[84]

With Allende's election, a decade's worth of hopes, skills, and resources poured into Chile under the Alliance for Progress appeared for naught. A socialist state on the Latin American continental landmass posed the threat of a contagion that could not—as in Cuba—be easily confined within the boundaries of a single state. Chile might become a base for continental terrorist and extremist groups allied to the Soviet Union or Cuba. At a minimum, Allende's victory offered Castro a major opportunity to breach the wall of isolation that the United States and its allies had sought to erect around him.

In a global perspective, Allende's victory was also a serious set-back for the United States. As Ambassador Korry subsequently remarked, at the very time when President Nixon was about to launch new diplomatic initiatives in Moscow and Peking, "to act indifferent to the disappearing . . . of a unique democracy in what was viewed throughout the world as [our own] backyard, could have a significant effect on those who make policy in the Soviet Union and the People's Republic of China." Further, with impending elections in Italy and France, "popular front tactics [could alter] the whole fundamental structure of Western defense, Western ideals." In this, he affirmed, "the Chilean model could have a certain effect."[85]

Whether such premonitions on the part of U.S. policymakers were fully justified is quite beside the point. These were the operative assumptions upon which the United States proceeded to deal with President Allende, notwithstanding some fulsome assurances by President Nixon that the United States was "prepared to have the kind of relationship with the [new] Chilean government that it is prepared to have with us."[86] Rather less clear, however, is the degree to which the United States was able to translate its concerns into an effective policy. Put simply, having established the fundamental hostility of the United States to the Allende experiment, we are still left to measure its effect.

Economic Relations and the "Invisible Blockade"

The onset of serious economic difficulties after the regime's euphoric first year almost inevitably focused attention on relations with Chile's formerly preeminent partner in matters of trade, credit, and investment. The Popular Unity view of this matter was most definitively expressed by President Allende himself in a speech to the United Nations General Assembly on December 4, 1972. On that occasion he declared his country was the victim of "a new form of imperialism—more subtle, more artful, and for that reason all the more effective in impeding the exercise of our rights as a sovereign state." In this address Allende made particular reference to a "financial-economic blockade," "not an open aggression . . . but an attack at once oblique, subterranean, but no less lethal for Chile," whose purpose, he maintained, was "to isolate us internationally, strangle our economy, paralyze the sale of our principal export, copper. And to deprive us of access to sources of international financing."[87]

Since the 1973 coup, the concept of an "invisible" or "informal blockade" has been raised to the level of an omnibus explanation for the regime's most critical economic disjunctions. The subsequent publication by the Church committee of CIA Director Helms's notes taken during his September 15, 1970, meeting with President Nixon and Kissinger seems to provide confirmation of Allende's charges from U. S. official sources, since on that occasion Helms quoted Nixon as having ordered the CIA "to make the [Chilean] economy scream."[88] A corroborative piece of evidence—also uncovered by the Church committee—was National Security Council Memorandum 93 of November 1970, which established U. S. policies toward the new government. In the economic field, that document called for "all new bilateral foreign assistance . . . to be stopped . . . . The U. S. would use its predominant position in international financial institutions to dry up the flow of new multilateral credit or other financial assistance. To the extent possible, financial assistance or guarantees to U. S. private investment in Chile would be ended, and U. S. businesses would be made aware of the government's concern and its restrictive policies."[89]

Given the fact that U. S.-Chilean economic relations were dispersed along a rather broad front of activities, they must be explored layer by layer. Here we discuss the foreign debt, relations with the multilateral banks, relations with private banks, private suppliers of equipment and spare parts, and public (that is, government-to-government) aid programs. Finally, we review the credit available to Chile from alternative sources. Only then will it be possible to measure the proximate dimensions of the "invisible blockade."

The foreign debt. For some years before Allende's election, Chile had come to depend heavily on foreign borrowing to cover its trade and fiscal deficits. Such negative balances arose in part out of fluctuations in the world price of copper, whose volatile movements were capable of depriving the country almost overnight of resources needed to meet medium- and long-term commitments. Infusions of foreign capital—whether from governments, multilateral banks, or private foreign banks—eventually imposed an increasing burden of debt services, which as early as 1960 constituted 11 percent of the country's export earnings. Ten years later—that is, the year of Allende's election—that figure had ballooned to 37 percent.

Consequently, even before the advent of Popular Unity, international economists were beginning to worry about Chile; perhaps only the temporary boom in copper prices during the mid-1960s, producing the first trade surplus in many years, was capable of drowning out their warnings. Nonetheless, as one authoritative study recounts, "even in those prosperous days, [financial experts] were predicting that copper prices would soon fall and that Chile would need more than a billion dollars in new loans if the country was to continue to develop." In addition, it would require $600 million more for debt service. Because of the Vietnam War and the inflated price of copper, the exchange crisis predicted for the final years of Frei's administration was postponed for several years and in fact fell during the Allende period. It is worth noting, however, that even during the apparently halcyon Christian Democratic era, "Chile continued to experience a current account deficit during all but one of these years [1965–1970], and the country maintained its surplus only because foreign investment and external lending continued to be substantial."[90]

Without doubt the willingness of foreign creditors to extend new lines to Chile during this period constituted a vote of confidence as much political as economic; this was particularly true of those in the United States. But that confidence rested not merely on evident ideological compatibility, but on a vigorous Chilean program of improved tax collections, the projected expansion of copper production, and respectful treatment of foreign investment and foreign obligations generally. Further, these creditors were operating on assumptions about future events in Chile quite different from those that subsequently occurred. The political difficulties that erased the profit balances of copper mining under Allende simply were not anticipated, and even the relatively conservative projections that forecast trouble for the late 1960s assumed a far lower bill for imports and foodstuffs than materialized under a socialist government.

The long-avoided moment of truth came in November 1971, when President Allende announced a moratorium on foreign debt servicing and requested a general refinancing of Chile's international obligations. Between February and April 1972, Chilean delegates met for this purpose in Paris with representatives of the eleven nations holding shares in the country's public foreign debt.[91] In spite of the fact that some $1.23 billion of the total principal of $1.86 billion was owed to the United States, the United States was unable to persuade other members of the "Paris club" to link refinancing to compensation of the expropriated copper companies.[92] Instead, the Chileans obtained a quite favorable settlement, which allowed them to roll over for an eight-year period 70 percent of the debts that matured between November 1971 and December 1972. In addition, a two-year period of grace was extended to the remaining 30 percent, which would otherwise have fallen due immediately. Finally, the Paris club members agreed to consider Chile's request for a rescheduling of the country's 1973 debt service at the end of 1972; preliminary talks on this subject finally opened after several postponements in May 1973, and were still in progress at the time of the coup.

Within the general framework of the Paris club agreements it was left to Chile to work out bilaterally the exact sums and interest rates with each of the creditor nations. As a result, the Allende regime obtained even more extensive relief. For no final agreement on the debts owed to the United States was ever reached, and the Allende government never actually serviced the amount that otherwise would have been remitted to Chile's principal creditor. This in itself constituted a de facto relief on foreign debt servicing for 1972 alone of approximately $243 million.[93] Based on the then-current dimensions of Chilean exports (one billion dollars a year), the Paris club renegotiations—taken as a whole—increased the foreign exchange availability to the Allende government by approximately one third.

The multilateral development banks. Chile fared somewhat differently at the hands of the Inter-American Development Bank and the International Bank for Reconstruction and Development, more commonly known as the World Bank. Although both bodies had long supported Chilean efforts in economic and social development, during the Allende years there was a perceptible contraction in their financing role. Given the preponderant voice that the United States at least reputedly exercised in the deliberation of both bodies, many have concluded—along with President Allende—that political rather than strictly economic criteria determined the policies of both banks towards the Chilean government.

Sensitive to charges of this sort, both agencies have been at considerable pains to refute them. To this end, each issued a white paper documenting its dealings with the regime. The IDB brief advances the following points: (1) that two new "soft" loans were approved in early 1971 to expand the Catholic

University in Santiago and the Universidad Austral in Valdivia; (2) that slightly more than $70 million—loans approved during the Frei administration—was disbursed to Chile during the Allende period, making the Popular Unity government the recipient of the largest annual disbursements in the bank's history; (3) that the bank received three new project requests during the Allende period, which were at various stages of study, none reaching the vote stage by September, 1973; (4) that the bank rewrote an ordinary capital loan approved in 1969 at the Allende government's request in 1971 and by June 1973, had committed $13.1 million to this project—involving thirty-nine industrial ventures in which the Chilean State Development Corporation (CORFO) would own 49 percent of the stock—in addition to which it organized funding from nonbank sources bringing the figure to $54.2 million; and (5) that during these years the bank financed several million dollars' worth of capital imports to Chile from other member countries.[94] This still left, of course, no major *new* loans both approved and disbursed during the life of the Popular Unity government.

An independent study of Chile's relations with the multilateral development banks found the IDB guilty of a lack of consistency in lending policies, compared both with its past treatment of Chile and in its dealings with other Latin American nations during this period; but the critical focus of the study centered on the failure to approve new loans (and what it regarded as an unreasonable delay in processing new applications), rather than on a lack of disbursements. It also suggested that IDB officials discouraged Chilean representatives from tendering certain kinds of loan applications in 1972 and 1973 on the grounds that, given Chile's lack of creditworthiness, such requests would not be favorably considered by the bank's executive board. Thus the fact that—apart from the two small university loans—no new projects actually came before the board for a vote during the Allende period could not, in this reasoning, have been due merely to technical problems or to Chilean restraint.[95]

What of the World Bank? Its own white paper recounted a close if increasingly troubled relationship with successive Chilean governments. On one hand, between 1948 and 1973 Chile received nearly $235 million worth of credit from this institution. On the other, in the half-decade before Allende's election, the bank began to worry about what it regarded as the country's gradually deteriorating creditworthiness, its general economic performance, and its relatively high rate of inflation. So much was this the case that, apart from a large burst in 1967, presumably related to the copper expansion program, Chile received relatively little assistance from the World Bank during the Christian Democratic period, particularly when compared with the IDB or, for that matter, the U.S. government and U.S. private lenders (see Table 7.1).

TABLE 7.1
Loans Approved for Chile by Multilateral Banks, 1965—1973
(millions of dollars)

Fiscal Year	World Bank	Inter-American Development Bank
1965	4.4	4.9
1966	2.7	62.2
1967	60.0	31.0
1968	—	16.5
1969	11.6	31.9
1970	19.3	45.6
1971	—	12.0
1972	—	2.1
1973	—	5.2a

Source: Covert Action in Chile, p. 34.

Notes: Does not reflect actual disbursements. Dashes indicate no loans approved.

a = Loan approved after September 11, 1973.

Against this background it is not surprising that the bank should voice serious reservations about Allende's economic policies, particularly his artificial acceleration of demand, cavalier treatment of inherited reserves of foreign exchange, and neglect of productive investment. Quite early (February 1971) bank officials warned Chilean representatives that the quest for wholesale "structural and institutional changes" added an element of "uncertainty" to the short-term economic outlook, and reminded them that "the basic criteria of economic rationality and efficacy apply to socialist as well as capitalist-oriented economies."

During the first year of the Allende regime, the World Bank completed the preliminary studies for three new loans: one for electric power, one for livestock development, and one for fruit and vineyard processing. A conflict over electrical rates to be charged consumers quickly caused the first to be shelved; the second and third were at various stages of completion when it became clear that the country could no longer service its foreign debt according to schedule.

During 1972 relations between Chile and the bank deteriorated, as the latter repeated its call for "an investment program setting priorities for the next several years together with an analysis of the monetary, fiscal, and balance of payments implications" that would allow a fuller evaluation of the country's creditworthiness. For their part, Chilean delegates at various meetings accused the bank of serving "not all its members, but [acting] as the mouthpiece or tool of special private interests of one of its member countries." On January 1, 1973, Chile suspended all payments of interest and principal on its obligations to the bank.

During the first six months of 1973 there were repeated attempts by both Chile and the bank to resolve their differences. By mid-year the Chileans had agreed to resume service on their debt to the bank, and to make good by December 31 the payments that were in arrears. In exchange, the bank authorized $5 million for feasibility studies that would justly future loans. At the time of the coup, however, no action on these had been taken beyond the preliminary paperwork.[96]

Unquestionably Chile's decision not to compensate the American copper companies damaged its credit standing in the United States, but whether this decision dictated bank policy is far from established. As World Bank President Robert McNamara reminded Chilean representatives in October 1972, the bank had a history of lending to countries that opted to nationalize basic resources—and this over the objections of one or more great powers. The difficulties between the bank and Chile occurred about (but not quite) simultaneously with the country's suspension of service on its public debt. And that the Special Copper Tribunal refused to hear appeals by Anaconda and Kennecott at just about the time the bank was concluding (as the result of a special mission) that economic circumstances did not justify new lending to Chile does, however, provide some space for the dark inferences drawn by Popular Unity spokesmen at the time (and sympathetic commentators thereafter).[97]

Although Chile thus received no new loans from the World Bank during Allende's presidency, it fared only slightly better in the first two and final three years of his moderate predecessor. This suggests a quite conservative lending policy generally—one that, on other grounds, might be the proper object of criticism. But with respect to the issue at hand, it strongly suggests—as the independent study cited above concludes—that the bank was "relatively consistent" in its treatment of Chile throughout both Christian Democratic and Popular Unity periods.[98]

Some confusion has been introduced into this controversy by the Church committee's publication of the contents of NSC Memorandum 93 and also by President Nixon's admission that after Allende's election he had instructed U.S. representatives at the multilateral banks to vote against Chilean loan applications.[99] But the truth is that—apart from the two university loans approved by the IDB in early 1971, no such petitions actually came before the executive board of either during the Popular Unity years.[100] Was this the result of U.S. efforts? At the IDB there was considerable delay in processing new applications, and it is known that bank officials actively discouraged new Chilean initiatives; when compared with its past role in Chile, and its contemporaneous treatment of other member states, this points strongly to U.S. pressures within the organization. It is far more difficult to document such patterns at the World Bank. Without discarding the possibility that the United States *attempted* to influence the latter's dealings with Chile, however, it must be noted that whatever political pressures may have been operative in the first instance would inevitably have been overwhelmed in short order by economic criteria. That is, if one can look past the bank's historical lending policies up to the autumn of 1971, Paul Sigmund may be justified in remarking upon "a certain disingenuousness [on the part of the World Bank] in the constant reference to creditworthiness at a time when Chile was still paying her debts";[101] for 1972 and 1973, however, Allende's own economic policies, undertaken independently and against the advice of World Bank technicians, were bringing about—ironically enough—precisely the situation that President Nixon would have willed if he could.

Relations with private U.S. banks. Private lending from the United States to Chile declined dramatically during the Popular Unity period. Cancellation of credit lines was gradual, however, and did not reach significant proportions until the fourth quarter of 1971—that is, after Allende's suspension of service on the foreign public debt.[102] The effect of this withdrawal of lending confidence was not negligible, since private U.S. banks had traditionally provided relatively low-cost money to finance imports and for rotating credits. There is no evidence of concerted activity, however, or even of financial "quarantine"; in mid-1973, for instance, the Bank of America was still involved in Chilean lending, both to local banks and to government corporations.[103]

Alexis Guardia, who served as an important economic adviser to President Allende, has since claimed that American banks withdrew credit lines pending resolution of Chile's external debt refinancing by the Paris club; however, he complains, "once an agreement was made . . . the U.S. banks did not modify their policy."[104] Guardia passes right over the fact that although the United States initialled the Paris club agreements, those documents released Chile from its most pressing credit obligations, while establishing that it would have to reach an individual understanding with each member country. The United States was never able to conclude a refinancing agreement with the Allende government. Nor can the conduct of U.S. banks be divorced from general business and economic conditions in Chile, and the Popular Unity government's treatment of its own private banking sector.[105]

Equipment and Spare Parts. At the time of Allende's election most of the equipment in use in the most critical sectors of the economy—copper, steel, electricity, petroleum, and transport—was of U.S. origin. By late 1972, according to data cited from Chilean sources by the Church committee, "almost one-third of the diesel trucks at the Chuquiquimata copper mine, 30 percent of the privately-owned city buses, 21 percent of all taxis, and 33 percent of the state-owned buses in Chile could not operate because of the lack of spare parts or tires."[106] What was the nature of these shortages, and to what could they be attributed?

Court attachments of the assets of CORFO and the Chilean State Copper Corporation (CODELCO) in New York State in early 1972 made some Chilean acquisitions in the United States more difficult—more difficult, but not at all impossible. First, these attachments did not affect private Chilean entrepreneurs, whose problems arose out of either a shortage of credit or their own government's foreign exchange constraints. Second, no restrictions were placed on the acquisition of parts by third parties, whether Chilean private citizens, Mexicans, or even Soviet intermediaries. Third, had the Chileans chosen to do so, they could have established purchasing agencies in other states.[107] Fourth, according to the testimony of two former functionaries of the Allende government, it was possible to acquire many spare parts from European and Latin American subsidiaries of U.S. companies.[108]

The problem of spare parts actually centered not on U.S. government restrictions, which did not exist, but on the availability of short-term credits. Indeed, in this connection it is not at all certain that the court attachments were really important, because by the time they were ordered in February and March 1972, the country's access to short-term financing had been seriously impaired by the moratorium on the foreign debt. Moreover, to the end of the Allende regime it was possible for Chilean government representatives to purchase critical spare parts *for cash*, and in fact Norman Gall reported in mid-1972 that such parts were acquired for the Chuquiquimata mine and flown directly to Chile. One of the managers he interviewed at that mine even remarked in passing that "the freezing of our New York bank accounts . . . does not seem now to prevent us from buying supplies in the United States."[109] Likewise, at the October 21, 1971 meeting of U.S. corporate representatives with Secretary Rogers, a spokesman for Ford Motor reported that his company had "been asked to continue to supply spare parts to Chile." It had "indicated that they will," he said, "with firm letters of credit on reputable banks." (This in spite of the fact that Ford's Chilean properties had just been expropriated and that the company had been forced to write off losses amounting to $16 million.)[110]

It is true that at the same meeting Secretary Rogers "raised the question of whether there should be an informal embargo on spare parts and materials being shipped to Chile." But according to the minutes, on this subject "the consensus of the group was quite mixed." Rogers urged the companies to hold periodic meetings with a view to "solidify[ing] a position."[111] No evidence has come to light suggesting that such an agreement was ever reached or implemented. Once again, by early 1972 Chile's credit standing imposed as serious a restraint on the acquisiton of spare parts as any "informal embargo" might conceivably produce.[112]

Public Aid Programs from the United States. U.S. public aid to Chile—as expressed in loans and grants—fell dramatically during the Allende years, from an annual average (for fiscal years 1965–1970) of $119 million to slightly less than $7 million (1971–1973). To some degree the comparison is inevitably skewed by the fact that the Christian Democratic period was one in which Chile received unusually heavy assistance within the Alliance for Progress; further, the Nixon administration, whose views on aid to Latin America were (to say the very least) more astringent than its predecessors, began cutting back a full year before Allende's election. Thus the figure for total loans and grants authorized for FY 1970 (Table 7.2) is significantly lower than for previous years, though still, of course, higher than the amounts appropriated during each of the three Popular Unity years.[113]

As the table demonstrates, U.S. public assistance during the Allende period was dominated by loans and grants for military acquisitions, which reached a historic high.[114] There was nothing particularly sinister about this development, however. Allende and his ministers, Ambassador Davis has recalled, "requested and approved all credits, sales, training, and other [military] cooperation between Chile and the United States." The ambassador adds that "the consistent thrust of President Allende's public and private posture was to support military cooperation and credit and to criticize us if we showed signs of cutting back." What is perhaps of equal or greater moment, U.S. arms sales to Chile during this period were overshadowed by purchases from the United Kingdom and other Western sources.[115]

Important as it was, military aid was not the only form of U.S assistance that continued under Allende. "Old" loans continued to be disbursed, amounting—according to one U.S. Treasury estimate—to "perhaps $200 million" for 1971 and 1972.[116] In addition, humanitarian aid—represented by the Peace Corps and the dispatch of surplus foods—was not withdrawn—it was shipment of the latter, including more than 10 million pounds of powdered milk in 1971, that "made it possible for President Allende to carry out his pledge to give a daily free pint of milk to every school child."[117] As Table 7.2

TABLE 7.2
Foreign Aid to Chile from U.S. Government Sources, Fiscal Years 1967–1973
(millions of U.S. dollars)

	1967	1968	1969	1970	1971	1972	1973
AID[a]	15.5	57.9	35.4	18.0	1.5	1.0	0.8
Food for Peace	7.9	23.0	15.0	7.2	6.3	5.9	2.5
Export-Import Bank	234.6	14.2	28.7	3.3	0	1.6	3.1
Total U.S. economic assistance	258.0	95.1	79.1	28.5	7.8	8.5	6.4
Military aid	4.1	7.8	11.8	0.8	5.7	12.3	15.0
Total military and economic aid	262.1	102.9	90.9	29.3	13.5	20.8	21.4

Source: Covert Action in Chile, p. 34.
Note: Corrections in addition made by author. [a] = Agency for International Development.

indicated, in spite of President Nixon's decision to end all bilateral assistance not already committed at the time of Allende's election, new appropriations — however token in proportion — were nonetheless authorized during every year of the Popular Unity government.

The episode that placed U.S. assistance policies in the most unfavorable light concerned a Chilean attempt to borrow $21 million from the U.S. Export-Import Bank for the purchase of three Boeing passenger jets for the national airline (LAN). In August 1971 — that is, one month after the expropriation of the copper mines but before a decision had been announced on compensation to American firms — officials of the bank suddenly announced that they were postponing a decision on financing. The political motivations of this step seemed all the more transparent since it came some months *before* Chile declared a moratorium on foreign obligations. It seems probable that this move was taken at the behest of Treasury Secretary John Connally as part of a new hard-line policy toward expropriating third world countries in general and Latin America in particular.[118] From the U.S point of view, however, the decision proved curiously self-defeating. The Chileans were not dissuaded thereby from deducting "excess profits" from the amounts due the American copper companies, and the Allende government — spurred by Washington — simply turned to negotiating with the Soviets for the purchase of Ilyushins.[119]

Alternative sources of aid. The withdrawal of lending confidence in Chile by the U.S. government, the multilateral banks, and private U.S. banks was — from a purely quantitative point of view — more than amply replaced by credits from alternative sources. The precise amounts have escaped documentation, but in a very general way it is known that in the period 1970–1973 Chile's medium- and long-term debt increased by 16.7 percent, while its short-term obligations grew nearly six-fold.[120] For 1972 alone, estimates of new credit lines range from $600 million[121] to $950 million.[122]

The universe of Chile's new creditors embraced a remarkable range of political systems and ideologies. With Argentina, for example, a neighbor with whom relations had rarely been cordial and which at the time was ruled by a right-wing military junta, there was a significant growth not only in trade (largely foodstuffs) but in short-term credits, which, according to former foreign minister Almeyda, were critical in helping Chile to overcome balance-of-payments difficulties.[123] A somewhat similar relationship evolved with Brazil, whose military rulers were, if anything, even cooler to the Allende experiment;[124] for 1972 Brazil allocated $32 million to Chile, and the following year the Argentines authorized lines amounting to $100 million.[125]

With Western Europe economic relations were characterized — again, in the judgement of Almeyda — by "a friendly, cooperative, and favorable attitude";[126] if another Popular Unity functionary is to be believed, by 1972 Western

European banks began to assume the role formerly played by their counterpart in the United States. By mid-1973, in his reckoning, "Chile had rebuilt and diversified its system of external finance." And, he adds, by June of that year the country had obtained from these sources short-term credits amounting to $547 million.[127] To which should be added the fact that Chile was able to draw from the International Monetary Fund for the period November 1970 to September 1973 an amount slightly greater than $100 million.[128]

Chile's economic relations with the socialist countries during the Allende period are still shrouded in controversy. According to the same Popular Unity source cited above, however, they were characterized by long-term grants of credit for the purchase of machinery and industrial plants, which reached $471 million by the end of 1972 (excluding grants from the Chinese). "In general," this commentator holds, "the monetary conditions attached to these credits were better than those of non-Socialist markets, at least as far as interest rates were concerned, for [these] varied between two and five percent, while no interest was charged for the Chinese grants, for which the first payment varied between 0 and 15 percent.[129] This seems a very generous interpretation of Soviet (and Chinese) accounting methods, but if it is true, in this particular area the refusal of U.S. credit sources to underwrite the Popular Unity experiment was for Allende an asset rather than a liability.

These figures are deprived of much of their grandeur in one, crucial qualitative dimension: for the most part Chile's new financial partners were unwilling to extend hard-currency loans. That is, most of the credits from sources both East and West were tied to specific projects or acquisitions; very little of them constituted "straight out balance of payments assistance — literally fully disposal convertible foreign exchange." Even the largest hard-currency credit from the Eastern bloc, a $50 million loan from the Soviet Union authorized in late 1971, may have been something other than what it appeared, at least in the opinion of some U.S. Treasury officials, who regarded it as largely "project oriented and therefore susceptible to delays in disbursements."[130] "The overall picture," one sympathetic observer concludes, "is therefore that [Popular Unity] successfully obtained aid and credit to replace that withdrawn from the United States. The bulk of this credit," he adds, "was, however, short-term, involving harsher financial terms than in the past."[131]

The "invisible blockade": Toward an evaluation. The most obvious conclusion to all the material presented above is that there was no "financial-economic blockade" of Chile, invisible or otherwise. In sheer financial flows, the country continued to receive credit assistance from the widest variety of sources, and in virtually unprecedented amounts. In fact, as Ambassador Davis has pointed out, on August 30, 1973, a few days before his fall, Allende had almost twice as much short-term credit available as he had upon assuming office three years before.[132] The refusal of the World Bank and the Inter-American Development Bank to countenance new loans (whether due to economic or to political motives, or a combination thereof) did not interrupt disbursements, which for the IDB reached record proportions. Even private U.S. banks and U.S. government agencies continued to transfer resources to Chile, though in greatly reduced amounts. At no time was an embargo on spare parts or equipment imposed upon Chile by the U.S. government, or, evidently, the supplying companies themselves.

Even the legal judgments sought by Kennecott against copper shipments had only a tangential effect; at least, this is what a senior CODELCO official of the period tells us. After 1971, he writes, "the market for Chilean copper did not change in any substanial way." Although some supply routes had to be changed to circumvent orders of attachment in specific countries, "the fact is that Kennecott was unable to block the sale of El Teniente copper in Europe."[133]

To say that there was no blockade does not mean that Chile under Allende did not experience problems in its economic relations with the United States. Quite obviously, the inability to reach a settlement on the portion of the public foreign debt owed to the United States and probably also on the compensation due the copper companies had repercussions throughout the banking community and among U.S. creditors actual and potential. Above all, the reduction of short-term lines of credit immediately convertible into any currency introduced an "element of rigidity" into Chile's foreign trade transactions.[134]

That the U.S. government sought to use debt renegotiations to extract from Chile what it did not wish to grant—an end to deducting "excess profits" from the sums owed to Anaconda and Kennecott—does not mean, however, that in the absence of such demands its creditworthiness would have been instantly restored. "Refusal to grant aid to a nationalizing government is, after all, a perfectly rational decision," two British friends of Popular Unity have tartly observed, "since there is reasonable doubt whether the loans will be repaid."[135]

In examining the sorts of credits Chile was able to obtain during the Allende years, two aspects command attention. First, they constitute attempts by newcomers to take advantage of the U.S.-Chilean impasse, whether for economic or for political reasons, often at Chile's expense.[136] Second, the terms offered were generally so much less favorable than in the past that one cannot but think that the judgement of U.S. private bankers about actual Chilean creditworthiness was not far off the mark.

Finally, no evaluation of Chile's financial problems in this period can omit mention of the *advantages* that accrued to Chile by its failure to service its debts to the United States. This constituted de facto relief of $243 million for 1972 alone, which more than offset the loss of commercial credits from the

United States,[137] although it could not fully cover the enormous balance-of-payments deficit. The dimensions of that deficit were indeed impressive, but due entirely to elements beyond Washington's control: a drop in world copper prices; the increasing cost of foodstuffs; a decline in Chilean industrial productivity (particularly copper); and above all, Popular Unity's own policies, which contemplated a painless transition to socialism—a transition in which the loyalty of some Chileans would be held in the one case, and the reluctance of others overcome in the other by an unremitting wave of consumption.[138]

Assistance to the Opposition, 1970–1973: The Dimensions of the Covert Effort

In its investigation, the Church committee found that between 1971 and 1973 the CIA was authorized to spend $7 million "in covert support to opposition groups in Chile." Of this amount, $6 million was actually spent during the Allende presidency, and some $84,000 thereafter for commitments made before the coup. If money spent during 1970 (that is, during the presidential campaign and before Allende's inauguration) is added, the figure rises to approximately $7 million, including project funds not requiring 40 Committee approval.[139] Obviously, it is these funds that lie at the heart of Representative Harrington's charge that the United States "destabilized" the Allende regime; therefore, the purposes to which they were put must be examined in careful detail.

Assistance to the Opposition Media. Ample evidence—both documentary and circumstantial—exists that significant portions of CIA money were passed to proprietors of opposition media during the Allende period. A Christian Democratic newspaper founded shortly after Allende's presidency, for example, closed for economic reasons within weeks after the coup. The television channel of the Catholic University and about two-thirds of the radio stations in Santiago were in the hands of opposition forces.[140] It is known for certain that *El Mercurio*, dean of Chilean dailies and the most sophisticated of conservative organs, received a covert subsidy from the United States of $1.5 million.[141]

The somber tones in which the Church committee presented these figures are considerably lightened, however, when placed in context. During the Allende period the media were subject to recurring waves of economic and political pressure. The Chilean government itself and state-owned industries together constituted the largest source of advertising in the daily press; the redirection of this business to exclusively progovernment papers, combined with the generally perilous state of private industry during this period, deprived the independent press of any visible means of support.[142] More to the point, efforts of the Allende government to bankrupt the only privately owned source of newsprint, the Compañía General de Papel y Cartones (the so-called "Papelera"), failed only because of National Freedom Fund assistance, and the intervention of Allende's service chiefs. As one of the conditions for entering his cabinet in late 1972, the generals insisted that the president observe the spirit as well as the letter of the Statute of Democratic Guarantees, and allow the company to raise its prices.[143]

Newspapers and radio stations, along with other elements of the private sector, sustained losses produced by government-declared wage increases and price freezes. Bills for back taxes were presented under new interpretations of the law. Fire codes and other municipal violations were invoked against opposition newspapers and radio stations. When students of the University of Chile voted to change the orientation of their institution's television station, Popular Unity militants organized a takeover of the studios by the local union. Import licenses and foreign exchange permits to acquire radio and television equipment and printing supplies were denied to unfriendly outlets.[144] In spite of all this it is true, as the Church committee somewhat artfully concluded, that "freedom of the press continued in Chile until the military coup of 1973";[145] this, however, was thanks not to Allende but to the CIA.[146]

Assistance to Opposition Political Parties and Movements. The greater portion of CIA money—approximately $4 million—went to the support of opposition political parties. This was used to underwrite the costs of their media, posters, campaign expenses, and salaries. The largest recipient was the Christian Democratic party, and smaller amounts were disbursed to the National party and various splinter groups. An effort was also made to split elements off from the Allende coalition, which may have played a role in the departure of the Radicals in late 1971. CIA funds subsidized the opposition in three by-elections in 1971, and in the congressional elections of 1973. "The CIA gave support in 1970 to one [unidentified] group whose tactics became violent over time," the Church committee's report somewhat torturously reasons. "Through 1971 [Patria y Libertad] received small sums of American money through third parties for specific purposes," which activities it defines as demonstrations or propaganda activities, rather than violence. "Such disbursements—some $7,000 in total—ended," the committee concludes, "in 1971." Nonetheless, it adds, "It is possible that money was passed to [Patria y Libertad and other] groups on the extreme right from CIA-supported opposition political parties."[147] For his part, Ambassador Davis, who assumed his post in the final weeks of 1971, has simply stated that "to my knowledge, no monies or support of any kind were passed to Patria y Libertad during my incumbency."[148]

The support of non-Communist political forces in Chile was nothing new for the CIA; what were different were the circumstances. The Christian Democratic party, as Ambassador Korry later recounted, ended the 1970 presidential campaign owing "large amounts of money to banks the Allende government would quickly nationalize; we reckoned that [the latter] would exploit nationalization to blackmail, to coerce, and to starve financially . . . numerous and influential members of the party." This premonition, he adds, was amply fulfilled "starting quickly in 1971." The vulnerability of the Christian Democrats was apparent in that their party "owned no national newspaper, had no TV outlet, and influenced few of Santiago's many radio stations at the time of the election"—a truly astonishing situation given the fact that it was the largest party in the country and had been in government for six years.[149] In the context of an ever–widening public sector under the control of Popular Unity, the prospects for the financial survival of the Christian Democrats, the Radicals, and other forces of the center were extremely problematic—or rather, would have been without external subventions.

Moreover, the Popular Unity government was far from helpless in the fact of this challenge. "Most domestic and foreign newsmen in Chile were aware," Ambassador Davis writes, "that government parties skimmed a percentage off foreign trade operations." Further, "government transport, communications equipment, supplies of paper and printing facilities were made available to the [Allende] forces on a large scale. Subventions came from abroad. I believe most foreign correspondents in Chile could confirm that [government] parties and candidates went into the elections of 1972–73 well supplied and supported."[150]

In addition to funding political parties, the CIA provided financial assistance to a wide range of private sector groups, including trade organizations and labor unions. It is here that the greatest controversy has arisen over the agency's role in Chile, since these groups were responsible for organizing the two great national strikes (October 1972 and July–September 1973) that shook the regime, required military participation in government, and arguably set the stage for the coup. The Church committee has extensively documented the degree to which the CIA make "a careful distinction between supporting the opposition parties and funding private sector groups trying to bring about a military coup." It confessed itself unsure, however, "given the turbulent conditions in Chile" and the close relationship between various sectors of the opposition, whether such a difference was operationally meaningful.[151] It goes on to say that

> with regard to the trucker's strike [July–September, 1973] two facts are indisputed. First, the 40 Committee did not approve any funds to be given to the strikers. Second, all observers agree that the two lengthy strikes . . . could not have been maintained on the basis of union funds.
>
> It remains unclear to what extent CIA funds passed to opposition parties may have been siphoned off to support strikes. It is clear that anti-government

strikers were actively supported by several of the private sector groups which received CIA funds. There were extensive links between these private sector organizations and the groups which coordinated and implemented the strikes. In November, 1972, the CIA learned that one private sector group had passed $2,800. directly to the strikers contrary to the Agency's grounded rules. CIA rebuked the group but nonetheless passed it additional money the next month.[152]

The funds made available to these private sector groups were intended for relay to opposition political parties—in other words, to be tendered to such forces from the sources which, under normal circumstances, they could expect to receive financial assistance. What was the "seepage factor" for non-electoral purposes? Ambassador Davis has addressed himself to this question very fully:

> Obviously, if one gives a political party money to meet its needs, somebody or some group which otherwise might have contributed to those needs could not contribute to the truckers. But that is not the same thing as the party acting as a conduit. And it is not so difficult to tell if money given to a political party for electoral purposes or advertisements, for example, is being used for that purpose.

To which he adds, with a droll touch: "The CIA has been paying monies in foreign countries ever since the Agency was formed, and has developed techniques of some effectiveness for determining whether its monies are being used for the purposes authorized and intended."[153]

This is not merely a matter of one man's opinion. Such information as has come to light on actual disbursements repeatedly points to a careful rein on such matters. In September 1972, for example, the 40 Committee authorized $24,000 in emergency support for one opposition group, but deliberately withheld it from others for "fear that these organizations might be involved in anti-government strikes." The following month, the committee allocated some $100,000 to private sector groups, which the CIA subsequently reported was spent exclusively on "election activity, such as voter-registration drives, and get-out-the-vote drives" in connection with the congressional elections of March 1973.[154] That this authorization took place in October 1972—a month characterized by widespread strikes against the Allende government— is far less suggestive than might appear at first glance, for such allocations required an additional six to eight weeks for disbursement. By that time, of course, the crisis in Chile had been temporarily resolved.

The most thorough account of CIA deliberations on this subject and perhaps, given the chronology, the most important, concerns August 1973. During that month the CIA station in Santiago recommended that an additional $1 million be granted to opposition parties and private sector groups. While the 40 Committee was considering the proposal, the station forwarded an additional plan to pass $25,000 to the striking truckers. The first proposal won approval, conditional, however, on the assent of the ambassador and the State Department. It remains unclear whether the second ever actually came before the 40 Committee. It is a matter of record that the initial proposal never received the necessary concurrence of the ambassador or the State Department, and therefore was not implemented; the second, strenuously opposed by the U.S. mission, was never approved. *None of these funds ever changed hands.*[155] Meanwhile, events in Chile raced ahead of the deliberations in Washington, and the Allende government fell.

All of this still does not exclude the possibility that small amounts of CIA money found their way to the strikers. But official U.S. policy on the matter is unmistakable; and, assuming that the Agency was faithfully pursuing the instructions it received (which the Church committee does not dispute), any major misallocation of funds by recipients would have been both obvious to it and the pretext for a policy review. Because the CIA believed that its money was being properly used,[156] no such occasion arose.

The United States and the Military Coup of September, 1973. "Was the United States *directly* involved, covertly, in the 1973 coup in Chile?" To this rhetorical question, the Church committee report responds that its investigation "found no evidence that it was." It goes on immediately to qualify these findings, however, by observing that "the United States sought in 1970 to foment a military coup in Chile; after 1970, it adopted a policy, both overt and covert, of opposition to Allende; and it remained in intelligence contact with the Chilean military, including officers who were participating in coup plotting."[157] By this it is not clear precisely what the committee means us to understand. Either it wishes to convey the notion that, in spite of being unable to find any evidence, it refuses to abandon the presumption of guilt; or possibly it believes that between opposing Allende and fomenting a military coup there can be no meaningful distinction. Let us examine the evidential premises upon which the committee based these statements.

That the United States favored a coup in Chile during October–November 1970 is beyond discussion; it is likewise reasonable to assume that the desires of the Nixon administration became a matter of common knowledge among the Chilean high command as a result of probes made in connection with the Schneider affair.[158] But once these efforts ended in disaster, how relevant were they to the subsequent U.S. role? On this the committee received two completely different views. One was the testimony of Thomas Karamassines, former CIA deputy director for plans and principal agency contact throughout Track II. In the excerpt published in the committee report, the following dialogue appeared:

MR. KARAMASSINES. I am sure that the seeds that were laid in that effort in 1970 had their impact in 1973. I do not have any question about that in my mind either. . . .

Q. Was Track II ever formally ended? Was there a specific order ending it?

MR. KARAMASSINES. As far as I was concerned, Track II never really ended. What we were told to do in effect was, well, Allende is now President, so Track II, which sought to prevent him from becoming President, was technically out and done. But what we were told to do was to continue our efforts. Stay alert, and to do what we could to contribute to the eventual achievement of the objectives and purposes of Track II. That being the case, I don't think it is proper to say that Track II was ended.

When summoned before the committee, Kissinger took issue:

THE CHAIRMAN. Would you take issue with that, with the [Karamassines] testimony?

SECRETARY KISSINGER. Totally. * * * It is clear that * * * after October 15 there was no separate channel by the CIA to the White House and that all actions with respect to Chile were taken within the 40 Committee framework. There was no 40 Committee that authorized an approach to or contact with military people, no plots which I am familiar with, and all covert operations in Chile after Allende's election by the Congress were directed towards maintaining the democratic opposition for the 1976 election. And that was the exclusive thrust, and if there was any further contact with military plotting, it was totally unauthorized, and this is the first time I have heard of it.[159]

Ambassador Davis some years later offered his own assessment:

Unfriendly sentiment in the White House toward Salvador Allende no doubt continued [after 1970]. Elsewhere in Washington, however, enthusiasm for covert action ebbed, and Washington policymakers focused increasingly on the importance of avoiding compromising acts. There was, also, progressively less Chilean institutional viability to 'destabilize'.[160]

The subsequent investigation of the committee, far from resolving this controversy, only added to it by gathering evidence for yet another version. This falls into three distinct chronological periods. Before October 1970 the CIA's contacts with the Chilean military were limited to two "assets," neither of whom—when President Nixon ordered implementation of Track II— was prepared to spark a coup. Under heavy pressure from the White House, the station rushed ahead to establish new contacts. After General Schneider's murder and the collapse of this initiative, the station was left "with only its initial assets in the military." It took the CIA another ten months to rebuild a network of agents "among the cautious Chilean military."

The second period began in the fall of 1971 and ran through the early months of 1972. By this time the Santiago station and CIA headquarters were discussing how to use the network of assets. The Church committee report continues:

> In November [1971] the Station suggested that the ultimate objective of the military penetration program was a military coup. Headquarters responded by rejecting that formulation of the objective, cautioning that the CIA did not have 40 Committee approval to become involved in a coup. However, headquarters acknowledged the difficulty of drawing a fine line between monitoring coup plotting and becoming involved in it. It also realized that the U.S. government's desire to be in clandestine contact with military plotters, for whatever purpose, might well imply to them U.S. support for their future plans.[161]

In spite of these inferences, the report concludes that it was this period—some nine to twelve months before the Allende regime confronted its first serious crisis—in which the CIA was "most active" within the Chilean military. In this context, it refers to a "short-lived" effort to subsidize a small anti-government news pamphlet aimed at the armed forces, the compilation of arrest lists and other operational data, and what it referred to as a "deception operation." The latter began as a plan to pass to senior Chilean officers counterfeit materials attempting to "prove" that Cuban secret police and the Investigations unit of the National Police (carabineros) were gathering intelligence prejudicial to the army high command. "It was hoped," the report explains, "that the effort would arouse the military against Allende's involvement with the Cubans, including the armed forces, to press the government to alter its orientation and to move against it if necessary." This proposal, it continues, was rejected by CIA headquarters, however, in favor of passing "'verifiable' [true?] information to the leader of the coup group [sic] which headquarters and the station perceived as having the highest probability of success."[162]

The third and final period embraced the second half of 1972 and all of 1973 up to the coup in September. Here the report concedes that CIA operations during these months were confined to intelligence gathering, but once again manages to convey at the same time the unmistakable impression that such activities were virtually inseparable from coup plotting. It reports, for example, that during this period the Santiago station collected operational intelligence necessary in case of a coup, such as

> arrest lists, key civilian installations and personnel that needed protection, key government installations which needed to be taken over, and government contingency plans which would be used in case of a military uprising. According to the CIA, *the data was collected only against the contingency of future headquarters requests and was never passed to the Chilean military.*[163]

Then it reports that CIA "penetration" of various military groups known to be coup-prone

> was to walk a tightrope. The distinction between collecting information and exercising influence was inherently hard to maintain. Since the Chilean military perceived its actions to be contingent to some degree on the attitude of the United States government, these possibilities for exercising influence scarcely would have to be consciously manipulated.[164]

As the careful reader will perceive, the second sentence in the paragraph above begins by presenting as a statement of fact what is nothing more than an opinion, and concludes by declaring the United States guilty for purely contextual reasons. What is more important, the first sentence suggests an insensitivity on the part of the CIA to the possible consequences of intelligence gathering far greater than was, in fact, the case. During the secret testimony of David Atlee Phillips, former chief of the agency's Western Hemisphere Division, the elaborate precautions taken by CIA headquarters to avoid involvement in a coup in Chile were outlined in considerable detail. In its report, however, the Church committee, for reasons of its own, chose not to take official cognisance of this evidence. It has only come to light in Phillips' subsequently published memoirs. There he explains that in May 1973 two cables were sent to the Santiago station.

> In a rather abrupt departure from CIA custom, these instructions pointed out the probability of an opposition move against Allende and the inevitability that CIA would be blamed as the instigator of any coup.
>
> The Station response to the first message reminded headquarters that CIA continued to have the responsibility of predicting a coup—ringing the gong—and that the Station could hardly be expected to do that unless its agents penetrated all conspiracies.
>
> The second headquarters cable countered this valid argument saying that, this time, keeping CIA's record clean was more important than predicting a coup. In short, the CIA Station Chief was ordered to do the best he could on forecasting a coup from the margin of plotting and to avoid contacts of actions which might be construed as supporting or encouraging those who planned to overthrow Allende.[165]

The United States and the Chilean Opposition: What Does the Evidence Support? The one incontrovertible fact concerning the period after Allende's inauguration that the Church committee uncovered in its investigation was that the CIA had played a crucial role in sustaining the opposition in Chile. But beyond this it offered no standard by which to measure the precise U.S. role in the larger context of developments. To weigh the importance of covert involvement properly, one would have to balance that single fact against several others. For one thing, control of the government armed Popular Unity with significant economic (and therefore political) resources of its own. For another, Allende unquestionably received subsidies of an unknown magnitude from Eastern bloc and Cuban sources. For yet another, there is no inevitable and direct relationship between heavy financial support and political success — as the Watergate affair and the subsequent presidential campaign of John Connally in the United States both illustrate. In Chile it is very possible, as Henry Landsberger has suggested, that foreign influence on one side "simply cancelled out" efforts on the other, "leaving factors internal to Chile as the more basic explanation of what occurred."[166]

Certainly one cannot automatically elide support for the opposition into support for a military coup—as the Church committee comes perilously close to doing any number of times—and then from there jump directly to the event itself. Quite apart from the fact that both the opposition and the armed forces shifted their stance toward the regime over time, CIA practice consistently differentiated between the purposes of the United States and the evolving goals of Chilean actors. Thus the agency withheld money from potential strikers, was repeatedly reminded by headquarters that support for a coup was not authorized, and—in the final, critical weeks of the regime—directly distanced itself from officers known to favor a coup and to be actively discussing that option. Finally there is no inconsistency whatever between a U.S. policy aimed at "maintaining the democratic opposition for the 1976 election" (Kissinger) and covertly subsidizing hard-pressed political parties, newspapers, and radio stations. Indeed, one can hardly imagine what *other* course of action—given that objective—the U.S. government could have been expected to take. Conversely, if a military coup (as opposed to contingency planning and intelligence gathering) was what Washington wished, why did the 40 Committee so persistently withhold what it could so easily have given: the necessary authorization?

The U.S. Role in Chile: Some Concluding Observations

What is truly remarkable about the investigation of the Church committee concerning U.S. involvement in Chile is how little its actual findings have altered the perceptions originally created by Representative Harrington's letter and Seymour Hersh's articles in the *New York Times*. For although the United States looked with extreme disfavor on the advent of a socialist government in Chile, it was unable to prevent Allende's election of confirmation by Congress. Nor was it able to facilitate a coup, of either the military or "constitutionalist" variety. Plans to "unleash economic chaos" (ITT) or "make the economy scream" (Nixon)—both conceived during the period between Allende's election and inauguration—remained on the drawing board because of the unwillingness of the banks and major multinationals (with the sole exception of ITT) to endanger their holdings, the possibilities of compensation, or their future relations with the new government.

Now, eventually the economy did "scream," but not as a result of U.S. government measures. There was no "invisible blockade," either of credit or spare parts; there *was* a drastic reduction (but never a total cutoff) of U.S. public aid to Chile, intensifying a trend already at work during the final year of the Frei regime. There was also a credit squeeze that eventually assumed proportions, largely as a consequence of the Allende government's own policies, which forced it to declare a moratorium on its foreign debt in November 1971. Although failure to reach an agreement with Washington within the context of the Paris club agreements grievously damaged Popular Unity's credit standing in the United States, it nonetheless afforded it very considerable short-term relief.

The U.S. government in all probability did lobby at the Inter-American Development Bank and may also have made attempts at the World Bank to shut off the flow of loans to Chile. But after 1971 such efforts — given the country's general economic perspective — would have been wholly gratuitous. In any event, the attitude of the multilateral banks was of less than crucial significance; Chile was able to turn elsewhere for credit, which it obtained in unprecedented amounts. The new terms were considerably less favorable than those traditionally obtained from U.S. sources, but so, indeed, were Chile's prospects for repayment.

Throughout the Popular Unity period the United States expended nearly $6 million to keep opposition political parties and forces alive. The subvention was most evident in the media, interest groups, and the electoral process. The CIA did not, however, generally fund groups committed to the violent overthrow of the regime, such as Patria y Libertad, and although its relations with the Chilean military after the Schneider debacle apparently experienced several shifts, by mid-1972 they were confined to contingency planning and intelligence gathering (monitoring coup plotting). The authorization to go beyond this was pointedly refused several times, and in the final six months of the regime, the Santiago station was specifically enjoined to distance itself from coup-prone elements in the armed forces, lest U.S. policy be misunderstood.

The CIA was not involved in promoting or sustaining the strike of October 1972, and although support for that of July-September 1973 was discussed in Washington, no decision was ever reached. The CIA did not, contrary to Seymour Hersh's report, "provide strike benefits for anti-Allende strikers and other workers in 1972 and 1973."[167]

Without question, these activities did have an impact in Chile, though not precisely in the fashion often suggested by critics. Subventions to elements of the opposition created difficulties for the regime, inasmuch as it found itself unable effectively to bankrupt or expropriate their sources of financial support. Allende was therefore forced to implement his policies—policies for which there was never a majority—within the context of a continuing pluralistic political system. That is not, however, the same thing as "destabilizing" a regime. As a matter of fact, there never was a decision to "destabilize" Chile. As William Colby later explained in a letter to the *New York Times* on September 18, 1974, the word was Harrington's in *his* characterization of the CIA chief's secret testimony.[168]

One might argue—as Harrington later did—that given the role the United States had played in Chile, withdrawal of support for any regime was bound to have far-reaching (and negative) consequences. But this amounts to nothing more than declaring the obvious: that the United States could have made life much easier for Allende by rushing forward with credits, grants, and other forms of material assistance. It had done this for Frei, in a vain attempt to provide an attractive alternative to Castroism in Latin America. But this perspective does not explain why the United States, having failed to avert the triumph of Marxism in Chile (at the cost of $2 billion in aid and millions more in Overseas Private Investment Corporation insurance premiums), should have ratified its error by throwing good money after bad. This point of view could only make sense if one believed (as Harrington surely does not) that the advancement of Marxism in Latin America and throughout the Third World should be an element of U.S. foreign policy.

Finally, whatever its intentions, the United States was utterly unable to conjure up the fundamental weaknesses of the Allende regime. These were a failure to obtain a decisive mandate at the ballot box, a governing coalition internally inconsistent and frequently at war with its constituent elements, an economic policy bound to polarize both its supporters and its enemies, and ultimately the need to recur to the military for the stability that only a genuine consensus could provide. It was here—not in the machinations of the CIA, real or (more often) imagined—that the seeds of disaster were planted. It is to these elements—not to external forces—that anyone wishing to understand the fall of Allende must inevitably recur.

Notes

1. Jack Anderson, *Washington Post,* March 22, 1972.
2. The investigation and the documents were subsequently published as U.S. Congress, Senate, Committee on Foreign Relations, Subcommittee on Multinational Corporations, *The International Telephone and Telegraph Company and Chile, 1970-71,* 93rd Congress, 1st session, 1973; a separate report of findings appeared under the same source and title as a committee print on June 21, 1973. Hereafter the hearings and documents are cited as *ITT, 1970-71,* the committee print is cited as *ITT-CP.*
3. Seymour Hersh, *New York Times,* September 20, 1974.

4. Seymour Hersh, *New York Times,* September 24, 1974. These and other charges are fleshed out with a wealth of baroque detail in Hersh's subsequent book, *The Price of Power: Henry Kissinger in the White House* (New York, 1983), pp. 258-296. It is not possible to examine them here; an exhaustive critique, which among other things sheds considerable light on Hersh's reportorial methods, is found in Nathaniel Davis, *The Last Two Years of Salvador Allende* (Ithaca, N.Y., 1985), pp. 316-347 and *passim.*
5. The precise designation of the documents is as follows: U.S. Congress, Senate, Select Committee to Study Governmental Operations with Respect to Intelligence Activities, *Covert Action* (Hearings), 94th Congress, 1st session, 1975 (hereafter *Covert Action*); idem, *Alleged Assassination Plots Involving Foreign Leaders,* 94th Congress, 1st session, 1975 (hereafter *Alleged Assassination Plots*); and idem, *Supplementary Detailed Staff Reports on Foreign and Military Intelligence,* 94th Congress, 2d session, 1976 (hereafter *Supplementary Reports*). The second document deals with alleged assassination plots in many countries; obviously, I shall only be concerned with its findings as they apply to Chile.
6. U.S. Congress, House of Representatives, Committee on Foreign Affairs, *The United States and Chile during the Allende Years,* 94th Congress, 1st session, 1975 (hereafter *The United States and Chile*).
7. President Carter at his press conference the next day characterized the Church committee as not having found "any evidence that the U.S. was involved in the overthrow of the Allende government in Chile." The United States had apparently given financial aid to "political elements that may have contributed to the change of government" in Chile, the president admitted, but he said that there had not been "any proof of illegalities here," which was surely beside the point. Ironically, President Carter's statement on that occasion was considerably at variance with his version of Chilean events as he expounded them in his 1976 debate with President Ford. At that time he accused the Republican administration of having "overthrown an elected government and helped to establish a dictatorship" in Chile. All quotations are from *Facts on File, 1977* (New York, 1978), p. 219.
8. *New York Times,* June 3, 4, 1980.
9. "Kissinger: Self-Portrait," in *Practicing History* (New York, 1981), p. 219.
10. *Covert Action,* p. 45.
11. "U.S. Policies in Chile under the Allende Government" (interview with William F. Buckley, Jr., on September 29, 1974), in F. Orrego Vicuña, ed., *Chile: The Balanced View* (Santiago, 1974), p. 292.
12. One of the problems with the Church committee report *Covert Action in Chile, 1963-73* (Washington, 1975) (hereafter *Covert Action in Chile*) is that it combines indiscriminately CIA activities of the 1960s with those of the Allende period, even though they unfolded under very different conditions. As will be shown further on, it is far easier to defend the necessity of covert action during the Allende period than in the years preceding it.
13. William E. Colby and Peter Forbath, *Honorable Men; My Life in the CIA* (New York, 1978), p. 191. For a fascinating personal account of how one agency official operated in Chile during the early 1950s, see David Atlee Phillips, *The Night Watch: Twenty-Five Years of Peculiar Service* (New York, 1977), pp. 14-28.
14. *Alleged Assassination Plots,* p. 229n; *Covert Action in Chile,* p. 9.
15. *Honorable Men,* p. 302.

16. *Covert Action,* p. 6.
17. *Covert Action in Chile,* p. 16.
18. Ibid., pp. 16-17.
19. Ibid., p. 9.
20. Korry, "U.S. Policies in Chile," pp. 289-90.
21. U.S. Congress, Senate, Committee on Foreign Relations, *Nomination of Hon. Cyrus R. Vance to be Secretary of State* (Hearings), 95th Congress, 1st session, 1977 (hereafter *Vance Nomination*), p. 51; *ITT, 1970-71,* vol. 1, pp. 281, 311. In the latter hearings Ambassador Korry remarked that representatives of all three candidates in the 1970 elections approached representatives of major U.S. financial interests in Chile as well.
22. Ambassador Korry estimates $425,000 (*Vance Nomination,* p. 52); *Alleged Assassination Plots,* pp. 20-21, 229, refers to $390,000 with an additional contingency fund of $500,000 set aside to influence the vote of Congress if Allende received a plurality; and *Covert Action in Chile,* p. 20, gives the high figure of "between $800,000 and $1,000,000."
23. *Covert Action* (testimony of Inderfurth), p. 13.
24. *Vance Nomination,* p. 52; *Covert Action in Chile,* pp. 12-13.
25. *Covert Action in Chile,* pp. 12-13; see also *The United States and Chile* (testimony of Sigmund), p. 245.
26. Henry Kissinger, *White House Years* (Boston, 1979), p. 659.
27. *Covert Action in Chile,* p. 20.
28. Colby and Forbath, *Honorable Men,* pp. 302-303.
29. *Covert Action in Chile,* pp. 17, 19-20.
30. Cord Meyer, *Facing Reality* (New York, 1980), p. 182.
31. Kissinger, *White House Years,* p. 663.
32. Ibid., p. 665.
33. Ibid., p. 667.
34. Ibid., p. 669.
35. Ibid., pp. 670-671.
36. *ITT, 1970–71,* vol. 1 (testimony of Broe), pp. 244–246.
37. *Covert Action in Chile,* pp. 12–13.
38. *ITT, 1970–71,* vol., pp. 608–615. The Chilean Constitution did not allow successive presidencies, but this technically would be circumvented by a twenty-four hour Alessandri administration.
39. Ibid., vol. 1 (testimony of McCone), pp. 102–103.
40. Ibid. (testimony of Neal), pp. 59–87; (testimony of Meyer), pp. 398–410; and vol. 2. pp. 599–600.
41. Ibid., pp. 622–623.
42. Ibid., vol. 1 (testimony of Broe), pp. 250–253.
43. *ITT–CP,* p. 11.
44. *ITT, 1970–71,* vol. 2, p. 627 (emphasis added).
45. Ibid., pp. 644–645.
46. *ITT–CP,* p. 11. See also the testimony of various bank executives in *ITT, 1970–71,* vol. 1 (Clark, Lillicotch, Greene, and Odgen), pp. 342–373; (Bolin, Raddatz), pp. 383–398.
47. As William H. Bolin, senior vice–president of the Bank of America, explained to the Church committee, any policy to undermine the Chilean economy "would have been directly contrary to our own interests at that point in time, because we

had every reason to expect that we would be approached by the Chilean Government with a proposal to sell out our branches and that we would be able to negotiate this satisfactorily if the environment of our negotiations were right, and that, in fact, did occur." *ITT, 1970–71*, vol. 1, p. 388.
48. Ibid. (testimony of Greene), p. 359.
49. Ibid. (testimony of Clark), p. 344.
50. To be sure, there were signs of massive bank withdrawals during the period after the September 4 election, but these were due to legitimate fears that Allende would rigorously fulfill his campaign promise to lower interest rates drastically. Broe emphasized in his testimony that this was a preexisting reality upon whigh the CIA had hoped to build the larger plan he presented to Gerrity. Ibid., pp. 250–251.
51. Ibid., vol. 2, p. 528.
52. Ibid., vol. 1 (testimony of Merriam), pp. 45–47.
53. Ibid. (testimony of Mecham), pp. 265–276.
54. Ibid. (testimony of Foster), pp. 373–377.
55. For example, Anaconda Vice–President Ralph Mecham stated in his testimony that he found it incomprehensible that the Nixon administration persisted at this time in continuing pipeline aid to Chile. Ibid., p. 267.
56. Ibid., p. 320.
57. Ibid. (testimony of Raddatz), p. 393.
58. *ITT, 1970–71*, vol. 2, pp. 943–953 and 964–965.
59. Ibid., pp. 951–953.
60. Ibid., vol. 1, p. 431.
61. At the time Allende's "excess profits" finding was pending before the Special Copper Tribunal.
62. This directed the president to suspend all foreign aid to a country that had expropriated U.S. property without compensation or had not taken steps within six months to move toward arbitration or other means of discharging its obligations under international law.
63. *ITT, 1970–71*, vol. 2, pp. 1091–1092.
64. *Covert Action in Chile*, p. 23; *Alleged Assassination Plots*, p. 225.
65. Kissinger himself describes the September 15 meeting at the White House in somewhat different terms. In his recollection, Nixon "told Helms that he wanted a major effort to see what could be done to prevent Allende's accession to power . . . Helms should bypass Korry and report directly to the White House, which would make the final decisions. The operational object at the time was still the 'Rube Goldberg' scheme [that is, the Alessandri gambit]. Nixon did not in fact put forward a concrete scheme, only a passionate desire, unfocused and born of frustration, to do 'something.'" In Kissinger's view either Track I or Track II would have involved military participation of some sort; therefore, the Church committee labels are not very meaningful (Kissinger, *White House Years*, p. 673). But at best this would not deny the coup-oriented objective of Track II, merely extend it to Track I, which is, by the way, also at times the position of the Church committee. It found, for example, that "the essential difference between Tracks I and II . . . was not that Track II was coup-oriented and Track I was not. Both had this objective in mind. The difference between the two tracks was, simply, that the CIA's direct contacts with the Chilean military and its active promotion and support of a coup *without* President Frei's involvement were to be known only to a small group of individuals in the White House and

the CIA." *Alleged Assassination Plots*, p. 232. Ambassador Korry disagrees. "Track I," he told the Church committee, "followed Mr. Frei, then the President of Chile and its constitutional leader. It adopted certain minimal and cosmetic suggestions put forward by one purportedly in President Frei's confidence . . . Track II, on the other hand, did not seek his concurrence, did not follow his lead, *did not pretend to be within any constitutional framework of Chile." Covert Action*, pp. 30–31 (emphasis added). Of course, Korry only learned of the existence of Track II some years later.

66. *Alleged Assassination Plots*, p. 230.
67. Kissinger, *White House Years*, pp. 674–675.
68. The full statement, originally passed to Frei through his defense minister, read, "Frei should know that not a nut or bolt will be allowed to reach Chile under Allende, Once Allende comes to power we shall do all within our power to condemn Chile and Chileans to utmost deprivation and poverty, a policy designed for a long time to come to accelerate the hard features of a Communist society in Chile. Hence, for Frei to believe that there will be much of an alternative to utter misery, such as seeing Chile through, would be strictly illusory." Quoted in *Alleged Assassination Plots*, p. 231n. Korry later explained to the Church committee that the statement was a "deliberate overstatement" to goad Frei into activity along Track I (the "Alessandri gambit") and relieve Korry of pressure emanating from Washington "to go to the military" (the "constitutional" coup). *Supplementary Reports*, pp. 127–128.
69. *Alleged Assassination Plots*, pp. 232–233.
70. Covert Action in Chile, pp. 23–24.
71. Meyer, *Facing Reality*, pp. 185–186; see also *Covert Action in Chile*, pp. 33–37.
72. In its report, the Church committee went to considerable lengths to establish that these two groups were not totally discrete entities. (See especially *Alleged Assassination Plots*, p. 239, n. 2); nonetheless, they were treated as such by the CIA, and, as will be shown, operated as if they were.)
73. Kissinger, *White House Years*, p. 676.
74. *Alleged Assassination Plots*, p. 243.
75. Ibid., pp. 243–245.
76. Ibid., p. 226.
77. Ibid., p. 226n.
78. *Covert Action in Chile*, p. 24.
79. *Alleged Assassination Plots*, p. 246. The murder of Schneider also led to the promotion into his position—by order of strict seniority—of General Carlos Prats González, who, it anything, was even more inflexibly "constitutionalist," and, as time would show, not at all unsympathetic to Allende. (See Chapter Eight.).
80. *ITT, 1970–71*, vol. 1 (testimony of Guilfoyle), p. 208.
81. *ITT–CP*, pp. 13–16; U.S. Congress, Committee on Foreign Affairs, Subcommittee on Inter–American Affairs, *Recent Developments in Chile*, 92d Congress, 1st session, 1971 (hereafter referred to as *Recent Developments*) (testimony of Mays), p. 6.
82. Embassy of Chile (Washington), press release, text in *ITT, 1970–71*, vol. 1, pp. 228–229.
83. Korry, "U.S. Policies in Chile," p. 292. Whether the U.S. taxpayer should in effect have borne the burden of such risks is a debatable matter, although at the

time such insurance was introduced it was believed that it would defuse potentially explosive investment disputes. Instead of isolating the sources of conflict, however, OPIC insurance in effect spread them into the political community — that is, made private disputes with foreign governments a matter of public interest. This curious bifurcation of intentions and results is fully explored in Paul Sigmund, *Multinationals in Latin America* (Madison, Wisconsin, 1980), especially pp. 302–337.

84. See excerpted texts, "The Nixon–Frost Interview," *Historic Documents of 1977* (Washington, 1978), pp. 351–352, and Clodomiro Almeyda, "The Foreign Policy of the Popular Unity Government," in Federico Gil et. al., *Chile at the Turning Point: Lessons of the Socialist Years, 1970–73* (Philadelphia, 1979), p. 101.

85. Korry, "U.S. Policies in Chile," pp. 294–295.

86. Richard Nixon, "Third Annual Report to the Congress of the United States on Foreign Policy, February 9, 1972," in *Public Papers of the Presidents of the United States, Richard Nixon, 1972* (Washington, 1974), pp. 263–264. This was, of course, a grossly hypocritical statement; nonetheless, President Allende, too, made florid statements affirming his desire for cordial relations with the United States, but, when offered the opportunity to reach an accommodation in early 1971 — in the concrete matter of compensation for U.S. mining properties — found himself unable to proceed. This was due to pressures from within the left wing of his own coalition, which, as Almeyda had since complained, was quick to see an "unjustifiable surrender in every negotiation and compromise." ("Foreign Policy of the Popular Unity Government," p. 85.) Doubtless Allende was sincere in his desire to minimize conflict with the United States, as long as it cost him nothing. "I don't know of a single instance," Ambassador Korry remarked to a U.S. congressional committee in mid–1971, "where the President of Chile has assured me or where his ambassador assured the Department [of State] of something that was going to happen that has happened yet, not a single instance where it involves our interests . . . It just hasn't worked out ever that their assurances have been fulfilled . . . I think when the President of Chile gives me these assurances, he is being sincere about them, but because of these internal contradictions within his own government . . . he can't carry them out." (*The United States and Chile*, p. 16.) For its part, the Nixon White House proceeded on the basis of a worst-case scenario, but it was constantly fighting against backsliders in the State Department and the embassy in Santiago, as Ambassador Nathaniel Davis — Korry's successor — makes abundantly clear in his own memoirs. Had the Allende government seriously addressed legitimate concerns, such as compensation for expropriated properties, events might have acquired a momentum of their own, and the two governments come to an understanding in spite of themselves. Ambassador Korry is preparing a memoir on this subject; pending its publication, readers are referred to his remarks in "U.S. Policies in Chile," pp. 291–294; *Covert Action*, pp. 32–33; and "Ambassador Korry on a 1971 Proposal to Allende," *Washington Post*, September 29, 1974.

87. "Sobre la independencia política y económica de los pueblos," official text released by the Chilean mission to the United Nations, mimeographed.

88. *Alleged Assassination Plots*, p. 227.

89. *Covert Action in Chile*, p. 33.

90. Jonathan E. Sanford, "The Multilateral Development Banks and the Suspension of Lending to Allende's Chile," in Orrego Vicuña, *Chile: The Balanced View*, pp. 127–130. Although this is an official Chilean government publication, Sanford's work is merely reprinted. It was originally commissioned by the Congressional Research Service, Library of Congress.

91. Belgium, Canada, France, Great Britain, Italy, Japan, the Netherlands, Spain, Switzerland, West Germany, and the United States.

92. Eventually, in fact, the United States—or more precisely, the Nixon administration—eventually desisted from this position for reasons of its own. For the details, see Davis, *The Last Two Years of Salvador Allende*, pp. 72–77 and Henry Kissinger, *Years of Upheaval* (Boston, 1982), pp. 385–388.

93. Virginia M. Hagen, "United States Relations with Chile under the Government of Salvador Allende: Background and Current Developments," in *The United States and Chile*, p. 401; Nathaniel Davis, "U.S. Covert Actions in Chile, 1971–1973," *Foreign Service Journal* (November, 1978), p. 38; $243 million is the figure estimated by the International Monetary Fund.

94. Background paper: Chile and the Inter-American Development Bank During the Administration of President Salvador Allende," in *The United States and Chile*, pp. 440–441.

95. Sanford, "Multilateral Development Banks," pp. 137–140.

96. International Bank for Reconstruction and Development (IBRD), "Chile and the World Bank," in *The United States and Chile*, pp. 441–448. According to Ambassador Davis, by mid–1973 pressures were mounting for the Inter-American Development Bank "to approve something for Chile," largely because Santiago was scheduled to host the annual meeting of the board in 1974. Davis, *The Last Two Years of Salvador Allende*, p. 128.

97. Sanford, "Multilateral Development Banks," pp. 137–140.

98. IRBD, "Chile and the World Bank," p. 447. The annual average under Frei was $15.6 million, under Allende $15.4 million.

99. "The Nixon–Frost Interviews," p. 351.

100. It is not clear that it would have made much difference if they had. At the confidential meeting with representatives of major American investors in Chile on October 21, 1971, cited above (p. 22), Secretary Rogers turned aside pressures "to curtail IADB [IDB] loans" with the remark that the United States "does not have veto power over loans." *ITT, 1970–71*, vol. 2. p. 975.

101. Sigmund, *The Overthrow of Allende and the Politics of Chile, 1964–1976* (Pittsburgh, 1977), p. 338.

102. See, for example, the figures offered by William S. Ogden, executive vice-president of Chase Manhattan, in *ITT, 1970–71*, vol. 1, pp. 366–367.

103. Ibid., vol. 1 (testimony of Bolin), pp. 386–392.

104. "Structural Transformation in Chile's Economy and Its System of External Economic Relations," in S. Sideri, ed., *Chile, 1970–73: Economic Development and Its International Setting* (The Hague, 1979), p. 76.

105. *ITT, 1970–71*, vol. 1 (testimony of Greene), p. 360; (testimony of Ogden), p. 366–373; (testimony of Bolin), pp. 386–387; and vol. 2, p. 536.

106. *Covert Action in Chile, pp. 32–33.*

107. This would have run the eventual risk of renewed legal action by the copper companies, and would also have necessitated relocating specialized personnel already settled in New York. But since it was never tried, we cannot know to what degree these obstacles would have been negotiated successfully.

108. Carlos Fortin, "Nationalization of Copper in Chile and Its International Repercussions," in Sideri, *Chile, 1970–73*, pp. 207–208; and Fernando Fajnzylber,
"The External Sector and the Policies of the Unidad Popular Government," in
ibid., pp. 144–145.
109. Gall, "Copper Is the Wage of Chile," *American Universities Field Staff Reports*
(West Coast South America Series), vol.19, no. 3 (1972), p. 10.
110. *ITT, 1970–71*, vol, 2, p. 1074.
111. Ibid., p. 1075.
112. For a persuasive but fundamentally misleading account of this issue from a
pro-Allende point of view, see Edward Boorstein, *Allende's Chile* (New York,
1977), pp. 89–107. It is worth noting that the issue of spare parts was not seen
as a particularly conflictive element in U.S.-Chilean relations at the time; instead, many Chilean officials effusively welcomed the opportunity to diversify
their country's foreign sources of supply. It was only after the fall of the regime
that this issue surfaced as an element in the debate, suggesting its polimical
rather than concrete value.
113. Figures from Kenneth Ruddle and Kathleen Barrows, eds., *Statistical Abstract
of Latin America, 1972* (Los Angeles, 1974), table 276; and James Wilkie and
Paul Turovsky, eds., *Statistical Abstract of Latin America, 1976* (Los Angeles,
1976), table 3000.
114. U. S. Arms Control and Disarmanent Agency, *World Military Expenditures and
Arms Transfers, 1966–75* (Washington, 1976), table II.
115. Davis, "U.S. Covert Actions in Chile," p. 39. See also Davis, *The Last Two
Years of Salvador Allende*, p. 99.
116. *ITT, 1970–71*, vol. 1 (testimony of Hennessy), p. 340.
117. Paul Sigmund, "The 'Invisible Blockade' and the Overthrow of Allende,"
Foreign Affairs, vol. 52, no. 2 (1974), p. 334.
118. Sigmund, *The Overthrow of Allende*, p. 153. Kissinger offers some piquant
collatoral evidence in *Years of Upheaval*, pp. 385–388. For alternative explanations of the transaction offered by Export-Import Bank Officials, see *Recent
Developments* (testimony of Sauer), pp. 5–6; and U.S. Congress, House of
Representatives, Committee on Foreign Affairs, Subcommittee on Inter-
American Affairs, *New Directions for the 1970s: Part 2, Development Assistance Options in Latin America*, 92d Congress, 1st session. 1971 (testimony of
Corette), p. 225.
119. After discussions with the Soviets, the Chileans returned to Boeing in early 1972
and purchased the three planes with funds that "according to speculation,"
could have come out of a $50 million credit from Moscow. Hagen, "United
States Relations with Chile," p. 400.
120. Philip O'Brien, "Was the United States Responsible for the Chileans Coup?",
in O'Brien, ed., *Allende's Chile*, p. 233.
121. *Covert Action in Chile*, p. 32.
122. *The United States and Chile* (testimony of Crimmins), p. 69.
123. Almeyda, "Foreign Policy of the Popular Unity Government," p. 87.
124. Ibid., pp. 89–90.
125. O'Brien, "Was the U.S. Responsible . . .," pp. 233–234.
126. Ibid., p. 93.
127. Guardia, "Structural Transformations in Chile's Economy," pp. 85–86.
128. International Monetary Fund, *International Financial Statistics, 1973 Supplement* (Washington, n.d.), p. 71.

129. Guardia, "Structural Transformations in Chile's Economy," pp. 82–83. For a U.S. estimate of bloc and Chinese assistance, which runs considerably higher, see Davis, *The Last Two Years of Salvador Allende*, pp. 130–133.

130. *The United States and Chile* (testimony of Crimmins), p. 69. For a similar observation with regard to Western Europe, see Guardia, "Structural Transformations in Chile's Economy," p. 86.

131. O'Brien, "Was the United States Responsible . . .," p. 233. An explanation of the more advantageous role formerly played by American banks is presented in *ITT, 1970–71*, vol. 1 (testimony of Greene), p. 363.

132. Davis, *The Last Two Years of Salvador Allende*, p. 129.

133. There was, he adds, a slight decline in sales to Western Europe and the United States, but this was compensated for by increased shipments to Japan, Latin America, and the socialist countries, particularly China, Fortín, "Nationalization of Copper in Chile," pp. 205, 206–207.

134. Guardia, "Structural Transformations in Chile's Economy," p. 86.

135. Clive Bell and David Lehmann, "The International Context of *La Via Chilena*," in J. Ann Zammit, ed., *The Chilean Road to Socialism* (Brighton, Sussex, 1973), p. 359n.

136. Markos J. Mamalakis, *The Growth and Structures of the Chilean Economy* (New Haven, 1976), pp. 260–261.

137. These fell from $219 million in August, 1970 to $32 million in August, 1972.

138. *The United States and Chile* (testimony of Crimmins), p. 69; (testimony of Lansberger), pp. 227–228; Henry A. Lansberger, "An Introduction to the Complexities of Assessing the U.S. Credit Squeeze," in *The United States and Chile*, pp. 527–528 and Guardia, "Structural Transformations in Chile's Economy," pp. 83, 86.

139. *Covert Action in Chile*, p. 27.

140. *The United States and Chile* (testimony of Sigmund), p. 247.

141. *Covert Action* (testimony of Treverton), p. 16. Some additional funds were spent for propaganda activities of a more general sort. According to the Church committee, the CIA also (1) subsidized several magazines of national circulation, and a large number of books and special studies: (2) developed material for placement in opposition press and electronic media; and (3) funded an opposition researched organization that channeled a steady flow of economic and technical material to opposition parties and private sector groups. Many bills introduced by opposition parliamentarians were drafted by this organization. *Covert Action in Chile*, p. 30.

142. By the end of the regime *El Mercurio*, normally comparable in size to the *Washington Post*, was reduced to an edition of six or eight pages, virtually devoid of advertising.

143. Davis, *The Last Two Years of Salvador Allende*, p. 117. Contrary to widespread presumption, apparently the CIA did not play a role in saving the Papalera. Ambassador Davis says that he flatly refused to support "a covert bailout of the Papalera— . . . I still shudder to think of how much money could have been absorbed by that operation." Ibid., p. 327.

144. Davis, "U.S. Covert Actions," p. 11; Everett G. Martin, "Did the Chilean Press Need CIA Help?", *Wall Street Journal*, September 18, 1974.

145. *Covert Action* (testimony of Treverton), p. 17.

146. Ibid. (testimony of Korry), p. 4. See also Ambassador Korry's letter to Senator Church dated October 23, 1975, reprinted in Ibid., p. 117; and his remarks to William Buckley, Jr., in Korry, "U.S. Policies in Chile," pp. 296–297.

147. *Covert Action in Chile*, pp. 31, 49.

148. Davis, "U.S. Covert Actions," p. 14.

149. Korry, letter to Senator Church.

150. Davis, "U.S. Covert Actions, Part II," p. 11 See also *The Last Two Years of Salvador Allende,* pp. 340–341. Osvaldo Puccio reveals that in the 1960s he and other members of the Socialist party set up the Sociedad Comercial Arauco, for the express purpose of raising money through trade operations with the governments of Poland, East Germany, Cuba and "other socialist countries." In 1970, he writes, Allende's entire presidential campaign was funded in this way. *Un cuarto de siglo con Allende* (Santiago, 1985), pp. 163–164, 166, 168, 205. It surpasses belief that once in government the Socialist party did not continue to use this method to raise campaign funds.

151. *Covert Action in Chile*, pp. 16, 22, 30–31.

152. Ibid., p. 31.

153. Davis, "U.S. Covert Actions, Part II," p. 14. In his book he adds, "As for the private-sector groups which received CIA money, they were given relatively small sums, and their own needs were pressing." *The Last Two Years of Salvador Allende*, p. 325.

154. *Covert Action in Chile*, p. 10.

155. Ibid., pp. 30–31; see also Davis, *The Last Two Years of Salvador Allende*, pp. 324–328.

156. Phillips, *The Night Watch*, p. 237.

157. *Covert Action in Chile*, p. 2.

158. Oddly enough, however, this is scarcely mentioned in the posthumous memoirs of General Carlos Prats, Schneider's successor. See *Memorias: testimonio de un soldado* (Santiago, 1985).

159. *Alleged Assassination Plots*, p. 254. Asterisks indicate material excised from the record for security reasons.

160. Davis, *The Last Two Years of Salvador Allende*, p. 328.

161. *Covert Action in Chile*, p. 37 (emphasis added).

162. Ibid., pp. 38–39.

163. Ibid. (emphasis added).

164. Ibid., p. 135. Ambassador Davis takes strong issues with this, arguing that that by mid-1973 "the gap between the desires of the Chilean opposition and the inclinations of our embassy widened. As [the year] progressed, anti-UP forces were coming to favor a coup . . . . The U.S. government could have done little to prevent or slow this trend, and seeing this, we tried to avoid bankrolling the plotters and to keep away from the plotting. As pro-coup sentiment spread, the effort became more and more difficult, but it was honestly sustained . . . it was becoming clear [by then] to responsible U.S. officials in Washington as well as in Santiago that the U.S. record of abstention from coup plotting was going to be more important than any resort to increasingly superfluous covert intervention." Davis, *The Last Two Years of Salvador Allende*, pp. 328–329.

165. Philips, *The Night Watch*, p. 238.

166. *The United States and Chile* (testimony of Landsberger), p. 226.

167. Hersh's other sensational allegation—that Ambassador Davis at some point was instructed "to aid the opposition by any means possible" and "to get a little

rougher''—was flatly denied by Davis at the time his articles were published, and, as the ambassador later had the satisfaction of observing, found no substantiation in the Senate investigation. ''U.S. Covert Actions in Chile,'' p. 38.

168. ''To insure that no mere difference in semantics is involved,'' Colby added, ''this term especially is not a fair description of our national policy [in Chile] from 1971 on of encouraging the continued existence of democratic forces looking to future elections.'' Newsman Daniel Schorr, who was later also permitted to read top secret materials on covert CIA operations in Chile, has corroborated Colby's statement. Daniel Schorr, *Clearing the Air* (Nashville, Tenn., 1977), pp. 130–133.

8

How Allende Fell

The Allende regime lasted approximately three years—a thousand days which were light years in terms of Chile's political culture and historical context. The abrupt and brutal fashion in which the country's Marxist president and his government were extinguished has distorted historical perspective. It cannot be recalled too often that at the time of its election, Popular Unity seemed inevitable and invincible, a view shared even to a certain extent by its opponents. Allende's prospects altered but gradually—so gradually, in fact, that he was late in recognizing the extent of their deterioration. The historian's task, then, is to plot the points at which they changed, and to recapture, insofar as possible, the way the world looked to those who were acting with no foreknowledge of the outcome.

As Chapter One has shown, from a certain perspective Allende's 1970 victory at the polls could be interpreted as nothing more than the culmination of long-standing trends in postwar Chilean political history. Certainly this was the regime's own view of itself, and at the beginning there were few facts on the ground to contradict it. Through mid-1971, in fact, the new government seemed to move from strength to strength. During its first nine months, it nationalized the banking system, expropriated foreign holdings in the copper industry, and launched a new and more radical version of land reform. On April 4 it scored a narrow victory over the combined forces of the opposition in municipal elections held throughout Chile. Within days, Allende and his colleagues were debating the convocation of a plebiscite which would alter the country's institutions once and for all, and put those created in their place forever beyond the reach of any opposition.

It was precisely at this high point that things began to slowly unravel. On June 8, the civility of Chilean political life suffered a stunning blow; Frei's former Minister of the Interior Edmundo Pérez Zujovic was assassinated by a band of leftist terrorists, the Organized Vanguard of the People (VOP). A few days later, Popular Unity lost a by-election for the Chamber of Deputies in

Valparaíso, establishing that April 4 would be its high-point of electoral popularity. By the end of the year, economic mismanagement and hoarding had led the government to take control of the distribution of foodstuffs, and pro- and antigovernment rallies and clashes were a common sight in the universities and on the streets. Most important of all, the Christian Democrats and the Right had overcome their mutual repugnance and concluded an electoral pact which bore fruit within a matter of weeks; in January the new combined Center-Right list soundly defeated Popular Unity at by-elections for senator in O'Higgins and Colchagua provinces and for a deputy in Linares.

The year 1972 was dominated by a single issue—the proper parameters of nationalization. In February Congress passed the Hamilton-Fuentealba bill, a series of constitutional amendments restricting Allende's efforts to socialize the economy. In April the President vetoed the bill, and warned that if the legislature persisted in an "obstructionist attitude toward the executive," he would ask for authority to dissolve it; if this ploy failed—as he must have known it would—he threatened to call a plebiscite on the future of Chile's economy. Meanwhile, seizures of factories and farms continued, some with, some without, the explicit support of the government—it was not always possible to know which was which. In October, the renewed threat of nationalization of small enterprises provoked the first serious massive response by the opposition—a trucker's strike which later spread to other sectors of the economy. Within days Chile's internal market was hopelessly disrupted; Allende succeeded in breaking the logjam, that is, ending the strike, in late November, but only by inviting the armed forces into the government and placing it in charge of food distribution.

The striking had been settled, but the fundamental issue—the boundaries of public and private property—were still undefined. The differences divided not merely government and opposition, but Popular Unity itself; thus in January 1973, Allende's coalition split on the main lines of a compromise government bill, with the President's own Socialist party opposing the return of several dozen "intervened" or "requisitioned" enterprises to their owners. The armed forces could not create a consensus where none existed, and in fact its presence in the government was predicted on the need to maintain a minimum of order and normality until the major political issues could be sorted out, presumably in parliamentary elections set for March 4.

Far from resolving the conflict, however, the midterm elections merely exacerbated it. Although Popular Unity read the results as a kind of triumph— the government did better than it or its opponents had expected—the opposition still commanded the support of a solid majority of voters (54.2 percent). More to the point, it was far more unified in its purposes than the government coalition itself, which was still divided into "revolutionary" and "legalist" wings. The election had merely documented what everyone knew: that the country was stalemated politically and ideologically. But now the armed forces were not present to mediate the differences between government and opposition, since the generals left Allende's cabinet on March 27.

The period March-September 1973 was characterized by three developments. First, the opposition, having failed to win the necessary two-thirds in parliament to impeach Allende, set about trying to immobilize his government through strikes and protests, the parliamentary impeachment of individual ministers, and, at the very end, by resolving in Congress that the government had placed itself outside the framework of Chilean legality. Second, Allende himself, conscious that the country had become ungovernable, tardily set to negotiating his differences with the Christian Democrats. These talks began on July 30, but ended abruptly on August 3, when the President of the Christian Democratic party declared that Allende was unwilling to accede to the "minimal demands" of the opposition.

Third and finally, from March to September both Allende and the opposition looked to the armed forces for a solution. The President continually importuned the service chiefs to rejoin his cabinet, which they finally did on August 9. However, the military could not carry out policies to which a majority of Chileans were opposed, and what is more to the point, to which its own members objected. The re-entry of the armed forces into the government was a Pyrrhic victory for Allende: it only succeeded in undermining the position of his principal supporter within the military, army commander General Carlos Prats González, who was forced into retirement by his colleagues on August 23. As for the opposition, having failed either to force the government to compromise its basic program, or to win enough congressional seats to impeach it, it now looked to the armed forces as the means to a *golpe seco*—a "white coup," whereby Allende could be immobilized for an indefinite period. Both were apparently unaware of the degree to which the military had acquired an independent political identity of its own, one which would become fully apparent only after the violent overthrow of the government on September 11.

About these broader contours, there is general agreement. When one descends, however, to the level of particulars—motivations, perceptions, and goals—the controversy begins. What did Allende and his opponents originally intend? How were their purpose altered over time? Why did the Chilean military play, first one role, then another? To what degree was the Allende regime the victim of opposition cabals with the military? To what degree did it fall into a trap of its own devising?

Allende and the Left

Salvador Allende was not merely the first Marxist chief of state freely elected anywhere; he was also the first to be forced to govern within the framework of open and democratic institutions. This meant that—unlike his friends Fidel Castro and Ho Chi Minh—he was accountable to an electorate which was to return to the ballot boxes twice during his presidency, and also to an independent judiciary and a vigorous opposition press. In order for Chile's transition to socialism to be irreversible—as Allende hoped and expected it would be—the economic policies implemented in the early months of his term had to be resoundingly successful; in no other case, could he expect an affirmative outcome in a plebiscite.[1] One can debate endlessly whether any set of economic and social transformations—particularly ones advertised as revolutionary—can ever be rendered irreversible within the broader framework of democratic values. In the case of Allende's Chile, however, such a discussion is irrelevant, since the issue was never put to the test. The plebiscite was postponed after the April elections in the hope of gaining yet more ground with the electorate. This was not to be: in fact, after mid-1971 the political indicators were less, not more favorable. Thus, Allende was forced to govern for another two and half years constrained by "bourgeois" legality, but—here the crucial point—still seriously committed to radical social change, while exposed to the mounting political costs of a deteriorating economic performance.

To add to the confusion, on a purely theoretical level Allende was never entirely clear as to the exact nature of Popular Unity's project. At times he spoke of "socialism" as something which might follow his government in the future, as if he were preparing a half-way house between two completely different systems. At others, he strongly emphasized the class nature of his government, with a "vanguard formed by predominantly working-class Marxist parties." On such occasions he openly professed his Marxism: "I am working through socialism for socialism." This phenomenon was repeated at the level of constituent parties within the ruling coalition. Thus, while the President's own Socialist party often spoke as if the country were on the immediate outskirts of their ultimate objective, "socialism," the Communists rarely used the word, "and never in conjunction with the immediate tasks of Popular Unity."[2]

The other components of Popular Unity shifted their stated goals over time, blurring the ideological frontiers in the process. The Radical party—the historic expression of Chilean Masonry and the provincial middle class, for whom all problems ultimately reduced themselves to expanded government employment—suddenly declared itself "Marxist" in August 1971, and promptily split in two; less than a year later, the "progressive" remnant, the Left Radical party (PIR) left Popular Unity altogether. Also in the same month of August 1971, MAPU went even further and formally embraced Marxism-Leninism, driving out one of its founders, Jacques Chonchol, together with three congressional deputies, who joined the new Christian Left party (IC);[3] it split again four days before the 1973 elections, expelling fifteen key members for being in contact with the ultra-Left.[4] This was a curious charge given the close ties that both the Christian Left and the MAPU were known to have with the MIR.[5] Generally speaking, the center of political gravity within Popular Unity lurched sharply to the left after 1971, even though Allende continued to select personalities for his cabinet identified with the moderate wings of their respective parties.

For the Soviet Union—and therefore, for the Chilean Communist party— the tasks of Popular Unity were a less ambitious sort. From a Western European perspective, Allende's experiment would fully accomplish its purpose if it succeeded in reassuring hesitating socialists in Spain, France and Italy who were then contemplating electoral alliances with their own Communist parties. In the larger context of Third World politics generally, the new government in Chile could best serve Soviet purposes by trimming its ideological and programmatic sails. By 1970 the bill for the Cuban revolution had long since fallen due, and setbacks in Indonesia, Ghana, and Egypt had imposed a less expansive view in Moscow of Third World revolutions generally. In such countries the desired strategy was now the "non-capitalist road to development," defined as "anti-monopolist, anti-imperialist measures with increased involvement of the state in the economy."[6] Such regimes were advised not to break with the West, but rather to maintain normal relations with it. In other words, the Communists and their allies would make the revolution, but the capitalist world would pay for it. This in turn presupposed that the new regime would be more broadly based than, say, in Cuba— incorporating "middle strata, petty bourgeoisie, intellectuals, even groups of progressive military men."[7] The local Communist parties would not disappear or necessarily be sacrificed (as in Egypt), but neither would they play a vanguard role. Rather, such parties would concentrate on forming "broad popular fronts." Regimes more or less resembling this model already existed at the time of Allende's election in Peru and Bolivia, and within three years there would be yet another in Argentina.

In effect, as Isabel Turrent has written, "by the beginning of the 1970s, Soviet doctrine itself virtually eliminated the possibility of Communists fulfilling their classic role: to be the 'vanguard of the proletariat' and to lead a process of socialist development."[8] This approach was not without contradictions of its own, but since Allende was not expected by Moscow to win the 1970 election,[9] the Soviets could not be expected to have thought through all of the consequences of their doctrine as it applied to Chile.[10] The Chilean party itself understood full well that in no other way could Popular Unity hope to triumph at the ballot box, since four of the six parties of the original coalition were strictly speaking populist rather than Marxist.

For the dominant wing of Allende's own party, the objective was different: whereas the Communists envisioned a vague compromise between populism and Marxism, most Socialists unambiguously advocated a revolutionary state. Here they reflected the influence of the Cuban revolution, and specifically of Fidel Castro himself. Though the Cuban dictator (under Soviet pressure) had apparently abandoned his rigid commitment to the violent road after 1968, and though, too, he made statements helpful in this sense to Allende on the eve of the 1970 elections, he never fully surrendered his earlier premises. According to Jorge Edwards, a career diplomat sympathetic to Popular Unity sent to reopen the Chilean Embassy in Havana, Castro regarded Allende's victory as "an apparently favorable accident which could, however, turn out to be a double-edged sword." Allende had no alternative, he insisted, "but to radicalize the process, leading it to the point of rupture." Otherwise, he warned, the Chilean President would "get bogged down in the swamps of legality." The Chilean situation, Edwards subsequently recalled, "he had not precisely encouraged Fidel to revise his theories, as some thought in all innocence, but rather to elaborate and confirm them in another fashion." In the course of a month-long visit to Chile in November–December 1971, Castro gave Allende a submachine gun, but also has tendered the same present to individual leaders of the MIR. "That is," Edwards adds, "after a first-hand look at the Chilean experiment, Fidel had given a pat on the back to the extreme left, whose policies were evidently and obviously incompatible with the government's fundamental strategy."[11] By directly passing over the So-cialists in favor of the MIR, Castro actually reinforced—rather than weakened—the insurrectionary line within its ranks.

Prior to 1970, the Socialists' disagreements with the Communists remained purely theoretical, since so many of the former professed not to believe in the possibility of acquiring power through elections. Once proven wrong, how-ever, they were forced to imagine how their revolution could be completed within the framework of "bourgeois-domocratic" institutions. Herein emerged two crucial differences between Allende's party and its Communist and non-Marxist allies. Whereas the latter favored economic redistribution as a mech-anism to acquire the final resorts of political power, for the Socialists this was putting the cart before the horse. "It is not economic success which opens the road to political power," argued Secretary-General Carlos Altamirano in proper Leninist fashion, but "the political solution that defines the control of power, which in turn will permit [the government] to resolve economic problems."[12] In practice, this meant opposing the very economic concessions which could have widened, or at any rate, consolidated the government's political base.

The other distinction was equally fundamental: the Socialists and their confrères on the farthest left were frankly skeptical of the possibilities of completing their ideological project through existing institutions. Instead, they favored the creation of "germs of popular power"—"organisms opposed to bourgeois power, but not for that reason to the government."[13] These included new revolutionary bodies created at the workplace or in the neighborhood which operated more or less independently of the government. The term "Soviet" was never used, but the metaphor was obvious, with the very important difference that Allende was not the Socialists' Kerensky (though it is difficult to say exactly what the proper historial metaphor should have been). For their part, the Communists were frankly puzzled as to how these "germs" could grow, take possession, and ultimately supersede the "bourgeois" state. When asked to explain what "popular power" meant to him, Communist trade union leader Luis Figueroa told *El Siglo*, "it is inconceivable that there could be a popular power residing outside that government over which Comrade Salvador Allende presides."[14] The Communists were consistently critical as well of attempts, as they put it, to "leapfrog stages in the revolutionary process."[15]

This division passed through the very center of the government itself. "One of the two lines could have been adopted, and pursued in depth." MAPU deputy Julio Silva Solar has written, "but this was not done because it would have produced the rupture of Popular Unity, and as a result, weakened the government." Yet by not choosing, President Allende "allowed the two lines to coexist, mutually annulling and blocking one another. The President tried always to conciliate, but the differences were irreducible. With neither rudder nor compass, it was impossible to sail the seas."[16]

Meanwhile, the emergence of new organizations became a matter of practical concern, since they took on something of a life of their own. First, there were *focos*—a term borrowed from Ché Guevara but more nearly resembling the Viet Cong-controlled areas of South Vietnam. That is, they were fortified populations under the control of the MIR rather than the government. Although few in number, they attracted international attention, particularly one on the southern border with Argentina, where a flamboyant young man who fashioned himself "Comandante Pepe" held sway. Then, there were *campamentos*, shantytowns on the edge of Santiago or other cities organized into militarized hamlets by the MIR and others. Some of these—with names like "Lenin" or "26th of July"[17]—actually predated the Allende regime; others, like "New Havana" were created afterwards. "Protected by barbed wire," U.S. Ambassador Nathaniel Davis has written, the campamentos often displayed "strong internal organization and, in some cases, impressive discipline." The *cordones* were worker-controlled industrial belts. The first of these was Los Cerrillos, along the avenue to the Santiago airport, created in June, 1972 when workers in local factories organized themselves to press for expropriations. Militants of the left-wing of the Socialist party and of the MIR almost immediately seized control of Los Cerrillos, and consolidated it through the introduction of vigilante squads.

Finally, the *comandos comunales* were organizations in working-class neighborhoods to mobilize people on behalf of the government, but independently
of it; these parallel bodies embodied what, in the parlance of the time, was
called "peoples' power." Organized by circumscription, they included delegates from the trade unions, the JAPs, mother's clubs, student organizations,
and so forth. A council of delegates was divided into working groups—
defense, education, justice, propaganda, and so forth. Manuel Dinamarca,
Socialist vice-president of the CUT regarded them as "the vanguard of pro-
letarian power," which would eventually reproduce themselves at provincial
and national levels, somehow eventually "replacing the bourgeois
institutionality."[18]

Ambassador Davis recalls that by mid-1973 "a dozen cordones ringed the
heart of Santiago, stretching out along the principal avenues . . . . Allende
never made it quite clear whether he was on the side of the mobilized workers
or his own governmental authorities, and the workers of the revolutionary
vanguard never made it clear whether they supported the government or were
trying to organize for their own revolution."[19] This was understandable, since
there was a perceptible if undefined overlap between the parallel organizations
of "people's power" and bodies more firmly responsive to government direction, particularly the trade unions. At times both were needed in the streets
to intimidate the opposition or to assume concrete tasks, such as reactivating
areas of the economy paralyzed during the October strike; or, as when, during
the abortive military coup of June 29, 1973, Allende himself urged workers
to take to the streets in defense of his government. Mobilization, however,
could not be turned off as easily as it had been turned on, and "even superficial demobilization generally requires some repression,"[20] to which Allende
was naturally reluctant to recur.[21] The result was that the president could not
control all of the bodies for whose conduct he was ostensibly responsible, and
therefore could not effectively negotiate with the opposition on concrete matters—
such as the return of factories seized by his followers in moments of crisis.

Allende's problem was organizational only in the first instance; it was at
heart political. It was not a case—as some would have it—of a "revolution
from above" versus a "revolution from below,"[22] but rather, whether organization and discipline could prevail over sheer numbers. The former were the
strong suit of the left-wing Socialists and the MIR, and to a lesser degree,
MAPU and the Christian Left—who in proper Bolshevik fashion sought to
exploit them to compensate for the popular support which they lacked.[23] "For
the most part," one Popular Unity functionary has since conceded, "the
[communal] commands were elected from above and were not always completely representative of the rank-and-file."[24] One Socialist worker interviewed in European exile recalls that once a factory was expropriated, "many
workers took no further part in activities at a cordon level," partly because,

he says, they were frankly put off by small coteries of professional activists who tended to get bogged down in ideological wrangles.[25]

By way of contrast, where trade union democracy continued to function in a regular fashion, "the Christian Democrat vote was spectacular, while the MIR and other extremist factions continued to be practically non-existent." More to the point, between the two large Marxist parties, the Communists continually gained on the Socialists, though in the final, highly polarized days of the regime the thesis of "dual power" gained ground even among the former.[26] By the time of the coup, however, the fundamental issue was still unresolved: Popular Unity was able to accomplish the "transition to socialism" through institutions (where it lacked the votes and the laws) nor through insurrection (where it lacked the arms, the will and a coherent leadership). Instead, it set down both paths more or less simultaneously, paying the price in order and legitimacy for an alternative strategy which frightened adversaries and alienated neutrals, but could neither prevail over the one nor convince the other.

Allende and the Christian Democrats

To transform an entire economic and social system by democratic means obviously requires a very broad political consensus. In the Chilean case, this meant some sort of understanding between Popular Unity and the Christian Democratic party, still the country's largest single political force.[27] Such an arrangement, which was beyond all possibility by September 1973, was far from inconceivable in 1970. The Christian Democrats considered themselves serious social reformers, and in a certain way, so they were; they had just nominated a residential candidate whose platform—however irresponsible and demagogic—was actually somewhat more radical than that of Popular Unity. Though long-term electoral and ideological trends strongly suggested that the left tide in Chile was receding rather than rising by the time of Allende's election,[28] this was not at all apparent to most Christian Democrats. Rather, they were overcome by the *triunfalismo* of the Marxist parties, and by the illusion which temporarily attends all newly-elected governments that the world is about to be remade.

Moreover, Allende and his new ministers were not creatures from Outer Space, but schoolmates, colleagues, and friends, often related by blood or marriage, people with whom the Christian Democrats had joisted and bargained within the give-and-take of Chilean politics for a quarter-century or more; thus it was natural to imagine that—rhetoric aside—business would continue more or less as usual. One of the few who sensed something new and dangerous at the outset was retiring President Eduardo Frei, and he found himself almost alone among his coreligionists at this time.[29] This point seems worth emphasizing in the face of repeated attempts by Allende's former collaborators to collapse the first and last days of the regime, as if—as one of them has written—the "bourgeois" nature of the Christian Democratic party inevitably led it to be captured "by the strategy and spirit of fascism."[30]

The truth is that the Christian Democrats began the Allende administration by proffering a hand of collaboration. In a certain sense, of course, they had made the new government possible in the first place by voting for Allende in the congressional runoff. But their intentions went considerably further than that, as Senator Narciso Irueta and the national council of the party made clear to the new president in a courtesy call in December 1970, a few days after Allende had assumed office. Irueta was in an expansive mood: as the standard-bearer of the Left, he had just defeated Andrés Zaldívar, Frei's handpicked candidate for party leadership, and most of the council members who accompanied him shared his views. His party, he explained to the president, interpreted its responsibility "as an obligation to help you govern." And he concluded his remarks by imploring the new chief executive to "help us to be good Allendistas."[31]

The visitors offered to work with the new government in those areas where there was a considerable ideological overlap: specifically, bank reform and copper nationalization. As they knew that further moves in both areas were contemplated, they asked to see the relevant draft bills before they were submitted to Congress. To both of these requests the president readily agreed. Within days, however, Allende had preemptorily nationalized Chilean banks without the benefit of any enabling legislation whatever, and shortly thereafter he expropriated all foreign holdings in copper without so much as discussing the matter with the Christian Democrats.[32]

The pattern of relationship was set very early, then: Allende promising things he would not (or could not) deliver. The effect over time was to undermine those very forces within Christian Democracy which favored a policy of critical support for his government, and to strengthen the hand of their more moderate and conservative rivals. Of particular significance was the way that Radomiro Tomic—who sought to play an intermediary role between the two forces—was preemptorily pushed aside.[33] At Irueta's request, the party's 1970 presidential candidate, a long time personal friend of Allende, renewed the initial offer of a working coalition (to include in some cases joint support for individual candidates) both before and after the April 1971 municipal elections, and again in June 1971 after the by-election in Valparaíso. It quickly became apparent to Tomic that Popular Unity's strategy—rather than to fashion an accord with the Christian Democrats—was to "force [us] to reach an understanding with the Right, and to divide [the party's] leadership from its mass, peasant, and youth base."[34] In other words, to replicate the schism of 1969 which had resulted in the creation of MAPU.

Popular Unity did in fact succeed in splitting Christian Democracy once more in July 1971, when six deputies left to form the Christian Left party. The political costs of this strategy turned out to be higher than contemplated; once it became clear that the government's purpose was (again, to quote Tomic) "never to collaborate with the Christian Democrats but to divide and destroy them,"[35] the left wing of the party found itself steadily undermined and eventually discredited.

The distance the Christian Democrats had to travel to a working alliance with the National party was immense, and nothing better illustrates the impact of the government's policies of intentional polarization than the celerity with which it was accomplished. By 1970, the Frei administration was so heartily disliked by the Right as to lead it to run a candidate of its own in the presidential elections, a risky strategy which at a minimum assured the defeat of almost anyone the Christian Democrats might nominate. The latter returned the compliment: almost all of Tomic's verbal artillery in the campaign was aimed at Alessandri. Throughout 1971 the Christian Democrats repeatedly turned away approaches by National party leaders; they even referred to the decision to run a joint list in the Valaraíso by-election as "circumstantial,"[36] and as late as December, Senator Renán Fuentealba, another leader of the party's left wing, who had played a large part in the negotiations in Congress by which Allende obtained the presidency in the first place, was still saying publicly that his party was ready to collaborate in the construction of a "socialist society, Chilean style, with democracy and pluralism." But, he added, it would oppose a "Cuban-style socialism that Chileans cannot accept."[37]

The turning point came on February 7, 1972 when Allende proposed that all Popular Unity candidates run on a single list in the March 1973 congressional elections. Though technically a violation of Chilean electoral law, it was eventually finessed through a complicated two-tiered system whose details need not concern us here. Of rather greater importance is the fact that the legal brief to reinterpret the rules was submitted to the electoral court of review jointly by a Socialist deputy (on behalf of Popular Unity) and a leader in the Alessandri campaign. The Christian Democrats, who had a long tradition of refusing to participate in coalitions, appealed the decision to the Supreme Court, which, on the basis of a technicality, declared its incompetence to rule in the matter. The Christian Democrats were thus faced with the choice of concluding an electoral pact with the Right or committing suicide. "It was absurd to assume," Tomic observed later, "that just because Popular Unity would prefer for the Christian Democrats to stand alone, the latter would sacrifice themselves resignedly. The real world does not work like that."[38] Nor did it.

In the meanwhile, the unique civility of Chilean public life was exposed to multiple lacerations. Not satisfied with having defeated the Christian Democrats in the presidential elections, Popular Unity—through its growing media network—launched a slanderous attack on the previous government, and particularly on the person of Eduardo Frei, who was probably still the most popular figure in the country. Nor was the violence purely verbal. The assassination of Pérez Zujovic shook the country to its foundations, not only because it was so radical a departure from Chilean tradition, but because the victim was a former high official of the Christian Democratic government, and the executioners a group of left-wing thugs some of whom had been beneficiaries of a presidential pardon in the first weeks of the Allende regime.[39]

By the end of 1971, much of Chile's political conflict was moving out of the halls of Congress and into the street. On December 1, the day before Fidel Castro's departure, about 5,000 women in Santiago organized a march to protest food shortages. Most were from middle class households (or their "gentrified maids," in the droll observation of Ambassador Davis)—the very constituency from which Christian Democracy drew the bulk of its support. Though the march began peacefully, young people from the Communist and Socialist parties, as well as the MIR, began throwing rocks at the women and their escorts. No one was hurt, but riot police found it necessary to fire tear gas pellets to disperse the crowd, and the Santiago garrison decided to declare a curfew.[40] More serious were threats to the lives of those who succeeded in defeating Popular Unity candidates at the ballot box. In January 1972, newly-elected Christian Democratic Sentator Rafael Moreno was stoned in Rancagua by persons shouting Popular Unity slogans, and the same month the MIR stood accused of kidnapping the son of the new National party deputy from Linares. In November the rector and vice-rector of the University of Concepción—both members of the opposition—survived two separate assassination attempts, both within days of each other.

There was a growing sense, as well, that the government was trying to use not merely "legal loopholes" but the discretionary powers of office or its less scrupulous supporters to alter unfairly the rules of the political game. A plan to establish "peoples' tribunals" in Chilean neighborhoods, which Congress forced Allende to drop, was seen by the opposition—not without reason, as Allende's justice minister subsequently admitted—as intending to create "a system of justice with a clear political bias."[41] There were attempts to silence the opposition press through the artificial generation of labor disputes, both at *El Mercurio* in Santiago and at two papers in Concepción. The new government publishing combine Quimantú (ex-Zig-Zag) denied normal quality paper supplies to the opposition newsmagazine *Ercilla* in blatant disregard of contractual obligations. "The leftists were candid about their fight against opposition media outlets," Ambassador Davis has written. "The Communist trade union chief Luis Figueroa had stated publicly that all mass media should be placed under state ownership."[42] In the 1972 trade union elections—the first such ever held on a national level—it took an inexplicable six weeks to count the ballots, and the results were so disproportionately favorable to the Marxist parties, and particularly to the Socialists, that even they thought the Communists had cooked the figures.[43] At elections at the University of Chile, where the opposition controlled the rectory and the governing assembly throughout the Allende period, Marxists used their control of student organizations to press for restructuring and for the dismissal of "reactionary" professors.[44]

Perhaps most important of all was a growing sense of dispossession which the government's supporters—if not precisely the cabinet or the president—purposely visited upon its opponents. Radomiro Tomic puts it thus:

> At the base level in public administration (both state and municipal), in the labor unions of workers and employees, in the neighborhood councils and other mass organizations with hundreds of thousands of members, in the peasant masses, and in youth, university, and student organizations—sectarianism in the exercise of power became general and acquired hateful forms.

> Millions of Chileans came to feel they were denied their citizenship or legitimate options. As Popular Unity did not use, and couldn't use, arbitrary arrests, torture, or the machine gun, this sectarian harassment of the "conquered" by the "conquerors" ultimately provoked a wave of blind resentment in the Chilean populace against the new governors.[45]

This was particularly the case in factories "requisitioned" by the Left, such as the SUMAR textile mill, where Christian Democratic workers were dismissed and their union representatives refused access to the premises.[46] Political discrimination could even be extended to non-political individuals for family reasons; thus, the son of President Frei, Eduardo Frei Ruiz-Tagle, an engineer, found himself in difficulty at his place of work after it passed into the hands of government "interventors."

By the time Allende recognized the need to compromise with the Christian Democrats, precious time had been lost, and he was no closer to control of his own coalition. The Hamilton-Fuentealba bill was passed by Congress in February 1972. Allende had sent his Justice Minister Manuel Sanhueza to work out a list of firms to be nationalized with Senator Fuentealba himself, but when news of the pending accord leaked out, Senator Carlos Altamirano objected and Allende was forced to repudiate his own minister's document and veto the bill outright. Jorge Tapia Videla, named to replace Sanhueza, was sent to resume talks with the Christian Democrats, but by then (June) the time limit for a Senate override of Allende's veto had expired. Even if Altamirano had not interposed, however, agreement would probably never have been reached, since the draft still left two crucial issues unresolved, namely, the time limits for intervention and the rules governing expropriation.[47] At no subsequent point did the two sides come any closer to closing the gap. Nationalization remained "a festering sore, and each requisition, or intervention, and each renewed wave of plant seizures, produced new crises, renewed frustration, and heightened outrage in opposition ranks.''[48] As Tomic put it at the time,

> considered alone, each takeover could have a reasonable explanation and a 'low social cost' (as has been the case up until now). But considered as a whole, multiplied by hundreds and thousands of cases that have occurred along the length of Chile, week after week, month after month, they end up having a cumulative effect on public opinion that is devastating for the government.[49]

By the second half of 1972 the government and the Congress were locked in a political stalemate. The opposition in the Senate and Chamber of Deputies impeached individual ministers for constitutional malfeasance, but Allende was fully empowered to keep them on in other capacities, which he often did. Thus the opposition could punish the government for transgressions committed by individual members, but it could not compel it to change course. The October strike refocused attention on the fundamental issue of property rights, but only to the extent of postponing its resolution until the mid-term congressional elections set for March 1973.[50]

In retrospect, in fact, it is obvious that the Chilean Democrats moved far slower against Allende than did opposition public opinion generally. There was, of course, from the very beginning violent opposition to Allende, archetypically represented by Patria y Libertad, an organization of right-wing terrorists who specialized in blowing up bridges and electric power pilons. These dramatic flourishes kept its name on the front pages, and periodically provoked recriminations by supporters of the government and the National Police. But for the first year, Patria y Libertad was utterly isolated politically, with no program and no possibility of seizing power on its own; though the ideological tide began to turn in its direction in 1972, it never went further than dramatic and largely self-defeating gestures.[51] A far more formidable opponent emerged from the ranks of small businessmen, shopkeepers, truckers, and so forth: corporate interest groups known collectively as *gremios*. These organizations were already politically active in the late Frei administration, but were galvanized into militant action by Popular Unity's penchant to politicize virtually every aspect of economic life, provoking—in the words of Henry Landsberger—"a vicious circle of suspicion and countersuspicion."

> The Government's creation of neighborhood committees to supervise the fair distribution of scarce goods [he writes] was seen by small shopkeepers as the beginning of nationalization of retail distribution and hence the end of their existence, quite apart from charges of political favoritism in distribution. Doctors felt threatened by proposals for a change in the organization of medicine . . . as well as increasing indiscipline in hospital staff. Truckers thought the shortage of spare parts was intended to squeeze them out in order to make way for nationalized truck lines.[52]

All of these frustrations eventually congealed into the October strike, a very nearly spontaneous movement which sent the Christian Democrats and even the Nationals scuttling to get in front of it. By the time the armed forces had entered the cabinet and convinced the strikers to return to work, *gremialismo* had evolved into an impressive grass-roots phenomenon "with impressive direct action capability"[53]; its leaders—Rafael Cumsille of the shopkeepers; León Vilarín of the truckers; Juan Jara Cruz of the National Confederation of Land Transport; Ernesto Cisneros of the microbus and taxi owners; and Julio Bazán of the professionals—viewed all politicians, including the Christian Democrats and the Nationals, with a generalized distrust, while representing a constituency no opposition leader could ignore or countermand.[54]

The cumulative effect of all these things—the arrogance, sectarianism, and triumphalism of the government toward the very members of the opposition closest to it ideologically; the erosion of political civility; the lack of authority to conclude binding agreements; the grass roots rebellion of small business-men, shopkeepers, and professionals—had the effect of pushing the Christian Democrats to the right. Even so, the process was remarkably slow, and responded to the gradual perception that there was no reasonable basis upon which to do business with the government. As it was, Senator Renán Fuen-tealba was replaced as party president by Particio Aylwin in May, 1973—under the circumstances, remarkably late in the day.[55]

The crucial turning point in relations between government and opposition came in March 1973, when mid-term congressional elections were held to renew the entire Chamber of Deputies (150 seats) and half the Senate (25 seats). The Christian Democrats and the National party, together with the Democratic Radicals, saw this as the definitive opportunity to obtain either a two-thirds majority of seats, which would enable them to impeach Allende constitutionally, or at least a simple majority capable of forcing him to change direction.[56] Instead, to their consternation, the joint opposition list (desig-nated under the acronym CODE) came nowhere near the desired two-thirds, and in fact lost six deputies and two senators. The government's performance was all the more impressive in light of widespread shortages, triple-digit inflation, and evident tactical and strategic internal divisions on the one hand, and the evident growth and militance of the opposition on the other.

In its euphoria, however, Popular Unity lost sight of the fact that it was still a minority government, resting now on 43.9 percent of the vote, which was considerably better than its performance in 1970, but rather worse than two years before. Moreover, the opposition was not merely larger numerically, but more unified in direction and purpose. In spite of the dramatic context, the parties of the left did about as well as usual in congressional races of this sort.[57] In fact, As Arturo Valenzuela has shown, with the exception of the Socialists—who gained 6.2 percent of the vote at the expense of the Radicals—

there was a change of only about one percent in the relative strength of the major parties. Though changes in the suffrage laws between 1971 and 1973 — lowering the voting age to 18 and expanding franchise to illiterates—brought 500,000 new Chileans to the polls, there were few qualitative changes of political geography. "There was no dramatic shift in the bases of support," Valenzuela finds. "Traditional working class regions and sectors continued their support of the government, while the opposition continued to have strength in the countryside and more affluent areas." There was some erosion of middle-class support for the Left, and a concomitant strengthening of the same in working-class and rural areas, but given the polarized environment, this is hardly to be wondered at.[58]

Towards Polarization and Stalemate

The midterm elections provided the government with a temporary psychological lift which it promptly proceeded to squander away by blundering into a new political minefield—educational policy. Like most Latin American countries, Chile possessed both private and public school systems, the former largely controlled by the Roman Catholic church. During its first two years, the Allende government—far from attacking the status quo—actually increased state subsidies to private education. Behind the scenes, however, a storm was brewing at the Ministry of Education, particularly among political appointees from the Socialist and Communist parties, as Jorge Tapia Valdés— himself a Radical—discovered when he assumed the portfolio in November 1972. For functionaries from the Marxist parties, the order of the day was to carry the revolution to Chile's classrooms, "in order to take the initiative against the enemy." Sensing trouble, Tapia Valdés appealed to Allende, and received authorization to defer action on several draft proposals, so that nothing would be done until March 1974 at the earliest.

Meanwhile, however, a reform went forward, and was released to the public immediately after the March elections, along with the announcement that the new syllabus would be tried out on an experimental class of ninth graders in June. The purpose of the reform, the document read, was to inculcate "values of Socialist humanism" so as to achieve "harmonious development of young people's personalities." Ultimately all schools in Chile, public and private, would be required to adopt the new syllabus which—to Tapia Valdés' horror—had not undergone the revision of language he had requested when he had seen it in draft.[59] Chilean parents found themselves wondering what the government had in mind, particularly since the proposal's blatantly Marxist vocabulary—in the words of army commander General Carlos Prats—"justified every suspicion."[60]

There was little reassurance forthcoming when Rear Admiral Ismael Huerta, commander-in-chief of the Chilean navy, led 100 officers to the Ministry of Education for a meeting with Tapia Valdés. In the course of the discussion the latter "reportedly admitted that the school system of East Germany had served as a model for drawing up the plan,"[61] which virtually guaranteed its wholesale repudiation by the armed forces. More important still, the new syllabus — known by its Spanish initials, ENU[62] — deeply offended Chile's Catholic bishops, who objected to its lack of a spiritual dimension, its scant respect for pluralism, and the government's failure to consult. This was the first time in nearly three years that they had spoken out in clear opposition to a government policy, and while an extended confrontation between church and state was avoided when Tapia Valdés announced on April 12 that the plan was being indefinitely shelved, the ENU "marked a cooling in the hierarchy's previously cordial relations with the government."[63] The new mood was evident in June, when the hierarchy took the Allende administration to task for what it called "tendencies toward statism," and warned against the threat of totalitarianism, defined as "systems which, although founded on different and sometimes contradictory ideologies, tolerate no opposition, no criticism, or countervailing forces."[64]

The ENU controversy was a blow from which the government never fully recovered. It provided a catalyist to rally once more th forces of the Center and Right, demoralized by the outcome of the mid-term elections. It pushed the church for the first time into an opposition role, however tentative. "And, to make matters worse," Arturo Valenzuela writes, "Allende's capitulation on the issue aggravated [his government's] already deteriorating relations with the left wing of the coalition."[65]

Fuentealba, retiring as president of the Christian Democratic party, clearly saw the configuration of the road ahead, and tried to warn Allende in mid-May that if his government persisted in its policies, it would be unable to "resist the current of popular discontent." In fact, that current reached something of a high tide in subsequent weeks. The copper miners of El Teniente were already on strike since April, and would not return to work until early July. In May there was another strike by owners of collective transport, demanding higher fares and a solution to the problem of spare parts. In June the Chamber of Deputies impeached Economy Minister Orlando Millas for political discrimination in the distribution of basic foodstuffs, and the thirteen members of the Supreme Court accused Allende of being a party to a "systematic campaign" to destroy the prestige of their institution. Finally, on June 29, one unit of the Santiago garrison attempted a military coup.

The putsch — though suppressed almost immediately — underlined the urgency of the situation. Within hours Allende, at the behest of the Roman Catholic primate, Cardinal Raúl Silva Henríquez, had contacted the Christian Democrats, and a new round of talks began. Unlike earlier discussions, these were held at the very highest level—between party president Patricio Aylwin and the president himself. In such circumstances Allende did not show his most attractive side; it was in his nature, Ambassador Davis recalls, "to make political bargains rather easily, always with the possibility of being able to wiggle out of them later." While an obvious asset in the short run, "this touch of frivolousness . . . may have been Allende's greatest political weakness in the longer term."[66] Writing from a wholly different perspective, the president's long-time personal secretary merely avows that his chief "detested people who proposed negotiations with conditions,"[67] which under the circumstances did not bode well for the new dialogue.

The Christian Democratic leadership with which Allende now had to deal was very different from the one Senator Narciso Irueta had led into his office in the last days of 1970. Though Aylwin had phoned the president his personal support on June 29,[68] his party's posture had hardened considerably.[69] Too many conversations had ended inconclusively; too many agreements made and broken; too many false assurances and delays had taken their toll in Allende's personal credibility, and he was now facing an opposition divided only by the question of whether he would resign or whether he should replace his cabinet with a "civil-military administration," which presupposed abandoning much of his program and making a clean break with the far Left.[70] The Christian Democrats believed—not without reason—that Allende was "being less than honest . . . and was merely buying time to implement his full program."[71] Thus the only way they could be sure their concerns were met was to stage, in effect, a "constitutional coup," one which left the President in office but ideologically and politically neutered.

For his part, Allende neither wished nor dared to abandon the most militant part of his constituency, and certainly not without assurances of genuine backing which at that late date the Christian Democrats could not have given him even if they had wished to. Even so, trouble was brewing within his own coalition. The Socialist party was threatening to leave the government in the unlikely eventuality that an agreement was reached. For their part, the Communists still wanted Allende to strike a bargain with the Christian Democrats, but not at the expense of splitting the left in two. They could not have forced matters in any case. After several days and nights of enervating discussions, the Christian Democrats looked up to find that Clodomiro Almeyda, who had been representing the president's own party, was no longer present; in his chair sat a Communist deputy.[72] The talks concluded abruptly on August 3, four days after they had begun, with Allende refusing to bring the military back into the cabinet, and the Christian Democrats insisting that there was nothing further to discuss because Allende had not acceded to their "minimum demands."

The same day the dialogue ended, 60,000 bus, taxi and jitney owned-operators joined private truckers, who had gone out on strike again on July 26. A week later, having called the military back into the cabinet, Allende warned the strikers that if they did not return to work by August 12, their vehicles would be confiscated and their owners prosecuted. Between August 16-18, the government requisitioned 2,000 trucks; on the second of these two days the Congress impeached transport undersecretary Jaime Faivovich; Allende replaced him with Army General Herman Brady. The Christian Democrats, who had proclaimed their support of the truckers, now advanced a motion which passed through the Congress on August 22 declaring the Allende government outside the law. By that time Chile was convulsed with a cascade of other strikes, and had become virtually ungovernable. The major question by the beginning of September was not whether the government would complete its term but whether it would succumb to a coup, "constitutional" or otherwise, or whether—as Cardinal Silva Henríquez and bishops feared[73]—the country would be plunged into a civil war.

Allende and the Armed Forces

Either possibility seemed extremely remote at the time Allende assumed office. In 1970 Chile, almost alone of Latin American nations possessed genuinely resilient political institutions and a tradition of civilian control of the military. Between the 1820s and 1973 there were only three episodes of serious military involvement in politics: the civil war of 1891 (in which the army and navy divided), a brief episode in 1924-25, and the dictatorship of Colonel (later General) Carlos Ibáñez del Campo in 1931-32. The first two were the product of divisions within the civilian political community; the last was an outgrowth of the depression, which hit Chile with a force unequalled almost anywhere in the world. When Ibáñez stepped down in 1932, fleeing the country and leaving it much the worse for his efforts, an entire generation of cadets and young officers resolved never again to surrender the prestige of their institutions to the intrigues of civilian politicians.

Certain long-term trends reinforced the withdrawal of the armed forces from politics. Between the 1880s and the First World War, the Chilean army was trained by German officers, from whom it absorbed the tradition of unquestioning obedience to superiors. More to the point the country's political leadership proved capable of resolving most of the problems that invited (or facilitated) military intervention in other Latin American republics. In addition, after 1932, the militarized national police—the Carabineros, modeled on Spain's Civil Guard—took over the unlovely task of putting down strikes, riots, and other disorders. Finally, in the nearly 40 years prior to Allende's inauguration, most administrations dealt severely with military intrigue and insubordination. Allende was, in fact, a direct beneficiary of this legacy, which among other things made it almost impossible for the U.S. Central Intelligence Agency to recruit officers for a "constitutional coup" to prevent him from taking office.[74]

The most important indicator of the low political salience of the armed forces in Chile was the meager provision made for pay, allowances, and equipment. From 1938 to 1970, one European specialist has found, the defense budget decreased in comparative importance "by almost any yardstick one cares to use." In 1965, the percentage of government resources devoted to military purposes (9 percent) was well below the Latin American average (15 percent); expressed as a percentage of gross national product, it had declined secularly from 3.3 (1931–32) to 2.2 (1958) to 1.7 (1964). Since military payrolls actually increased during this period, "it follows that the army must have sacrificed its officers' real salaries and new equipment to cope with the reduction in its budget that was periodically being imposed by the Chilean Right."[75]

The Christian Democrats were no friendlier; apart from their more compelling interest in other budgetary rubrics—education, health, land reform—their principal ally, the United States, specifically discouraged military spending. In the second half of the 1960s the U.S. Congress—in a fit of what Kissinger later called "doctrinaire antimilitarism"—had placed country-specific ceilings on the sale of arms throughout Latin America, and terminated military aid programs.[76] "The Chilean military appealed to me to intervene with Frei to get this kind of hardware, that kind," Ambassador Korry recalls. "We just didn't do it ... instead, we deliberately wound down our presence."[77]

On October 21, 1969 civil-military relations received their first serious shock in nearly forty years when the officers and men of the Tacna and Yungay regiment of the Chilean army—both garrisoned in the capital—took control of their own headquarters and also of the main arsenal, the Non-Commissioned Officers School, and the main recruiting center. The apparent purpose of the *tacnazo* was not to overthrow the government, but to dramatize the army's need for higher salaries and better equipment. The rebels selected as their leader General Roberto Viaux, who had been forced into retirement a few days previous for raising these issues publicly, and in somewhat intemperate terms; in addition to greater budgetary consideration, they also asked for the resignation of Defense Minister Tulio Marambio. Within hours President Frei agreed to all of the demands, and the rebellion rapidly dissolved.

In spite of its prompt resolution, however, echoes of the *tacnazo* reverberated across the Chilean political stage for months and even years thereafter. Viaux himself became something of a cult figure in the armed forces, particularly among younger officers and NCOs and also "the object of attraction by diverse political forces, both left and right."[78] Patria y Libertad, founded

TABLE 8.1
Military Expenditures Before and During Popular Unity, 1963–1973

Year(s)	Millions $U.S.
1963–1965 (annual average)	92.07
1966–1968 (annual average)	114.76
1969	124.76
1970	145.11
1971	173.83
1972	138.95
1973	245.33

Source: U.S. Arms Control & Disarmament Agency. *World Military Expenditures and Arms Trade, 1963–73* (Washington, D.C., 1975), Table II.

a short time before, claimed the general as its spiritual leader (a distinction he did not explicitly acknowledge), but the Socialists, too, expressed their ambivalence towards his movement by maintaining a discreet silence during the crucial hours of the *tacnazo* while other parties (including the Communists) rushed to express their support for the government. Later, several of the rebellious officers were defended in courts-martial by Socialist lawyers.[79] For its part, the Chilean army command was deeply shaken by the evident erosion of discipline, and during the last year of the Frei administration (1970) its leaders, particularly commander-in-chief General René Schneider, were above all interested in expunging the stain of the Viaux incident.[80]

The *tacnazo* also suggested that by exploiting latent resentment against the traditional political elite, Popular Unity might move the armed forces beyond mere neutrality and actually co-opt them for the ongoing political project. After all, at the time Allende took office, immediately to the north in Peru, a military government, was already carrying out a social revolution similar in content to his own. And across the Andes in Argentina the recrudesence of military populism (that is, Peronism) was evidently only a matter of time. Both these examples provided what one specialist has called "a cogent foundation" for the notion—held by many of Allende's people—"that nationalist and progressive elements existed within the officer corps, and that civilian authority would continue to be respected, particularly if Popular Unity policies responded to the major institutional problems of the armed forces."[81]

Thus throughout his term of office, but particularly during his first year, Allende uninhibitedly courted the military. Two of his defense ministers, though civilians, had service backgrounds.[82] One of the president's first official acts was to reaffirm his predecessor's decision to go ahead with the building of two submarines and two frigates in Great Britain, and also to acquire other equipment from a variety of Western European sources. To meet these commitments, the defense budget was increased in 1971 by nearly 20 percent, and by 1973 it was nearly double what it had been the year Allende took office.(Table 8.1)

TABLE 8.2
U.S. Military Assistance to Chile, 1965–1973
(millions of dollars)

1965–1970 (annual average)	1971	1972	1973
7.4	5.7	12.3	15.0

Source: U.S. Senate, Select Committee to Study . . . Intelligence Activities, *Covert Action* (Washington, D.C., 1975), p. 181.

While much of the increase was due to new equipment, specific provision was made for salary improvement, particularly for the middle and lower ranks. New housing projects for military families were begun; top ranking officers were given automobiles specifically imported for them. In the final phase of the regime, when Allende was trying to convince the military to remain in his cabinet (June 1973), he offered to double housing allowances and increase salaries by another 10 percent.[83] As Ambassador Korry told a congressional hearing in July 1971, the initial package of pay, benefits, and equipment was "the best deal that any president in modern Chile history had given to the military." As far as material was concerned, Korry reported, Allende had given his officers "almost everything" they had asked for.[84]

Partly because of commitment made under the Statute of Democratic Guarantees, partly out of prudence, Allende did not overtly tamper with patterns of military assignment and promotion. In this area Chilean presidents normally enjoyed considerable discretion; under the Statute to the Armed Forces (DFL-1, 1968, Title 111) they could pass any serving officer onto the retired list without offering any reason. Up to 1972, however, this provision had been used by Allende only twice: once in connection with Rear Admiral Víctor Bunster del Solar, naval attaché in Washington, who was accused by the Socialist party press of undue contact with the Central Intelligence Agency and once with regard to Colonel Alberto Labbé Troncoso, long-time commander of the Military School, who had permitted one of his officers at a public ceremony to critize the alleged veneration of "foreign international figures alien to the Chilean tradition," which, coming at the time of Fidel Castro's state visit, was read as an act of insubordination against the civilian authorities.[85]

Prudence also dictated an initial circumspection with regard to external military aid. Allende therefore left relatively untouched the traditional service-to-service relationship with the United States, to the extent that assistance in the forms of grants and credits experienced a three-fold increase during his first year, and a doubling in 1972.[86] (Table 8.2) Between this and acquisitions from Great Britain and Sweden,[87] the armed forces were able for two years to fend off pressures from Allende and other Popular Unity leaders to accept "incomparably more generous" offers from the Soviet Union and Eastern Europe.[88]

Because of the early relationship of the Socialist party with the air force,[89] and also because of his own Masonic affiliations, over the years Allende had occasion to know many retired Chilean officers.[90] Once in the presidency, he took it upon himself to become better acquainted with those on active service. He visited garrisons up and down the length of the country; he took meals in the officers' and non-commissioned officers' messes, and turned his considerable personal charm upon his hosts; he began to refer to himself as "Generalissimo" and wore medals at ceremonies involving the military.[91] He never missed an opportunity to praise the armed forces and to express his confidence in them. Moreover, the president sought actively to draw the armed forces into the work of his government: flag officers were named to the leadership of public sector companies (both those inherited from the previous administration and those subsequently "intervened"); military representatives for the first time joined other sectors of society at ODEPLAN; military men participated in development effort in the far southern provinces. They took part in the distribution of milk to needy children; in the planning of the third meeting of the United Nations Conference on Trade and Development (UNCTAD III), held in Santiago in 1972; and in the government agency for developing national sports.[92]

While the armed forces obviously welcomed Allende's attentions and the budgetary solicitude of his government, neither fully succeeded in their purpose. Instead, there was a growing climate of alienation within military circles, which can be charted along two separate but intersecting curves. The first related to issues of specific professional concern. These included attempts to alter the traditional sources of external military aid, and perceived threats both to the armed forces' monopoly of weapons as well as to discipline and order within the ranks. The other arose out of the broader political context, and the unusual role into which Allende sought to cast his officers and men.

Throughout the Popular Unity period, the Chilean armed forces were encouraged by the government to broaden the base of their acquisitions (that is, to begin purchasing some equipment from the Soviet Union and the Eastern bloc). Thanks to the tight-fisted arms sales policies of the Nixon administration, by the third year of the Allende regime those pressures began to bear some fruit. Though U.S. military aid had been sharply increased in 1971 and 1972, given the extremely low base line established during the Frei administration, the arms balance between Chile and its neighbors, particularly Peru,

was still strongly unfavorable. The Chilean service chiefs took every opportunity to complain to U.S. officials of the neglect which, they claimed, was
undermining their historic pro-Western orientation; in September 1972, Prats
even sent his chief of staff, General Augusto Pinochet Ugarte, to Panama to
explain to General Underwood, chief of the U.S. Southern Command, that if
Washington continued to deny Chile the arms it wanted to acquire, it would
have no choice but to turn to the Soviet Union, just as the Peruvians had done
after 1968. "The political results" of the visit, Pinochet later wrote, "were
very meager."[93]

By mid-1973, Prats felt compelled to make a trip to the Soviet Union (as
well as to Eastern and Western Europe) in search of additional provisions.
How the Army commander felt personally about his mission to Moscow is a
matter of conflicting testimony. Ambassador Davis says that Prats came to see
him before departing to express "his reluctance to become involved with the
Soviets," and sought to neutralize appearances by visiting the United States
en route. The general's reluctance, Davis believes, "was genuine."[94] But
Jorge Edwards, by now Chilean chargé d'affaires in Paris, who saw the army
commander enroute home from Moscow, recalled Prats as strongly tempted to
acquire Soviet tanks, which were of good quality, of the type Chile needed,
and offered at fire-sale prices. Prats was restrained not by geopolitical considerations, but by the probable domestic political fallout in Chile.[95] Thus
only a $50 million logistical agreement was concluded with the Soviets, a
modest line of credit which—according to U.S. intelligence analysts—
"Allende could not get [his] military to use."[96] Thus without making serious
inroads into Chile's traditional pattern of arms acquisitions, Allende ended up
paying almost as high a political price as if he had, since by sending Prats—
his principal supporter in the armed forces—to Moscow in the first place, he
undermined his stature with Chile's strongly anti-Communist officer class.

Of even greater concern to the Chilean military was the prospect of losing
its historic monopoly of force through the creation of new paramilitary formations, typically provisioned with arms from highly non-traditional sources.
To begin with, the president's personal bodyguard, the "Group of Personal
Friends" (GAP) was recruited directly from the principal terrorist organization of the Left, the MIR; was trained outside the purview of the Defense
Ministry; and drew its provisions from separate, undisclosed budget lines. In
addition, as the political conflict sharpened in 1972, the parties of the Left—in
clear violation of the Statute of Democratic Guarantees and Allende's own
repeated assurances[97]—created their own paramilitary units: the Ramón Parra
Brigade (Communist), the Elmo Catalán Brigade (Socialist), and an unde-
nominated formation recruited from the MAPU.

While Patria y Libertad obtained its arms and explosives from sympathizers or for cash in neighboring Argentina, the formations of the Left looked to Cuba, East Germany, Czechoslovakia, and the Soviet Union, all of which maintained oversized military missions in Chile during the Allende period. In addition, by 1972 munitions of a primitive sort, including even a jerry-built "tank," were being produced semi-clandestinely in certain "intervened" factories. Arms of both foreign and domestic provenance proliferated in the industrial belt ringing Santiago, where paramilitary training activities proceeded apace; Chilean military intelligence even discovered Cuban, Czech and East Germany military instructors making visits to Los Cerrillos, one of the largest of these industrial areas, and it was alleged that a paramilitary training center had been established near Valparaíso, in a prefabricated housing plant financed by the Soviet Union. By April and May of 1972 the evidence of expanding paramilitary activities on the part of the MIR led Prats and his chief of intelligence, General Mario Sepúlveda, to press Allende for authority to search for illegal arms caches.[98] Allende temporized and delayed, while the activities of paramilitary formations grew in size and importance, broadly synchronized with the deteriorating political situation. By the second quarter of 1973, there was a "quantum leap" in their activities, both in the cities and in the countryside.[99]

Not surprisingly, one of the concessions exacted by the armed forces as a condition of entering Allende's cabinet in November 1972, was the president's immediate signature on an arms-control law which had cleared Congress some months earlier. Introduced by Senator Juan de Dios Carmona, Frei's former Defense Minister, it specifically reserved heavier armaments (such as submachine guns, large-caliber high-penetration automatic weapons, grenades, tear gas launchers, and bombs) for use only by the three branches of the armed forces, the national police, the investigative police, and by prison guards. More important, it gave the courts, other civil authorities, and the armed forces the right to authorize and carry out military searches for the prescribed munitions. It also gave the armed forces the right to license smaller weapons by permit, and to try violators in military courts, a provision that, if strictly applied, would have eliminated Allende's private bodyguard.[100]

The arms control law failed to eliminate private or "party" armies; instead, it generated a new round of recriminations between the government and the armed forces on one hand, and the opposition and the government on the other. Generally speaking, Allende's people felt that the military were not sufficiently interested in suppressing the activities of Patria y Libertad; this was also the view of General Prats, and, apparently, of General Pinochet as well.[101] On the other hand, the evident proliferation of weapons in factories, trade union officers, and working-class communities suggested to the opposition that on balance the government had no real intention of enforcing the law either. Prats' two colleagues who left the cabinet with him after the March elections said so publicly, as did former President Frei in a major address on July 8.

It was not merely a case of the government's critics and opponents scoring debating points; particularly after the abortive putsch on June 29, leading personalities of Allende's own party spoke as if the time had come to arm and prepare for a decisive confrontation. Even one Communist leader suggested openly that "if the reactionary sedition becomes worse, passing into the arena of armed struggle, no one should doubt that the people will rise as one man to crush it with speed." A widely distributed pamphlet, which cannot have escaped the purview of military intelligence, urged workers to "develop at an accelerated pace the accomplishment of military tasks in the party and among the masses . . . Form organizations necessary to assume the self-defense of the masses in industries, services, neighborhoods, communes, and cordones, developing "armed popular power" and developing the future Army of the People."[102]

Between March and September the military took matters in its own hands and accelerated the search for arms. In April, May, and June, they averaged three searches a week; by July, almost one a day; in August, forty-five in all. According to one advocate of the insurrectional line, of the twenty-four in July, ten were carried out in factories, three in government offices, four in offices of Popular Unity, three in trade unions offices, and two in organizations of the opposition.[103] "The harder the military searched, the more arms they found," Ambassador Davis recalls. "The more this went on, the louder the left-wing Socialists and their allies screamed in public protest—and the harder the Leftists worked to distribute and conceal more arms in the industrial belts."[104] The irony was, he adds, that while "the workers were being trained for violence and possible civil war, . . . they were not being trained or armed fast enough to enable them to stand against the country's military forces. At the same time the mobilization of workers produced a sharp reaction among armed services leaders."[105]

Finally, there was the specter of politically-inspired acts of insubordination within the ranks. At the outset of his government, Allende sought to reassure the military and the opposition that nothing would be done to tamper with traditional service heirarchies; in the Statute of Democratic Guarantees, for example, he agreed to leave intact Article 24 of Law 14.853 (1962) which deprived enlisted men and non-commissioned officers of the armed forces and national police of the right to vote. By 1972, however, there were disturbing signs that some of the president's allies and followers were attempting to subvert individual units of the armed forces; in August of that year General Prats laid the evidence before the president, with the dry observation that he was unsure whether Allende's "most dangerous enemies were to be found in the ranks of the opposition or in the parties of Popular Unity."[106]

By mid-1973, the far Left was boasting unapologetically of its activities within the armed forces—whether real, exaggerated, or imagined. The pro-government press, particularly the political weekly *Chile Hoy*, published interviews with NCOs and enlisted men and their families, purporting to show that their class origins were a far greater source of identification than their professional affiliation. In one such reportage, and unidentified soldier depicted the high command in disrespectful terms, and expressed the hope that "the workers would continue to hit harder, take over more industries, and demonstrate the power that they have." The soldiers, he is supposed to have said, "are much impressed by the strength of the workers. To the degree to which that force is demonstrated, they will be more inclined to lean in their direction." The pièce de résistance came a few day before the coup, when someone, identified only as a "senior NCO," told the magazine that a "sergeant's revolution" within the armed forces was a distinct possibility. With a proper word from the Defense Ministry, he affirmed, "we can do the rest. Because within the unity themselves . . . the people who really run things are the NCO's; officer just sign the papers, that's all."[107]

The first concrete act of insubordination occurred not in the army, but in the navy, whose authorities announced on August 7-8 that they had discovered a subversive movement in two units of the fleet, the cruiser *Almirante Latorre* and the destroyer *Blanco Encalada*. Authorities of the Naval Prefecture in Concepción-Talcahuano announced that the plotters, some twenty-three out of nine hundred men, aimed at taking over their ships, and that under questioning, those arrested had implicated Miguel Enríquez of the MIR, and also the secretaries-general of the Socialist party and the MAPU, Senator Carlos Altamirano and Congressman Oscar Guillermo Garretón, respectively. The naval prosecutor asked for Enríquez' detention and the denial of parliamentary immunity for the other two. For its part, the Left—far from denying the charges—insisted that the plotters were forced to act to confound navy involvement in a new putsch. In addition, it asserted that the detainees had been horribly tortured, and therefore their confessions improperly obtained.

This confrontation between the navy and the Left "stretched Allende's policy of compromise with the military to the very breaking point."[108] The government "could not simply arrest those who argued they were doing their best to protect the government from a coup," Arturo Valenzuela observes. On the other hand, subversive activities within the ranks struck at the very heart of military interests. "For a majority of officers, it was no longer a matter of objecting to erroneous government policies, but ... of defending themselves and their institutions from the possibility of destruction."[109] By this time it hardly mattered how Allende proposed to cut this Gordian knot, since the tide had turned decisively against him within the armed forces; the day of reckoning was only hours away.

The Path to the Coup (I)

The Chilean military was never as "apolitical" as it represented itself to be, but neither was it the Trojan horse which some have since decided it must have been all along. As Ambassador Davis has put it succinctly, "the generals and admirals did not rush to their task of overthrowing their president." Rather, in their growing sense that things were falling apart,

> they went to see [Allende] again and again, mostly through their commanders-in-chief, but sometimes collegially, and asked the president to reconsider his policies and control the extremists. They squirmed, temporized, and looked for ways out, and it was a reluctant, uncertain, inconclusive process. The distinction was not always clear between seditious plotting and troubled consultation.
> . . .
> Again and again, the record indicates that 'serious planning' commenced, that conclusions were reached, or that judgements were made. In actuality there were ebbs and flows of planning and activity which followed successive pulls of national crisis, and subsided when the nation's politics moved to quieter ways. Each flowing tide of plotting reached farther than the last, but it was not a continuous advance.
> [The passage] from planning to talk to decision and action was made slowly. It was late—only days before the coup—when the armed forces moved collectively beyond the point of no return.[110]

To chart this course accurately—to pinpoint specific dates and events, and assess the full significance of each—is technically impossible, all the more so because so many of the surviving participants, whether civilian or military, government or opposition, recall the Allende period largely in terms of their subsequent political agendas. Nonetheless, certain points can be established without difficulty. The first is that the environment for military plotting was distinctly unfavorable well into the first months of 1972. The Chilean military resisted not merely foreign pressures to prevent Allende from taking office, but also the blandishments to which its members were subjected by politicians, businessmen, and retired military officers.[111]

By the third quarter of 1972, the government's economic policies had generated a new style of protest politics, culminating in the October strike. It was this event which first brought the armed forces into the cabinet, where they remained until congressional elections the following March. By agreeing to take over key ministries, the generals were able to strike the compromise necessary to put the country back to work. Above all, their mere presence guaranteed the opposition that the elections would be held as scheduled, with no irregularities or preemptive actions by the government or its constituent parties.[112] In a certain sense, the military's role during these five months would seem, then, to have underlined its vaunted political neutrality, though many supporters and critics of the government were not entirely inclined to think so.

For the left wing of Popular Unity, particularly the Socialist party, by inviting the armed forces into the cabinet, the president had accepted a *de facto* consolidation (rather than a deepening) of the revolutionary process. On this particular point the party was not mistaken: between November and March the size of the Area of Social Property did not expand; in one or two cases Allende was even forced to reduce its boundaries. And no new decrees of insistence were issued during the entire period.[113] As Joan Garcés has acutely remarked, the same "constitutionalism" which led the army to defend Allende in 1970 was now proving to be a double-edged sword. The only solution to the impasse, in his view, was to "close the Congress and govern by decree-laws." But for this, he adds, the president "could not have counted on the support of a single regiment."[114]

Meanwhile, some elements of the opposition began to view the close working relationship between Allende and the armed forces, and particularly with General Prats, his Interior Minister, in a sinister light. Was this, they asked, the beginnings of a qualitatively new development in Chilean politics—an informal coup, but reversing the Latin American pattern of generals hiding behind civilians? By co-opting the military—so the worst-case scenario ran—would Allende finally consummate economic transformations over the heads of the Congress, the courts and the comptroller-general, that is, the country as a whole? Secretary-General Luis Corvalán of the Communist party seemed to confirm this possibility in a newspaper interview in December 1972, when he said that the military presence in the government could conceivably become "a permanent and original feature of the Chilean transition" (e.g., to socialism).[115] As farfetched as the idea seems in retrospect, at the time it was less improbable, particularly against the background of contemporary developments in neighboring republics. Moreover, throughout late 1972 and early 1973 the relationship between the military and the opposition was often adversarial. The job of the armed forces in the cabinet, and particularly the Interior Ministry, was to restore and maintain order. And since the line between protest, legitimate dissent, and what the government and its supporters regarded as subversion was constantly shifting back and forth, General Prats, the Interior Minister, found himself becoming the focus of the opposition's deepest (perhaps, even most lurid) preoccupations.[116] Thus apparently both the opposition and the left wing of Popular Unity was relieved to see the military leave the cabinet shortly after the March elections.[117]

It is also evident that by mid 1972 unrest was spreading among the officer corps. The forcible retirement of Colonel Labbé Troncoso in December 1971 stood out at first by its exceptionality; thereafter, Prats' diaries record a cascade of incidents. In the first days of the year he learned that General Oscar Bonilla was meeting behind his back with Senator Carmona. In February, a regimental commander in Concepción confided to Prats his concern for "the enthronement of Marxism in the government"—apparently the first time a senior officer had dared to raise the issue with the army commander. A few days later he learned that the same officer had begun suggesting to colleagues in Santiago that Prats was "weak, totally in the pocket of the government."[118] In March, officers of the Second Armored Regiment and the Airborne School were discovered conspiring with Arturo Marshall, an ex-army major cashiered for his involvement in the *tacnazo*.

After a lengthy tour of units in the provinces, Prats returned to Santiago in early September with "the unpleasant sensation of 'plowing the desert', given the mentality of field-grade and junior officers, who are evidently afflicted with psychotic fears of Marxism." The same month he found serious questions raised about the government at the School of Naval Engineering and in the air force, and was compelled to ask General Alfredo Canales to retire for unspecified but evidently political reasons. Then, in late October, General Bravo, whom Prats had assigned to command of the Southern region where the trucker's strike had raised political passions to a white heat, asked to be retired ahead of schedule.[119] Nonetheless, as late as June 11, 1973, Prats concluded after meeting with his generals that there was "a consensus that the worst outcome would be military intervention."[120] More than anything else, this attested to the army commander's growing isolation from his colleagues, who no longer trusted him enough to say what was fully on their mind.

The Path to the Coup (II)

Once it was clear that the March elections had solved nothing, both government and opposition resumed their offensives. A few days after the military left the cabinet, Allende defied the comptroller-general by signing a decree of insistence affecting forty-three enterprises whose requisition had been previously declared illegal. The moratorium on agrarian expropriations lasted another 2 months; then, in June, July, and August, there was a rush to confiscate as much land as possible. Of the approximately 1,700 farms (1,560,500 hectares) affected throughout the entire Popular Unity period, nearly a third of these were seized during those three months.[121] The opposition matched this by moving in Congress to declare the government illegal; some civilians began unofficially to visit military installations, begging on an almost daily basis for some action against the government.[122] Not all of these encounters were marked by perfect cordiality: some officers were even pelted with chicken feed by particularly militant opposition women, who found the armed forces' apparent devotion to the Constitution and the political status quo an affront to conventional notions of Chilean manhood.

During these weeks Prats was pressing both Allende and his opponents for a political truce which would have required, among other things, a clear definition of the three areas of the economy, and a more prudent monetary and fiscal policy. On June 14, the president agreed to make an effort, but the following evening his chief of staff dropped by Prats' house with somber news that Allende had failed to convince the constituent parties of his coalition.[123] Three days later, Prats asked Oscar Guillermo Garretón, leader of the hardliners in MAPU, what, given the refusal, "was the way out of the present bottleneck." Garretón acknowledged—apparently without regret—that there was a real possibility of civil war.[124] For their part, the Christian Democrats told General Bonilla on July 1 that their price for an understanding was a "civil-military administration." This meant, Prats correctly observed, an end to the Popular Unity government, something he could not possibly broker.[125]

The stalemate was broken again on June 29, when the Second Armored Battalion under Colonel Roberto Souper surrounded the Moneda Palace with tanks and tracked vehicles, and exchanged fire with Allende's bodyguard. Prats himself rushed to the scene to personally direct loyalist troops, who broke the siege within two hours. Apparently no other unit in the country had joined the rebels, but the army commander confided to his diary that the Second Armored Battalion could not possibly have been alone in the adventure. "At a minimum, part of other units must [have been] committed or at least waiting to see what the initial reaction would be." An admiral subsequently confirmed what Prats suspected: that the younger officers had all sympathized with the rebels.[126] As it was, those soldiers who died trying to overthrow Allende were buried with full military honors alongside fallen loyalists, while supporters of the government, gathered outside the military cemetery, clamored for summary justice and the firing squad for those "putschists" who had survived.[127]

The events of June 29 had a profound impact upon the political situation and on civil-military relations. During his brief period of confinement, Allende had taken to the radio and begged his supporters, particularly in the unions, to demonstrate their support for him by marching to the center of the city. Instead, they seized their factories—nearly doubling those then occupied from 282 to 526. When the crisis passed more rapidly than he had anticipated, the president could not easily undo what he had in effect ordered. Thus after June 29, Ambassador Davis recalls, "workers extended their control over industrial belt neighborhoods, organizing sentries and militias, assuming internal police functions, and excluding or impeding the entry of uniformed carbineros. They also expelled Christian Democrats and other opposition-oriented workers from their industrial belt redoubts.'' In the affected factories, production plummeted "as paramilitary activities interfered with labor discipline. The industrial belts increasingly competed for power with the government rather than following it."[128] This was a virtual invitation to the armed forces to implement the arms-control law with full rigor, even if it meant a series of violent confrontions with supporters of the government—which, in the event, was precisely what occurred.

Ever since the March elections, Allende had been urging the military to return to his cabinet. A few days before the June 29 incident, he renewed his request to his service chiefs, but Prats concluded that since Allende could not coax a compromise out of his coalition, such a situation "would merely undermine subordination of the military to civilian authority."[129] By August 9, against a background of widespread strikes, work stoppages, and sabotage, the president finally prevailed, with Prats rejoining the cabinet as defense minister. Navy commander Admiral Raúl Montero was named finance minister; air force commander General Cesar Ruiz Danyau, transport minister; national police chief General José Maria Sepúlveda, minister of lands and colonization. Prats' earlier reluctance to form part of the new government was now justified by events. When General Ruiz Danyau, whose job it was to deal with the striking truckers, found his authority questioned by his subsecretary, a political appointee, he resigned his portfolio. Allende accepted his resignation, but—to the surprise of the officer corps—he also relieved him of command of the air force and relegated him to retirement. This action undermined the position of generals considered sympathetic to the government: Sepúlveda, Pickering, and above all, Prats.

For some time the army commander had been under considerable strain, both personally and professionally. Though not a man of the Left, the frequent attacks upon his integrity by the opposition press tended to drive him into the arms of the government. To some degree it was simply a case of a common enemy suddenly bringing two neutrals together. But there was a qualitive element present as well: General Prats' civilian critics were generally the more shrill and irresponsible elements of the opposition, while those Popular Unity personalities with whom he had occasion to deal—normally, cabinet and subcabinet officers—tended on the whole to be more moderate than their coreligionists in Congress, the unions, universities, press, or "organs of popular power." Prats also forged a particularly intimate relationship with the president. Though he had never met Allende prior to succeeding General Schneider in 1970, the two men found that they could work well together, and came to hold each other in considerable esteem. For his part, the president did all he could to solidify the relationship, as any clever politician would.[130] No doubt the army commander sincerely saw his role as one of defending the constitution and the democratic system, of which the Popular Unity government was momentarily the legitimate expression. Basically insensitive to the deeper ideological issues, he tended to regard all politicians—including the most radical—as roughly equivalent. In normal times Prats' posture would have been unexceptionable; in the context, however, of the quasi-revolutionary situation through which Chile was passing in 1973, it amounted to a concrete political statement. Or so his critics and colleagues thought.

A few even began to tell him so. At a meeting of general officers a few days after the Souper putsch, General Arturo Araya, whom Prats had always considered one of his protégés, suggested coldly that the army commander retire and join the government as a civilian minister of defense. When Prats asked him why—he harbored no political ambitions—Araya informed him that his image was "negative among the junior officers." If that was so, Prats replied, "it is because the generals have not been faithful interpreters of my professional philosophy."[131] What his subordinates dared not say to his face, others told him surreptitiously. In June and July he received anonymous phone calls and letters, both at his office and at his home, urging him to resign. Wives of officers congregated outside his house, shouting oaths and casting aspersions on his masculinity.

Returning from lunch on June 27, he noticed someone in another car making an obscene gesture. He ordered his driver to force the vehicle off the road; he dismounted, pulled out his pistol, and discovered to his horror that the other driver was a woman. A group of people rapidly gathered at the scene—a corner of a fashionable suburb—and began to taunt Prats for attacking a helpless, unarmed housewife. Journalists and photographers materialized from nowhere. Someone let the air out of his tires, forcing the general to escape in a taxi. "That day," Pinochet writes, "General Prats was the victim of the most extensive nervous crisis I had ever seen."[132] By August 23, having failed to bridge the widening gap between government and opposition, and near emotional collapse, Prats retired from the cabinet and the army.

The Final Obstacle Removed: Prats Resigns

In the weeks prior to his resignation, Prats had made the rounds of the governing coalition, arguing that if "putschism was no solution for Chile's future, neither could Marxism impose a dictatorship of its own."[133] Whatever its undeniable intrinsic merits, this formulation failed to take full cognisance of political realities. The middle had disappeared from Chilean politics, and neither the Left nor the opposition believed things could continue as they were. This left the Chilean generals with only two choices. As Ambassador Davis has phrased it, "They could, with Prats, march on to a lonely destination called honor; or they could step down in their gleaming uniforms, and wade through dark waters towards what they might hope was higher ground, and a destination called power. A few followed Prats, but not many."[134]

By now Allende was aware of extensive plotting within the armed forces, and if Prats' successor General Pinochet is to be believed, the president even pressed him early on to purge the army of four generals he suspected of deep involvement with the opposition.[135] Yet even though Santiago was rife with rumors of a new military uprising, Allende seems not to have taken the threat as seriously as the situation warranted. Almost to the very end he continued to act as if all problems might yet be resolved with a new tactical *démarche*— renewed discussions with the opposition, or a new arrangement with the armed forces. These were the techniques, after all, by which he had survived a thousand days in office, and he could not imagine any other. In that sense, the coup of September 11 rescued the president from the cul-de-sac into which his own policies had forced him, and allowed him to pass into history as a martyr rather than a failure.

There was a fatalistic side of Allende's personality which was often remarked upon by those who knew him well.[136] Thus it was not out of character for him to tell Prats on Saturday, September 8 that he was planning to convoke a plebiscite so that Chileans could determine whether they wished him to continue in office. He knew, he told his guest, that he would lose, "but it will be an honorable defeat for Popular Unity, an expression of the majority will, [thus] avoiding a civil war, something never justified by even the most cherished of partisan considerations."[137] Prats was dumbfounded at this news, since Allende proposed to convoke the exercise only two days hence, on Monday, September 10.

He told the President that the idea was ridiculous; that at least thirty to sixty days would be required to prepare a national scrutiny; he assured him that long before that—"within the next ten days"—he would confront a military pronouncement. Allende acted as if this was the first time he had considered the possibility. Were not his service chiefs still loyal to him?, he asked. Prats imagined so, but it hardly mattered. "They will be superseded by putschist generals . . . so fast that there will be no break whatever in the chain of command. And the most constitutionalist of officers will understand that any division of the armed forces means civil war." When Allende asked him what, then, did he recommend, Prats replied, "On Monday you should ask constitutional permission to take a year's leave of absence and leave the country. Under this arrangement, you will eventually be able to return in glory to finish out your term." The President's own response was "Never!"[138]

Was There Another Way?

Looking back on the events leading up to the coup, it is difficult to see how Allende could have proceeded other than he did. Both a Marxist and a democrat, he failed to perceive a contradiction between the two value systems until he was forced to reconcile them in practice; by that time it was too late to shift decisively in favor of one or the other. Nor did he wish to: to the last day of his life, Allende sought to represent the most radical tendencies in Chilean politics and also some of the most conservative—to be both the fiery evangel of revolution and the repository of the Constitution and the laws. Popular Unity was held together by common aspirations and common illusions, but these could flourish only at the threshold of power. Once in full possession of political responsibility, it fell into contending pieces, unified only by the notion that each was the revolution for which Chileans—some Chileans—had voted in September 1970 and again in March 1973. The only possible arbiter was Comrade Allende himself, and he was not saying. Meanwhile, radicals and reformers, constitutionalists and insurgents, each went about their version of the Chilean road, while the country's economy verged on the point of collapse.

Given the extreme polarization which prevailed in the last days of the regime, it is easy to forget the continuities which led from practically every Chilean government since at least 1938 to the election of Allende in 1970. Over the years statist tendencies, the enlargement of the public sector, price controls, even the expropriation of foreign properties under certain circumstances and in certain industries had become the common currency of politics. Every government promised more than it could deliver, and every one found it necessary to pull back from its most advanced positions, as economic realities exacted their cost. This meant disillusionment for intellectual sectors of first, the Radicals, and later, the Christian Democrats. These periodic reassessments had one virtue, however: they protected each government from the ultimate consequences of its own policies.

When Allende came along, promising that he would succeed where others had failed, that he would, in effect, resolve economic difficulties by political means alone, more than a few Christian Democrats, Radicals, and independents, perhaps even a few conservatives, must have wished him well. In fact, for the first year Popular Unity seemed to have wrought something of a miracle. But by 1972 there were serious distortions in the economy, which any other Chilean government would have been forced to correct. Instead, Allende postponed decisions to March 1973, in the hope of increasing his support in Congress. This he did, though not definitively; meanwhile, the basic economic conditions had worsened, and had made the stakes in the by-elections intolerably high, not merely for the contending parties, but for the political system as a whole.

In subsequent years it was common for Popular Unity historians or their foreign sympathizers to take the Christian Democrats to task for advocating revolution, but lurching into the arms of the military once it finally came along. But in this they were no different from reformers of any age: they imagined they could have widespread abundance through the simple expedient of punishing the wealthy. When another government proved that this was not the case, they naturally reacted against its policies, the consequences of which were felt directly in the marketplace, in the pocketbook, at the kitchen table. It would have been odd indeed if, under these circumstances, the Christian Democrats had persisted in some of their own (or Allende's) more expansive economic notions.

In theory Allende could have reached out to these people early on and struck a compromise. In practice it was never possible. In 1971 there seemed no need to do so. In 1972, when circumstances were still propitious and the left wing of Christian Democracy was still in the ascendency, the temptation was too strong to let redistributionist economic policies reshape the country's political geography. By the next year it was obvious that this was not going to happen, at any rate, not at any time soon. The Christian Democrats themselves had hardened their position, and Allende was hardly able to soften his own.

Allende's recurrence to the military in 1972 seemed inspired enough at the time, it put an end to the October strike and temporarily gave his government the stability which otherwise could be obtained only by reaching a costly political truce with his opponents. General Prats' presence in the Interior Ministry (and that of his colleagues in Supply, Transport and Agriculture) provided an easy and even pleasant way around settling on the three areas of the economy or demarcating the lower limits of agrarian expropriations. But it carried with it a yet higher price; in effect, it made Allende dependent upon the armed forces for the survival of his government—a support which could not be purchased with weapons, pay raises, or flattery alone, but with respect for the profoundly conservative nature of military society and its members. It is very possible that the extraordinary personal rapport between Allende and General Prats ill-served the president, in that it deluded him into underestimating the growing discontent within the armed forces. In the end, Allende would not, of course, give to the generals and admirals what he could not give to opposition politicians. It was only a matter of time before the latter two would recognize the convergence of interest.

Notes

1. Some personalities and forces within Popular Unity, particularly the non-Marxist components, genuinely expected the expansionary economic policies of 1971 to be successful, and not just in the short term. Thus they had no strategy to offer when in fact this proved not to be the case. Jorge Tapia Valdés, ''The Viability and Failure of the Chilean Road to Socialism,'' in Federico G. Gil et. al., *Chile at the Turning Point: Lessons of the Socialist Years, 1970-73*, tr. by John S. Gilitz, (Philadelphia, 1979), pp. 298-299.

2. Isabel Turrent, *La Unión Soviética en América Latina: el caso de la Unidad Popular chilena, 1970-73* (Mexico, D.F., 1984), pp. 72-73.

3. Created by the insurgent youth wing of the Christian Democrats in July, 1971 to protest their party's decision to run a joint list with the Right in the Valparaíso by election.

4. Those expelled promptly fashioned themselves MAPU-OC (MAPU-"Worker-Peasant"), though in fact most were well-to-do young people from the *haute bourgeoisie* of Santiago.

5. Davis, *The Last Two Years of Salvador Allende*, pp. 86-87.

6. Turrent, *La Unión Sovietica en América Latina*, p. 29.

7. Ibid., p. 33.

8. Ibid., p. 37.

9. Ronald Russell Pope, "Soviet Foreign Affairs Specialists: An Evaluation of Their Direct and Indirect Impact on Foreign Policy Decision-Making Based on Their Analyses of Cuba, 1958-61 and Chile, 1969-73," Unpublished Ph.D. diss., University of Pennsylvania, 1975, pp. 135-136.

10. These were not as apparent in Peru and Bolivia because the local Communist parties were junior partners in military-populist ("Nasserist") regimes, and therefore did not bear the fullest responsibility—as their analogue did later in Chile—for the architecture of economic and social policy.

11. Jorge Edwards, *Persona non grata* (versión completa) (Barcelona, 1982), pp. 339-340.

12. Quoted in Genaro Arriagada Herrera, *De la via chilena a la via insurrecional* (Santiago, 1974), p. 294. In practice this meant that some (presumably Socialist) leaders of Popular Unity even welcomed hyperinflation as a means to "destroy the bourgeoisie"—a position which Communists like Pablo Neruda (serving as Allende's ambassador in Paris) found utterly senseless, Edwards, *Persona non grata*, p. 398.

13. Arrigada, *De la via chilena*, p. 293.

14. Quoted in ibid., p. 296.

15. Quoted in Patricia Santa Lucia (pseud.), "The Industrial Working Class and the Struggle for Power in Chile," in Philip O'Brien, *Allende's Chile* (New York, 1976), pp. 140-141.

16. Silva Solar "Errors of the Unidad Popular and a Critique of the Christian Democrats," in Gil, *Chile at the Turning Point*, p. 317.

17. The anniversary of the Cuban revolution.

18. Quoted in Arriagada, *De la via chilena*, p. 301.

19. Davis, *The Last Two Years of Salvador Allende*, pp. 88-89.

20. Henry A. Landsberger and Tim McDaniel, "Hypermobilization in Chile, 1970-73," p. 516.

21. Tapia Valdés, "Viability and Failure . . .," pp. 304-305.

22. Peter Winn, *Weavers of Revolution: The Yarur Workers and the Chile's Road to Socialism* (New York, 1986); Michel Raptis, *Revolution and Counter-Revolution in Chile* (tr. John Simmonds) (New York, 1974).

23. For a close look at the original model, see Leonard Schapiro, *The Russians Revolutions of 1917: The Origins of Modern Communism* (New York, 1984), esp. pp. 73-119.

24. Santa Lucia, "The Industrial Working Class . . .," p. 142.

25. Colin Henfrey and Bernardo Sorj, *Chilean Voices* (Hassocks, Sussex, 1977), pp. 63-64.

26. Arriagada, *De la via chilena,* p. 297-98, 307.
27. Popular Unity held 57 seats in the Chamber of Deputies at the time of Allende's election, as opposed to 92 for the combined forces of the opposition, 55 of them Christian Democratic; in the Senate, the figures were 23 and 27 respectively, with 20 of them Christian Democratic. Though Popular Unity improved its representation in the mid-term elections of March, 1973, it still failed to win a working majority. Radomiro Tomic points out that in 1970 the Christian Democrats also controlled 70 percent of Chile's peasant organizations, one third of the trade union federation—the Central Unica de Trabajadores—and "an overwhelming majority" of neighborhood councils, mother's clubs, technical and professional organizations, five of the eight universities, and an important part of the media. Tomic, "Christian Democracy and the Government of the Unidad Popular," in Gil, *Chile at the Turning Point,* p. 214.
28. See Chapter One.
29. Interview with Eduardo Frei Montalva, Santiago, March 20, 1980. Reproduced in Appendix. Nonetheless, during the first months of the regime Frei felt obligated to put the best possible face on the matter; thus in a press conference in Madrid on April 12, 1971—a few days after the municipal elections—he insisted that democracy was not in danger in Chile because it was stronger than individual governments.
30. Silva Solar, "Errors of the Unidad Popular . . . ," p. 323.
31. Radomiro Tomic, "Some Clarifications of Certain Historical Facts," ibid., pp. 190-191.
32. Interview with Patricio Aylwin, subsequently President of the Christian Democratic party, Santiago, August 26, 1982. At this initial meeting Allende also agreed to the Christian Democrats' request to allow Bosco Parra to accede to his now vacant senatorial seat (the Xth circumscription—Magallanes-Chiloe); on this too he broke his word.
33. As Tomic bitterly recalled later, the intentions of Popular Unity were clear: "Nothing to do with the Christian Democrats, and with Tomic, not even to go to Mass!" "The PDC During the Allende Years and Some Comments on the Origin of the Christian Democratic Left Wing," Gil, *Chile at the Turning Point,* p. 330. In his posthumous memoirs Allende's long time personal secretary claims that Tomic approached Allende in the pre-electoral period in 1970 (that is, before either had been formally nominated) and offered his support for the Presidency "in exchange for some very subtle conditions. They were so subtle that many politicians would have accepted them. And at times I asked myself why Allende didn't . . . . But in the course of the discussions I realized that Allende, like a chess player, had already thought two or three moves ahead." He offers no further details, except to say that Tomic (who had recently served as ambassador in Washington) told Allende "a UP government was impossible without a steady flow of American credits." Osvaldo Puccio, *Un cuarto de siglo con Allende* (Santiago, 1985), p. 330.
34. Tomic, "Christian Democracy and the Government of Unidad Popular," pp. 228-229.
35. Tomic, "Some Clarifications . . . ," p. 190.
36. Lester A. Sobel, ed., *Allende and Chile* (New York, 1974), p. 43. Actually, there was no joint list properly speaking; there was a "gentleman's agreement" to support the strongest candidate each put up in a given circumscription. Up to that point Chilean law forbade joint lists.
37. Ibid., p. 49.

38. Tomic, "Christian Democracy and the Government of the Unidad Popular," pp. 332-333.
39. The assassination of Pérez Zujovic was heartily condemned by all sides, but interpreted in quite different ways. For the Christian Democrats it underlined Allende's ambivalent relationship with the violent left; they were particularly disturbed by the curious fact that all of the guilty were killed in a shoot-out with the police, so that there were no witnesses. For their part, the Socialists, Communists, and MIR took refuge in the notion that the CIA was involved. As late as May, 1975, former Christian Left congressman Luis Maira was still claiming that "the U.S. had played an important role in the perfectly executed operation," though the report of the Church committee of the U.S. Senate *(Alleged Assassination Plots Involving Foreign Leaders)* published a few months later, found no such evidence. See Chapter Seven. Maira's claim appears in "The Strategy and Tactics of the Chilean Counterrevolution in the Area of Political Institutions," Gil, *Chile at the Turning Point*, p. 258.
40. Davis, *The Last Two Years of Salvador Allende*, pp. 47-48.
41. Jorge Tapia Videla, "The Difficult Road to Socialism: The Chilean Case from a Historical Perspective," Gil, *Chile at the Turning Point*, p. 43. Tapia Vadela was not the serving minister at the time the plan was introduced.
42. Davis, *The Last Two Years of Salvador Allende*, pp. 337-340.
43. Ibid., pp. 91-92. The official returns gave the Communist slate 170,000 votes, the Socialists 145,000, and the Christian Democrats 144,000.
44. Ibid., pp. 92-93. Among those professors targeted for attack was Claudio Véliz, the distinguished internationalist, who was locked out of his office. He eventually emigrated to Australia. The university's television station was seized by Popular Unity partisans in January, 1973 and held illegally for eight months, while government authorities "postponed" the execution of several court orders mandating the eviction of the invaders.
45. Tomic, "Christian Democracy and the Government of the Unidad Popular," p. 227.
46. Interview with Patricio Aylwin (cited).
47. For the crucial implications of both, see Chapter Five.
48. Davis, *The Last Two Years of Salvador Allende*, pp. 59-61.
49. Quoted in Tapia Videla, "The Difficult Road to Socialism . . . ," p. 43.
50. The Chilean political calendar has a peculiar configuration, at least for people living in the northern hemisphere. Since the seasons are reversed, the Chilean summer begins around Christmastime; the political year is thus in recess from January to March. The October strike actually ended in November, making the congressional elections the next important political date.
51. "If truth be told," Ambassador Davis recalls, "provocative wall slogans and grandiose schemes were probably Patria y Libertad's strong suit—along with efforts to subvert rightist military officers. Patria y Libertad also encouraged the organization of vigilante squads in the wealthy suburbs, and maintained gangs of youths who appeared on the streets whenever violence was the order of the day." Apparently the organizations also engaged in a clandestine arms traffic in Chile's northern provinces bordering Argentina, but by mid-1973 these activities had come to an end with the arrest and exile of a number of leaders. In the end, of course, the regime was overthrown by the armed forces, which did not depend upon subversive organizations for firepower. Davis, *The Last Two Years of Salvador Allende*, pp. 153-154.

52. Henry Landsberger, Prepared statement, U.S. Congress, House of Representative, Committee of Foreign Affairs, *The United States and Chile During the Allende Years,* 94th Congress, 1st session (Washington, 1975), p. 233.

53. Davis, *The Last Two Years of Salvador Allende,* p. 151.

54. The term "bosses' strike" is ideologically satisfying to Popular Unity sympathizers, but inaccurate. Most of the participants were not well-to-do and in fact did not feel particularly close to the Chilean establishment, which they regarded as having abandoned them.

55. As Tomic has pointed out, for the more "progressive" Fuentealba-Leighton slate to win "depended to a great extent on its capacity to be heard by the government and exercise some influence." Two weeks before the meeting to vote on new party leadership, the official organ of the Socialist party, *Ultima Hora,* owned by three ministers of the Allende government, began attacking Fuentealba in what Tomic calls "pornographic" terms. "The PDC During the Allende Years . . . ," pp. 336-337.

56. In his interview, Aylwin denied that his party put much stock in the two-thirds figure. The prospects for actually obtaining that many seats in both houses were extremely remote, and it was intolerably risky for National party President Sergio Onofre Jarpa to announce the goal as if it were within reach. As the U.S. Embassy calculated, the opposition would have to score between 67 and 70 percent of the popular vote, something which no party or coalition of parties had done in Chile for over a generation. Davis, *The Last Two Years of Salvador Allende,* pp. 139-140.

57. In 1969, FRAP (as it was then known) obtained 43 percent—practically the same as the combined left in 1973.

58. *The Breakdown of Democratic Regimes: Chile* (Baltimore, 1978), pp. 86-87. Then and later it was argued that Popular Unity owed its performance in 1973 to blatant electoral fraud. It was certainly true that for the first time in modern Chilean history the results were not announced within 24 hours. Ambassador Davis believes that there was some fraud, "but not enough to make a significant difference." *The Last Two Years of Salvador Allende,* p.142. A sophisticated case for fraud, advanced by faculty members at the Catholic University of Chile, is reproduced in Augusto Pinochet Ugarte, *El día decisivo* (Santiago, 1980), pp. 187-192. Nonetheless, it has been satisfactorily refuted by Paul Sigmund in *The Overthrow of Allende and the Politics of Chile, 1964-1976* (Pittsburgh, 1977), pp. 219-220.

59. Tapia Valdés, "The Viability and Failure of the Chilean Road . . . ," pp. 312-313.

60. Carlos Prats González, *Memorias: testimonio de un soldado* (Santiago, 1985), p. 378.

61. Davis, *The Last Two Years of Salvador Allende,* p. 135.

62. Escuela Nacional Unificada-National Unified School.

63. Brian H. Smith, *The Church and Politics in Chile: Challenges to Modern Catholicism* (Princeton, N.J., 1982), p. 196-199.

64. Ibid., pp. 200-201.

65. *The Breakdown of Democratic Regimes,* p. 90. Tapia Valdés calls it "the final weapon" for the Right to "mobilize . . . the middle sectors in its favor." "The Viability and Failure of the Chilean Road . . .," p. 303.

66. Davis, *The Last Two Years of Salvador Allende,* p. 50.

67. Puccio, *Un cuarto de siglo con Allende,* pp. 62-63.

68. Tomic, "The PDC During the Allende Years . . . ," pp. 334-335.
69. The Christian Democrats had, for instance, publicly supported the strike at El Teniente, and also the recent stoppage of collective transport owners.
70. Prats, *Memorias*, p. 424; Valenzuela, *The Breakdown of Democratic Regimes*, p. 96. Specifically, Aylwin demanded that six of the ministerial portfolios be given to serving officers; the rest to "apolitical personalities." But he also asked that military men be given all of the intendencies (roughly, the governorships of Chilean provines, traditionally appointed by the President).
71. Valenzuela, *The Breakdown of Democratic Regimes*, p. 96.
72. Interview with Patricio Aylwin.
73. Smith, *The Church and Politics in Chile*, p. 203.
74. See Chapter Seven. This summary of Chilean military history draws upon Alain Joxe, *Las fuerzas armadas en el sistema político de Chile* (Santiago, 1970), and Frederick M. Nunn, *The Military in Chilean History: Essays on Civil-Military Relations* (Alburquerque, N.M., 1976).
75. Alain Joxe, "The Chilean Armed Forces and the Making of the Coup," in O'Brien, *Allende's Chile*, pp. 255-256. In 1964, the last year of the Alessandri administration, the Army's share of the defense budget was 40 percent of its prewar level.
76. Kissinger, *White House Years*, p. 664.
77. Korry, "U.S. Policies in Chile under the Allende Government," in F. Orrego Vicuña, ed., *Chile: The Balanced View* (Santiago, 1975), p. 298.
78. H.E. Bicheno, "Anti-Parliamentary Themes in Chilean History: 1920-70," in Kenneth Medhurst, ed., *Allende's Chile* (London, 1972), p. 133.
79. Cristián Zegers Ariztia, "The Armed Forces: Support of a Democratic Institutionality," in Pablo Baraona Urzua, ed., *Chile: A Critical Survey* (Santiago, 1972), p. 313.
80. Joxe, "The Chilean Armed Forces . . .," pp. 259-260.
81. Liisa North, "The Military in Chilean Politics," in Abraham Lowenthal, ed., *Armies and Politics in Latin America* (New York, 1975), pp. 171-172.
82. Alejandro Ríos Valdivia (1970-72) was an elderly, well-liked former instructor at the military school; Orlando Letelier (1973) had been a cadet there, though never actually commissioned.
83. Prats, *Memorias*, p. 410.
84. Korry, *The United States and Chile During the Allende Years, 1970-73*, p. 4.
85. Zegers Ariztia, "The Armed Forces . . .," pp. 315-317. On this occasion General Prats covered for Allende by assuming responsibility for the decision. For his own account, see *Memorias*, pp. 233-236. Apparently Allende toyed with the idea of using his discretionary powers more widely than he ever did; for example, in December 1971 he tried to alter the promotion list for 1972, but Prats talked him out of it "after an arduous debate." Ibid., pp. 200, 229.
86. At Allende's request, however, the size of the U.S. military mission was reduced from sixty-eight (where it stood in 1967) to thirteen (in 1973). Korry, "U.S. Policies in Chile Under the Allende Government," p. 296.
87. Zegers Ariztia, "The Armed Forces . . .," p. 323.
88. Davis, *The Last Two Years of Salvador Allende*, p. 99.
89. Joxe, "The Chilean Armed Forces . . .," pp. 252-254.
90. See Puccio, *Un cuarto de siglo con Allende*, passim.
91. Nunn, *The Military in Chilean History*, p. 272.
92. Ibid., p. 277.

93. Pinochet, *El día decisivo*, p. 82.
94. Davis, *The Last Two Years of Salvador Allende*, p. 132.
95. Edwards, *Persona non grata*, p. 424. See also Prats, *Memorias*, p. 389.
96. *The United States and Chile during the Allende Years* (testimony of Litsinger), p. 162. For complicated legal and technical reasons, which may have reflected political problems, the Comptroller-General refused to register Prat's agreements with the Soviets in any case.
97. In a speech in Temuco on March 28, 1971, Allende declared, ''I have said it before and I say it again: the Popular Unity government has committed itself . . . to seeing that in Chile the only armed forces are the Army, the Navy, the Air Force, and the National Police. The people require no other forces to defend themselves than the unity and respect for the Armed Forces of the Fatherland.'' *Nuestro camino al socialismo* (Santiago, 1972), p. 128.
98. Prats, *Memorias*, p. 262.
99. Davis, *The Last Two Years of Salvador Allende*, p. 157.
100. Ibid., 116.
101. Prats, *Memorias*, p. 401.
102. Quoted in Valenzuela, *The Breakdown of Democratic Regimes: Chile*, p. 101.
103. Jorge Palacios, *Chile: An Attempt at "Historic Compromise"* (Chicago, 1979), p. 334. Palacios was a militant of the Revolutionary Communist party. (PRC).
104. Davis, *The Last Two Years of Salvador Allende*, pp. 156-157.
105. Ibid., p. 158. Even so sympathetic a figure as General Prats openly confronted Altamirano and Almeyda at a cabinet meeting in August, accusing both of conniving with ''left extremism'' and the MIR. Altamirano calmly (and duplicitously) denied the charge. Prats, *Memorias*, p. 283.
106. Prats, *Memorias*, p. 281.
107. Quoted in, Arriagada, *De la via chilena*, pp. 316-317.
108. Ibid., pp. 318-321.
109. Valenzuela, *The Breakdown of Democratic Regimes: Chile*, p. 103.
110. Davis, *The Last Two Years of Salvador Allende*, p. 165-66.
111. Prats, *Memorias*, pp. 165-189; Pinochet, *El día decisivo*, pp. 52-53.
112. Tomic, ''Some Clarifications . . . ,'' p. 189.
113. Tapia Videla, ''The Difficult Road to Socialism ...,'' p. 52; Arriagada, *De la via chilena*, pp. 309-310. Of equal significance was the fact that Air Force General Alberto Bachelate, who replaced a Socialist at the Secretariat for Distribution and Commerce, purposely set about recovering that portion of the supply network for basic foodstuffs—some 30 percent of the whole—which had been seized by ''popular'' organizations (JAPs, workers and neighborhood councils, etc.). Silva Solar, ''Errors of the Unidad Popular . . .,'' pp. 268-269.
114. Joan Garcés, *El estado y los problemas tácticos en el gobierno de Allende* (Mexico, D.F., 1974), pp. 24-25.
115. Quoted in Joxe, ''The Chilean Armed Forces,'' p. 268.
116. See Prats, *Memorias*, pp. 190-375 and passim.
117. Tapia Videla, ''The Difficult Road to Socialism . . . ,'' p. 57.
118. In his memoirs Pinochet claims that when he became chief of staff in early 1972 he tried on two or three occasions to elicit Prats' views on the political situation, but the latter purposely steered the subject to professional matters. Pinochet also claims to have ventured an observation which drew a sharp response to his chief (''Are you saying that you are thinking of some little military adventure? How

could such an idea occur to you?'') *(El día decisivo,* pp. 71, 77-78). There is no suggestion of such attitudes on Pinochet's part in Prats memoirs, even though the latter had the opportunity to revise them later in full knowledge of the outcome.

119. Prats, *Memorias,* pp. 234, 244-245, 286, 289.
120. Ibid., p. 402.
121. Arriagada, *De la vía chilena,* pp. 309-310.
122. Pinochet, *El día decisivo,* p. 97.
123. Prats, *Memoirs,* p. 402.
124. Ibid., 408.
125. Ibid., 424.
126. Ibid., pp. 417-422.
127. Valenzuela, *The Breakdown of Democratic Regimes: Chile,* p. 99.
128. Davis, *The Last Two Years of Salvador Allende,* pp. 171-175.
129. Prats, *Memorias,* pp. 410-411.
130. Two American diplomats who dealt with Prats found his apparent ''conversion'' to the cause of Popular Unity paradoxical and even unbelievable. Ambassador Korry has remarked to me that when he was leaving in 1971, Prats held a dinner in his honor, ''and invited some of the most awful, reactionary people imaginable—caricatures of the Chilean upper class. Were these the people, I wondered, with whom Prats feels most comfortable?'' (Remark in a private conversation, June, 1980). Ambassador Harry Shlaudeman, who was deputy chief of the mission in Santiago, recalls that Prats made much of his status as acting chief of state during Allende's trip to the United States and Moscow in late 1972; ''he even invited me to the ceremony where he received the presidential symbols of office; his father was there. For Prats it was an enormously important event—I couldn't see why, since it was just a temporary formality.'' (Private conversation, March, 1983). Undoubtedly Allende noticed these weaknesses and played upon them for all they were worth.
131. Prats, *Memorias,* p. 425.
132. Pinochet, *El día decisivo,* p. 112; Prats, *Memorias,* pp. 414-416.
133. Prats, *Memorias,* p. 400.
134. Davis, *The Last Two Years of Salvador Allende,* p. 190.
135. Pinochet, *El día decisivo,* pp. 114-115.
136. See Appendix interview with President Eduardo Frei (cited).
137. Joan Garcés, Allende's adviser, relates the president's intentions in his own book, but carefully omits the latter's prediction of the outcome. *Allende y la experiencia chilena* (Barcelona, 1976), pp. 365-369.
138. Prats, *Memorias,* pp. 509-510.

9

Pinochet's Chile, 1973-1989

On September 11, 1973, the Chilean armed forces seized power and overthrew the government of Popular Unity. President Allende died in an attack on the Moneda Palace; his widow was allowed to fly to exile in Mexico. But those of his cabinet ministers and closest associates who failed to find refuge in foreign embassies were imprisoned, some in concentration camps in the inhospitable Chilean Antarctic. The entire country was placed under a state of siege which lasted for years; individuals friendly to the Allende government or active in Popular Unity organizations were arrested, many tortured, hundreds murdered. The fate of some 1,500 is still unknown. As late as 1975 the number of political prisoners remained relatively constant at 5-6,000; it began to drop only the following year, when Decree-Law 504 released a number to go into immediate exile in Western Europe, the United States, or other Latin American countries.

Up to the day of the coup Chile enjoyed prestige unusual for a Latin American republic in the community of civilized nations. This was due to its historic adherence to the rule of law, *habeus corpus,* and other freedoms common to Western societies. This made its sudden reversion to barbarism all the more shocking; what was more, far from denying the use of torture, the authorities in Santiago "put arguments forward in justification."[1] In spite of gradual improvement, more than a decade later the U.S. Department of State was still reporting that "as in the past, there were reliable and documented reports of torture and mistreatment of those detained by Chilean security forces. . . . Members of the security and military forces are widely believed to be responsible for the kidnappings, beatings, torture, and in a few cases, murders for which no suspects have been identified or apprehended." Meanwhile, "the diplomatic community was routinely denied access to Chileans detained by the Government for violations of the various state security laws."[2]

By 1980 Chilean life had resumed a degree of normality which would have surprised those foreigners whose only knowledge of the country was the few weeks of intense international news coverage following the coup. Many exiles had returned, and many more would do so in subsequent years. Chilean political life resumed to the extent of visible opposition parties, including Socialists and Communists, and an independent press and radio (though not television). But the coup itself was the final act in a drama which destroyed, apparently forever, the texture of the country's institutional civility. After September 1973, too many crimes were committed in the name of—or at the secret behest of—the country's highest authorities to make it easy to return to the disinterested rule of law. The only choices open to Chileans were the most fundamental and therefore the most difficult: whether to continue to live under authoritarian institutions, or resume in some form the political life interrupted in 1973.

In the weeks preceding the coup, Santiago was awash with rumors that the armed forces would either create a government of "apolitical personalities," of force Allende and the Christian Democrats to compose their differences and create a government of national concentration. As General Prats' diaries make clear, while the Christian Democrats were agreeable to the former, the latter was never even considered by the military. Instead, a four-man junta composed of the chiefs of Chile's four armed services[3] assumed quasi-legislative power, turning the executive power over to the army commander General Augusto Pinochet Ugarte, Prats' protege and successor. In the months and years that followed, Pinochet emerged to personify the regime, which became in a sense an extension of his (arguably demented) messianic personality.

The Emergence of Pinochet

To the day of the coup there was nothing to distinguish Pinochet from thousands of other commissioned officers in the armed forces, or the dozens of cautious military bureaucrats who had climbed to the top of the service hierarchy. Born to a middle-class family in 1915, he entered the military academy while still an adolescent and was commissioned a second lieutenant in 1933. For the next forty years, his professional life followed a curve well-defined by an army which knew neither wars abroad nor *pronunciamientos* at home. The high points were a tour as military attaché in Ecuador; teaching in service schools where he cultivated an interest in military history and geopolitics; and a period as zone commander in Chile's arid north, source of its mineral wealth, and the epicenter of its militant trade union politics. The election of Allende found him in command of the garrison in Iquique.

In his autobiography published six years after the coup[4] Pinochet describes his years before the presidency as a time of political maturation and growing awareness. He claims to have studied the writings of Marx and Engels, which caused him to view the Chilean Communist party in a wholly new light: "it was not one party more, as I had thought . . . [but] a movement which, as Pope Pius XI so rightly said, is a purveyor of an 'intrinsically perverse' political and social doctrine."[5] He tells of being shocked by the decision of the government to re-legalize the party in the late 1950s, and even more by the supposed indulgence of the Frei government towards "violent political groups, who unfurled red and black banners right under the noses of the authorities."[6] Only later, he writes, did he realize that "there was considerable Marxist infiltration in the [Christian Democratic] government."[7] The election of Allende only confirmed his worst suspicions about the particular weaknesses of the Chilean democratic system, and he set to work to counter its effects almost immediately.

If Pinochet did in fact hold these views at the time, he did an excellent job of keeping them a secret for years. The highest civilian officials of the Frei and Allende administrations knew nothing of them; neither did key figures in the military establishment. Beyond all doubt, had either Generals Schneider or Prats suspected Pinochet's loyalty to the political system, he would have been retired sometime in the 1960s. Instead, in 1971 he was promoted to major general and assigned to the military district of Santiago, the most important (and politically salient) troop command in the country. A year later he was ascended to army chief of staff. When Prats was forced out in August 1973, he convinced Allende to promote Pinochet into his job, a choice which did not seem to trouble the beleaguered president. Indeed, by that time Allende thought he knew who the plotters in the armed forces were, and the new army commander was not among them. Prats himself only began to sense a change in Pinochet's attitude after his retirement: the new commander-in-chief no longer returned his calls.[8]

Whatever the route by which Pinochet reached his present eminence, his position as commander-in-chief of the Chilean army is the crucial factor underpinning his political power. It is an army vastly different from the one Chileans have known throughout their history—larger, better paid, better-equipped, fully integrated into the administrative framework of the state. The social prestige of the military is much higher than before 1973; places in the service academies are now oversubscribed by young men from the traditional upper class—a pool which in the past disdained the profession of arms. Likewise, military wives have gained entreé into social circles in Santiago and the provincial cities which were heretofore closed to them. Generals and admirals have served as intendants, ambassadors, ministers, and sit on the boards of banks and industries either inherited from the Allende regime or forcibly taken over by the government after a financial collapse in 1983. There are also more flag officers serving on active duty, and the norms of retirement have been changed in such a way as to allow Pinochet a discretion in the composition of his general officer corps known to no other president of Chile.

For the first few years after the coup Pinochet ruled more or less as a chief of state who owed his position to the accident of seniority in the most important branch of the armed services. But the gap between him and other officers began to open almost from the beginning. Of the generals who planned the coup (according to his account in *El día decisivo*), three (Torres, Viveros, Nuño) were in retirement less than a year after the event; Bonilla died in an airplane accident in 1975; Arellano retired in 1976, and Palacios in 1977.[9] By 1989, if Pinochet succeeds in remaining as chief of state, the highest ranking military man under him will have been commissioned in 1953—separated from him by seventeen graduating classes, and from the youngest generals by twenty-five years of service.[10]

Pinochet's relationship to the other service chiefs has also changed. In 1978, when the air force member of the junta, General Gustavo Leigh, quarreled with Pinochet over the pace of political devolution, he was replaced by the (presumably more tractable) General Fernando Matthei. Of the original junta members, only Admiral José Toribio Merino, the navy representative, remains at the helm. Many look to Merino as a counterweight to Pinochet, and in fact he has periodically made statements which could be taken as vetos to proposals by the president-generalissimo. But as the army has grown in size and importance, and as Pinochet has tightened his grip upon it, the need for consensus within the service chiefs has declined, a crucial point to which we shall return.

The Transformation of Political Institutions

Three years after the coup, the junta appointed a council of state to redesign Chile's future political institutions. Though its most distinguished member was former President Jorge Alessandri, its leading spirit—and certainly the author of the draft Constitution it produced—was Jaime Guzmán, a right-wing intellectual who first gained fame by confronting Popular Unity spokesmen on a weekly television program[11] during the Allende years. Though some members of the council—traditional conservatives or retired Supreme Court justices—favored an early return to civilian rule, Guzmán and Pinochet working together excised from their draft the provision which would have ended military rule sometime in 1985. Characteristically, Alessandri resigned from the Council, apparently in protest, though he refused to explain to the press the reasons for his decision.

As put to the vote of a plebiscite in September 1980, the charter granted

Pinochet (named personally in the document) an eight-year term to end no later than March 1989. Sometime before then a new plebiscite would be held to determine whether to install for yet another eight years an (unnamed) candidate "proposed to the Chilean people by the junta"; that person would be eligible in 1997 for yet another eight year term, bringing the life of the regime up to 2005.

Between 1980 and 1989 Chile would be ruled by certain "transitory articles" which gave the government extraordinary discretion in legislative, judicial, and other matters. In 1990, a Congress would be elected for the first time since March 1973; this body would be almost powerless, at least compared to its predecessors. For example, the Senate will be only partially elected by popular vote, and cleverly crafted provisions give the executive the opportunity to "pack" it, and therefore to veto all of its decisions from within. More to the point, almost no important subject is left to parliamentary initiative. It deprives the Chamber of Deputies—the only fully representative body—of such historic privileges as the power to review quasi-legislative executive acts. The charter virtually abolishes the need to obtain parliamentary approval for decrees that restrict constitutional guarantees. Finally, a new Constitutional Court, named by the military, will be empowered to expel a deputy or senator for drafting or even voting for a motion or bill subsequently found to be "unconstitutional." In spite of all of these precautions, the Constitution takes the trouble to statutorily prohibit the Left from participating in the new legislative assembly.[12]

The Chilean road to socialism thus had led to a curious and unexpected destination—a dictatorship which combines the authoritarian personalism so often found in the histories of Spain and Spanish America, with a perverted version of constitutionalism, the far-right equivalent of Joan Garcés' "legal loopholes." From a sociological point of view, the Pinochet government is a step backward in time, an alliance of the armed forces with the traditional upper classes who had largely withdrawn from direct participation in government after the victory of the Popular Front in 1938. Figuratively, and in some cases literally, the men who have served in Pinochet's cabinets and embassies abroad since 1973 have been the grandsons and greatgrandsons of the men who served as ministers and diplomats for President Arturo Alessandri (1932-1938) and his predecessors. At the same time, however, the regime has made possible the emergence of a class of "new men"—entrepreneurs and financial technicians whose careers would probably have been impossible in the restrictive, regulation-laden Chile of Allende, Frei, or even Jorge Alessandri or Carlos Ibáñez del Campo. Many small businessmen, shopkeepers, and farmers have likewise profited (or believe they have done so) from the continuity, order, and a lack of serious labor unrest.

The Chilean "Economic Miracle"

The coup put an end not merely to Chilean politics as traditionally practiced, but to the statist economic policies which had characterized every
government since the Great Depression. Under the direction of a group of
technocrats, some trained at the University of Chicago, Chile became a showcase for neoclassical economics, sometimes over the protests and disclaimers
of liberal economists in the United States and Western Europe, who bore no
particular brief for Pinochet or his methods. Nonetheless, a combination of
free market incentives, careful management, and a neutering of the labor
movement created a mood of business confidence unknown there since before
the First World War. By 1986 the rate of inflation had been pushed down to
19.5 percent;[13] Chile's creditworthiness was without parallel in Latin America, and indeed within the developing world; new export lines, particularly
seasonal fruits, experienced a phenomenal growth. The diversification which
had been the goal of every government since the 1940s seemed nearly at hand.

Certainly in two areas where the Allende regime was notably deficient—
savings and investment—its successor has managed to restore Chile to the
levels of the Frei years, and in some cases, even beyond them. (Table 9.1)
This was an accomplishment all the more impressive, given the lack of
foreign aid and concessionary credits, such as the Christian Democrats had
received in the 1960s, and in the face of a four-fold increase in the price of
oil since 1973, and, after 1981, a catastrophic drop in the price of copper.

TABLE 9.1
Gross National Saving and Gross National Investment,
Selected Years Since 1965
(expressed as a percentage of Gross Domestic Product)

Year(s)	Percentage
Gross National Savings	
1965–1970	14.6 (annual average)
1971–1973	10.8 (annual average)
1983	12.5
1984	12.6
1985	16.5
1986	18.4
Gross National Investment	
1965–1970	16.0 (annual average)
1971–1973	13.6
1980–1983	16.2
1984–1986	14.2
1987	15.2
1988	15.9 (projection)

Sources: World Bank, *Chile: An Economy in Transition* (Washington, D.C., 1979) and *Chile:*
Adjustment and Recovery (Washington, D.C., 1987).

In a very general way, the economic policies of the Pinochet regime could be characterized as the reversal of almost all of the trends evident in Chile since the 1930s. The relative size of the public sector has been reduced; deficits have been sharply eliminated or greatly diminished; the social security program has been privatized, as have been a number of government-owned enterprises, including the National Telephone Company (ENTEL), the Pacific Steel Company (CAP), the Chilean Electrical Company (CHILECTRA). The state copper enterprise, CODELCO, has remained in government hands, but foreign exploration firms and providers of up-to-date technology have been brought in to assist it on a contract basis.[14] Steps have been taken to privatize the social security system, once dispersed into dozens of individual pension funds, each administered by a state agency. In agriculture, the government has utilized legislation inherited from the Christian Democrats to grant fee simple title to peasants, releasing large numbers of *asentados* from the limbo into which the ideological squabbles of urban politicians and intellectuals had consigned them. This, combined with a lifting of price controls on foodstuffs in the urban marketplace, has created a modest boom in food production.

By the end of the 1980s, the government's economic performance is presumably its one strong suit, to be pressed at every opportunity when outsiders seem overly concerned with its human rights record. However, during Pinochet's fifteen years of power the indicators have risen and dropped more than once. During the late 1970s, when copper prices reached record highs, and private banks were awash in liquidity recycled from oil producing countries, Chile experienced a heady economic boom, climaxing in 1980. The following year, copper prices began to fall, and the peso—which had been rigidly pegged at 39 to the dollar—was suddenly devalued, leaving many Chileans with dollar-denominated debts they could not service.[15] In 1982 and 1983 several of Chile's private banks collapsed and were taken over by the government. Unemployment reached record levels, and family incomes dropped by almost a third.

The country experienced a modest recovery between 1984 and 1986, during which the gross domestic product averaged 4.6 per year, and employment generation at double that rate. Even so, throughout the entire Pinochet period joblessness has far exceeded the previous two governments, mitigated slightly by public service programs and some other strongly redistributive transfers: basic education and family subsidies. By way of comparison, during Frei's last year, 1970—one of recession—the unemployment rate was 5.9 percent; at the time of Allende's overthrow, (1973), 4.8. At the height of the 1980 boom, it was 11.7; in 1985, 16.0, and in 1987, considered a year of recovery, 12.6.[16]

A study by the Department of Economics, University of Chile found that in 1987 household shares of income were comparable to that of the late 1960s.

TABLE 9.2
Some Indicators of Income Distribution
(Selected Years)

Year	GNP Per Capita (US$ 1977)	Gini Coefficient (%)	Social Expenditure Per Capita (US$ 1978)
1968	29,616	50	*
1970	30,313	50	9,451
1973	29,182	45	*
1980	32,730	53	8,222
1984	29,291	55	8,684

Source: Aristides Torche Lazo, "Distribuir el ingreso para satisfacer las necesidades basicas," in Felipe Larraín. *Desarollo economico en democracia* (Santiago, 1987), p. 186.

There is, of course, no consensus in major industrial democracies like Great Britain or the United States on the degree to which the government should attempt to close the gap between income groups, but if one accepted the fundamental premise that it should—which most Chileans did—then the country was either moving backwards or at any rate, had slipped twenty years behind. There were some methodological problems with the study,[17] but other data confirmed its broader contours. (Table 9.2)

These figures measure not merely a regressive transfer of income, but of economic and social power. Unemployment and a new labor law introduced in 1980 (which forbade industry-wide strikes), effectively neutralized the trade union movement, once so crucial to Chilean politics. In the countryside many peasants granted definitive ownership of their plots were forced to sell them for lack of credit, technical assistance, or simple entrepreneurial skills— the final destiny of almost every land reform since the French Revolution. The white collar bureaucracy, once entrenched in the ministries, in the school system, and in various agencies and inspectorates, was disarmed politically by the fear of privatization, dismissal, or the persecution of excessively vocal leaders.

Perhaps in time the macroeconomic indicators will "trickle-down," neutralize, and even reverse the inegalitarian tendencies of the economic model, but this presupposes a straight-line extrapolation of political conditions into the indefinitive future—an eventuality nobody is willing to predict. In the meanwhile, by making free market economics so conspicuous by a part of its ideological baggage, the military government all but assured that a dispassionate discussion of economic options would never be possible, at least as long as democratic choice and democratic responsibility were banished from public life.

However one might feel about the tenor and direction of economic policy under Pinochet, it remains a fact that such progress as the country has made since 1973 has depended upon heavy foreign borrowing. This explains in

TABLE 9.3
Ideological Preferences of Chileans, 1986

Tendency	Percentage
Left	13
Center-Left	21
Center	33
Center-Right	18
Right	15
No response	9

Source: Encuesta sobre la realidad chilena . . ., cited in note 19.

large part why the current account balance, which was U.S. $(-) 134 million in 1970, had reached U.S. $(-) 1,091 million by 1986. Put another way, 1970, the year Allende took office, the country's long-term foreign debt was slightly more than two billion dollars; by 1985, it had increased six-fold. In 1970 debt service accounted for two percent of gross national product, and 19.1 percent of the export of goods and services; in 1985, the numbers were 8.7 and 26.2 percent, respectively. This was somewhat mitigated by an ingenious system of debt-equity swaps; nonetheless, the World Bank reported that "even during 1985-86, Chile paid about a tenth of its GDP (and half its domestic savings) in foreign interest payments abroad, leaving little room for expansionary programs or marginal investments." And, it continued, "in spite of good policies. . . . continued fiscal prudence, growing investment, and a stable (if not improving) international environments are necessary to enable Chile to grow despite its heavy debt burden."[18]

Perhaps the most important economic fact about Chile today is that, whatever the regime may have accomplished, it has clearly failed to reorient the public's basic economic values. These remain, in fact, remarkably unchanged since 1970. For example, in a poll conducted in 1986 by one of the major research institutions in Santiago, 66 percent of those queried placed primary responsibility for giving employment on "the government"; only 19 percent, "private enterprise." By even greater majorities (79 and 82 percent, respectively), they affirmed the responsibility of the government to fix prices of articles of prime necessity, and to provide health services.[19] This was fully coherent with the country's general ideological profile. (Table 9.3)

These numbers acquire enhanced significance when compared to the historic performance of the Chilean electorate over the past twenty-five years. By aggregating Center and Center-Right, one arrives at 54 percent, less than a point short of the figure reached by the anti-Allende coalition (CODE) in the congressional elections of March 1973. Or, by joining together Left and Center-Left, one very nearly replicates the percentage received by President

Allende in the elections of September 1970. By combining two-thirds of the self-described "Center" vote with "Center-Right" and "Right," one closely approaches the share of the Chilean electorate which supported Eduardo Frei against Salvador Allende in 1964.

It would seem then, that in spite of nearly a decade and a half of military rule, during most of which politics in the ordinary sense of the word was forbidden, Chileans have remained remarkably consistent in their basic views and commitments. In the past, the failure to channel these views into broad, coherent, and durable coalitions rendered politics somewhat unstable and unpredictable; each election was seen as a referendum on the system as a whole. Now, however, the possibility of overcoming these problems was loaded onto a plebiscitary mechanism, in which Pinochet himself was proposed for yet another eight, or even sixteen years.

The Survival of Traditional Political Forces

If broader political orientations seem frozen in time, so, too, does political history itself. The Allende years—or rather, what people made of them—continue to dominate political discourse, particularly on the Right and the Left. The government's rationale for Pinochet's perpetuation in power is the need to prevent a wholesale reversion to 1970 or 1973, as if the Chilean people were bound to lurch towards Marxism unless permanently harnessed to an authoritarian system. Ironically, this view is very nearly identical to the one advanced (on very different premises) by the Communists and the far Left. The Chilean Democrats are caught in the middle—firmly opposed to the military government, but somewhat lacking in moral leverage as a result of their role in the events leading up to the coup.

To be sure, the Christian Democrats operated in the Allende period under a wholly different set of expectations, and also in a radically different political environment.[20] This did not prevent the Left, particularly the radical Left, from pointing the finger at the party, though by the late 1980 it is Pinochet, not the Socialists, who most often remind the Christian Democrats of their role during the Allende period. As he remarked tauntingly on April 12, 1988, "these sectors owe their very existence to the armed forces and the forces of order—or have they already forgotten that they once knocked on the doors of the barracks, clamoring for shelter, protection, and justice?"[21]

The same arguments, the same issues—in many cases, the same actors. Allende died in the coup, probably by his own hand; the MIR's Miguel Eníquez shortly thereafter, in a shootout with the police. Frei and Alessandri succumbed to natural causes in 1982 and 1986, respectively. General Prats (and his wife) were brutally murdered in a car bomb in Buenos Aires in 1974, presumably by agents of the DINA, Chile's new secret police.[22] But all of the major personalities of the Alessandri, Frei and Allende periods were still on hand in 1988, including Sergio Onofre Jarpa, who had once led the National party; Patricio Alwyn (once again, president of the Christian Democrats), and his coreligionists Radomiro Tomic, Renán Fuentealba, Juan Hamilton, and Gabriel Valdés. On the Left there was Clodomiro Almeyda; Carlos Altamirano (in Paris); and Luis Corvalán (in Moscow). Even General Viaux was still dabbling in politics, reported in February to be favorably entertaining a proposal to "normalize the country" by leading "the political transition that will follow the 1988 referendum."[23]

The lack of real political life tends to inhibit the development of newer and younger cadres, and seems to confirm Pinochet's frequent assertion that party leaders are nothing but superannuated hacks with no new ideas to offer the country. In the same poll cited above, politicians enjoyed remarkably little credibility with the general public—only 3 percent. But with the exception of the Roman Catholic church, which had the confidence of 60 percent of Chileans, no other institution did much better, whether the armed forces (10 percent); professional associations (10 percent); businessmen (5 percent); or trade unions (5 percent).[24] On the other hand, the elaborate institutional paraphernalia of the 1980 Constitution had not created a new polity, as many within the government once hoped they might. Instead, Chile was divided as firmly in 1988 as it was in 1973; the only difference was that this time the government enjoyed the support of the armed forces and the Right, but confronted a far larger coalition of the Center and Left.

Pinochet and the World

The brutal fashion in which the military assumed power in Chile drastically reshaped the country's relationship to the outside world. This was particularly true in Western Europe, a region to which generations of Chileans from all walks of life always professed a special affinity. There, the very name of Chile became a synonymn for the resurgence of the fascist threat supposedly extinguished once and for all in the Second World War. Though the political realities were different, the visuals were extremely evocative—piles of books consigned to flames, generals in Prussian uniforms reviewing goose-stepping troops,[25] civilians scuttling for cover in massive police and army sweeps of public squares. And then, as supporters of the fallen government began to emerge from prison and into exile, there were the stories of torture and murder, accounts too rich in grisly detail, too possible to corroborate in their essentials, to be discounted. The fact that the new regime was the indirect beneficiary of U.S. aid to Allende's opponents—in the narrow technical sense that it could not have come into existence had Popular Unity prevailed—added a whole new dimension to the controversy, and piled Chile onto the already troubled agenda of European-American relations.

In the United States, the fullest impact of the coup was delayed until after the resignation of President Nixon in 1974, and the report of the Church committee in 1975. Few Americans bothered to read the latter; what they knew or subsequently remembered were the newspaper headlines, which in the best of cases crudely summarized a complex situation in which the choices were neither simple nor easy. Needless to say, neither Senator Church nor the partisans of the Allende regime had any particular interest in delineating these crucial distinctions, so for most Americans, including those normally quite well-informed, they were lost altogether.[26]

The investigation of the Church committee also coincided with the withdrawal of the United States from Vietnam. Both events led to a generalized distrust of government, as well as a distaste for intelligence activities abroad, covert action, even the anti-Communism which served as the organizing principle of American foreign policy since World War II. The stage was set for a "revisionist" moment in American culture, an exercise in national self-repudiation and self-hatred whose emblematic personalities were Noam Chomsky, Daniel Ellsberg, the brothers Berrigan, Ramsey Clark, Bishop Paul Moore, among thousands of lesser imitators in pulpit and press, classroom and legislative chamber. In this setting, a small South American country, eleven hours' flying time from New York, became a treasured exhibit in the chamber of horrors of American foreign policy, based on an undifferentiated recital of activities from CIA assistance to the Christian Democrats in the 1960s to the latest atrocity committed by Pinochet's police.

During the 1960s, the United States sought to strengthen democracy in Latin America by championing social and economic reforms; in some countries, local allies were either powerless or nonexistent. In Chile things were different: the Christian Democratic party was, in a sense, made to order for Washington's agenda. Policies, however, often have an outcome far from the one intended. In the case of Chile, rather than strengthening the Center, the United States' support for Frei tended to polarize political forces, revitalizing the Right and throwing the 1970 election to the Left. At that point the choices became more difficult, but, as Ambassador Davis subsequently wrote, they were "not between CIA intervention and a hands-off policy that would leave the Chilean political process to function undisturbed." Rather, "it was between covert action and abstention in a skewed political struggle."[27]

In effect, U.S. policy towards Allende's Chile was intended to prevent another Czechoslovakia. Had the circumstances permitted the survival of democratic institutions up through the 1976 elections, that policy would require no subsequent justification. Unfortunately, the United States could not control all of the variables on the ground; consequently, it has to accept partial responsibility for an outcome which was acceptable only in negative terms. The price for a non-Communist (or at least non-Marxist) Chile turned out to be extraordinarily high, and apparently to require periodic replenishment. For one thing, Pinochet and his associates never cease to emphasize the supposed political affinity between their purposes and those of the United States and the "West" (rather curiously defined in a way which excluded countries like France, Italy, or Holland, but included Taiwan, South Africa, and South Korea). For another, Chilean exiles in Western Europe took it upon themselves to detail their own version of the U.S. role, often in blatant disregard of the facts. A particularly egregious example was Isabel Vargas, Chilean wife of the vice-president of the Norwegian parliament, who had fled her country in 1973. Fourteen years after the event she told Oslo's most prestigious daily that "the [Chilean] generals would turn their backs on [Pinochet] if the United States would stop giving him weapons and loans."[28] At the time an arms embargo established by the U.S. Congress was in its eleventh year, and aid to the Chilean government was virtually confined to surplus foods and other humanitarian resources, facts which the Norwegian newspaper reader was unlikely to have at hand.

The persistence of a military dictatorship also undermines the posture of the United States in its quest for hemispheric security—specifically, its efforts to prevent the replication of Castroite regimes in Central America. Thus in the congressional debates over aid to the Nicaraguan resistance in 1985 and 1986, more than one opponent cited Chile as proof that the most logical—if indeed not the inevitable—result of assistance to the opposition in any Latin American country under Marxist rule was a tyranny far worse. Quasi-public assistance to the beleaguered newspaper *La Prensa* in Managua was even likened to CIA support of *El Mercurio* during the Allende period! And this in spite of the fact that, unlike Allende's government, the Sandinistas in Nicaragua displayed not the slightest ambivalence with regard to their goals, their purposes, or their international alliances. Indeed, some Americans, including some members of Congress, appeared to have decided that by preventing the creation (or consolidation) of a Marxist regime in Chile, their country had apparently incurred the obligation to make sure that more rigorous efforts elsewhere did not fail in the future.

The Unexpected Harvest of the Left

In Chile itself, the coup and the events which followed it turned the tables on the political forces as they had existed in 1973. By the end of the Allende regime, a majority of Chileans had repudiated the Socialist and Communist parties—as well as their allies—for their conduct inside the Popular Unity government. As the years passed, however, their discredit was neutralized, then cancelled out, by martyrdom. In addition, the undifferentiated contempt with which the military treated all political forces except those on the far right threw people together who, in August and September 1973, were facing off for civil war. The Allende regime also benefited retrospectively from its evident association with the old democratic order; how much longer it could have remained part of that order, which it was busily undermining, must remain a matter of controversy. But to the day of its overthrow, it enjoyed a degree of legitimacy which has persistently eluded its successor. In a certain sense, then, General Pinochet and his associates have rescued for Allende and his government a place in Chilean history which they did not earn and to which they could not otherwise have looked forward.

As for Popular Unity's allies abroad, things turned out better for them than might have been anticipated. The Soviet Union was proven right in its assessment of the Chilean situation; it was also relieved of the burden of underwriting another profligate socialist regime in the Western hemisphere. Moreover, in the murky frontier where Marxism, democratic socialism, and liberal sentimentality met and commingled, Allende dead proved far more valuable to the Soviets than Allende alive. His failures could be blamed upon his opponents; his widow periodically exhibited at "peace" conferences; his truncated experiment moved to the mythological pantheon of international Communism—much like the Shanghai Commune of 1972 or the Second Spanish Republic (1936–1939). As for the Cubans and the nearly 14,000 Latin American "refugees" who poured into Chile during the Popular Unity period, and who generally identified with the far Left, the failure of the Chilean road only strengthened their commitment to revolutionary violence, but paradoxically, also provided them with an apparent moral justification for it.[29]

Frei and Allende Compared

For two of its three years, the Allende regime profoundly divided Chileans; but the issues around which they parted company were not new. Almost every policy issue on the docket during those months—land reform, the size of the public sector, income policy, the role of foreign investment, particularly in non-replaceable raw materials, tax policy—had been at the center of public debate since at least the late 1930s. What was new was the intensity and the finality with which the questions were posed, as well as the costs exacted by applying them with excessive zeal. The Chilean Right has long emphasized the continuities between the Frei and Allende periods. And though it does not do so disinterestedly, for all that it is not wide of the mark. Both the Christian Democrats and Popular Unity were populist (multi-class) alliances which had won power with the argument that the principal obstacle to Chile's development was the unequal distribution of wealth. Both envisaged a predominant role for the state in the promotion of economic growth. Both inherited an economy in recession; both sought reactivation through wage increases and the taking-up of idle capacity in industry. Both experienced early, temporary successes—a surge forward in the growth rate and a drop in the rates of inflation and unemployment—subsequently rewarded by victories at the ballot box. For each government the booms were followed by crises of investment and foreign exchange, the falling away of political support, a revival in the fortunes of the opposition. Both temporized over equally distasteful alternatives to retrenchment, and both sought to transfer sectoral conflicts through nationalizations and heavy foreign borrowing.

There were, of course, some crucial differences. The Frei years coincided with generally high copper prices, though largely toward the end of the administration, when some of the benefit could be passed on to Allende. The Christian Democrats also envisaged a different role for foreign investment. By entering into agreements to produce copper jointly with American companies ("Chileanization"), Frei laid the groundwork for an expansion of the country's principal source of foreign exchange. (Here, too, many of the actual benefits were bequeathed to his successor.) By refusing to nationalize copper outright or to expropriate foreign property, Frei encouraged a modest growth in fixed capital investment, and preserved Chile's credit standing; private banks, foreign governments, and multilateral lending agencies were very generous to Chile during the Christian Democratic years. Some of this was the consequence of diplomatic and political alignments, but alone neither could have elicited so much concrete economic support.

However burdensome the subsequent service on Frei's debt, it was largely long-term and predicated on an increase in Chile's industrial plant, rather than conceived as a direct subsidy to immediate consumption. When faced with the need for stabilization and retrenchment in 1968 and 1969, the Christian Democrats accepted a schism within their party (the creation of MAPU) rather than to pursue a policy of social polarization. Conceivably, this cost the party the 1970 presidential election, but also served the larger purpose of preserving the country's basic and social political fabric, as well as the democratic order and the rule of law.

The point is not that the differences made Frei a success; rather, they prevented him from being an egregious failure. Allende not only discarded the notion that capital formation was the principal motor of economic growth, he did all he could to assure that, should he ever change his mind, there would be no bridges left to recross. When the negative results of his policies made themselves manifest, the president was left with no choice but to print more paper money and borrow wherever he could, on whatever terms he could. No doubt Allende also hoped, ultimately, for a bailout from abroad. This surely could not have come from the United States, which had invested so much in the Frei administration, but it was not forthcoming from the Soviets and their allies either. It was not a matter of resources or ideology but of basic ethos: perhaps without realizing it, Allende's "socialist consumerism" cruelly mocked the austerity and rationing central to Marxist socialism wherever seriously practiced.

The real difference between the Frei and Allende years, however, is one that can never be resumed in statistics, since it was cultural, moral, even spiritual in nature. While the Christian Democrats came to power in 1964 convinced that they were destined to rule Chile for a generation or more, Allende proposed a still more ambitious project—to introduce once and for all a whole new order of things. By apparently confounding economic orthodoxy in 1971, the new government temporarily created a mood of abundance and freedom Chileans had never known. People seized the opportunity to do "crazy" things they would never otherwise have done—buy a house or a car, get a divorce, even emigrate. By 1972, however, the choices had narrowed. The sudden shortage of the most basic articles of consumption announced in the most direct and brutal way that if there were to be winners in the new Chile, there would have to be losers as well. Indeed, the people were told as much more than once, if not by Allende himself, then by people who occupied a position of even greater authority within his own party.

At that point, the public mood shifted from euphoria to impending doom and visions of imminent apocalypse. That is what led thousands of Chileans— most of no great social distinction, lacking special skills, foreign languages, contacts abroad—to take to the streets in defense of their interests. "Class consciousness," after all, is no monopoly of the proletariat, and in a given political and economic context, its "bourgeois" or "petty-bourgeois" expression can be a powerful revolutionary force of its own. The fact that the Chilean opposition unwittingly paved the way for a quasi-fascist regime no more invalidates its basic grievances than those of the Russian soldiers in 1917 who—wanting only peace and bread—nonetheless helped to destroy the only democratic government in their nation's history.

1989: Chile at the Crossroads

Pinochet's Chile has been driven by a curious vision, which looks both forward to a post-political epoch, and backward to the period prior to 1938. On one hand, it has sought to create new institutions; on the other, it has taken refuge in the oldest practices of Hispanic political life. For much of the time the opposition, too, has looked backward as well as forward—to the years 1938–73, or rather, selected periods associated with Conservative-Liberal,

Christian Democratic, or Socialist ascendancy. Indeed, one of Pinochet's enduring strengths has been the inability of the opposition as a whole to define which is the particular moment in Chile's democratic past at which the nation should resume its subsequent course.

Ironically, Pinochet's Constitution, whose purpose was to perpetuate him in power and to enthrone his system for all time, has played a role very different from that envisioned by its authors. In its original draft, this charter gave the general sixteen years of uninterrupted power. But persuaded by his advisers that so long a mandate stood little chance of winning approval at the ballot box (the document was submitted to a plebiscite in September, 1980), the dictator agreed to submit to a new test at the polls sometime before March, 1989. At the time, eight years seemed like an eternity, the opposition was hopelessly divided, and the country in the midst of an economic boom which— had it continued uninterruptedly—would presumably have assured a victorious outcome for the government.

Until the very last year, the regime's gamble seemed likely to pay off. Repeated polls showed that while a civilian "consensus" candidate proposed by the junta was more likely to win than Pinochet, the "yes" and "no" votes seemed to run very nearly in tandem, with as much as a third of the electorate declaring itself "undecided." Once Pinochet was unambiguously proposed as the candidate on August 30, 1988, however, the "undecideds" began to move in the direction of the "no" vote. By then Chileans were little more than a month away from the hour of decision. As in the case of Alessandri in 1970, the weakness of the candidate fielded by the Right was discovered too late in the day to do much about it.

The prospect of another eight years of Pinochet—perhaps another sixteen, if the Constitution permitted, as some thought it did, his candidacy in a new plebiscite in 1997—was sufficient to unite the most disparate elements of the opposition. Moreover, the very act of declaring a plebiscite gave out-of-work politicians, ambitious newcomers, and restless young people something to do; energies could be focussed on a concrete task with discrete boundaries and a far-reaching outcome. This, combined with an imaginative advertising campaign, and a deliberate attempt to project a moderate or even conservative image, proved a formidable challenge to the government, whose appeal to the people was based exclusively on the fear of a return to the Allende period. On October 5, somewhere between fifty-four and fifty-six percent of Chileans— government and opposition figures varied slightly—voted "no" to Pinochet's aspirations. The decision was all the more shocking to the government for being unexpected; indeed, until the very night of the plebiscite Pinochet had believed in the assurances (and the favorable, and now it appears, fraudulent polls) tendered him by his courtiers. When October 6 dawned, the regime had no choice but to declare itself defeated, or break with its own institutionality.

By choosing the former, rather than the latter, the government opened the road to a return to democratic life, at least to the extent of activating the mechanisms which called for a competitive presidential election (as well as elections for both houses of a new Congress) in December, 1989. But that same institutionality gave extraordinary residual powers to the armed forces, and allowed Pinochet himself to remain on as commander-in-chief of the army for an additional eight years. (Whether from a temperamental, personal, or political point of view this was really possible, remained to be seen.) It was also an open question how the opposition and the armed forces—if not Pinochet himself—would sort out their separate agendas, and arrive at some sort of understanding. The entire democratic world awaits the result with deep concern.

Chile is, after all, not just another country. For much of the twentieth century it was one of the few nations in the Third World where positivist presumption seemed to have some continuing validity. The definitive extinction of democracy there, a victim of the very same forces which divide Western societies under more favorable circumstances, would be a serious blow to the political faith which inspires and sustains free societies. One can only hope that the issues raised by its contemporary history—equality and growth, legality and legitimacy, the costs and values of democratic order—can somehow be resolved, lest the fate of Chile become a parable of continuing and disturbing relevance.

Notes

1. *The Amnesty International Report 1 June 1975–31 May 1976* (London, 1976), pp. 92–96.
2. *Country Reports on Human Rights Practices for 1987* (100th Congress, 2d, Session), (Joint Committee Print), February, 1987, pp. 407–408.
3. Army, navy, air force, and national police (carabineros).
4. Pinochet, *El día decisivo: 11 de septiembre 1973* (Santiago, 1980).
5. Ibid., p. 29.
6. Ibid., p. 41.
7. Ibid., p. 43.
8. Moy de Tohá, "La amiga de los militares," in Patricia Politzer, *Miedo en Chile* (Santiago,1985), pp. 340–341.
9. Arellano has since repented of his role in the coup, and through his son, a journalist and lawyer, published a remarkable confession, Sergio Arellano Iturriaga, *Más allá del abismo: un testimonio y una perspectiva* (Santiago, 1985). Characteristically, he blames the United States for "trying . . . to force South American military men into becoming political actors and considering as valid and legitimate the seizure of power for purposes of national security, a preachment that North American society would never practice itself." Ibid., p. 71.
10. Genaro Arriagada H., *La política militar de Pinochet, 1973–1985* (Santiago, 1985), pp. 100, 136–206 *passim*.
11. *A esta hora se improvisa*—a program which featured representatives of different

political tendencies. It survives today in a radio version, broadcast each Sunday evening on the network of the Roman Catholic Archdiocese of Santiago.

12. Article 8 declares unconstitutional persons or groups who propogate doctrines which promote violence, or a totalitarian conception of society, or one based on class struggle.

13. All figures cited here unless otherwise indicated are from the International Bank for Reconstruction and Development, *Chile: Adjustment and Recovery* (Washington, D.C., 1987).

14. The Chilean experience seems to have played an important role in convincing many of the large industrial metals enterprises in the United States, Western Europe, and Japan, that service contracts with nationalized firms were a much safer investment, and perhaps more profitable too. Predictably, Popular Unity figures (and also Christian Democrats of the stripe of Radomiro Tomic) protested this policy, too.

15. After Allende's fall, the peso was introduced to replace the escudo, which had lost all value in the hyperinflationary spiral.

16. Fernando Colomo Correa, "Crear Empleo: Uno Tarea Urgente," in Felipe Larrain, ed., *Desarollo económico en democracia* (Santiago, 1987), p. 249.

17. Cited in *Chile, Adjustment and Recovery*, p. 22. The bank noted, however, that "given the notorious uncertainty surrounding most income distribution surveys (the poorest and richest often understate their income) and the limited comparability between the various studies done on income distribution, any conclusion must be cautious."

18. *Chile: Adjustment and Recovery*, Synopsis (n.p.).

19. FLACSO-Chile, *Encuesta sobre la realidad chilena: resultados preliminares* (Santiago, 1986).

20. As Arturo Valenzuela points out, in the predominantly Christian Democrat "centrist" historiography of the Allende period, "there is little . . . self-criticism . . . There is no analysis of the dialectical interplay between political forces, or the unanticipated consequences of political actions and and events." "Visions of Chile," *Latin American Research Review*, X, 3 (1975), p. 165. It is at least arguable, however, that the Christian Democrats have made their own self-criticism more implicitly, in their opposition to the Pinochet regime. To go further would be to regret a course of action which, whatever else it failed to do, prevented Popular Unity from consolidating a totalitarian Marxist state.

21. *Foreign Broadcast Information Service–Latin America*, April 14, 1988.

22. The same agents evidently murdered Orlando Letelier, Allende's former ambassador to the United States, in September 1976. The method was the same—a bomb attached to the engine of his car; the incident occurred a block from the Chilean Embassy residence at Sheridan Circle in Washington.

23. *FBIS–LAT*, February 8, 1988.

24. FLACSO—Chile, *Encuesta sobre la realidad socio-economica chilena . . .*, p. 3.

25. Europeans were probably unaware of the fact that the practice had been introduced by Prussian drill instructors sent to Chile in the 1890s; it survived under all governments thereafter, including Frei's and Allende's.

26. Interestingly, Senator Church soon forgot the findings of his own committee (see Chapter Seven), and endorsed some of the more lurid conspiracy theories. When asked by the press to comment on Costa-Gavras' *Missing*, which portrayed the

American mission in Santiago as having "all but engineered a military coup that claimed thousands of lives through torture and execution," he could only remark, "I think it hits pretty close to home, and it happens other places, too." *Washington Post*, February 8, 1982.

27. Davis, *The Last Two Years of Salvador Allende* (Ithaca, N.Y., 1985), p. 342.
28. *Aftenposten*, October 31, 1987.
29. Two personalities who later became cabinet ministers in the Sandinista regime in Nicaragua—Jaime Wheelock and Miguel d'Escoto Brockmann—spent time in Allende's Chile and were strongly influenced by their experience there. Unquestionably, they also derived from the subsequent backlash in the United States an appreciation of the potential of the U.S. Congress and press to undermine U.S. purposes overseas, a lesson which they would put to good use a decade later.

Appendix

Interview with Former President Eduardo Frei Santiago, Chile, March 28, 1980

FALCOFF: I wonder if we might begin with your commenting to me on what might be called the *political* personality of Salvador Allende.

FREI: That's a question I've asked myself over and over during the last ten years or so. What *happened* to Salvador? What *happened* to him? You know, we were very good friends; our wives and families were friends. But something happened to drive us apart (*distanciarnos*).

I think it was the [Chilean presidential] election of 1964. He was sure he was going to win, and his loss was a great shock to him. You may recall the famous phrase he used when he addressed his followers on the night of his defeat— "We will deny them [the Christian Democrats] salt and water!" After that our relationship changed. During my presidency he never once came to the Moneda [Palace], even though on many occasions it corresponded to him in his capacity as President of the Senate, such as the state visits of the President of Italy and the Queen of England. There could be no mistaking his intentions, since he had no problem attending a dinner for the Queen of England at the British Embassy. After the election of 1970, when the actual outcome was still in doubt, he finally came to see me, and all of a sudden it was the old, warmhearted, gregarious Allende, full of jokes and good company. The object of the visit, however, was not long in revealing itself. He said, "With your support, I can be President tomorrow."

To which I replied, "No, Salvador, we will have to await the verdict of Congress. If Congress gives you its approval, you can be sure that I will hand over the sash, seals, and symbols of office to you—but not by any private deal between us. The Congress must vote, and I shall accept the decision of the Congress."

Now, Allende was a man of great *natural* intelligence, great capacity at speaking and improvising—but he had very little systematic education (*muy poca formación*). I can remember once in the days when we were still close, overhearing his wife say to him, "For God's sake, Salvador—why don't you read a *book* sometime!" He never read *anything*, and in a certain sense, as a politician, he didn't seem to need to.

So to return to your question, what happened to Salvador Allende? I have formulated three hypotheses over the years.

One, he expected to be able to out-manipulate and outmaneuver everyone, pull all the strings, and somehow ride out the internal contradictions of his own government.

Two, there was an element of fatalism about the whole Popular Unity experiment. At times Allende seemed reconciled to the fact he was going to fail, and predisposed to accept it. During the last phase there was much talk about death and suicide, about the example of Balmaceda, etc.

Third, at times this fatalism and gloom would alternate with an unwonted optimism, informed by the idea, or rather the delusion, that he was going to inaugurate here in Chile a whole new political system, and become, say, someone like Tito. Allende was going to go down in history as the man who had finally found a legal, peaceful road to socialism, the road which had eluded so many others.

Allende was capable of wide swings of mood, depending on the political prospect. Sometimes he was optimistic, then—when difficulties would begin to close in on him—he would sink into suicidal gloom. He would sometimes utilize the first syndrome (manipulative tactics) to try to break out of difficulties.

A good example was his use of "discussions" with people. He would invite, say, a bunch of military men to a long lunch and dinner, and try to convince them of his point of view—with characteristic charm and wit—but actually reach no agreement. Nonetheless, rumors would run throughout Santiago that "Allende had met with some military men, etc., etc., etc.," and for the moment many would assume that Allende and his opponents had reached some agreement which in fact had *not* been reached. This nontheless would give the government some additonal breathing space—for a time.

We were particularly sensitive to this technique during those periods in which there was an attempt by the Cardinal [Silva Henriquez] to get some sort of dialogue going between Christian Democracy and Popular Unity, particularly in 1973. At one point, I told Allende on the phone that I would be glad to meet with him, but only at the Moneda [Palace] and only in full public view, and that I would make no statement to the press unless in fact an accord had been reached.

When [Christian Democratic Party President Patricio] Alwyn undertook a series of discussions with Allende, the result was the same—no agreement, just advertising in the rumor mills of Santiago that an accord either had been reached or was about to be. On one of these occasions (you should really talk to Alwyn about this) the Christian Democratic people were with Allende at [the presidential residence of] Tomás Moro from about 11 in the morning to 11 in the evening. After a long and exhausting day interrupted by two meals, Alwyn finally said, "Well, Mr. President, did you invite us here just to *talk*, or do you want to sign some agreement?" Allende suggested—it being Friday—that the agreement be postponed to Monday.

"No, President," Alwyn replied, "if not tonight, then tomorrow. Or the next day. There must be no break between the talks and the final agreement." Alende could not agree to this, and, of course, no agreement was reached. I hope this rather long exposition answers your question.

FALCOFF: Well, I think it pretty much does. My intention in asking it was to elicit your opinion as to whether—from what might be called the point of view of *temperament*—whether Allende's personality was really suited for democratic politics, the give-and-take, the respect for the rights of the opposition, and so forth.

FREI *(making a sign with his hands which meant "neither here nor there"):* It's hard to say. He was a very ambivalent man. I don't think he himself ever quite made up his mind.

FALCOFF: Well, of course, he *had* functioned more or less successfully, in fact, quite successfully, in the context of Chilean democratic politics for over 30 years at the time he was elected president.

FREI: Yes, but times had changed, too. You have to remember what was going on in the late 1960s—the Mao cult, the Baader-Meinhof gang in Germany, a whole atmosphere of *ideological delerium*, a world-wide phenomenon which had serious repercussions here in Chile. We had serious problems within our own party—Chonchol, all the people who later joined the MAPU, etc. They clamored, for example, for "a rapid and massive agrarian reform," as if it were as simple as that. I told them "Look, gentlemen, if I give you what you ask for—'a rapid and massive agrarian reform'—you're not going to be able to handle the consequences." In the last two years of my government I spent an enormous amount of energy just asserting my authority over the hotheads of my own party—you know that all night meeting [in 1969] at which we managed to regain control over the PDC assembly?

Well, Allende never felt the need or the desire or the responsibility to do the same thing with his own people.

And then, there was the problem of the MIR, with whom he was deeply involved. Shortly after his inauguration ceremony, I made a formal visit to him, and I said, "President, this government of yours is going to end in horror and blood—in horror and blood. The result is something you yourself cannot even imagine." Allende looked at me genuinely surprised, and said, "Why do you say that?" I told him that I did not have much confidence in his ability to control the violent Left, and that Chileans—a people who have a decided tempermental preference for order and tranquility—would react very badly to this. He looked at me, amazed, and said, "You're all wrong. The MIR are my best friends. I have nothing to worry about from that quarter."

I repeated the same predictions to a group of Christian Democratic senators who came to my house for lunch a few days after Allende's inauguration. Nobody said much afterwards, but I later learned that when they left the house, they gathered around their parked cars and discussed my comments. At the time only one of the eleven thought there might be something to my views. Nonetheless, two years later more than one reminded me of my prediction and its tragic accuracy. At that point people were already visiting military bases imploring the military to intervene. The miracle of it all is not that the coup came at all, but that the military resisted civilian pressure as long as it did.

FALCOFF: What do you think of Allende's constant threats to call a plebiscite? I've studied the UP program over and over, and for the life of me I can't imagine why Allende thought that a plebiscite would somehow solve all of his problems—that is, if you assume that democratic practices, the right of an opposition to function, etc., would not be abolished. What made him think that the very same electorate which had returned *one* favorable, let us say, "Assembly of the People," would not eventually return another, opposed to the government, at some later date, if something went wrong?

FREI: If what you're asking me is what I *think* you're asking me, then, yes, I would agree—there is no doubt whatever that what was eventually envisaged was a government of a totalitarian type. No doubt whatever.

FALCOFF: What about the Cuban role in all of this? I mean, apart from the obvious ideological pressures. I understand that the Cubans were very, very busy here. They had a very large embassy, and apparently their diplomatic baggage often contained arms. To what degree do you think they played a role in trying to set Chile up either for a civil war or a left-wing coup?

FREI: Well, it's really hard to say with any degree of precision. Quite obviously—as you point out—the Cuban presence here was very visible. No doubt arms *were* being smuggled in—although how much no one can say, really. There were arms all over the place. Insofar as Chilean domestic politics was concerned, the Cuban presence was felt largely at the level of the Marxist political parties, the Communists and the Socialists.

On balance, however, I think that the conspicuous Cuban support for Allende cost him more politically than it was worth.

There was the visit of Fidel Castro—

FALCOFF: Which was very long.

FREI: Yes, *very* long. It naturally raised questions about what was going on in the Moneda between Allende and Castro.

Moreover, I don't think Allende himself really appreciate the condescending manner with which Castro treated him. This was particularly true at public events, where Castro would undertake to read Allende revolutionary lessons. I feel sure that—in spite of the outward cordiality—in his intimate feelings as a Chilean, Allende felt injured and insulted.

Furthermore, the Cuban leaders as a group didn't particularly "sit well" with the Chilean public, which is accustomed to a somewhat more sober and serious political style. I remember, for example, the visit of Raúl Castro, Fidel's brother. The long ponytail, the fatigues, the unkempt beard just didn't wash with the Chileans—it's not what they think a political leader should look like. When Raúl Castro visited the public market, the police had to rescue him from a hailstorm of rotten tomatoes thrown by the grocers, or more often, by their wives.

FALCOFF: What do you think of the authenticity of the White Book, issued by the present military government?

FREI: I must admit, I haven't seen it. What is it?

FALCOFF: A collection of documents purporting to show that the Socialist party was planning a left-wing coup of its own, the so-called Plan Zeta—which apparently involved the assassination of Allende. . . . I'm sure the *Mercurio* must have published something about it.

FREI: I really don't know myself how to evaluate such thing. The documents themselves might be valid enough, and yet not really very important. There was so much going on during those months. . . .

FALCOFF: What do you think of the idea that Allende himself was intending to reach an agreement with Christian Democracy, but that some people within his own party had other ideas, and went ahead—say, with plans for a coup—without consulting him?

FREI: Who knows? Maybe so. The Socialist party was always a very undisciplined group of anarcho-Trotskyists, of anarcho-Trotskyists. Look at them now, split into three pieces—one leadership in Caracas, one in Mexico City, and one here (in clandestinity)—all fighting with each other, accusing one another of selling out to the Chinese, the Russians, whatever. Talking endlessly about what Allende *should* have done, etc., etc. (*throws his hands up in the air*).

And now, you must excuse me, as I have another meeting.

FALCOFF: Thank you, Mr. President.

Index